Samuel Beckett's New Worlds

Samuel Beckett. Photograph by John Minihan, courtesy of Tom Bishop.

SAMUEL BECKETT'S NEW WORLDS

Style in Metafiction

by

Susan D. Brienza

UNIVERSITY OF OKLAHOMA PRESS

Norman and London

Permission is gratefully acknowledged from Grove Press to quote extensively from the following works by Samuel Beckett, all of which are published by Grove Press, Inc.: *Cascando and Other Short Dramatic Pieces* (© 1968), *Company* (© 1980), *Disjecta: Miscellaneous Writings and a Dramatic Fragment*, ed. Ruby Cohn (© 1984), *Endgame* (© 1958), *Ends and Odds* (© 1976), *First Love and Other Shorts* (© 1974), *Fizzles* (© 1976), *Happy Days* (© 1961), *How It Is* (© 1964), *Ill Seen Ill Said* (© 1981), *Krapp's Last Tape and Other Dramatic Pieces* (© 1960), *Lessness* (© 1970), *The Lost Ones* (© 1972), *Malone Dies* (© 1956), *Mercier and Camier* (© 1974), *Molloy* (© 1955), *More Pricks Than Kicks* (© 1972), *Murphy* (© 1957), *Poems in English* (© 1961), *Proust* (© 1957), *Rockaby and Other Short Pieces* (© 1981), *Stories and Texts for Nothing* (© 1967), *The Unnamable* (© 1958), *Waiting for Godot* (© 1954), *Watt* (© 1983), and *Worstward Ho* (© 1983).

Library of Congress Cataloging-in-Publication Data

Brienza, Susan D. (Susan Dolores), 1949–
 Samuel Beckett's new worlds.

  Bibliography: p.
  Includes index.
  1. Beckett, Samuel, 1906–   —Style. 2. Experimental
fiction—History and criticism.   I. Title.
PR6003.E282Z5785   1987   848'.91409   86-24919
ISBN 0-8061-2047-9

The paper in this book meets the guidelines for permanence and durability of the Committee on Production Guidelines for Book Longevity of the Council on Library Resources, Inc.

This book has been published with aid of a grant from the Andrew W. Mellon Foundation.

Dedicated to my parents

Joseph John Brienza and Florina Vagnoni Brienza

And to the memory of my brother

Patrick Joseph Brienza

(1951–1972)

Acc 1551/3

TO END YET AGAIN

To end yet again skull alone in the dark pent
up bowed down on a board to begin. Long thus to
begin till the place fades followed by the board
soon after. To end yet again then skull alone in
the dark the void no neck no face just the
last (remaining) place in the dark the void. Place
of remains where once used to gleam in the dark
on and off used to gleam a remain. Remains of the
days of the light of day never was light so weak
as theirs so pale. So then the skull starts to
glimmer again instead of going out. There in the
end all of a sudden or little by little there
dawns and magic a leaden dawn. Little by
little less dark till the final grey or sudden as
if switched on grey sand as far as eye can see beneath
grey cloudless sky same grey. Skull last (remaining)
place black void within without till (all of a) sudden
or little by little this leaden dawn frozen no sooner
dawned. Grey cloudless sky grey sand as far as eye
can see long empty to begin. Sand pale as dust ah but
dust indeed deep to engulf the proudest monuments
which it once was (incidentally) here and there. There
at just same grey invisible to any other eye the expelled bolt erect among his ruins. Same grey the entire little body from head to feet sunk ankle deep
were it not for the eyes last (remaining) lustres
(grey). The arms still cleave to the trunk and to
each other the legs designed for flight. Grey cloudless
sky ocean of dust not a ripple
mock bourne upon bourne hell air not a breath. Sinking
mingled with the dust many already only barely
emergent the debris of the refuge. First change
of all at last a fragment comes away and falls. Slow
fall for so dense a body it comes to rest like cork
in water and immerges barely. So then the skull last
(remaining) place starts to glimmer again instead of
going out. Grey cloudless sky bourne upon bourne
grey timeless air of those nor for God nor for his

A typescript of the opening of "To end yet again [*sic*]" with corrections and revisions in Beckett's hand. This is not the final version of the text. This translation of "Pour finir encore" becomes Fizzle 8, which is discussed in Chapter 10. This page, catalogued as part of item 1551/3 at the Beckett Archive in the Library of the University of Reading, England, is reproduced here with the Archive's permission.

ESTRAGON: I tell you I wasn't doing anything.

VLADIMIR: Perhaps you weren't. But it's the way of doing it that counts, the way of doing it, if you want to go on living.
—*Waiting for Godot*

There are many ways in which the thing I am trying in vain to say may be tried in vain to be said. I have experimented, as you know, both in public and in private, under duress, through faintness of heart, through weakness of mind, with two or three hundred.
—"Three Dialogues"

I take no sides. I am interested in the shape of ideas. There is a wonderful sentence in Augustine: 'Do not despair; one of the thieves was saved. Do not presume; one of the thieves was damned.' That sentence has a wonderful shape.
—Samuel Beckett, in an interview

A (*nervously*): Keep going, keep going!

B: ". . . for as long as they entered my awareness, and that in either case, I mean whether such on the one hand as to give me pleasure or on the contrary on the other to cause me pain, and truth to tell—" Shit! Where's the verb?

A: What verb?

B: The main!

A: I give up.

B: Hold on till I find the verb and to hell with all this drivel in the middle. . . .
—*Theatre II*

Contents

Illustrations

Halftone Illustrations

Figures

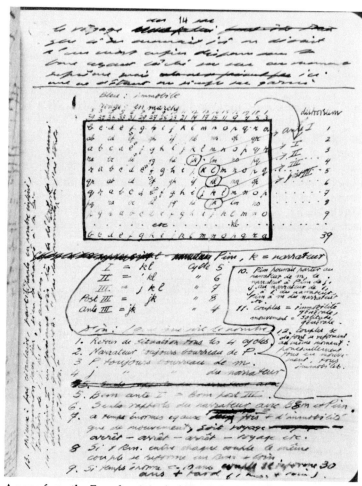

A page from the French original of *How It Is, Comment c'est*, in a note-book Beckett entitled "PIM IV." This recto of leaf 14 contains notes and charts detailing the journey of Beckett's creatures in the mud, color-coded in blue and red for *immobile* ("still") or *en marche* ("moving")—see the top of the page. *How It Is* discussed in Chapter 5. Courtesy of The Harry Ransom Humanities Research Center in The University of Texas at Austin.

Preface

One Saturday afternoon, David handed me the latest *New Yorker* opened to a short story and playfully challenged, "Read the first paragraph and guess who wrote it." So I read:

From where she lies she sees Venus rise. On. From where she lies when the skies are clear she sees Venus rise followed by the sun. Then she rails at the source of all life. On. At evening when the skies are clear she savours its star's revenge. At the other window. Rigid upright on her old chair she watches for the radiant one. Her old deal spindlebacked kitchen chair. It emerges from out the last rays and sinking ever brighter is engulfed in its turn. On. . . .

Taut phrases. Staccato rhythms. Lyrical surprises. Looking up I answered, "Well, if this weren't the *New Yorker*, I'd say Samuel Beckett, obviously." And so it was, a story called *Ill Seen Ill Said*, and with his name clearly printed at the end of the piece. But what exactly made my hypothesis so sure, even in an incongruous context? What marks Beckett's style as unmistakably his? Especially in the later fictions, which distinct features make the style(s) so distinctive? These sorts of questions have been answered for other master stylists of the twentieth century—Joyce, Hemingway, Faulkner—but not for Beckett, whose verbal effects seem as elusive as they are elegant.

Some approaches to Beckett's new styles in the following chapters derive from linguistics, some from stylistics, and some from reader-response criticism, while others are imported from standard critical methodologies (for example, the tracing of motifs) which here are applied more quantitatively than usual. I use the term "stylistic analysis" to mean a close verbal study adopting methodology and rigor from linguistics when critically profitable—an analysis always bearing in mind the reader's difficulty in deciphering the text's language purely at the word level, both temporally and spatially. Launching outward from a close reading of the text as a point of departure, I then use stylistic analysis to journey toward discussions of narrative technique, covert characterization, point of view, tone, imagery, minimal themes, allusions and allegories, tableaux, and cinematic techniques.

The residual elements of fiction in Beckett's new worlds, which at first appear to have vanished, surface in compressed forms and subtle guises and often are visible only through the window of style.

Always to be avoided is arbitrary linguistic description: for each piece verbal analysis is not an end in itself but a means to critical interpretation. When examining *Texts for Nothing*, for example, it is not sufficient to catalog pronoun shifts; the next step is to correlate this pattern with the theme of the search for self. Also, unlike linguists or stylisticians, who often observe a text in a vacuum, as a sample of a given language or grammar, the (non-New) critic obviously places each piece in the context of genre conventions, literary history, or of the author's canon. In the case of Beckett's work, it is irresponsible and almost impossible to discuss the later stories without glances toward his poetry and drama as well as his earlier fiction.

Since Beckett himself translated the French texts into English (concurrently revising slightly, so that the two versions may differ), and since statements about English prose do not necessarily apply to French prose, and vice versa, I concentrate on the English editions of these fictions, occasionally introducing features of the French versions to amplify an interpretation. Beckett's unpublished material surrounding both English and French texts also reveals much about his later styles: besides providing evidence of meticulous rewriting, his manuscripts, typescripts, and working notebooks are filled with doodles, marginal calculations, tables, diagrams, and rephrasings—that is, with numerous insights into his creative process. Unfolding the revisions of post-*Unnamable* fictions (usually a series of alternating manuscripts and typescripts), and uncovering abandoned or unpublished ends and odds of writing, helps to explain (1) how the styles of many fictions are further condensed with each rewriting, (2) how Beckett composed some of the most repetitive texts from phrasal units, and (3) how some of the later stories grew out of each other, or developed from the same conceptual seed.

I continued to read *Ill Seen Ill Said*, realizing that warnings to the character could also be interpreted as warnings to the critic: "Already all confusion. Things and imaginings. As of always. Confusion amounting to nothing. Despite precautions. . . . Gently gently. On. Careful."

Acknowledgments

The starting point for this study of Beckett's later styles was a linguistics course taught by Michael Peinovich at the University of Pennsylvania. Since he included a section on stylistics, that topic became one option for a final paper, and I want to thank him for saying Yes when I asked if I could try a stylistic analysis of a bizarre text called *Lessness*. This project led to my attempt to apply linguistic methodologies to all of Beckett's fiction after *The Unnamable*, and the fun began.

An early version of the manuscript benefitted from the comments of Stan Gontarski and Alice Kelley, who generously took the time to write detailed criticism. Marjorie Perloff, who helped me to view Beckett's later prose through the prism of poetry, read a later version of the study and offered wise advice and steady encouragement toward revision. Rubin Rabinovitz carefully read two chapters, and shared some of his ideas on late Beckett fictions of mutual fascination.

Other Beckett scholars have influenced my work indirectly—through criticism of their own that has constructed a framework for my thinking; I especially want to thank Porter Abbott and Hannah Copeland. Of course, Ruby Cohn has shown many Modernists how to read a text closely, listening for patterns and echoes; her work on Beckett, now classic, has provided a level of precision that is simultaneously a guiding model and an impossible goal. Still other Beckett scholars became acquaintances, then correspondents, then friends, through conferences and MLA sessions over the years: Porter Abbott, Tom Bishop, Katherine Burkman, Mary Doll, Marty Fehsenfeld, Jim Knowlson, Dina Sherzer, Dougald McMillan, and Hersh Zeifman.

Many librarians, curators, and research staffs—at Trinity College, Dublin, the University of Reading in England, Washington University in St. Louis, and the Humanities Research Institute at Austin, Texas—have aided my work on Beckett manuscripts and typescripts. I particularly want to express appreciation for the open scholarly spirit of the late Richard Admussen. While teaching at Washington University, he precisely cataloged the Beckett holdings there, and then graciously gave of his materials and time. Also, the secretary at Reading, Rosemarie, was a special person as well as a special assistant. You knew you had made her list of favored researchers when, at high tea time, she brought you sugar cookies with your coffee.

UCLA friends and colleagues—Albert Braunmuller, Albert Hutter, Robert Kinsman, Ken Lincoln, and Richard Yarborough—kindly read and commented on some individual chapters, and I have with appreciation incorporated their suggestions. Two other department friends, Martha Banta and Karen Rowe, gave careful readings to articles of mine on Beckett's drama, and their comments gave me new glimmers about the later fiction.

My friend and UCLA colleague Jeffrey Rubin-Dorsky meticulously read the entire manuscript and offered numerous thoughtful recommendations, chapter by chapter. In addition, he freely advised me when my language became too condensed and fragmented, like an unintentionally poor imitation of Beckett's style (in return I let him know when his prose became wordy and redundant—too much like bad Washington Irving).

My research assistants over the years—Kevin Dettmar, Emilia Puma, and Pat Rose—deserve much thanks for all the library and proofreading hours they put in. Also earning my gratitude is Nora Reyes, who spent part of a long hot summer retyping the entire manuscript and trying to decide who was crazier—Samuel Beckett, for writing such strange stories, or me for analyzing them.

My friends Margaret McBride and Janice Karlton helped in subtler ways, by lending support and good cheer, and by sharing the similar pains and joys of their long projects—Margaret's on James Joyce, and Jan's on her own painting.

One of the last people to be mentioned was my best support, a loving and caring partner. David Jefferson stands behind the pages of this book in many ways: he would buy me each tiny new Beckett text as it hit the bookshelves; he convinced me that literary criticism need not slight logic; he taught me how to use my first computer and then a second text-editing system, and miraculously produced copies of early chapters on a laser printer. Thus David changed the way I processed words—literally and figuratively, mechanically and mentally. Moreover, as I worked, or as we discussed contemporary novelists, he brewed innumerable pots of Darjeeling tea to keep me warm and alert.

Portions of this book in different form appeared in *ELH, Journal of Modern Literature, Journal of Beckett Studies,* and *Style.* I appreciate their permission to reprint this material. Finally, I would like to thank Samuel Beckett for granting me permission to quote from some of his manuscripts and for going on with such beautiful fictions.

IMAGINATION DEAD IMAGINE

No trace anywhere of life, you say, pah, no difficulty there, imagination not dead yet, yes, good, imagination dead imagine. Islands, waters, azure, verdure, one glimpse and vanished, endlessly, till all white in the whiteness the rotunda. No way in, go in, measure. Diameter three feet, three feet from the ground to the summit of the vault. Two diameters at right angles AB CD divide the white ground into two semicircles ACB BDA. Lying on the ground two white bodies, each in its semicircle. White too the vault and the round wall eighteen inches high from which it springs. Go back out, a plain rotunda, all white in the whiteness, go back in, solid throughout, a ring as in the imagination the ring of bone. The light that makes all so white no source, all shines with the same white shine, ground, wall, vault, bodies, no shadow. Strong heat, surfaces hot but not burning to the touch, bodies. Go back out, move back, the fabric vanishes, ascend, it vanishes, all white in the whiteness, descend, go back in. Emptiness, silence, heat, whiteness, wait, the light goes down, all grows dark together, ground, wall, vault, bodies, say twenty seconds, all the greys, the light goes out, all vanishes. At the same time the temperature goes down, to reach its minimum, say freezing-point, at the same instant as the black is reached, which may seem strange. Wait, more or less long, light and heat come back, all grows white and hot together, ground, wall, vault, bodies, say twenty seconds, all the greys, till the initial level is reached whence the fall began. More or less long, for there may intervene, experience shows, between end of fall and beginning of rise, pauses of varying length, from the fraction of the second to what would have seemed, in other times, other places, an eternity. Same remark for the other pause, between end of rise and beginning of fall. The extremes, as long as they persist, are perfectly stable, which in the case of the temperature may seem strange, in the beginning. It happens too, experience shows, that rise and fall stop short at any point and mark a pause, more or less long, before resuming, or reversing, the rise now fall, the fall rise, these in their turn to be completed, or to stop short and mark a pause, more or less long, before resuming, or again reversing, and so on, till finally one or the other extreme is reached. Such variations of rise and fall, combining in countless rhythms, commonly the passage from white to black and from heat to cold, and vice versa. The extremes alone are stable, as is stressed by the to be observed when a pause occurs at some intermediate stage, no matter what its level and duration. Then all, ground, wall, vault, bodies, ashen or lead en or between the two, as may be. But on the whole, experience shows, such a passage is not common. And most often, when the light begins to fail, and along with it the heat, the movement continues until, in the space of some twenty seconds, pitch black is reached and at the same instant say freezing-point. for the reverse movement, towards heat and whiteness. Next most frequent is the fall or rise with pauses of varying length in these feverish greys, without at any moment reversal of the movement. But whatever its uncertainties the return sooner or later to a temporary calm seems assured, for the moment,

Typescript of *Imagination Dead Imagine* with revisions in Beckett's hand. Note the diagram in the right-hand margin. Beckett drew two lines, AB and CD, which would determine the two semicircles mentioned at the beginning of the text: ACB and BDA. Courtesy of Samuel Beckett Papers, Washington University Libraries, St. Louis, Missouri.

Samuel Beckett's New Worlds

Alan Mandell in the 1984 English-language premiere of Beckett's *Company*, which was adapted for the stage by the playwright, directed by S. E. Gontarski, and produced at the Los Angeles Theatre Center by Diane White. Photograph by Ian Dryden, reproduced by permission of Mary Dryden.

1

Samuel Beckett's New Styles

Excellence of style has until recently been one thing on which all readers of Samuel Beckett could agree. The most indifferent or hostile reviewers of the early plays would grudgingly admit that Beckett's (to them) ugly world was at least presented in well-structured forms and beautiful or fascinating language. Even though the short fictions of the 1960's seemed fragmented and frustrating, their condensed style was admired at the same time that their strange substance was either disliked or misunderstood. Lately, however, some Beckett readers are losing patience with his stylistic economy; his prose as well as his content is becoming too thin, too rarefied, they complain. We can hear this exasperation in two reviews of a 1980 story, *Company*:

> Is the mind, then, on its back in the cradle or the coffin, consciousness itself? In doubting the fictions of time, space, memory, light, sound and language and the very notion of a 'we,' does it condense to a vanishing point? [John Leonard, *New York Times*]

> A man is lying on his back in the dark. There is a voice, now distant, now less distant. The voice is repetitive and enigmatic. . . . This goes on (without even the occasional flash of humor with which Mr. Beckett customarily rewards our patience) for fifty-seven short pages, or about ten thousand words. [*New Yorker*, Feb. 9, 1981]

Conversely, though, *Company* elicited a new hymn of praise for Beckett's style from another reviewer: "This is the most wonderful prose I have ever read by him—sleek, ironic, gloom-cadenced, self-dissolving, eye-pure, at peace—and perhaps the most wonderful prose I have *ever read*" (Karl Keller, *Los Angeles Times*). And ironically, the *New Yorker*, which had sounded so bored with *Company*, would eight months later publish Beckett's next story, *Ill Seen Ill Said*, in one sense another repetitive text of "about ten thousand words." Whether Beckett is damned or praised, the way he arranges his words must be arresting. First, what mystifies readers about Beckett as a stylist is how he can possibly continue to write sentences at all when he has apparently taken grammar to its limits in *The Unnamable* (1958). And the next question is how over the past thirty years he has produced a series of condensed prose pieces, a babel of silence and words, similar-sounding at first yet each a slightly or drastically different stylistic innovation. The most general issue, though, is how to make sense of such forbidding texts when style remains the foremost element of Beckett's fiction, and when even the style is coming unravelled.

Since the conclusion of the trilogy ("I can't go on, I'll go on") Beckett's narratives have been attempts to "go on" artistically and stylistically, without normal syntax and minus functional parts of speech. No wonder, then, that his post-*Unnamable* stories are difficult to read, describe, or classify using the standard critical terms. The Beckett reader, simultaneously intrigued and irritated by his later fiction, needs new guidelines on how to read prose when he encounters language like this from the beginning of *Ping*: "All known all white bare white body fixed one yard legs joined like sewn. Light heat white floor one square yard never seen. White walls one yard by two white ceiling one square yard never seen. Bare white body fixed only the eyes only just. Traces blurs light grey almost white on white."

The best hint for interpretation of his work that Beckett has given is that he cares deeply about the shape of a sentence: "it is the shape that matters," he says.[1] And his implied credo on imitative style (the style imitating the content in some way) compels us to analyze the smaller units of clauses and phrases when sentences themselves lose their shapes, dissolve and fragment, in the later prose. Stylistic patterns help a reader (especially a Beckett reader) to determine meaning: as one jumps consecutively from sentence to sentence and paragraph to paragraph, one makes linguistic and narrative inferences all the while. But with the recent fictions readers have become bogged down by a morass of Beckettian fragmentation, contradiction, and non sequitur, so that finally, it seems, they can connect nothing with nothing. Usually a reader assimilates the language of a narrative well enough to reconstruct the author's fictional world, but here again the traveller through late Beckett tends to lose the way. Rather than mapping any remote areas of the real world, Beckett's recent fictions delineate, as many scholars have noticed, "closed systems" of language that are about writing—and often about interpreting.

Hannah Copeland has taught us to read Beckett's novels as

narratives about narrating,[2] and now we must train ourselves to analyze later Beckett stories as compositions about composing at the phrase level. These strange fictions make us ponder anew the relationship between writer and text, and between text and reader: we learn about the writing process and the reading process—about imagination, creation, and imaginative reconstruction. Parsing is usually an activity that the reader performs intuitively, a step in reading far below the more conscious process of interpreting a piece of literature. But for the *Ping* passage above, and others in late Beckett fiction, we are forced initially to supply syntactic divisions and determine phrasal and clausal units, and then to align subjects with verbs (if any) and modifiers with modified. Instead of looking *through* the style to a story, as we do for many narratives and most nonfiction, we must (to use Richard Lanham's distinction) stare *at* the style itself.[3] Not so coincidentally, around the time that Beckett's styles took off in new directions, David Lodge wrote *The Language of Fiction*,[4] in which he proposed that we read novels with the same close attention to syntax that we usually devote to poetry; it is no accident that Lodge published the first sensible explication of *Ping*. If Beckett's recent narratives, what Ruby Cohn calls "lyrics of fiction," initiate a new form of prose poetry (Marjorie Perloff convincingly argues this and calls them "associative monologues"[5]), then readers—guessing that they are caught between two genres—must bring to these dual constructions their sensibilities for analyzing poetry as well as their conventions for responding to prose. The readings of Beckett's narratives from *Texts for Nothing* to *Worstward Ho* in the following chapters raise theoretical issues about the limits of language, the boundaries of contemporary experimental fiction, and the very activity of understanding and interpreting literature when a text is generically and stylistically unique.

Beckett's radical change in style in his later fiction demands a radical change in critical method—one that originates with stylistic analysis. Significantly, in a 1957 interview Beckett expressed his artistic and formal impasse in linguistic terms: "In the last book, 'L'Innommable,' there's complete disintegration. No 'I,' no 'have,' no 'being.' No nominative, no accusative, no verb. There's no way to go on."[6] Beginning with *Texts for Nothing*, he has written self-reflexive fictions that are studies in and experiments with language (especially with syntax), attempts to achieve a condensed, minimal style, and glosses on the writing and understanding of narrative at the sentence and phrase level. Despite their refusal to tell a traditional story in conventional language, Beckett's stark later pieces manage to suggest a poetic richness which surpasses that of his earlier novels. For indications about how to approach these fictions through their styles, it is useful to examine Beckett's statements on style and content, explore various definitions of style, and evaluate methods of stylistic analysis.

Of course, Beckett, like Proust and Joyce, is even more concerned than are most writers with matters of form and style. All three authors, in their creative work, in essays, and in their correspondence, express great interest in grammar, syntax, rhythm, semantics, etymology, and proper names. Primarily they strive in each text for a form that will reflect the content appropriately although "reflect" is misleading here because it implies a split between the two that these writers deny should exist. Beckett expresses this idea of imitative form imagistically in his own famous verbal analysis:

> For Proust, as for the painter, style is more a question of vision than of technique. Proust does not share the superstition that form is nothing and content everything, nor that the ideal literary masterpiece could only be communicated in a series of absolute and monosyllabic propositions. For Proust the quality of language is more important than any system of ethics or aesthetics. Indeed he makes no attempt to dissociate form from content. The one is a concretion of the other, the revelation of a world.[7]

The young Beckett's reading of *Finnegans Wake* displayed sophisticated knowledge of linguistic properties: etymologies, syntax, and prose rhythm. His defense of the novel against those who complained about its impenetrable style has been quoted uncountable times as a commentary on Beckett's own art, but it merits another recall, because it applies with special force to his later fictions, where content seems to reduce to the arrangement of words:

> Here form *is* content, content *is* form. You complain that this stuff is not written in English. It is not written at all. It is not to be read—or rather it is not only to be read. It is to be looked at and listened to. His [Joyce's] writing is not *about* something; *it is that something itself*. . . . When the sense is dancing, the words dance. . . . How can we qualify this general esthetic vigilance without which we cannot hope to snare the sense which is for

ever rising to the surface of the form and becoming the form itself?[8]

Without a stylistic analysis we cannot truly look at, cannot hope to snare the sense of a late Beckett fiction, since now style and substance are intricately intertwined. The complex relationship between form and content, style and substance, cannot be fully explored within the covers of one book, or through a study of one author. It has become a multifaceted theoretical question subsuming linguistics and narratology, and everything in between; it takes up issues from the smallest units of grammar (verb tenses and pronoun referents) to the largest (story and discourse). Thus the problem will not be solved here, only further extended and partially illuminated: for some of Beckett's later fictions, style embodies the meaning; for others, the language itself provides the best route to meaning. Looking intently at individual sentences and phrases we will ask: What are the salient stylistic features? In what ways do these present new verbal choices for Beckett? How do stylistic patterns embed the meaning of the text as a whole? What effect do the linguistic properties have on the reader? Not ever abandoning what little content remains—in fact, beginning with a close reading of each story—I will shuttle back and forth between substance of sentence and shape of sentence.

While Stanley Fish believes that his emphasis on the reader's experience dispels the dichotomy between style and meaning, process and product,[9] this answer begs many other questions (for example, What actually is "the meaning of experience"?). Still, his focus, allowing for critical oscillation between style and substance, reveals some convergence points. Fish's most useful suggestion, especially for Beckett's fictional new worlds, is that we become aware of our own reading process at the linguistic level: "Essentially what the method does is *slow down* the reading experience so that 'events' one does not notice in normal time, but which do occur, are brought before our analytical attentions. It is as if a slow-motion camera with an automatic stop action effect were recording our linguistic experiences and presenting them to us for viewing."[10] Curiously, Beckett himself repeatedly invokes camera imagery to describe the vision of his protagonists—particularly his narrator/observers—and the language in some fragments resembles series of verbal snapshots.

Samuel Beckett's fiction after *The Unnamable* can continue by photographing itself; style comments on writing in these new worlds. In *Texts for Nothing* Beckett "goes on" artistically through linguistic sleights of hand with verbs and pronouns. *From an Abandoned Work* is the monologue of a disjointed narrator who speaks in distorted and inverted syntax. In *Enough* the narrator's self-delusion expresses itself in wistful and contradictory language. The self-destructive short novel *How It Is* spews out bits and scraps of a life in fragmented phrases of "midget grammar," and thereby records the torture of composing. In *Imagination Dead Imagine* paradoxical language mirrors the impossible feat (for author and reader alike) of creating something out of nothing. The mythlike story of *The Lost Ones* tauntingly leads the reader on a search for meaning (mirroring the climbers' attempts at escape) in language that mocks man's need for order and structure. The style of *Ping* embodies the suffering of the artist (represented as an imprisoned creature), a figure as constrained as the few recycled phrases of the text. By the time we get to *Lessness* the artist has regressed to a fetus, unable to stand, described with incomplete, "issueless" phrases, as Beckett achieves the "syntax of weakness" he set as his goal around 1960. In *Fizzles* the narrative voice is fizzling out, and bodies are either "Still" or going on in zigzag paths as their sentences collapse or meander in parallel ways. Language itself is the narrator's only companion in *Company*, and both imagination and expression are doubted in the highly self-conscious prose of *Ill Seen Ill Said*. Finally, regressing from *The Unnamable*'s vow "I'll go on," the most recent piece promises only to move *Worstward Ho*, and manages to do so through the creation of "worse" words and "un-" words.

Seeking models for a study of Beckett's later styles, one reaches first for Lawrence Harvey's thorough explication of the poetry, which explores imitative style and even imitative phonetics. Harvey argues that "[t]he fragmentation of form into discrete particles in Beckett's poems is on the one hand a resolution of 'no confidence' in the logical order of grammar and beyond this in the order of human rationality itself, and on the other an effort to transmit an experience of relative chaos perceived as more real."[11] Unfortunately, Beckett scholars have yet to apply the same intensity and scope of verbal analysis to the later prose, prose that often reads as poetry. More recently H. Porter Abbott's analysis of the novels as specimens of imitative form[12] has dissected the structural properties of the early and middle fiction. But studies of form become problematic with the very short and seemingly formless recent prose works: "style" must often be substituted for "form" in the critical vocabulary for Beckett's fiction after *The Unnamable*, since in the "fragments," "residua," "miniatures," and "fizzles," structure exists mainly at the sentence, or even the phrase, level. Analyses of Beckett's imitative style in the trilogy[13] and in *How It Is* have been guiding scholars toward a linguistic approach. For example, Hugh Kenner perceives Beckett's narrators as striving to maintain subject-verb-object order to impose "tidy control" over their lives;[14] by *How It Is* the narrator is desperately "struggling to utter sentences," but his unorthodox syntax reveals that local (if not global) harmony has been shattered.

Even more foreign-looking than *How It Is*, two of these fictions, *Ping* and *Lessness*, are constructed in prose that seems to invite computer analysis. These short, highly repetitive texts composed of a small number of permuted phrases lend themselves easily to mechanical methods, though two factors make IBM undesirable or unnecessary: first, the required tabulations can be done by hand; second, computational analysis usually produces obvious results and shortsighted views of literary texts, reducing them to strings of characters, and falling short of an actual interpretation. Nonquantitative stylistic analysis in the respected tradition of Louis Milic and Ian Watt is suitable for initial depictions of Beckett's new styles, but here too difficulties arise. A sentence often serves as the basic unit for analysis in a verbal study, certain sentences being tagged ungrammatical. Then, working with grammatical units, the traditional stylistician may count proportions of sentence types, for example, simple, compound, and complex, or periodic and running. An evident feature of Beckett's later style, however, is that much of the syntax is highly unconventional and woefully incomplete. Furthermore, classification of general syntactic patterns would not adequately typify these stripped-down languages, or help interpret these fragmented fictions. To paraphrase Watt's uncertainty with the object "pot," what can the reader do when he determines about a unit of prose that it resembled a sentence, it was almost a sentence, but it was not a sentence of which one could say, Sentence, sentence, and be comforted?

Working primarily at the clause level, a Chomskian linguist will tabulate the types and frequencies of transformation rules a particular writer favors. If the aim is to contrast the prose of different authors, this transformational-generative approach works, having produced precise characterizations of the styles of Gibbon and Hemingway,[15] and Faulkner;[16] and a similar method could be applied to Beckett's earlier novels. But after the *The Unnamable*, his fictions are syntactically as well as narratively fragmented: not even deletion transformation rules (for example) can operate on "sentences" from which so much has been deleted; and often it is hard even to determine the demarcations of clauses. It is almost as if Beckett is creating a new language with its own grammar rules, and in fact, there is some manuscript evidence that he was intentionally devising his own paradigms for phrasal constructions.

Observing Beckett's late style from an historical perspective, we can envision the young experimental poets and novelists of Paris in the literary world of the 1920's. Beckett's early contact with the Surrealists may have had a delayed influence on the development of his later "ungrammatical" prose, an influence that can be detected as early as Lucky's monologue in *Godot* of the fifties.[17] The Surrealists were striving for a dissolution and reconstruction of language similar to that Beckett achieves in the recent fictions, particularly in the random arrangement of *Lessness*.[18] For them as well as Beckett, logic, and therefore, syntax disintegrates. Maurice Nadeau described the aim of the Surrealists as the abolition of traditional grammar systems: "First of all, no more logic. In language especially it must be hunted down, beaten to a pulp, reduced to nothing. There are no more verbs, subjects, complements."[19] Beckett's narrators, from the trilogy onwards, discuss their slippery sentences and their willful annihilation of certain parts of speech, and the recent voice in *Ill Seen Ill Said* concedes his fondness for manufacturing new terms.

All this grammatical freedom implies a rebellious attitude toward orthodox fictional prose. Eugene Jolas, whose articles and editorials in *transition* evolved into a liberated style manual for the Parisian writers of the 1920's, declares that the artist is free "to disintegrate the primal matter of words imposed on him by textbooks and dictionaries . . . to use words of his own fashioning and to disregard existing grammatical and syntactic laws."[20] In *Lessness*, Beckett does precisely that: he creates a large class of "-ness" words to compensate for an absence of verbs and arranges them in carefully composed, yet strangely un-English, structures. In 1932, Beckett, never an official member of Verticalism but sympathetic to its theories, signed a statement called "Poetry is Vertical," which reads in part, "The final disintegration of the 'I' in the creative act is made possible by the use of a language which is a mantic instrument, and which does not hesitate to adopt a revolutionary attitude toward word and syntax, going even so far as to invent a hermetic language, if necessary."[21] In later texts like *The Lost Ones* and *Fizzles*, Beckett has made this ideal of a "hermetic language" a reality with new closed systems of language obeying their own rules of grammar. Judith Dearlove also sees the earlier philosophy applied in the later fiction—"In his residual works, Beckett successfully accomplished what his Verticalist pieces failed to do . . ."—but she argues that here "he expresses the chaos by avoiding it."[22] Conversely, perhaps the later styles are more accurate and direct accommodations of the chaos than was the early prose.

Lurking behind any stylistic method, and behind studies of stylistic change through cultural time, is the baffling question of what style is. Although there are many meanings of "style," and no one definition that holds for all of Beckett's fictions, examining various ways of characterizing style helps to isolate some of the formal problems in the texts. One way of viewing style is as a particular writer's particular language—his idiosyncratic syntax and diction. This framework, which makes sense of the "ungrammatical" and nonsensical languages of Dylan Thomas and e.e. cummings,[23] is especially useful when analyzing Beckett's new condensed and repetitive prose in *Ping* and *Lessness*. In fact, on one level these texts are linguistic experiments obeying language rules that Beckett had invented for himself; they define their own "micro-grammar," a subset of English. A related definition of style presents it as the sum of all the linguistic choices— semantic, syntactic, figurative, and rhetorical—that a writer makes within the language.[24] While author attribution studies must consider subconscious preferences, stylistic interpretations for texts of known authorship, especially those favoring imitative style, can concentrate on the writer's deliberate linguistic choices. Why has Beckett chosen to use many conditionals and hypothetical constructions in *Texts for Nothing*? What does he gain by exploiting syntactic non sequitur in *From an Abandoned Work*? Why does he use no present-tense verbs in *Lessness*, and no definite articles in *Ping*? Why has Beckett chosen to parody convoluted syntax in *The Lost Ones*, and to obliterate traditional punctuation altogether in *How It Is*? Clearly these linguistic decisions affect how we read and respond to each piece; and in the case of cryptic minimal narratives like these, stylistic differences offer significant clues to meaning.

Style can also be viewed as a deviation from a linguistic norm: a writer's canon may deviate in particular ways from the language as a whole, containing, for example, a high frequency of doubles or triplets. But over the years linguists have debated the workability of this definition, asking, Is there such a thing as a "normal" usage of a word or a construction? Which of many possible norms should we maintain as the standard? A poem will deviate from the stylistic norm of fiction in one way and from the norm of, say, journalism in another. Also, one circles around in a tautology with this theory, since the language of every work will necessarily deviate from the norm of which it is a part.[25] A refinement of the deviation theory which considers a particular piece as a stylistic deviation from a writer's works as a whole, rather than from the English language, suffers the same tautological fallacy. Furthermore, "deviation" analyses of style depend on accurate frequency charts of constructions for those texts taken as the norm. Despite these drawbacks, locating the "deviating," low-frequency, words within a text can be a first step in verbal analysis; these deviations become "foregrounded" elements which stand out against the "background" of a text.[26] Significant foregrounded properties can then be grouped according to semantic or syntactic similarities, much as image clusters are gathered and compared in a poem.

One variation of the deviation view of style treats the entire text as a weaving together of these foregrounded segments, or as a recurrence of certain converging deviant forms. Stylisticians in this school look for coherence and convergence of linguistic patterns, that is, for grammatical and lexical "cohesion."[27] A synthesis of the foregrounding and converging methods becomes effective for analyzing highly repetitive texts such as *How It Is*. Yet since overwhelming redundancy becomes the stylistic norm in so many of Beckett's later fictions, even the combined power of existing theories and techniques is not strong enough. A reader requires new analytic methods when a recurring pattern does not surface from the background of a text, but rather itself forms the background. Then, in a reversal of the usual procedure, locating an ordinary but infrequent word as a deviant element becomes a key to interpretation. Such a technique helps "break" the linguistic code of *Ping*, enabling the reader to extract some minimal images, to combine them, and then to interpret them as metaphors for writing. Another possibility is to consider rampant repetition as itself the meaning, as the enactment of a continuous present in Beckett's world.[28] This phenomenon, in which repetition becomes virtually another verb tense, operates in the drama *Play* and accounts for the verbal "changelessness" and the lack of present-tense verbs in *Lessness*.

By now it should be evident that even though reviewers speak of "Beckett's new condensed language" as if there were just one style, actually—as is inherent in the definition of imitative style—the style of each later piece is necessarily different. Also, there is no continuous development from early late style to later late style (as there is in, say, Henry James), no single line of regression that we can draw from *Texts for Nothing* to *Worstward Ho*. Lucky's monologue in *Waiting for Godot* gives a preview of the style in *How It Is* (1964), yet post-trilogy *Enough* (1966) and *From an Abandoned Work* (1956) display syntax more conventional than that in the Unnamable's page-long sentences of the 1940's. In describing precisely what has happened to a Beckett "sentence" since *The Unnamable*, and in deciding how these units of fiction are to be read and interpreted, a first approximation is that Beckett's late experiments with style vary along three coordinates: point of view, tone, and syntax. A descendant of the self-conscious, first person narrator/writer from *The Unnamable* continues in *Texts, Abandoned Work, How It Is, Enough*, and some of the *Fizzles*. But a new voice appears in *The Lost Ones* and *Ill Seen Ill Said*—a third person, deadly neutral observer (almost a camera eye) that models the role of the reader; and in *Imagination* a clinical guide issues second person imperatives to the reader. *Ping* and *Lessness* seem to be written in zero point of view, and for *Company* an alternating second- and third-person perspective contributes to its unique language and structure. Tone in Beckett's new styles registers in two general variants: the impassioned, lyrical memory passages of *How It Is* and *Company*, and the detached, matter-of-fact statements of *The Lost Ones*. It is possible to describe the style of *Imagination Dead Imagine* as an oscillation between scientific language and poetic language,[29] and objective and emotional tones are interwoven in most of the later fictions.

This hybrid style, developed and varied for different purposes depending on which late text is in question, is reminiscent of Joyce's achievement of a mechanical yet lyrical blend in the "Ithaca" chapter of *Ulysses*:

Alone, what did Bloom feel?

The cold of interstellar space, thousands of degrees below freezing point or the absolute zero of Fahrenheit, Centigrade or Reaumur: the incipient intimations of proximate dawn.[30]

Beckett too writes of atmospheric and galactic conditions in metaphorical and rhythmic phrases that sound like poetry; and a merging of highly precise and freely figurative language becomes the embodiment for visual and verbal imaginative creation in Beckett's new worlds, such as *Lessness*: "Figment dawn dispeller of figments and the other called dusk."

The new syntax also takes two extreme forms, reduction and expansion. Some Beckett sentences shrink to discontinuous strings of verbless clauses, often echoing the voice's disjunction from himself and his world, and his frantic inability to create a harmonious whole. Conventional grammar—subject, verb, object—implies pattern, order, and causality in the world,[31] a statement of order that would be a lie for Beckett's new worlds. The author alluded to this conjunction between syntax and meaning when he said to Lawrence Harvey that "perhaps the most perfect expression of Being would be an ejaculation":

On one occasion Beckett said, "I write because I have to," and added, "What do you do when 'I can't' meets 'I must'?" He admitted to using words where words are illegitimate. "At that level you break up words to diminish shame."[32]

Thus the nonsense sound "ping" at scattered intervals in a phrasal text imitates consciousness better than any syntactic complexity could describe it. In the opposite direction, a late Beckett sentence can inflate to an intricate structure relying on elaborate and convoluted clauses. Here syntax itself is foregrounded to the point that it becomes the hero of the story, or else a parody of elaborate syntax mocks the mental order that well-structured language reflects and promotes. For both grammatical end points— and all the variations in between—Beckett blends rhythm and rhyme (with more sonorous qualities in the French than in the English) and plays on clichés and literary allusions.

Because composition of these later fictions overlaps, because Beckett's style apparently defies chronological evolution, and because Beckett himself admitted[33] that *Enough* was "out of place in the series," the fictions are not analyzed in the chapters to come strictly in the order of composition. Here is a table of chronology for the texts I discuss:

Textes pour rien, 1950 (*Texts for Nothing*, 1967)
From an Abandoned Work, 1956
Comment c'est, 1960 (*How It Is*, 1964)
Imagination morte imaginez, 1965 (*Imagination Dead Imagine*, 1967)
Assez, 1966 (*Enough*, 1967)
Le Dépeupleur, 1966 (finished in 1970; *The Lost Ones*, 1972)
Bing, 1966 (*Ping*, 1967)
Sans, 1969 (*Lessness*, 1970)
Pour finir encore et autres foirades, 1976 (trans. 1972–1975; *Fizzles*, 1978)
Company, 1980
Mal vu mal dit, 1981 (*Ill Seen Ill Said*, 1981)
Worstward Ho, 1983

Texts for Nothing, From an Abandoned Work, and *Enough* form a natural sequence stylistically as an intensification of *The Unnamable*'s musings, an attempted return to pre-trilogy prose, and then a verbal compromise between the two (see Chapters 2, 3, and 4). *How It Is* stands alone as a stylistic turning point, departing dramatically from the earlier narratives, and forecasting linguistic experimentation to come (Chapter 5). *Imagination Dead Imagine* and *The Lost Ones* have obvious links in pseudo-setting, paradoxical language, and cinematic technique (Chapters 6 and 7). And *Ping* and *Lessness* form another logical pairing (Chapters 8 and 9) because of their similar parsing difficulties for the reader, their phrasal repetition, and their tractability to similar stylistic approaches. Six of the eight *Fizzles* ("foirades") were written in the sixties in French and translated in the early and middle seventies, but not collected until 1978. They employ—except for the innovative piece "Still" (1972)—variations of previous syntactic patterns, yet exploit new imagery (Chapter 10). With *Company* and *Ill Seen Ill Said*, Beckett returns to more grammatical, though severely condensed, sentences to produce an accessible yet bizarre prose with an autobiographical aura and a nostalgic tone (Chapter 11). The latter two pieces comment not just on fictional language but also on Beckett's career as fiction writer. By *Worstward Ho* (Chapter 12) sentences become "unsaid" as soon as uttered, as the prose moves on only through repeated urgings of "On."

Each fiction takes either a hesitant or a headlong step, artistically and linguistically, away from conventional forms and styles and toward a prose that imitates the narrator's, protagonist's, or reader's predicament. Previous discussions of Beckett's fiction—even when they confront his later texts—do not dissect his difficult new styles, do not work minutely enough with the prose at the phrase level. Brian Finney's fine short monograph *Since "How It Is"* treats only five later texts (up to *Lessness*), and his approach is philosophical, thematic, and imagistic. In a later article, *"Assumption* to *Lessness,"* Finney makes some useful observations about the style of the short fictions, although his main argument concerns thematic continuity from Beckett's earliest prose works to the most recent pieces.[34] H. Porter Abbott's valuable book on imitative form in the novels, *The Fiction of Samuel Beckett: Form and Effect*, needs to be extended in two ways: beyond *Texts for Nothing* (1950), the last fiction Abbott analyzes fully, and below the strata of structure to the sentence and phrase levels. James Knowlson and John Pilling's *Frescoes of the Skull*, on Beckett's later work, contains compelling discussions of each recent fiction. Although Pilling offers some insightful comments about Beckett's syntax and narrative techniques, and excels at hearing allusions to major poets echoing behind Beckett's lines, his analysis (sometimes questioning those critics who count and catalog) stops just short of the deepest workings of Beckett's new styles.

A recent study of this later prose by J. E. Dearlove expresses an interesting minority opinion that Beckett has been inconsistent in his pursuit of imitative form, and that for *How It Is* he breaks with his own tradition.[35] Yet *Comment c'est* can be seen as Beckett's most elegant overlay of content and style. Dearlove's argument that in the later fiction we find "nonrelation" between style and content and between voice and world is shaken when her categories for these recent pieces cause misinterpretations of the texts themselves. For example, the classification of *From an Abandoned Work* as a retreat to conventional fiction appears plausible until we reread the piece and notice discrepancies between the critic's characterization of the style and the author's actual words. Is it accurate to say that, with all its false starts, arbitrary episodes, and internal contradictions, *Abandoned Work* "returns [Beckett] to the structures and certainties of earlier literatures," and that "Apollonian assumptions overwhelm" the story? Here is a representative speech from our abandoned narrator: "why the curses were pouring out of me I do not know, no, that is a foolish thing to say. . . . Is it the stoats now, no, first I just sink down again and disappear in the ferns. . . . "When the new reading of this language concludes that, "Instead of crossing out lines or deleting passages, the narrator retains what he has said and explains it" (p. 132), then judgments about other late fragments and the classifications they are grouped in become suspect. A few of Beckett's works fit almost too easily into Dearlove's new schema, while others seem uncomfortable in their new literary homes. Placing *Enough* with fictions marked by a "sense of sufficiency" ignores the narrator's contradictions, paradoxes, and fears. Beckett early in his career warned against the dangers of neat critical pigeon holes; the overgeneralizations in Dearlove's *Accommodating the Chaos* obscure the unique stylistic innovation of some later texts.

While many contemporary fiction writers do not necessarily strive for a style to imitate their content (Saul Bellow explores modern scepticism, despair, and voids in standard English sentences), and while other novelists achieve only one mirroring form (Borges pursues uncertainty, chance, and probability with similar motifs and metaphors in each story), Beckett performs his artistic task of reshaping our modern confusion by creating several different styles. Through his dying narrator Malone, Beckett favors various containers for the void: "the forms are many in which the unchanging seeks relief from its formlessness" (*Malone Dies*, p. 121). A stylistic reading of the post-*Unnamable* fictions traces Beckett's groping toward new grammatical (and ungrammatical) structures that make imperative different ways of reading. Beckett abandoned traditional characters long ago, and what remains for the reader to follow in the recent metafictions are half-human creatures metaphorically struggling through fields of language, represented by dense forests, thick mud, or barren moors. As Ruby Cohn has shown,[36] the physical journey reflects a verbal quest; and this identification can be taken one leap further. With the wandering figure of *From an Abandoned Work*, the crawling creature of *How It Is*, the fallen body on the brink of a step in *Lessness*, and the drifting woman in *Ill Seen Ill Said*, Beckett chronicles his grappling with new vehicles, new styles.

Hermetic languages become the enclosed spaces of Beckett's later metafiction, constricted styles delimiting constrained domes, oblongs, cylinders, and boxes in which his recent characters are confined either moving or straining to be still. The reader too experiences a claustrophobic atmosphere when floundering in limited structures, or along mazelike paths, or inside sentences themselves—descending to the phrase level, getting lost or drowned in syntax, and then surfacing for white spaces. As the later Beckettian character becomes increasingly slow and then altogher immobile in an incrementally smaller area, he comes to represent both writer and reader, frustrated yet challenged by the borderlines of creative thought and linguistic expression: he can't go on, he'll go on.

In fact, Beckett on occasion has described himself when composing as a destitute traveller either stuck in or thrashing through forbidding terrain. Explaining in a letter to director Alan Schneider his problems with *Endgame*, Beckett writes, "I'm in a ditch somewhere near the last stretch and would like to crawl up on it."[37] Later in the same year (1956), as he was beginning to stage the play, Beckett wrote to Schneider again, this time sounding like the wandering protagonist of *From an Abandoned Work* (also 1956), and panting like the crawling body yet to be created in *Comment c'est* (1961): "I am panting to see the realization and know if I am on some kind of road, and can stumble on, or in a swamp."[38] Beckett, as well as his narrators and voices, analyzes his progress through a story or sentence by using journey metaphors in terms both tactile and linguistic.

If these recent fictions present (interrelated) solutions to artistic and stylistic problems, verbal ways of going on, then an accurate formulation of the problems appears in *Texts for Nothing*. Through the narrator of *Texts*, Beckett discusses the difficulty of continuing to write narratives, and finally the inability to complete even a clause: "The words too, slow, slow, the subject dies before it comes to the verb, words are stopping too."[39] As Linda Ben-Zvi has shown, Beckett inherited from the philosopher Fritz Mauthner a profound scepticism about language, especially about the power of language to express the inner being. Mauthner believed that thinking is reducible to language, the self is contingent on language, and language is reducible to the memory of sensory experience. Also, he held that communication is suspect because each person's expression is only a metaphorical approximation of his own reality. If all that language can do is make "pictures of pictures of pictures" (*Critique of Language*, I, 129), then all that human beings can do is resort to laughter—or to silence.[40] Beckett characters futilely search for the self, or at least for silence, while every sentence they speak or hear betrays them.

At a more specific level as well, language is not to be trusted by the novelist. Particular words, certain parts of speech, must be abandoned or Beckett is tricked into traditional plot and character again, as in the early fiction. The very mention of "he" creates at least the illusion of humanity, as even the Unnamable realizes. With the simple verb "to be" Beckett implies some type of existence, and this stylistic equation leads to a paradox inherent in grammar. The simple declaration "I am" is either illusory or deceptive. Often in the later fiction, Beckett circumvents a metaphysical issue by erasing it; in many stories he deletes verbs altogether, especially the copulative. Starting with *Texts for Nothing*, language itself arises as Beckett's main subject, as his creatures weigh each unit of thought, question nouns, and revise phrases, all the while wandering along strange syntactic paths. Style in Beckett's late fiction means not just a way of writing but a way of thinking.

2

Texts for Nothing
"Going On" Through Stylistic Devices

After *The Unnamable*, Samuel Beckett realized that he faced a problem of how to go on artistically and linguistically. By the last novel in the trilogy, character, setting, and plot had all disintegrated, the paragraph had disappeared, and even the sentence had stretched out of shape. What is left is a babble of words, yet the next Beckett storyteller, the narrator of *Texts for Nothing*, describes his predicament with surprising good humor: "No, no souls, or bodies, or birth, or life, or death, you've got to go on without any of that junk, that's all dead with words, with excess of words . . . they'll find some other nonsense, no matter what, and I'll be able to go on. . . ."[1] At least words themselves continue in *Texts for Nothing*, "texts" meaning by one definition simply the wording of something written. The Unnamable ends his monologue paradoxically, "I can't go on, I'll go on," and the narrator of the texts continues this sense of a linguistic impasse: "Suddenly, no, at last, long last, I couldn't any more, I couldn't go on" (p. 75). Yet he does go on with nothing but style, "text" by another definition having "the Latin sense of literary tissue or style."[2] Where words are not cohesive units of grammatical sentences and paragraphs, and where these in turn do not compose the traditional elements of a novel or short story, how does a fiction writer manage to string words together and still have them mean something, or—more difficult still—have them convey "nothing" at all?

By employing a noncharacter as a narrator, Beckett opens up a world of possible content, the creation of a protagonist. Also, by attempting to produce a main character, Beckett links the thirteen texts and thus provides a kind of dramatic unity, despite the lack of plot and of coherent sentences. Acting on the premise that the modern writer has nothing to express and yet the urge to express, Beckett uses several tricks of language which enable him to multiply the number and variety of words and phrases without having them add up to a narrative expression. This allows his fiction to "go on," and thus by about 1950, stylistic devices emerge as Beckett's most important means of continuing his fictional voices' murmurings. As with the Unnamable (who reasons, "If only I were alive inside one might look forward to heart-failure . . ."—p. 64), the goal of the narrator throughout the text is to create himself so that he can then cease to exist—to be truly born so that he can unequivocally die. As he labors to be delivered, he calls up or invents memories of things and beings, and all these provide material for his murmurs. The invention of more than one voice makes possible a dialogue with the self— and again other words: "My den, I'll describe it, no, I can't. It's simple, I can do nothing any more, that's what you think" (p. 75). Already, in Text 1, both a first- and a second-person pronoun exist, reflecting the Cartesian mind/body dichotomy that has intrigued Beckett since *Murphy*. Soon we will hear a "he" and a "they" as the split self becomes a multi-persona, as in *Molloy*, an inner and outer voice at the very least, and often a voice in three parts: "Ah yes, we seem to be more than one, all deaf, not even, gathered together for life. Another said, or the same, or the first, they all have the same voice, the same ideas" (pp. 75–76). Echoing the layered voices in *The Unnamable*, the murmurs in *Texts* bounce back yet more rapidly and with even more fragmentary structure and uncertain tone.

Since in French the title phrase *Textes pour rien* suggests "mesure pour rien,"[3] a musical silence, a bar's rest, it is not surprising that at times the different selves seem to be orchestral parts singing in a kind of harmony—"I can follow them well, all the voices, all the parts"—and that the voices sing as a "duo" or "trio," seeking a coda of silence. As the texts regress, however, the "we" breaks down increasingly into an "I" and a "he," or an "I" and a "they," who try to trick each other. A Cartesian universe includes potential deception by an evil demon (occurring in Beckett's work since the French stories)[4] who strives to confuse man about his own physical existence and the physical reality of the world. Beckett invokes this deceptive spirit subtly by changing a verb in an earlier version from "taken in" to "deceived";[5] and later he actually brings the demon out into the open: "if there was a way out, if I said there was a way out, make me say it, demons, no, I'll ask for nothing" (p. 119). As Beckett himself searches for a "way out" of his artistic predicament, a fictional retrenchment becomes attractive.

Whereas, in a traditional story, action usually develops through conflict between two main characters, in these texts

Beckett derives all the conflict he requires (to keep the dialogue and the words in general going) within one noncharacter. As the antagonism between the different parts of the self reaches a crescendo, disharmony shatters the silence and plays itself out through a clashing of pronouns: ". . . what's to be said of this latest other, with his babble of homeless mes and untenanted hims, this other without number or person whose abandoned being we haunt, nothing" (p. 134). Here Beckett self-consciously employs the grammatical classifications "person" and "number" to depict this pronoun with no noun to back it up. Use of a pronoun implies a noun referent, but our narrator is never given a name (not even "Unnamable") so that all his pronouns falsely refer to a nothing, analogous to two-dimensional cardboard figures that are facades only, that have nothing behind them. Different parts of the "I" serve as both subjects and objects, both speakers and addressees; and fictional personas created by the narrator also populate the text, beings who nearly become other characters he can interact with or merge into. The narrator hypothesizes that one way to "get born" is to tell a story and then to infuse himself into a character. Like the Unnamable, though, his pensum is to relate the *correct* story, the "right aggregate" of words. At first he tries calling up memories, but people from his past do not provide inspiration because in these recollections he is limited to the past tense, while true stories must be told in the present in order to earn the character an existence in time. Thus he experiments with different verb tenses as well as with various pronouns in order to compose a proper story in which he can embody himself. (By tracing the series of manuscripts and typescripts leading to *Texts*, one can observe Beckett himself trying out different tenses and temporal signals, even inserting the word "tenses" into a phrase about time.)

In Text 3 the voice tries to imagine events in the future tense: "I know how I'll do it, I'll be a man, there's nothing else for it, a kind of man, a kind of old tot, I'll have a nanny, I'll be her sweet pet, she'll give me her hand, to cross over, she'll let me loose in the Green, I'll be good, I'll sit quiet as a mouse . . ." (p. 86). But the narrator soon realizes that all the contracted "will's" in the world cannot will him into being—especially if he is trapped in limbo between childhood and old age. His wistful "if only it could be like that" refers not only to the impossibility of being a child with a nanny, but also the impossibility of creating a self-defining story with this device. "I know it's not me," he admits.

Later in this text he again laments that he has no current existence, and this directs him once more into the future tense, but a future that implies a past. In a wonderfully comic passage, the speaker invents an old army buddy—because, after all, every man must have old war stories on tap:

No no, I'll speak now of the future, I'll speak in the future, as when I used to say, in the night, to myself, Tomorrow I'll put on my dark blue tie . . . I'll have a crony, my own vintage, my own bog, a fellow warrior, we'll relive our campaigns and compare our scratches. Quick, quick. He'll have served in the navy, perhaps under Jellicoe, while I was potting at the invader from behind a barrel of Guinness, with my arquebuse. We have not long, that's the spirit, in the present, not long to live, it's our positively last winter, halleluiah.

[P. 87]

After starting in the future tense, moving through the future perfect construction "he'll have served," and arriving at the present tense, the narrator concludes this section with the conditional verb "would," the verbal mood for speculation, for imagination: "He'd nourish me . . . he'd ram the ghost back down my gullet . . . he'd prevent discouragement . . . I'd say to him, come on, gunner, leave all that. . . . We *were*, there we are past and gone again . . ." (pp. 88–89, my italics). The "I" continues for a while in the past tense, but then rejects it with "no, that's all memories, last shifts older than the flood" (p. 89). Only in a present-tense chronicle can he create a current, living self: ". . . I'd join them [black dancers] with a will if it could be here and now, how is it nothing is ever here and now?" (p. 102).

His next attempt to situate himself, though, falls back on the conditional and the subjunctive: "And what if all this time I had not stirred hand or foot from the third class waiting-room of the South-Eastern Railway Terminus . . . and were still there waiting to leave . . ." (p. 108). A return to the past tense, a reversion to mere memories, produces self-condemnation; to pretend he is alive and therefore capable of the peace of death, of silence, he must try again to tell a self-creating story. But this narrative incarnation fails because neither the present tense nor the third person pronoun can be maintained: the man he imagines disintegrates into an amorphous mass of flesh and bones, an impersonal "it."

Making a detour in Text 8, the narrator—instead of attempting to relate a story—tries to fabricate a character (himself) by dra-

matizing place, time, costume, and props. "But what is this I
see, and how, a white stick and an ear-trumpet, where, Place de
la République, at pernod time, let me look closer at this, it's perhaps me at last" (p. 114). Bowler hat and brown boots "advance
in concert, as though connected by the traditional human excip-
ient," but the "I" rejects the temptation of infusing himself into
the body of this other vagrant because "I would know it was not
me, I would know I was here." As this bum begs for money, the
narrator acknowledges that he himself is begging for the greater
alm "of being or of ceasing"; and this disparity between the
physical, practical beggar and the metaphysical, figurative
quester is too wide—even for the lies and self-deceptions of this
persona.

For his last try at self-creation in Text 12, the narrator evokes a
setting with a combination of present, future, past, and present
participle verbs: "It's a winter night, where I was, where I'm
going, remembered, imagined, no matter, believing in me, believing it's me, no, no need . . ." (p. 133). The introduction of a
third-person "he" who is viewing his own body delineates a
character, a shell the narrator then tries to enter. But the timing
of the he/I merger is tricky here (as reflected in the various verb
tenses juggled), and some outside force ("the others"?) must
finesse it: "Will they succeed in slipping me into him, the memory and dream of me, into him still living, amn't I there already,
wasn't I always there . . . and from now till he dies my last
chance to have been . . ." (p. 134). This last gamble must have
failed; in Text 13 the "I" admits that he is an "unmakable being."
Nonetheless in all the futile attempts to make a being, Beckett
has gone on with sixty-five pages of words, words that depict
imagination, invention, and creativity even if they never create a
character or define a self.

Thus it is possible to construct a formal text without any traditional elements of narrative, elements that are mocked by the
narrator of *Texts for Nothing*. After "I" starts to depict a realistic
setting and the religious atmosphere of a Sunday for the Mr. Joly
episode, he catches himself with "Here at least none of that, no
talk of a creator and nothing very definite in the way of a creation" (p. 83). While he concedes that a narrator usually requires
characters, he rejects the typical romantic themes of adventure
novels in one of the most humorous passages of the work:

there has to be a man, or a woman, feel between your legs, no need
of beauty, nor of vigour, a week's a short stretch, no one's going to

love you, don't be alarmed. No, not like that, too sudden, I gave myself a start. And to start with stop palpitating, no one's going to kill you, no one's going to love you and no one's going to kill you. . . . [P. 86]

Although the "I" here debunks both romances and murder mysteries, he feels that something must happen in his narrative. By Text 6 he is still promising to tell "a little story, with living creatures coming and going on a habitable earth crammed with the dead" (p. 105), almost a *T.V. Guide* summary of a later Beckett fiction, *The Lost Ones.* Finally, by Text 13, the possibility of a narrative, and even the word "story," has been abandoned; now the "I" would be content with merely a "trace" of its existence. All traces, all murmurings vanish because "to speak of instants, to speak of once, is to speak of nothing." As for the voice, "it breathes in vain, nothing is made," but this nothing is still conveyed in words, and these words are arranged in an intricate shape.

Beckett advertizes not nothing, but *texts* for nothing. In this piece, more than in earlier Beckett fiction, the process takes precedence over the endproduct, and the creative process forms the only plot. Alternating with a search for the self-defining story is the theme of "giving up" the search for self, and this vacillation between hope and despair, this cancellation of yes by no,[6] determines that in each of the thirteen texts the "I" must start again; there is no cumulative solution. For the artist struggling with words, each piece, each sentence, is a continual re-beginning: an oscillation between the yes of creation and the no of revision. *Texts'* form mirrors the configuration of the narrator's artistic journey: every text starts with the illusion of progress but ends in a thwarted circle.[7] In the larger structure of the whole, the "I" finally decides that the time has come for him to begin at the conclusion of Text 7, about the midpoint of the work. As in *Endgame,* the literary process consists not in a building up but in a winding down. The "I" starts with a body, a head, a heart, and several selves, and ends with a voice. He begins with a setting, memories, and stories, and ends with only lies and murmurs. He commences with plans and hopes for being, and concludes by despairing of existence itself.

In Text 1 the narrator is the closest he will ever be to a conventional character of fiction; all he needs is to collect himself—literally. Beckett lends him a mother, a father, and a home he can

see in the distance, all realistic touches; but surrealism supercedes when the narrator cannot locate himself precisely in space
and time. Moreover, any story line dwindles when he is para-
lyzed in determining whether to remain or to go on; thus "I
can't" becomes the refrain for the first text. His inability to decide or to act produces a desire to rest: thoughts about the close
of day and memories of bedtime stories lead to sleep—and thus
to perfect poetic closure.

Text 2 elaborates on the idea that the "I" is in some sort of dead
world and that above, in the light, are the living. Still concerned
with time and location, he differentiates himself, down below,
with, "Here you are under a different glass . . ." (p. 81). When
he considers going above again (the same phrase occurs repeatedly in How It Is, "above in the light"), he contemplates a return
to conventional fiction, since the term "above" recalls realistic
scenery from Text 1: the sea, valleys, cliffs, and forests. This possibility calls up memories of people from above: Mother Calvet,
Mr. Joly, and (apparently) Piers Plowman. Ironically, though, the
"I" repudiates memory, wishing, "If only it could be wiped from
knowledge." Throughout this text, it is his present, not his past,
that he wants to understand; but time has expanded and become
indivisible, "one enormous second." Wherever he is, he knows
he must continue to utter words until he is at home, and "home"
now means silence.

The beginning of Text 3 thrusts aside the ending of Text 2—
"Leave, I was going to say leave all that" (p. 85)—and yet undercuts this very rejection. An earlier desire to know what happens,
to reconstruct history, becomes now a need to tell a story; the
narrator must fabricate his own past as life yields to art. Stories
and departures, the two motifs of Text 3, are logically linked because either narrating a self-defining story or moving in time will
create the "I." He fails at both and, even worse, cannot will himself a head or a body through either method. (We have regressed
from Text 1, where a body was implied, and from Text 2, where
the "I" was inside a head.) Both present and future appear dis-
mal and uncertain for this non-being: "Here, nothing will happen here, no one will be here for many a long day" (p. 90). Like
the Unnamable, whose first sentence is "Where now?" and
whose last sentence begins "The place," this "I" strives to locate
himself in space and time, to be "here and now."

Text 4 begins with already familiar queries: Where will I
go? and, Who am I anyway? The new addition here is a split

between the "I" and a "he," maintained (with a few denials) throughout the text. Either the "I" is making his figments talk, or "he" has created "I" as one of *his* figments, or there is only one "I" who tells lies, or. . . . (Similar nested layers of speakers and listeners determine the style and substance in the more recent Beckett fiction, *Company*, displaying a near-infinite regression of pronouns and voices.) The advantage of doubling an "I" and a "he" is that they can argue about who is at fault for the story's failure, and thus a dialogue of sorts can fill the void. Recriminations and accusations preface the courtroom scene of Text 5, but there the "I" ultimately escapes blame by denying the necessity of a story; simply his life will do. The split selves in Text 4 prepare us for the separation of the "I" into defendant and scribe in Text 5, and another foreshadowing occurs in the term "accusative"—"It's the same old stranger as ever for whom alone accusative I exist"—with its grammatical and legal connotations. (This word was added to the English version in the middle of the translation process; there is no equivalent in the French.)[8] In this imaginary courtroom, both being and nonbeing are punishable: "to be is to be guilty." On the witness stand of existence "nothing appears, all is silent, one is frightened to be born, no, one wishes one were, so as to begin to die" (p. 95). Although death's silence is the goal, the silent void is continually filled with phrases—one of the many transgressions of this linguistic criminal. The "I" still wonders where he is, wonders if he should go, yet ends up staying; as his degrees of freedom are more constricted, analogously his artistic choices become constrained.

Besides serving as both speaker and recorder at court, the "I" digresses on such literary topics as nature, setting, atmosphere, and the hero: "the sky and earth, I've heard great accounts of them . . . I've noted, I must have noted many a story with them as setting, they create the atmosphere. Between them where the hero stands a great gulf is fixed, while all about they flow together more and more, till they meet, so that he finds himself as it were under glass . . ." (p. 97). This is exactly where the protagonist found himself earlier. Like a guilty defendant psychologically unable to pronounce a victim's name, he is reluctant to utter the disturbing words "nearness" and "life": "Out of the corner of my eye I observe the writing hand, all dimmed and blurred by the—by the reverse of farness" (p. 96); "they want to create me, they want to make me, like the bird the birdikin, with larvae she fetches from afar, at the peril—I nearly said at the

peril of her life!" (p. 99). Frequently insisting that he is "far"
(from those above?), his birth is never complete, and thus genuine death is impossible. Text 1 ended with sleep after toil and
play; Text 5 ends with fatigue after toil only. Regression
continues.

The apparitions which begin Text 6 may derive from Text 5's
court scene or from resident phantoms, but the "keepers" surely
refer to prison wardens. Here the "I" seems imprisoned in his
own body, a fate also suffered by the Unnamable:

. . . I'm in something, I'm shut up, the silence is outside, outside,
inside . . . nothing but this voice and the silence all round, no need
of walls, yes, we must have walls, I need walls, good and thick, I
need a prison, I was right, for me alone, I'll go there now, I'll put me
in it . . . [*The Unnamable*, pp. 173–74]

Worse than that, the "I" of Text 6 has metaphorically become an
insect imprisoned in a display case—hence the repeated description of him as "under glass." Feeling self-conscious and
vaguely guilty, he shares J. Alfred Prufrock's fear of observation
and condemnation as when "formulated, sprawling on a pin."
Like a butterfly, he was "quick dead," becoming merely "a little
dust in a little nook, stirred faintly this way and that by breath
straying from the lost without. Yes, I'm here for ever, with the
spinners and the dead flies, dancing to the tremor of their
meshed wings . . ." (pp. 102–103). In translating from the French
to the English *Texts*, Beckett enhances the butterfly imagery: *flot-
tant* becomes "flaunting and fluttering," and *perspectives*, that is,
"openings," are rendered as "glades."[9] As butterfly, the narrator
possesses first an ephemeral life and in death a kind of permanence: "What can have become then of the tissues I was, I can
see them no more. . . . The eyes, yes, if these memories are
mine, I must have believed in them an instant, believed it was me
I saw there dimly in the depths of their glades. I can see me still
with those of now, sealed this long time, staring with those of
then, I must have been twelve, because of the glass . . ." (p. 103).
Here, in a linguistic shift, the glass over insects becomes a "round
shaving-glass" which the mother and father of the narrator (suddenly a real little boy) share. In French the equivalent word *glace*
means both "mirror" and "ice," and this double sense may have
prompted Beckett to slide surrealistically from earthly life to an
afterlife. Besides having lived for a time on earth, the "I" insists
that he also inhabited purgatory and hell. Instantly he is one of

Dante's damned—buried in ice up to his nose, and crying frozen tears. Between the weeping and the speaking he will, like a tormented sinner, be compelled to confess his errors, to recount somehow the required painful story; he, ironically, gives us his "word."

But in Text 7 he considers abandoning the search for identity because, clearly, he is not talking of himself; *he* is a creature who can just barely remember what it was like to move (p. 107), yet a real being requires locomotion. Rather, he is discussing, and has been discussing, "X, that paradigm of human kind, moving at will, complete with joys and sorrows, perhaps even a wife and brats, forbears most certainly, a carcass in God's image and a contemporary skull, but above all endowed with movement . . ." (p. 108). Meanwhile, the narrator may actually be sitting motionless in a railway terminal. Nothing is certain, and Beckett ironically uses legal, logical language recalling the courtroom scene to underline this scepticism: "In that case. . . . Whence it should follow, but does not . . . that this lump is no longer me and that search should be made elsewhere. . . . That is why one must not hasten to conclude, the risk of error is too great" (pp. 109–10). His linguistic maneuver is to narrate a third person story and then to translate it into the first person, to glide from "he" to "I"; but often these personal pronouns give way to the vague "one." Finally, the notion of night as a starting point, which has recurred, especially in the conclusions, ends this text as the "I" decides (near the midpoint of the book) that it is "time too for me to begin."

Text 8 recapitulates many of the themes we have already heard: the flow of words as tears, the location of the self, the possiblity of nonexistence, the light above, the hope of a story, the feeling of living inside a head, the inability to know anything, the guilt of being, and the search for the right words in order to find rest. Much of Text 8 is a lament for an ending: "But it will end, a desinence will come," where "desinence" means a termination or a final line of verse, and also—in linguistic contexts—an inflection or a suffix. Lov*ed* differs from lov*ing* by the terminal letters only, yet "loved" is over while "loving" continues; in words, in sentences, in stories, and in lives, the ending determines the interpretation of the whole: ". . . it's for ever the same murmur, flowing unbroken, like a single endless word and therefore meaningless, for it's the end gives the meaning to words" (p. 111). The new note introduced into Text 8 is the motif of begging, ultimately a seeking for the end of time. As he begs, the narrator shies away from any selfhood with his inability to utter the possessive "mine": "And the hand old in vain would drop the mite and the old feet shuffle on, towards an even vainer death than no matter whose" (p. 115). Even grammatically, he will not grant himself being.

Both the style and the substance in Text 9 seem more disjointed and confusing than those of the others, so a hint from the narrator is welcome: "What am I doing now, I'm trying to see where I am, so as to be able to go elsewhere . . ." (pp. 120–21). Specifically, he wants to ascertain if he ever had a physical body, if he ever died, and if there is a "way out" now, where "way out" may represent an escape from life or from mimetic fiction. However, he ultimately becomes drowned in a meaningless drift of words—or, as he puts it, buried in an "avalanche" of "wordshit"—and temporarily abandons his former pursuit of a story. The prison motif continues from Text 6, and a comparison with the French original confirms that the narrator's crime is still that of existence: "par lequel malgré eux les gens vous accusent" [10] becomes "with which the fellow-creature unwillingly betrays your presence" (p. 119). Guiltily questioning his origins, the "I" decides that he is lost somewhere between womb and tomb, and he recalls a time when he was slinking "to and fro before the graveyard" asking to be killed. The phrase "gates of the graveyard" cumulatively gains the force of a chant as, spinning in a frenzy, the "I" cannot recall whether he is "here" or "there, coming and going before the graveyard." Caught between the "here" of potential reality and the "there" of the imagination, he becomes so distraught that he confuses the recurring motif of the previous texts, "it's not me," with the refrain of Text 9, "There's a way out there"; and now the "way out" fervently desired is a departure from all these words. He concludes, with circularity, "The graveyard, yes, it's there I'd return, this evening it's there, borne by my words, if I could get out of here, that is to say if I could say, There's a way out there . . . ," as if the sentence itself would effect an escape. With even greater force than in *Malone Dies*, the saying makes it so; assertions forge reality. If the "I" plays God the creator, if he has only to say "Let there be X" for there to be X, then with the correct solution to the variable he can speak himself into existence.

"Give up" begins Text 10, but since the narrator has already capitulated in Text 7, he wryly concedes "it's nothing new."

Taking a personal inventory, the "I" tries to assess what he has lost: a head, a hand, a heart (all present in Text 1); and the senses as well are failing. Later the "I" asserts that he must go on without body or soul. Any more content than this, however, evaporates because Text 10 is composed almost entirely of devices of language which permit words to continue without allowing any narrative to creep in. At the barest minimum, the narrator will "have gone on giving up," yet even this minimal effort requires more words.

By Text 11 the narrator's self-consciousness and confusion prevent him from merely beginning the text. His mind (and his syntax) wanders, and he is literally at a loss for words. The new refrain here becomes, "I don't know, I shouldn't have begun," as every term raises some doubt about its very legitimacy. The only words that hold the others in the text together, "when come those who know me," were carefully chosen: as a subordinate, dependent clause it cannot complete its thought until followed by an independent clause. Beckett refuses to finish the sentence until the end of the text, keeping the first clause in suspension and thus unifying the passage. When the "I's" thought finally is completed, though, it reveals itself as a false solution to his problem of self-creation: "when comes the hour of those who knew me, it's as though I were among them, that is what I had to say, among them watching me approach, then watching me recede, shaking my head and saying, Is it really he, can it possibly be he . . ." (p. 131). The "I" temporarily achieves being through the Berkeleyian/Beckettian method of being perceived, but the perceiver, who should be the Other, is "I" also; and thus we circle back to the predicament of split selves. Although realizing that he moves nowhere with his ramble of words, that he is no closer to an answer now than when he started, the narrator almost deludes himself that conditions have improved; "it's not true, but I say it just the same . . ." (p. 130). If the utterance itself would make it so, if words indeed had ritualistic, magical powers, then the artist could succeed. Perhaps, then, all he lacks is *fewer* words.

Trying to remove all but the essential terms for his formula of self-creation, the narrator cancels out (with the phrase "no, no need") the unnecessary inventions: belief that the creature "going" is himself, belief in the presence of "others," and in the power to move somehow. (A similar revision-in-process occurs in a later fiction, "All Strange Away," with the title phrase used to delete unwanted details.) What remains is simply a winter's night with a light emanating from neither stars nor moon, but needed—light necessary so that the being, created with the mere mention of a "he," can see his own body. The "I" will capture the body and voice of this other, and haunt him in a kind of ghostly possession. When this fails, the protagonist reverts to the notion that creating his existence requires only the presence of others, now not as possible bodies to inhabit but as possible eyes to witness him. In despair, however, the "I" (like Watt) follows an infinite regression and realizes that a god, an unwitnessed witness, would also be necessary. He consoles himself with the thought that, unlike in Text 11, here fortunately he did not even begin anything: ". . . what a blessing it's all down the drain, nothing ever as much as begun, nothing ever but nothing and never, nothing ever but lifeless words." Ironically though, these words pulsate with linguistic life—with parallel structure, prose rhythm, and even internal rhyme (ever/Never). Paradoxically, a lamentation that nothing has begun re-begins the begetting of words.

After twelve texts, we have rich textures but still no hope of a story, or any other means to the narrator's embodiment. At the conclusion even the voice "that tried in vain to make me" is dying down. Text 13 provides excellent closure of *Texts for Nothing*, suggesting that despite their circularity the texts could not go on indefinitely: "there it dies, it can't go on, it's been its death, speaking of me . . ." (p. 137). Gradually, the "I" has lost his spirit, body, heart, head, and hand, but the voice becomes totally disembodied only in Text 13. Stressing the death of the voice in the English *Texts*, Beckett translates "elle se fait lointaine . . . ou elle baisse" [11] as "Dying away . . . or dying down" (p. 137). Grammatically the narrator has diminished from an "I" to an "it." Many other physical and emotional regressions reach their zero points in Text 13. Although one critic prefers to speak of "progression" rather than "regression," "counterpoint" rather than "contradiction," and "reintegration" rather than "fragmentation," [12] it is difficult to discern any positive conclusion in *Texts*— unless it exists solely in the reader's mind. In Text 6 the "I" described himself as dust blown by breath; in 13 he finds stasis in the still air that hardly disturbs the still dust. A weary voice now describes its first goal in the past: "that was the only chance, get out of here and go elsewhere . . ." (p. 138). This last text, like others, is punctuated with a refrain; but here, instead of driving a frenzied pace and a frantic tone, the repetition of "it says" creates a sense of distance and non-urgency. The "I" no longer pursues himself by spilling out torrents of words in order to find the answer to the riddle of existence. Now the "it" almost calmly "wonders what has become of the wish to know, it is gone, the heart is gone, the head is gone, no one feels anything, asks anything, seeks anything, says anything, hears anything, there is only silence" (p. 139). Yet the compulsive rhythmic reiteration of "[verb] anything," the enumeration of nothing, produces strings of something; and the last words, "it says, it murmurs," still disturbs the silence. The truth of "Weaker still the weak old voice," the start of Text 13, is illustrated by its final clause, in which "murmurs" has a much weaker volume and connotation than the verb "says." Ultimately, the "going on" of this voice produces the circularity of the piece, while its softening produces the overall structure of decline.

Texts for Nothing, if graphed, might appear as a curve from some negative number to some miniscule negative fraction approaching zero, but its structure is obviously circular as well. A return to one's starting point accomplishes "nothing," and Beckett has stylistically managed to "go on" and to go nowhere simultaneously. Most of the individual texts turn back on themselves so that a model of *Texts for Nothing* would consist of thirteen small overlapping circles within one large zero. There is a marvelous irony in that Beckett's picture of the void is intricate indeed, that nothing is filled with such linguistic brilliance.

In *Texts for Nothing*, when Beckett has reduced the novel to a murmuring narrator, and has further restricted the protagonist to a voice talking "for nothing," each word bears the horrible and paradoxical responsibility of meaning as little as possible. The circular imitative form of the work as a whole is reinforced by an imitative style in which the narrator's struggle with language, with finding the right words, takes place at the phrase level. Porter Abbott sees this reduction to strings of words in both *The Unnamable* and *Texts for Nothing*: "Without story, without people, without things, without space and time, the books become their words and syntax. It is here that we get the direct attempt to imitate in form the experience the speaker is going through."[13] Of course, one difference between the two works is the tight formal structure of the *Texts*—just the opposite of *The Unnamable*'s rambling and amorphous flow. The thirteen divisions, rebeginnings, repeated narrative attempts become the only story within a style that embodies its own futility. It is possible to classify four elements of this imitative style: absurd hypothesis, cancellation, the analysis of words, and the incomplete sentence.[14] Other characteristics, including authorial comment, literalism, and self-contradiction, have been analyzed as comic devices.[15] These and more subtle verbal maneuverings, when used in concert, compose an orchestrated opus of silence.

One method of approaching but never reaching a linguistic deadend, as Beckett's Watt knew very well, is the sheer repetition of words and phrases, compounding the confusion with permutation of words in a phrase and of phrases in a sentence, until all words lose all sense. Analyzing repetition in Watt, Bruce Kawin differentiates three variations of the permutation strategy: (1) "Listing every relevant fact or object in an attempt to fence in the phenomenon . . ."; (2) "Listing the logical permutations in an attempt at problem solving . . ."; and (3) "Carrying logical permutation to the language itself . . . ,"[16] as in Watt's inversion of letters. In Texts, words sometimes are simply transposed within phrases: "I am alone, I alone am." Whole clauses can be essentially repeated, for instance when Beckett uses parallel construction (repetition in syntax) substituting different adjectives or predicate nominatives: ". . . I won't be any more, it won't be worth it any more, it won't be necessary any more, it won't be possible any more, but it's not worth it now, it's not necessary now, it's not possible now . . ." (p. 130). The shift of the verb "be" from intransitive to transitive doubles its function, and negation of these resulting variations then multiplies the possible phrases by two. When this device is combined with paradox and extended by self-conscious remarks on style, then the (humorous) result is a string of self-propelling phrases, each one set into motion by the grammatical patterns of its predecessor:

What variety and at the same time what monotony, how varied it is and at the same time how, what's the word, how monotonous. What agitation and at the same time what calm. What vicissitudes within what changelessness. Moments of hesitation not so much rare as frequent, if one had to choose, and soon overcome in favour of the old crux, on which at first all depends, then much, then little, then nothing. [P. 118]

At first the 'I' simply echoes the same ideas using a slightly different clausal structure so that the nouns are in a sense "repeated" as adjectives. At the phrase level Beckett uses repetition to urge the narrator onward by extracting a segment from an earlier sentence to begin some later sentence in the same text. For example, in Text 7 part of the first sentence ("Did I try everything, ferret in every hold, secretly, silently, patiently, listening?") launches the third sentence: "In every hold, I mean all those places where there was a chance of my being . . ." (p. 107).

In other passages, before a clause can be restated, or even fully stated, half its terms are challenged, and this very fussiness over semantics consumes more words. A quibble about meaning can evade a question instead of answering it: "How long have I been here, what a question, I've often wondered. And often I could answer, An hour, a month, a year, a century, depending on what I meant by here, and me, and being, and there I never went looking for extravagant meanings, there I never much varied, only the here would sometimes seem to vary" (p. 76). A semantic twist or an eccentric redefinition also names words while not allowing a sentence to finish: "Another thing, I call that another thing, the old thing I keep on not saying till I'm sick and tired, revelling in the flying instants, I call that revelling, now's my chance and I talk of revelling . . ." (p. 108). Also, this narrator shares stylistic quirks with the narrators of the trilogy, the reversal or distortion of a cliché or proverb which pulls the reader up short. He maintains that he is "dead and kicking above," and promises that he will learn to keep quiet "if nothing foreseen crops up."

Conversely, the "I" often insists on the literal meaning of a word, thus providing a gratuitous pun: "The day had not been fruitful, as was only natural, considering the season, that of the very last leeks" (p. 84). A pun initially appears to produce a doubling of meaning, taking us far from the ideal of narrative emptiness; but by insisting upon two or more definitions simultaneously, a pun produces a paralysis of interpretation. For Beckett's characters "the only supremely satisfying form of language is the *pun*—the absurdity of words turned in upon themselves, where meanings cancel each other out and leave yet another Néant, a sudden reverberating silence within the 'big blooming buzzing confusion' of sound and significance. . . ."[17] At least once in the English version Beckett adds a play on words not present in the French original: "you may even believe yourself dead on condition you make no bones about it" (p. 93). Even the "end sheets" in Text 13 can refer to sheets of paper as well as to death. One of the narrator's favorite phrases, "in a manner of speaking," repeatedly plays over the surface; this aside "takes on an ironic smile when the whole work is concerned with the manner of artistic speaking. . . ."[18] At times Beckett exploits the literal meaning of a figurative expression to absurd limits of signifiers and signifieds: "And I'm in good hands again, they hold my head from behind, intriguing detail, as at the hairdressers . . ." (p. 123).

With the phrase "intriguing detail," the narrator critiques his own verbal handiwork, and throughout *Texts for Nothing* self-reflexive judgments about language inflate his narrative. More so than Beckett's trilogy narrators, he is ludicrously self-conscious about his style as well as about his story: "Never had the sea so thundered from afar, the sea beneath the snow, though superlatives have lost most of their charm" (pp. 83–84). In Text 5 the narrator/scribe remarks on his punctuation and dictation with "full stop, got all that." Moreover, in some stylistically self-defeating passages the narrator's critical evaluations consume as much space as the original statement:

And it is possible, just, for I must not be too affirmative at this stage, it would not be in my interest, that other fingers, quite a different gang, other tentacles, that's more like it, other charitable suckers, waste no more time trying to get it right, will take down my declarations, so that at the close of the interminable delirium, should it ever resume, I may not be reproached with having faltered. This is awful, awful, at least there's that to be thankful for. [P. 124]

Of course a pedantic search for the perfect word obsessed Molloy and Malone too, but the difference in *Texts* is that linguistic journeys subsume physical ones and obviate any plot whatsover. In the passage above self-references impede the progress of the sentence, while in many utterances they kill the sentence outright: "When I think, no, that won't work, when come those who knew me, perhaps even know me still, by sight of course, or by smell, it's as though, it's as if, come on, I don't know, I shouldn't have begun" (p. 127). For encouragement and impetus, the narrator provides positive as well as negative criticism: he counsels himself on what to utter (using the imperative mood) and plans how he will proceed (using the future tense): "somehow somewhere calm, what calm here, ah that's an idea, say how calm it is here, and how fine I feel, and how silent I am, I'll start right

away. I'll say what calm and silence . . . yes, I'll say all that tomorrow . . ." (p. 125). By playing with verbs and commenting
on comments (and by humorously contradicting himself) the
voice goes on manufacturing words without finally making a
statement.

Following the fine example of Molloy, the narrator poses countless queries to ascertain his nature, his location in time and
space, his task, and his future. In the tradition of the tramps in
Godot, he also cross-examines himself simply to pass the time.
The movement of Text 1 proceeds through several problems:
"Who are these people anyway? Did they follow me up here, go
before me, come with me? . . . Do they see me, what can they
see of me? . . . How long have I been here, what a question . . .
And that other question I know so well too, What possessed you
to come?" But by Text 13 there is only one question mark to be
seen, because the "I" has lost the desire for knowledge. He de-
cries the "old questions, last questions" despairingly: "Unfortunately it is not a question of elsewhere, but of here, ah there are
the words out at last . . ." (p. 138). In the interim, the inter-
rogative quality of the texts serves its purpose—getting on with
the words—for replies provide numerous opportunities for lists,
for "ors," for "ifs," and for "perhapes." The narrator poses questions quite consciously because he hopes that someday the answer will be the correct one and thus be the road to silence. In
the courtroom scene of Text 5 the narrator becomes increasingly
self-conscious about his sentence forms and their punctuation:
"And now birds, the first birds, what's this new trouble now,
don't forget the question-mark" (p. 99). But Beckett does "forget" the question mark, especially when queries are one clause
long and embedded in lengthy sentences. For a confused voice
questions are often the only possible statements.

In seeking solutions to his problem of nonbeing, the "I" pursues rhetorical questions to lend validity to a newly posited self.
In fact, queries about a hypothetical existence almost create
being: "Is it there I came to a stop, is that me still waiting there,
sitting up stiff and straight on the edge of the seat, knowing the
dangers of laissez-aller, hands on thighs, ticket between finger
and thumb . . . it's there, it's me" (p. 109). No, it can't be he—at
least not for very long—because the narrator is not located in
time, but rather in a timeless state of pre-birth reflected in the
jumbled verb tenses of "at first I only had been here, now I'm

here still, soon I won't be here yet. . . ." And, no, the "I" cannot be "me" because the "I" drowns in the profusions of pronouns in Text 13.

Many times the response to a question will be both yes and no—a double answer which is in reality a null answer. Contradiction, exploited by Beckett so effectively in the trilogy, becomes both a stylistic device and a thematic issue in *Texts for Nothing*. In Text 13 the "I" reviews previous testimony and concludes that there were "so many lies, so many times the same lie lyingly denied." Vacillations and cancellations reach a climax in this last text, as style and substance both sum to zero: "It's not true, yes, it's true, it's true and it's not true, there is silence and there is not silence, there is no one and there is someone, nothing prevents anything" (p. 139). Here even the word "prevent" balances conflicting meanings: its archaic meaning of to come before, to prepare, or to anticipate, and its modern one of to keep from happening or existing. In *Texts for Nothing* the striving for nothingness anticipates the something of its structure, and yet this nothing reduces the probability for creation. Often, the "I" contradicts itself to deny its own existence: "That's so that I'll never stir again, dribble on here till time is done. . . . It's not me, it's not true, it's not me, I'm far" (p. 87). Contradiction alone succeeds in forcing the narrator backwards, and used in conjunction with questioning, repeating, and quibbling over semantics, it results in near nothingness: "How many hours to go, before the next silence, they are not hours, it will not be silence, how many hours still, before the next silence?" (p. 104). Like many of the texts, this sentence moves in a circle and describes a void; yet this denial of language's meaning paradoxically requires the reassertion of language.

A child would link a flow of words with the simple conjunction "and," but a mature, reasoning voice like the narrator of *Texts* speaks in logical options joined with "or"s: "What possessed you to come?, unanswerable, so that I answered, To change, or, It's not me, or, Chance, or again, To see, or again, years of great sun . . ." (p. 77). Many sentences begin with "or" because a new clause is less a new proposition in *Texts for Nothing* than a further possibility. The "I" wonders about the fate of dead bodies and souls in Text 10: "Or has it knelled here at last for our committal to flesh, as the dead are committed to the ground . . . or for our reassignment, souls of the stillborn, or dead before the body, or still young in the midst of ruins, or never come to life through incapacity or for some other reason, or the immortal type, there must be a few of them too . . ." (p. 124). As this passage shows, the use of alternatives within alternatives deflects the speaker further away from the initial issue, and therefore closer to a diffused nothingness. In a tree diagram sentences like the one above might appear as in Figure 1.

Other times proliferating "or's" produce comic effects, a kind of linguistic burlesque: "I stay here, sitting, if I'm sitting, often I feel sitting, sometimes standing, it's one or the other, or lying down, there's another possibility, often I feel lying down, it's one of the three, or kneeling" (p. 93).

Reasoning about events occurring in various atmospheres necessitates frequent use of the conditional mood; and "perhaps" with other related locutions allows the voice to multiply his word output without committing himself to a statement of narrative fact. In Text 10 the voice proceeds rationally from "I'm nothing new" to "Ah so there was something once, I had something once. It may be thought there was." In Text 9 the narrator uses the phrase "what if" to consider past events, but more often the little word "if" enables Beckett's voice to take two steps forward and then three steps back. Specifically, the clause "if it's me" repeatedly undermines character incarnation, and permits the "I" to spin one false story after another. In the courtroom scene the narrator tires of playing scribe, defendant, and judge simultaneously: ". . . I'd be tired of it, if I were me. It's a game, it's getting

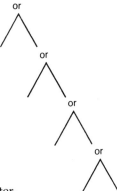

Fig. 1. A tree diagram of the alternatives within alternatives in *Texts for Nothing.*

to be a game, I'm going to rise and go, if it's not me it will be someone, a phantom . . ." (p. 98). Here the conditional mood slides into the future tense as a stylistic device to avoid a present existence.

Most of these stylistic techniques produce an accumulation of sentences with a dissolution of meaning. Taking the beginning as a high point, Mary Ann Caws traces a "line of reductions and diminutions" in the *Texts*: "definite statement is reduced to qualified determination, . . . the easiest clichés of natural speech to linguistic fumblings. . . . [and] [t]he most frantic cries diminish in tone to a helplessly polite monotony. . . ."[19] Other critics, however, praise the lyrical richness of *Texts for Nothing*. When rearranged, the opening of Text 4, albeit full of conditionals, shows "duple rhythm, caesural pauses, even rhyme":[20]

> Where would I go, if I could go,
> Who would I be, if I could be,
> What would I say, if I had a voice,
> Who says this, saying it's me?

It is almost as if rhythm replaces plot; the lyric supplants the narrative. But although the narrator of *Texts* is capable of imagistic poetry, he never manages a simple first-person story.

Instead, in these thirteen pseudostories, experiments of all kinds with verb forms of all sorts occur so often that the voice itself despairs of ever maintaining the authorial present. In trying to create a fictional origin, the narrator shifts from the conditional mood to an even more remote past conditional: "I'd have a mother, I'd have had a mother" (p. 118). Besides failing to situate his stories in the present, he cannot locate himself chronologically: "It's me all right, and ceasing to be what is more, then quickening my step, so as to arrive before the next onslaught, as though it were on time I trod . . ." (p. 119). Beckett's concern with time and its grammatical markers is revealed in his numerous revisions of verb tenses and in other changes that highlight this same obsession in the narrator: "all mingles, times mingle" becomes in a revised typescript "all mingles, times and tenses."[21] By Text 13 the "I" still has no time frame, as it speaks of past events with present participles and infinitives ("of being past, passing and to be"), and murmurs of endings in the present tense ("we're ended who never were"). Readers had been warned of this confusion as early as Text 3, where the narrator, then playing Shakespearean actor, advises, "let us be dupes, dupes of every time and tense, until it's done. . . ." The rapid switching of tenses expands the text because it permits repetition of similar clauses with different verb phrases, thus obviating continuity of plot or story line. The chronologically fragmented anecdotes and memories represent the temporally fragmented narrator, able to create only a minimal narrative about the struggle to invent a character. With changing tenses Beckett ensures that the "I" will never arrive at any continuous existence—one criterion for being. In these ways Beckett works against his own narrator, allowing him neither to stop nor to succeed.

Besides exploiting tricks with verbs, Beckett also manipulates pronoun changes to prevent the narrator from achieving being. The Unnamable has a similar problem: language cannot bring him into existence and "it's the fault of the pronouns, there is no name for me, no pronoun for me, all the trouble comes from that . . ." (*The Unnamable*, p. 164). In Text 11 the "I" almost succeeds in fabricating a body through a fantasy memory racing from infancy to schoolboy days to old age. Here words truly invent, as the fiction forces itself to become reality with "sobs made mucus, hawked up from the heart, now I have a heart. . . ." But undermining construction of being is destruction of the "I" through a modulation of pronouns. One phrase recurs in the story, but with significant variation: "having terminated my humanities," "having terminated his humanities," and "having terminated their humanities." This shift from "my" to "his" to "their" distances the fiction's events further from the "I," so that the attempt to forge a self degenerates into the old question, "who is this clot . . . who takes himself for me."

A possible answer to the question "who?" is the impersonal pronoun "one," a pronoun also exploited by Virginia Woolf in her short fictions about the imagination, particularly in passages about mirror reflections (a common metaphor for identity). With this pronoun Beckett can have his "I" speak of himself under false pretenses and evade the harsher realities of his nonexistence. In Text 5, when the voice learns that to be is to be guilty, he muses, "That is why nothing appears, all is silent, one is frightened to be born, no, one wishes one were, so as to begin to die. One, meaning me, it's not the same thing . . ." (p. 95). Thus the narrator seems aware of his linguistic ploy, as he attempts yet another method of evasion—denying responsibility and culpability in the courtroom scene by relying on the passive voice so that the action's agent need not be specified: "it's noted"—but by whom? This grammatical passivity continues, with the help of null pronouns, to the end of Text 5, until, "Yes, one begins to be very tired, very tired of one's toil, very tired of one's quill, it falls, it's noted" (p. 99). By the end of all the texts, the "I" masks his identity in multiple pronouns—"it and me, it and him, him and me, and all our train, and all theirs"—until he is buried far below the impossible affirmation of being, "I am."

These devices to keep empty language going on are quite effective solo, but arranged in counterpoint they sing of nothingness with an immense variety. Speaking of a way out in Text 9, the voice seems hypnotized by its own repetition, contradiction, permutation, and alternation: "down the long tunnels at first, then under the mortal skies, through the days and nights, faster and faster, no, slower and slower, for obvious reasons, and at the same time faster and faster, for other obvious reasons, or the same, obvious in a different way, or in the same way, but at a different moment of time, a moment earlier, a moment later, or at the same moment, there is no such thing, there would be no such thing . . ." (p. 118). The "way out" has been lost forever after this wordplay, and other texts similarly combine questions, authorial comments, changes in tenses, and shifts in pronouns to go on producing words for nothing, "in vain." The following proposition begins with some preconditions for the "I" and ends by dismissing the "I" altogether:

If I were here, if it could have made me, how I would pity it, for having spoken so long in vain, no, that won't do, it wouldn't have spoken in vain, if I were here, and I wouldn't pity it if it had made me, I'd curse it, or bless it, it would be in my mouth, cursing, blessing, whom, what, it wouldn't be able to say, in my mouth it wouldn't have much to say, that had so much to say in vain. [P. 138]

In this sentence, like many others in *Texts for Nothing*, syntax is so disjointed that, as the narrator puts it, "the subject dies before the verb." In this case the consequent, what should be the independent clause, is stated but then contradicted, and reasons for the contradiction are exhaustively pursued. Thus, "I would pity it" eventually becomes "I would bless it"; however, before the sentence can end, the "it" is analyzed out of existence. These sleights of language produce very long "sentences" with no direct line between subject and predicate, that is, no relationship between the actor and his action, or between a cause and an effect. This is one given of the texts: absence of standard characters and genuine action. So Beckett has created an appropriate imitative style for *Texts for Nothing*, a work in which there is "no talk of a creator and nothing very definite in the way of a creation."

Each linguistic device helps to make style and content reflect each other endlessly as in a fun house mirror. Since the voice is searching for the correct utterance, it is only natural that he should employ repetition and permutation, that he should try all possible word strings. He shuffles different phrases hoping to find some formulation that is stable; "that's why I say it, patiently, variously, trying to vary, for you never know, it's perhaps all a question of hitting on the right aggregate. So as to be here no more at last . . ." (p. 114). Because the "I" can be certain of nothing, he resorts to questions, contradictions, and conditionals: his very existence is one big "if." In a world of polar opposites like life and death, being and non-being, and speech and silence, the only sincere means of expression reduces to contradiction and paradox. And if the "I" must define himself through the texts, then using semantics to compose a self becomes logical: "With a cluther of limbs and organs, all that is needed to live again, to hold out a little time, I'll *call* that living, I'll *say* it's me . . ." (p. 85, my italics).

Separate voices never really harmonize, contradictions are never resolved, questions are never answered; and words merely cancel out each other to form texts for nothing: "Blot, words can be blotted and the mad thought they invent . . . wipe it out, all you have to do is say you said nothing and so say nothing again" (p. 103). The narrator's analysis of his writing style in *Texts* recalls Celia's analysis of Murphy's speaking style: "She felt, as she felt so often with Murphy, spattered with words that went dead as soon as they sounded; each word obliterated, before it had time to make sense, by the word that came next; so that in the end she did not know what had been said. It was like difficult music heard for the first time" (*Murphy*, p. 40). Through carefully chosen stylistic devices Beckett can go on writing without characters or plots. Using circular structure and a style that freezes his content near zero he can continue—as he demonstrates in *How It Is* and the more recent prose fragments—as long as there are words.

Texts for Nothing has gotten mixed reviews (some critics arguing that it merely provides a sequel to *The Unnamable*, for example), but it did extricate Beckett from an artistic impasse through experiments with short, discrete, and structured sections. Beyond this it anticipates several of the subsequent fictions;[22] in particular, its images provide points of departure for many a later fragment. The narrator's situation at the start of *Texts for Nothing* resembles that of the speaker in *From an Abandoned Work*: "Quag, heath up to the knees, faint sheep-tracks, troughs scooped deep by the rains. It was far down in one of these I was lying, out of the wind" (*Texts*, p. 75). The bracken and larch of Text 1 reappear as the thicket of *Abandoned Work*. Both narrators are obsessed with butterflies, fluttering things in general, and clocks, but primarily with wombs and tombs. *From an Abandoned Work* can be imagined as an expansion into story form of one sentence from Text 8: "Yes, my past has thrown me out, its gates have slammed behind me, or I burrowed my way out along, to linger a moment free in a dream of days and nights, dreaming of me moving, season after season, towards the last, like the living, till suddenly I was here, all memory gone" (p. 112).

Another *Texts* location consists of hills and valleys, and such terrain, of course, provides the setting for *Enough*. The narrators of *Texts* and of *Enough* both deny any independent knowledge (all information comes from "them" or from "him"), and both plead "not guilty" to an unnamed crime. Just as the "I" at the beginning of *Enough* watches a disembodied hand write the words of a disembodied voice, the "I" of *Texts* divides into a scribe and a speaker: "Yes, I see the scene, I see the hand, it comes creeping out of shadow, the shadow of my head, then scurries back, no connexion with me" (p. 97). At the end of *Enough* the narrator wipes out all but the flowers, thus cancelling out most of its fiction; similarly, as we have seen, the "I" of Text 13 "blots" and "wipes out" segments of his non-story. If the narrator of *Enough* is taken to be male and an older version of its former self, then one passage from Text 1 condenses the substance of the later fiction:

> Yes, I was my father and I was my son, I asked myself questions and answered as best I could, I had it told to me evening after evening, the same old story I knew by heart and couldn't believe, or we walked together, hand in hand, silent, sunk in our worlds, each in his worlds, the hands forgotten in each other. That's how I've held out till now. And this evening again it seems to be working, I'm in my arms, I'm holding myself in my arms, without much tenderness, but faithfully, faithfully. Sleep now, as under that ancient

lamp, all twined together, tired out with so much talking, so much listening, so much toil and play. [P. 79]

Similarly, we leave the couple in *Enough* faithfully "wedged together bent in three" after much talk.

The struggling, panting creature of *Texts for Nothing* is also related to Pim in *How It Is*. Resonances between these two works— short, stacatto phrases; and the theme of expiation for past sins—suggest that some of *How It Is* grew out of the courtroom scene in Text 5. Verbal echoes are numerous: "I say it as I hear it," "it's noted," "above in the light," and "bits and scraps." And the same motifs—the split self, the need to be witnessed, and the curtain and drama images—permeate both works. A long series of attackers and victims in the third section of *How It Is*, depending on each other for existence, is foreshadowed in Text 12: "That's the accountants' chorus, opining like a single man, and there are more to come, all the peoples of the earth would not suffice, at the end of the billions you'd need a god, unwitnessed witness of witnesses . . ." (p. 135). The narrator of *Texts* predicts of its imaginary artistic creation "perhaps it will end on a castrato scream," which is exactly how *How It Is* does end. More important is their similar phrasal structure. In *Texts for Nothing*, Beckett's style develops from the very long, unbroken linguistic strings of *The Unnamable* to sentences of reasonable length composed of repeated short phrases and clauses separated by commas. Sentences like these, when written as individual jagged, condensed segments, form the paragraphlike passages of *How It Is*, while *Text*'s phrases and clauses become short spurts of syntax that are now minus all commas, most connectives, and most verbs, to form the tortured language, the "midget grammar," of Pim and friend.

Beckett's conception for *Ping* also may have derived from a metaphor in *Texts*, but its style marks a new departure from the comparatively traditional style of *Texts*. The "ragdoll rotting" in Text 2 is transformed into the puppetlike white body of *Ping*. In Text 5, eyes—so prevalent in Beckett's later fictions—are mentioned explicitly: "It's an image, in my helpless head, . . . or before my eyes, they see the scene, the lids flicker and it's in. An instant and then they close again, to look inside the head, to try and see inside, to look for me there, to look for someone there . . ." (p. 95). The repeated phrase "fixed ping fixed elsewhere," which could refer to the blinking motion of eyes, may be *Ping*'s condensed version of clauses like those in Text 7: "an evening shadow you follow with your eyes, thinking of something else, yes, that's it, the mind elsewhere, and the eyes too, if the truth were known, the eyes elsewhere too" (p. 107). Also, "ping" suggests the ticks or bells of a clock, and analogously, in Text 11 the narrator remarks that "time devours on. . . . Or it's in the head, like a minute time switch, a second time switch . . ." (pp. 127–28). Repetitions of "one second" mark time in *Ping* and may measure the duration of eye movements or of memories. The narrator decides in Text 13 that the only requisite for a story is "something somewhere that can leave a trace," and the minimal action of *Ping* reduces to "traces blurs signs."

The white vault of *Imagination Dead Imagine* had its blueprints drawn in *Texts for Nothing* as well, where "perhaps we're in a head, it's as dark as in a head before worms get at it, ivory dungeon." An alternating hot and cold environment in *Imagination*'s white rotunda is elucidated by passages in *Texts*: "It's mechanical, like the great colds, the great heats, the long days, the long nights, of the moon . . ." (p. 117). While the narrator of *Imagination* tries to invent some sort of story despite imagination's death and all traces of life vanished, the "I" of Text 6 has a similar but more feasible goal: "I have high hopes, a little story, with living creatures coming and going on a habitable earth crammed with the dead, a brief story, with night and day coming and going above . . ." (p. 105). Two static creatures in *Imagination*'s vault may wait for a small society in another tale, in a different storm.

The small society of *The Lost Ones* comes and goes within the same alternation of cold darkness and hot light hinted at in *Texts* and appearing in *Imagination*; finally the brief story of "creatures coming and going" gets told. The "I" of *Texts* wonders if he will find the "way out"—"Shall I never see the sky again"—just as the lost ones wonder if they will ever return to the sky and stars, which they believe to be outside their cylinder. Twisting tunnels are searched for a "way out," but all journeys end in death, just as the narrator of Text 9 had predicted: "if only I could say, There's a way out there, there's a way out somewhere, then all would be said, it would be the first step on the long travelable road, destination tomb, to be trod without a word, tramp tramp, little heavy irrevocable steps, down the long tunnels at first, then under the mortal skies . . ." (p. 118). The lost creatures never escape from the long tunnels out into the skies, but with *Lessness* the "refuge" has fallen open and the later Beckett traveller is exposed to the void.

Thus a similar stylistic journey is reduced to the one step the creature in *Lessness* is vainly trying to make. The narrator of the *Texts* posits the sine qua non of a narrative: "Start by stirring, there must be a body, as of old . . ." (p. 85), and later imagines a story of "faint stirs day and night, as if to grow less could help, ever less and less and never quite be gone" (p. 112). This lesser movement prepares the way for the "little body" of *Lessness*. Or its aborted being could reincarnate one of the phantoms of Text 5, "those of the living and [those] . . . who are not born." Also, the "issueless" body in the ruins of *Lessness* recalls the souls contemplated by the "I" in Text 10, "souls of the stillborn, or dead before the body, or still young in the midst of the ruins, or never come to life through incapacity . . . among the unborn hordes, the true sepulchral body . . ." (pp. 124–25). Figments, blessings, curses, and screams that are discussed in Text 13 materialize in *Lessness*. In *Texts* day is a "disperser of phantoms," and in *Lessness* dawn is a "dispeller of figments." But while many of the motifs of *Lessness* come from *Texts for Nothing*, its form is innovative, in fact startling.

New forms, new arrangements of words, are the somethings Beckett has left after *Texts for Nothing*. These thirteen texts offer stark yet rich images which serve as catalysts for the minimalist stories to come; but more important, the texts provide testing grounds for the stylistic experimentation of the later fictions. Many critics, and the author himself, judged *Texts for Nothing* to be a failure, although, if it redeemed Beckett's language and gave birth to the stylistic varieties of the later prose, it was a fortunate fall indeed. Writing *about* the impasse itself provides a "way out" of the impasse, as Beckett chronicles his struggle to go on despite and through linguistic challenges by creating self-reflexive fictions.

From an Abandoned Work
"Breaking up I Am"

From an Abandoned Work,[1] a short monologue beginning an abandoned English novel of the early 1950's and first broadcast by the BBC in 1957, has been largely abandoned by the critics. Most recently, one critic has relegated it to the category of more conventional fiction, as retreating to "the structures and certainties of earlier literatures," and as "a return to people and objects . . . too easily explained."[2] Other scholars ignore this piece entirely, while some mention it in passing as insignificant.[3] But the significance of *Abandoned Work* declares itself in many areas: as a condensation, from Beckett's earlier novels, of the writer/ composing motif (and thus as a step toward further refinements in the later metafictions); as an autobiographical statement of the man and the artist; as an early approximation of phrasal imitative style which anticipates the style of *How It Is*; and as a self-conscious exercise in reader interpretation. For all of these aspects a close examination of the text's language is essential, and leads one to conclude that the narrator's rambling style "goes on" with as many jerks and swerves as does his ambling walk—similar to the style of *Texts for Nothing*. Porter Abbott, arguing for imitative form in early and middle Beckett fiction, compares the two works: "The forward progress of its narrator provides as good a model as any for the violent juxtaposition of opposites which characterizes so much of Beckett's other work."[4] After *Abandoned Work* the substance of the prose texts continually shrinks, and Beckett's style in some 1960's pieces approaches a Watt-like string of words, but the form/content relation still holds true, expressing itself through the metaphor of movement.

In a comparative study of the styles of *More Pricks Than Kicks*, *Murphy*, *Watt*, and *Abandoned Work*, John Coetzee, using statistical analyses on 800-word samples, computes the following results. *Abandoned Work* has the smallest vocabulary, and thus a high concentration of select words account for most of the text. It has the lowest number of words used only once, the smallest number of Romance/Greek words as a percentage of the sample, and is three times as monosyllabic as the three earlier works.[5] Coetzee concedes without irony that "if we investigate the features that stylostatistics traditionally investigates—sentence length, word length, etc.—we find precious little about Beckett that we might not have guessed."[6] The stylistic trends listed above do reveal that as early as the 1950's, Beckett was developing a more spare, repetitive, and condensed prose (and any reader could predict that a second computer study of *Abandoned Work* in a continuum with *How It Is*, *Ping*, and *Lessness* would show an acceleration of the same trends). But as a means to explicate an individual text, this school of stylistics is not a great deal of help. Instead, verbal analysis that includes content can show that Beckett's new language in this piece questions logical connections between narrative events, comments on the patterning that transforms life into art, and suggests the processes of creation and interpretation.

The plot of *Abandoned Work* seems trivial and nonsensical, as a lone character recalls three random days of his life: on the first his mother, in white nightdress, waves to him from a window of their house as he walks off, and later he sees a white horse; on the second he is chased by stoats (predatory creatures akin to ermines and weasels); and on the third he is stared at by an old man on the road. All three days appear to be haphazardly chosen from disparate times in the narrator's past. Our nameless first-person hero is even more of an aimless quester than was Molloy: he is always on his way, destination unknown. By the end he thrashes around in a thicket (in a scene similar to the initial setting), fearing that he will drop into a hole. A reader searching for some structure in such a plotless story may find it in the little clause "breaking up I am." The disintegration of the narrator's past and the fragmentation of his mind and body are conveyed in a form in which the language and syntax themselves are breaking up. Yet somehow, in fragments from abandoned works, Beckett is able to synthesize the essentials of the human condition. The narrator of *Abandoned Work* represents all mankind in his aimless journey from his mother to a hole in the ground, from birth to death. Acting out Murphy's motto that all life is "a wandering to find home" (p. 4) and Molloy's lament that all his life he "had been bent on settling this matter between my mother and me, but had never succeeded" (p. 87), *Abandoned's* wanderer adopts mythic elements of a journey to identity.

Procedural concerns as well as mythic patterns link Beckett's early and middle heroes. For example, Molloy has a similar difficulty organizing his documentation: when he recalls some sheep, he notes, "That then is how the second day began, unless it was the third, or the fourth . . ." (p. 38). Later, "[o]ther scenes of my life came back to me. There seemed to be rain, then sunshine, turn about. Real spring weather. I longed to go back into the forest" (*Molloy*, p. 124). Descriptions of random chronology, weather, and emotions echo each other in the language of non sequitur, which has its Beckettian origins in the French nouvelles,[7] and is perfected in the first section of *Abandoned Work*. Some inexplicable events of this abandoned novel are foreshadowed in several passages from *The Unnamable*:

. . . I would have liked to lose me . . . close my eyes and be in a wood . . . it's the town of my youth, I'm looking for my mother to kill her. . . . [P. 146]

. . . if I could be in a forest, caught in a thicket, or wandering round in circles, it would be the end of this blither. . . . [P. 158]

While places and motifs from the trilogy reappear in *Abandoned Work*, now they have quite a different tone: the bitterness found throughout the trilogy becomes softened in the autobiographical atmosphere of the later story.[8]

A son leaving his mother, the memory of a dead father, and the recollection of a lost career as professor all obviously derive from Beckett's own life—elements he was trying to understand in the 1950's. An added hint that the creature wandering about in the thickets represents its author surfaces in a curious remark Beckett wrote to a friend about his father, who had recently died and had habitually gone on long hikes with his son: "What am I to do now but follow his trace over the fields and hedges."[9] Beckett's fondness for his father and his memory of William going on walks across the moors surface again in the recent story *Company* in vignettes of recollection. Similar woods and thickets recur in Beckett's poetry, for example in "Serena I":

>   alas I must be that kind of person
>   hence in Ken Wood who shall find me
>   my breath held in the midst of thickets
>   none but the most quarried lovers[10]

Later in the poem the repetition of the query "but in Ken Wood/ who shall find me" underscores the solitude of the writer;[11] and Goethe's *Hagreise im Winter* (which influenced Beckett's "The

Vulture") also uses as a metaphor for the lonely artist a man im-
mured in thickets:

> But who is it that stands
> Apart?
> His path is lost in the thicket
> Behind him the bushes
> Close up
> The grass stands again
> Deserts engulf him.[12]

Goethe's verse could easily describe the last scene of Beckett's
abandoned story; thus one may view its wandering narrator as
meandering artist.

Since the protagonist enacts man as writer, the phrase "as I go
along" depicts his verbal journey as well as his physical one; and
his stick, like Malone's, aids in writing as well as in walking. A
further connection between wanderer and author is that in the
French translation, *D'un ouvrage abandonné*, "stick" is translated
as *baton*, which also means "a straight stroke" in writing, instead of as *canne*, which is the usual word for walking stick.[13]
Logically, the loss of the stick impedes the narrative progress of
the story along with the mechanical progress of the hero: "But I
was hardly down the stairs and out into the air when the stick
fell from my hand and I just sank to my knees to the ground and
then forward on my face . . ." (p. 47). (Malone's writing stick, a
Venus pencil, sets up an association between composing and
sex—the pencil and the penis—and *Abandoned Work*'s narrator
derives a similar physical power through his implement, through
the force of words.) A long digression on falling follows the accident, and only when the hero rises does the story, such as it is,
pick up: "But let me get up now and on and get this awful day
over and on to the next" (p. 47). Often the narrator uses a sentence of this form to prod himself verbally, and three of these
clauses (beginning with "but" or "so" and interrupting a passage) divide the one-paragraph-long monologue into its three-
part, three-day structure. Ruby Cohn suggests that the word
"now" serves the same purpose—recalling the narrator from the
ten or so digressions back to his narration about the three days.[14]
Frequently the word "now" appears in a conversational tone and
either introduces or continues a digression, as in, "Now the jog
trot on the other hand, I could no more do that than I could fly";
"Now why this sudden rage I really don't know . . ."; "Now

is there nothing to add to this day with the white horse and
white mother. . . ." This colloquial, nontechnical usage of "now"
has no reference to time; here it does not mark the present tense
but rather serves as a filler, grammatically as an absolute, in a
sentence.

More often the narrator uses the normally nontemporal word
"but" to shift from musing about the present to reminiscing
about the past. He heralds the events of the first day with "But
let me get on now with the day I have hit on to begin with . . .
yes, on with it and out of my the and on to another . . ." (p. 40).
To end his tangent on whiteness, the narrator chides himself,
"But let me get on with this day and get it over"; again he
drowns in seemingly irrelevant details and must extricate himself from his verbal muck by urging, "But let me get on now
from where I left off . . ." (p. 43). Pages pass, however, before
the narrator focuses on the second day: "So on to this second day
and get it over and out of the way and on to next" (p. 46). Here
the short phrases, linked by repeated "and's" and rushed by
repeated "on's," emphasize his hurried pace. Interrupting a
frenzied digression on the subject of stoats and death, he stops
to remind himself to narrate chronologically: "But let me start as
always with the morning and the getting out." After day three,
the reader assumes the story to be over, although the narrator
has farther to go: "But let us get on and leave these old scenes
and come to these, and my reward" (p. 48). All these sentences
indicating structural breaks have in common—besides "but" or
"so"—a tone of compulsion, of being driven. In the French translation the comparable sentences have added connotations of
speed and of narrator passivity: "Mais vite la suite de cette jour-
née qui m'est venue pour commencer" (p. 12). The protagonist is
haunted by a presence similar to the "voices" of Molloy, Moran,
Malone, the Unnamable, and the hero of *Texts for Nothing*; thus
he admits that his thoughts are "not mine." (In *Abandoned Work*
we hear the narrator talking *about* the voices, whereas in later
pieces like *Company* we hear the voices themselves.) His monologue then becomes a compulsory dictation; paradoxically, the
verbal outpouring is both expressive and exacted. Continually
critical, the narrator comments on his own plot and language:
"enough of my mother for the moment"; "I'll come back on this
perhaps when I feel less weak"; "strange expression, it does not
sound right somehow"; "There's that word white again"; "no,
that is a foolish thing to say" (appearing twice); "Schimmel, nice

word, for an English speaker"; and "awful English this." Of course, the fact that *Abandoned Work* was Beckett's first fiction in English since *Watt* (1944) can produce an amused smile. Often the wording indicates that mental composition of the piece is synchronous with its written record. The narrator tries to create an image of the questions confusing him—"Suddenly they are there, no, they float up"—and later the word "no" again cancels out and reformulates a thought: "but had to get through somehow until I came to the one I am coming to now, no, nothing . . ." (p. 46). His explanations of feelings toward his wardrobe change as is fictionally convenient: ". . . I could never bear the long coat, flapping about my legs, or rather one day suddenly I turned against it, a sudden violent dislike" (p. 47). This usage of "or rather" and "no" to graph instantaneous composition and revision (a stylistic practice begun in the trilogy) reaches new depths later in *Imagination Dead Imagine* and *The Lost Ones*.[15] Like Molloy, the narrator compliments himself on some of his emendations: "how is it I wonder I saw him [Balfe] at all, that is more like it . . ." (p. 48). Finally the self-conscious amanuensis anticipates then mocks the reader's supposed quibbles about his story: "What time of year, I really do not know, does it matter"; "Now was this my first experience of this kind, that is the question that immediately assails one." As did Sterne's *Tristram Shandy*, our narrator gives the gentle reader instructions: "Now is there nothing to add to this day with the white horse and white mother in the window, please read again my descriptions of these . . ." (pp. 45–46). Thus the verbal wanderer reveals his need to be understood—to be followed on his journey—and initiates a personal and immediate relationship with an audience.

By substance as well as by style, the narrator reveals himself as a writer, specifically through his three loves: stillness, whiteness, and words. Perhaps the hero inherited his love of whiteness and bright light from Murphy, and his love of stasis from Malone, who had remarked that he sought darkness and "the things that would never stir." Although the narrator feels ambivalent about motion (his words proclaim a desire for stillness while his behavior betrays sudden action and violent change), his preference for stasis is illustrated early in the story: "Great love in my heart too for all things still and rooted, bushes, boulders and the like. . . . Whereas a bird now, or a butterfly, fluttering about and getting in my way, all moving things, getting in my path, a slug now, getting under my feet, no, no mercy" (p. 39). His hatred seems to encompass the entire animal world, although it centers on the mother, who in her fluttering resembles a butterfly. The mother displeases him precisely because she is "always changing," and initially what he most desires is a frozen, static image; yet it is not clear whether the mother is the cause or the effect of aversion to movement. He himself "fidgets" too much, while what he would rather do is to sit still and watch a pendulum clock—literally and figuratively watch time passing.

However, the only way he can halt or manipulate time is through art, which he learns as he contrasts the freedom from temporal order he enjoys as a writer with his bondage to chronology as a man: "nothing to add before I move on in time skipping hundreds and even thousands of days in a way I could not at the time, but had to get through somehow . . ." (p. 46). Since the word "still" can mean no movement, no change over time, or no sound (a triple association Beckett exploits in "Still," Fizzle 7), the hero's love of stasis translates into the quest for silence, for an end to writing. Only after this story is told does the writer achieve a kind of stillness; he escapes present time by retelling his past, and he gradually sinks into the earth, where he finds temporary rest—a freedom from "going on," from compulsion.

As in *Murphy*, the absence of motion in *Abandoned Work* corresponds to an absence of color; the hero's love of stillness is equalled only by his love of whiteness: "White I must say has always affected me strongly, all white things, sheets, walls and so on, even flowers, and then just white, the thought of white, without more" (p. 41). Significantly, the main images of the remembered three days are white mother, white horse, and white rabbit. Stasis and the nothingness of white obviously promise the death and silence so prized by the narrator, and symbolically, the white of a page that need never be filled could console the narrator/author with its blankness. When leaves of paper have stopped turning, the transformation of life into art will be accomplished and the narrator can be still:

Then it will not be as now, day after day, out, on, round, back, in, like leaves turning, or torn out and thrown crumpled away, but a long unbroken time without before or after, light or dark, from or towards or at, the old half knowledge of when and where gone, and of what, but kinds of things still, all at once, all going, until nothing, there was never anything, never can be, life and death all nothing, that kind of thing, only a voice dreaming and droning on all around, that is something, the voice that once was in your mouth. [Pp. 48–49]

But the narrator realizes that his life can never be completely "over," that he can never reach nothingness, because the exacting voice subsists, this murmur echoing even in Beckett's most recent fictions. We last see the traveller "lashing about with the stick," metaphorically still trying to write.

For this writer/character, as for Beckett's future narrator in *Company* (1980), words comfort as well as frustrate: "Over, over, there is a soft place in my heart for all that is over, no, for the being over, I love the word, words have been my only loves, not many" (p 48). Revision from "over" to "the being over" reveals that it is a state of mind he wants to achieve, a condition free from being compelled. Obviously "over" can denote an end or a beginning or a continuity—"all over" or "over again" or "over and over"—like the phrase "winding up" in *Endgame* (which Beckett was writing at about the same time as *Abandoned Work*). The narrator himself gives the phrase a double meaning: he wants to be "all over," to be dead, and to be spread "all over" the earth when he disintegrates. Another favorite phrase, "vent the pent," is an incantation used to vent the very pent-up emotions mentioned; thus words can be marshalled to order life as well as to escape or precipitate death. Through rhythm and sound patterns, art effects some control over life: "Where did I get it [the thought of a ton of worms in an acre], from a dream, or a book read in a nook when a boy, or a word overheard as I went along, or in me all along and kept under till it could give me joy . . ." (p. 45). His initial question about the origin of a thought ("where did I get it") gets sidetracked as sound deflects sense: he rhymes book/nook, word/heard, along/along, and boy/joy as he plays with language, probably to evade disturbing images of earthworms and burial.

In less playful moods, the narrator uses words—almost as a philosopher would—both to articulate the problems of life and to analyze their solutions, thus giving the story the flavor of a comic Cartesian meditation. The difficulties of this abandoned wanderer stem from metaphysical and epistemological dichotomies: between mind and body, appearance and reality, art and life, and between two different modes of time. An overly cautious empiricist, the narrator expresses doubts about his own cogitation, demonstrated in the repetition of "I don't know,"

"perhaps," "seemed," "I think," and "I suppose." He bemoans
ignorance about both his life and his story and is skeptical about
the power of reason to afford any understanding because "I
know I could never think." With a brain "always on the alert
against itself," he detects no logic in his discourse: "But what is
the sense of going on with all this, there is none" (p. 47). A sudden rage follows his sighting of the horse, but "there's no accounting for it, there's no accounting for anything"; and later he
repeats "the white horse and then the rage, no connexion I suppose." Yet the qualifier "I suppose" calls into question the previous conclusion about no connections. Is the narrator teasing the
reader, coyly suggesting that there *could* be links between the
events, or is he deceiving himself and thus avoiding some deep
psychological association? His mother's waving also lacks rational connections; it may have been directed at him, or she may
have been "not bothering about me at all": "Then I raised my
eyes and saw my mother still in the window waving, waving me
back or on I don't know, or just waving . . ." (p. 40). This is the
same kind of randomness in life that so disturbed Watt, a disjunction between gesture and emotion, signifier and signified.

Since our narrator used to be "a very fair scholar," he relishes
precise distinctions (Not x, but y. Not that x; no, y. Not y, just
x.) and measuring both sides of a proposition (on the one hand,
A; on the other, B). By means of a question/answer method, his
humorous and disjointed pseudo-philosophical discourse stum-
bles on: "How shall I go on another day? and then, How did I
ever go on another day? Or, Did I kill my father? and then, Did I
ever kill anyone? That kind of way, to the general from the particular I suppose you might say, question and answer too in a
way, very addling" (pp. 44–45). Answers are never forthcoming,
however, and questions are especially addling for a fragmented
consciousness, "questions that when I was in my right mind
would not have survived one second, no, but atomized they
would have been, before as much as formed, atomized" (p. 44).
The narrator's mental and physical selves are both disintegrating,
and their links are straining as well, so that even for something
as animal as running, the mind—not the body—becomes the
impediment: "But I could not go on at that speed, not for breath-
lessness, it was mental, all is mental, figments" (p. 42). By the
end of the story, the two elements have parted company: the narrator concludes as a disembodied voice,[16] and thus resembles the
"I" of *Texts for Nothing*. The mind "just [goes] on, my body doing

its best without me." Only by denying, enclosing, or constraining the body can the Beckett consciousness continue.

A lesser dichotomy, but still a baffling one, is that between appearance and reality; for example, moving objects appear motionless at a distance: "Birds with my piercing sight I have seen flying so high, so far, that they seemed at rest, then the next minute they were all about me . . ." (p. 39). For the narrator, quick change in others is evidently most annoying, revealed by his repeated phrases "then a moment later," "then the next minute," and "suddenly." Ironically, he too is subject to sudden shifts (of emotion), and his turbulent passions are verbally allied to the moving animals: "Ducks are perhaps the worst, to be suddenly stamping and stumbling in the midst of ducks . . . few things are worse" (p. 39); of himself he decides, "the rages were the worst." In addition to relativity of speed, the narrator notices relativity of size when his mother's figure in the window is "all small because of the distance"; and the person behind the white horse which is "at a great distance" might be a boy, a small man, or a woman. All these instances of an unstable reality produced by subjective perception mean that epistemological certainty continuously eludes the narrator.

Other unsettling dichotomies for him are those between past and present, and between opposite ways of measuring duration, since time is simultaneously circular and linear in the story. Compulsion to "get on" to the "next" day presupposes a series of days, yet the narrator remarks that, "When a day *comes back*, whatever the reason, then its morning and its evening too are there . . ." (p. 46, my italics). Here a day represents another revolution of time (through the action of memory), and the hero who repeatedly exits and enters his house becomes identified with the sun, which determines days by apparently circling around its earthly home. In the French version of the story, "birth" is associated with "day" since "all I regret is having been born" is rendered as "tout ce que je regrette c'est d'avoir vu le jour" (p. 17). Locally as well as cosmically, time seems discontinuous or warped as our hero runs in spurts at great speeds: "five or ten yards, in a second I was there" (p. 42). More revealing than the narrator's method of running is his futile wish to observe a pendulum clock continuously, "moving my eyes to and fro, and the lead weights dangling lower and lower till I got up out of my chair and wound them up again, once a week" (p. 48). The rotation of the hands on the clock face and the swinging of the pendulum connote circular time, while the lengthening lead weights measure linear progression. With this clock, the narrator would merge the two modes of time and become a one-week chronometer himself (his eyes and head swinging like a pendulum). As it is, he internalizes circularity by cursing in reiterated phrases, "the same words over and over," by narrating his story in cycles, and by speaking of youth and age as if they were superimposed.

The words "new" and "old" recur with an almost obsessive frequency in the text of *Abandoned Work*, yet no clear distinction between the two can be made with phrases like "a new place soon old." Past events turn into current events in circular time, and life itself depends on the cycle of respiration, stale air becoming fresh: "So in some way even olden things each time are first things, no two breaths the same, all a going over and over and all at once and never more" (p. 47). This rhythmical passage, with its overlay of linear and circular time, is contradictory, though; here again the word "over" signifies both an ending and a rebeginning. Because the hero wants life to be over, a new thing becomes as hateful to him as it is to Hamm in *Endgame*: "if it was the end I would not so much mind, but how often have I said, in my life, before some new awful thing, It is the end, and it was not the end . . ." (p. 45). He looks forward to a suspended state, "a long unbroken time without before or after," yet his closest approximation to a timeless world lies in creating the circular structure of the text as a whole.

Some critics have commented on the story's lack of a conclusion (Beckett did in fact abandon this work), but the fiction is nonetheless finely shaped so that its ending circles back to its beginning—a standard closural device, and very common in Beckett—similar to the structure of the individual vignettes in *Texts for Nothing*. The piece starts with the hero's departure, and towards the end we read: "Well once out on the road and free of the property what then, I really do not know, the next thing I was up in the bracken lashing about with my stick . . ." (p. 49). At the beginning the hero remarks that he never has a goal, "And in this way I have gone through great ferns, like starched, very woody, terrible stalks"; and in the conclusion, the narrator speaks of dying. Midway through, he begins to relive day two once more: "Is it the stoats now, no, first I just sink down again and disappear in the ferns." These ferns (woody stalks) conjure up an image of giant pencils (wood-shafted), metaphorical forests of writing through which the narrator has travelled. If he can truly vanish in the ferns then he might reach the silence of an ending, of nonbeing. Malone in *Malone Dies* has a green pencil (green and woody) that diminishes as he dies. At the end of the novel Lemuel's (Samuel's?) wooden hatchet becomes confused in Malone's mind with a pencil or a stick, in the same way that the abandoned narrator conflates pencil and stick. The writer can kill as well as create characters; in fact, he can—as Malone does through Lemuel's hatchet/hammer/stick/pencil—self-destruct with a story's conclusion.

However, because the ending of *Abandoned Work*—unlike the fading out of *Malone Dies*—replays its beginning, the narrator will never be finally "over," will never get his "reward." Since the narrator's discourse is breaking up, the critical reader is teased into fastening the pieces together, just as he is taunted into shaping the sections of *The Lost Ones* towards allegory. It is left to the reader to infer the meaning and draw the connections between these episodes, for Beckett, at least, has chosen these particular events to depict. A story based on the recollection of three days might imply a triple structure with three equal sections. Although a scanning of *Abandoned Work* gives this orderly impression, a closer look reveals that the events of day one take up much more than the first one-third of the story, that the second and third days' actions occupy progressively smaller spaces, and that there is actually a fourth section which returns us to day one and thus adds weight (and emphasis) to this first episode. A count of periods quantifies this imbalance. Section one describing day one is eighty sentences long. Section two, beginning "So on to this second day. . . ," has eighteen sentences (if section three begins with "But let me get up now and on to get this awful day over and on to the next"). Direct description of day three takes up only two sentences, though the total for this section may be pushed upward (to include a preface giving indirect background) to yield nine sentences. A final section beginning "But let us get on and leave these old scenes" consists of only seven sentences.

Just as the apparently meaningless episodic adventures in Beckett's French stories prove to contain patterns (an alternation of expulsions and shelters, for example), so the three episodes of *Abandoned Work* have patterned motifs in common. Each of the creatures met during the three days shares some attribute with the narrator, and they appear to him in his subconscious search for identity. The son has apparently inherited the mother's characteristics: she has "no tenacity of purpose," and he is "simply on my way"; she is always changing, and he continuously alternates between violent rages and periods of calmness; both seldom speak, or talk mainly to themselves. Finally, the narrator recalls his mother's death and anticipates his own as he becomes identified with her. Both mother and horse are seen as bright white with the full sun on them; the narrator himself calls attention to this correspondence (p. 41). A pun on "hoarse" links the white horse with the narrator, who boasts about his fast run, and who hates the "jog trot." The white horse disappears suddenly, and at the end of the story our narrator fears suddenly vanishing among ferns. Also, two passages on the narrator's violent behavior have equine echoes: ". . . then I suppose the slow turn, wheeling more and more to the one or other hand, till facing home, then home" (p. 44); "I strive with them [questions] as best I can, quickening my step when they come on, tossing my head from side to side and up and down, staring agonizedly at this and that . . ." (p. 45). In the French translation Beckett has added, crossed out, and revised several lines after the disappearance of the horse. This section was obviously quite important or difficult for him.[17]

On the second day the narrator identifies with a hypothetical rabbit, chased as he is by stoats. He chides himself for not following the example of the submissive hare when confronted with predators, and later plans to "gather up my things and go back into my hole." Earlier the narrator depicts himself "going on" in a way which appears quite rabbit-like in retrospect, when we infer that the ominous "they" may stand for stoats: ". . . I have gone through great thickets, bleeding, and deep into bogs, water too. . . . And that is perhaps how I shall die at last if they don't catch me, I mean drowned . . ." (pp. 39–40). Knowing that a stoat resembles a weasel, we can perceive—even if the narrator cannot—a subtle correspondence between the stoats and the mother. In a discussion of taboos on animal names, the linguist Stephen Ullmann notes of the weasel that

the fear inspired by this animal has given rise to a multiplicity of propitiatory euphemisms which are very similar in different languages: in some of them it is described as a 'little woman' (Italian *donnola*, Portuguese *doninha*) or as a 'pretty little woman' (French *belette*, diminutive of *belle*, Swedish *lilla snalla*) while elsewhere a pretense is made of including it within the family by turning it into a 'bride,' a 'daughter-in-law,' a 'sister-in-law' or a 'gossip.'[18]

If stoats and mother somehow "connect," then we can sense an ambivalent fear and attraction caused by both, one signal of a love-hate relationship with the mother that may well be autobiographical.[19] Finally, the narrator himself, a man on the road, notes his correspondence to Balfe, the "roadman": "Now he is dead and I resemble him" (p. 48). In short, either the narrator locates himself in the creatures discussed in these three days, or we discern his characteristics in the beings that his memory calls up. Each of the narrator's voyages to the past is launched by some apparently chance encounter, thus paralleling Beckett's description of Proust's recovered instants: "The source and point of departure of this 'sacred action,' the elements of communion, are provided by the physical world, by some immediate and fortuitous act of perception. The process is almost one of intellectualized animism."[20] But whereas Proustian characters later analyze their madeleine moments, tracing the workings of memory, reconstructing temporal and causal links, Beckettian characters utterly reject such analysis: "no connexion I suppose."

In addition to the pattern of identification, another motif which joins three of the hero's four experiences, and which permeates all of *Abandoned Work*, is visual perception. Walking with his head bowed, the narrator is continuously "on the look out for a snail, slug or worm." He twice calls attention to his "piercing sight," and records in detail the sight of his mother waving. This picture, despite some motion, gives the effect of a tableau, "very pretty really the whole thing." Here vision is frustrated: "if only she could have been still and let me look at it all. No, for once I wanted to stand and look at something I couldn't . . ." (p. 40). A white horse affords the next visual experience, but it is curious that initially the narrator does not say that he *saw* it. In fact, the sentence introducing the horse is introduced does not contain a main verb at all; and later what is perceived is change: "all I noticed was the sudden appearance of the horse, then disappearance." Paradoxically, the sighting of the horse causes a figurative loss of sight: "suddenly I flew into a most savage rage, really *blinding*" (p. 41, my italics). The two extremes of vision, "piercing sight" and "really blinding," contradict each other, producing a temporary verbal stasis.

Eyes in this fiction are crucially important, literally and metaphorically. First, their motion seems to describe a circle, as do time, the sun, and the character's movements: "the eyes raised and back again, raised again and back again again . . ." (p. 43). The whole story concerns a cyclical veering towards and then away from the mother—both biological mother and mother earth. (Similarly, Molloy searches for his psychological origins by pursuing his alter ego through the forest of the mind and by journeying to his mother's room.) Blinding rage against the horse, more so perhaps at its disappearance, could connect to anger at the mother, especially her rejection, "the body turned away." During maternal encounters in *Abandoned Work*, communication seems to be more visual than verbal: "Sometimes she cried out on me, or implored, but never long, just a few cries, then if I looked up the poor old thin lips pressed tight together and the body turned away and just the corners of the eyes on me" (p. 44). By day three, reciprocal vision is equated grammatically (through the copula "was") with the day itself: "The third day was the look I got from the roadman . . . leering round and up at me . . . how is it I wonder I saw him at all, that is more like it, the day I saw the look I got from Balfe . . ." (p. 48). Here the syntax of the sentence emphasizes a meta-experience—not just Balfe's stare, but the perceiving of the look from Balfe, an indication of self-awareness.

From the French version of *Abandoned Work* we learn a second function of Balfe. "I went in terror of him as a child" becomes "enfant je le craignais comme le mauvais oeil" (p. 28). A figure like "the evil eye," Balfe recalls Basil in *The Unnamable*: "One in particular, Basil I think he was called, filled me with hatred. Without opening his mouth, fastening on me his eyes like cinders with all their seeing, he changed me a little more each time into what he wanted me to be. Is he still glaring at me, from the shadows?" (p. 13). Edith Kern cites this passage to argue that the Unnamable achieves substance only if seen by an Other (in the Sartrean sense); in *The Unnamable* the Self is petrified with the Look.[21] If such analysis is transferable to *Abandoned Work*, then it is appropriate that after describing the look from Balfe, the narrator contemplates invisibility through disappearance among the ferns. Like all Beckett characters, he must be perceived in order to be, but among the stalks in *Abandoned Work* one could "fall and vanish from view, you could lie there for weeks and no one hear you . . ." (p. 49). Although this situation is tantamount to nonbeing in Beckett's world, silent cessation ("the being over") is desired as well as feared.

The theme of death and the pervasive death imagery ultimately provide links among all four episodes of the story, thus helping the reader to "account" somewhat for juxtapositions for which the nearly mad, disintegrating narrator cannot. Initially, the scene of the transparent mother at the window presents a ghostly image: "The window-frame was green, pale, the house-wall grey and my mother white and so thin I could see past her . . ." (p. 40). Because of her movement, the mother provokes violence in the narrator, and the sighting of the horse causes unhealthful rage. Of course, the "pale horse" in Revelation represents Death,[22] and all four apocalyptic horses, one of which is white, are instruments of destruction. Also, a riderless white horse representing the deceased, marches in the funeral procession in some formal ceremonies. The narrator's word for the horse, "Schimmel," which translates as "mildew," also means "mold," a term even more connotative of decay and death.

On the second day the narrator's own death becomes a possibility. Earlier, after a series of regrets, he had commented that "dying is such a long tiresome business"—which explains his feelings toward the stoats, his anger that he had not seized the opportunity for a rapid demise. Thus a cliché about danger rings false in this case: "Indeed if I may say so I think I was fortunate to get off with my life, strange expression, it does not sound right somehow" (p. 46). By the third recounted day the narrator is a very old man, probably dying, perhaps already dead (if we take literally his statement that now Balfe is dead and "I resemble him"). While the roadman Balfe as the evil eye is terrifying enough, the speaker's horror has yet a deeper source. A "road-man" simply means one who repairs or constructs roads, but the image of a ragged brute down in a ditch with a spade, in a position such that he is barely visible (a six-foot-deep hole would conceal a man) certainly calls to mind a gravedigger. In addition, that "Balfe" looks like a condensation of "baleful" implies evil or destructive attributes in this creature.[23]

When the narrator leaves his negative memories, he yearns for a peaceful future with "life and death all nothing": life is hateful because it necessitates dying slowly; parents are hateful because they create life. Therefore, again like Hamm, the narrator of *Abandoned Work* ends by cursing both parents and God—for the "gift" of being. Much preferring the stillness of inanimate objects to the mobility of living creatures, he wants to unite with the earth or the sea. This desire, and his realization that in storytelling he can "move on in time skipping hundreds and even thousands of days in a way I could not at the time, but had to get through," links the narrator to Proust's projection of the ideal character, as quoted by Beckett:

. . . [Proust] will refuse to measure the length and weight of man in terms of his body instead of in terms of his years. In the closing words of his book he states his position: 'But were I granted time to accomplish my work, I would not fail to stamp it with the seal of that Time, now so forcibly present to my mind, and in it I would describe men, even at the risk of giving them the appearance of monstrous beings, and occupying in Time a much greater place than that so sparingly conceded to them in Space, a place indeed extended beyond measure, because, like giants plunged in the years, they touch at once those periods of their lives—separated by so many days—so far apart in Time.'[24]

Beckett's hero tries to touch at once three days of his life; he denies temporal continuity ("on to another day") and logical chains, offering instead only juxtaposition of events, a juxtaposition the reader must explain.

For *Abandoned Work*, Beckett had to devise a form suitable for a character isolated in space and time; he invented a structure of circularity and a narrative voice of disorder and alogic to portray an addled and ambivalent mind. By means of fragmentary chronology and a discontinuous style, Beckett gives the impression of a world and a being falling apart. This story is thus in the stylistic tradition established by the trilogy and *Texts for Nothing*, but it simultaneously ventures stylistic innovations necessary for its new kind of narrator. Taking our cue from the narrator's phrase "breaking up I am," we can conclude that the language of this text is "breaking up" in many ways: Beckett uses both imitative diction and imitative syntax to produce a monologue of a confused and half-sane consciousness. Ruby Cohn's hypothesis that "the syntactical fragmentation seems to reflect a fragmentation of [the narrator's] personality"[25] sets the correct course for a full analysis of correspondences between substance and syntax.

Even a first impression tells us that our narrator does not think in finished thoughts or speak in complete utterances. If a sentence is defined simply as a string of words beginning with a capital letter and ending with a period or other terminal punctuation, then there are 113 sentences in *Abandoned Work* (counts may vary because of question marks within longer constructions). Of these, only 30 are complete sentences syntactically, that is, consisting of at least one independent clause (with a finite main verb) and other independent and dependent clauses connected with the proper conjunctions or punctuation. The "run-ons" consist of several independent clauses separated only by commas or by "no," the narrator's idiosyncratic conjunction. Usually the fragments are otherwise well-structured and grammatical clauses lacking a subject and/or predicate. By the middle of these sentences some verbs, possessive pronouns, articles, and relative pronouns are missing:

[My] Throat [was] very bad, to swallow was torment, and something [was] wrong with an ear, I kept poking at it without relief, old wax [was] perhaps pressing on the drum. [An] Extraordinary still [was] over the land, in me too all [was] quite still, [this was] a coincidence. . . . [P. 49]

These deletions produce a contracted, stunted, elliptical style with a conversational tone: "All [was] well then for a time, [there was] just the violence and then this white horse . . ."; "Love too, [was] . . . often in my thoughts . . ."; "So [I was] up then in the grey of dawn . . ."; "[It was] not wet really. . . ." Besides conveying the "breaking up" of the I, this condensed language heightens the impression that the narrator is hurried and compelled to speak.

Even complete sentences are disjointed, suffering from another stylistic characteristic of this narrator—a penchant for inversion, shown most directly in his representative clause "breaking up I am." Inversion is a linguistic symptom of this narrator's breakdown as it was of Watt's. Many examples of objects appearing before their subjects and verbs occur in *Abandoned Work*, sometimes compounded by deletion: "Birds with my piercing sight I have seen flying so high"; "and the sound of my voice all day long muttering the same old things I don't listen to, not even mine it was at the end of the day"; "Just under the surface I shall be"; "Harsh things these great ferns [are]"; and "awful English this [is]." Of course inversion is a common characteristic of Anglo-Irish dialect (Compare "Is it me you're after?" or "fields it was"),[26] which Beckett might have chosen for this monologue since it was written expressly for the Irish actor Jack McGowan.

But the decision to use this dialect (with inversion as its predominant feature) is still Beckett's deliberate stylistic choice, and numerous syntactic inversions are maintained in the French translation as well.

Inversion of sentence parts causes further difficulty in reading—even in parsing—the text. For example, often a relative pronoun near the end of the sentence refers back to a noun phrase at its head. This delayed reference creates circular syntax patterns, since the reader must return to the start of a sentence in order to interpret the ending. (Beckett's "that" is emphasized in the following examples.) When a clause is short, few problems arise: "No tenacity of purpose, *that* was another thing I didn't like in her" (p. 40); "Now the jog trot on the other hand, I could no more do *that* than I could fly" (p. 42). However, in longer structures the reader must actually rescan the noun phrase later referenced, in order to avoid confusion and ambiguity: "One day I told him about Milton's cosmology, away up in the mountains we were, resting against a huge rock looking out to sea, *that* impressed him greatly" (p. 42). One clause with especially convoluted syntax requires the reader to replace a deleted "was" and to review several lines to remember that "all that" means the house, window, and mother: "The window-frame was green, pale, the house-wall grey and my mother white and so thin I could see past her (piercing sight I had then) into the dark of the room, and on all that full [was] the not long risen sun . . ." (p. 40).

Beyond grammatically repositioning objects in a sentence, the narrator sometimes avoids objects altogether, and in this he again resembles the heroes of the trilogy and the French stories.[27] Verbs may be intransitive, and thus actions initiated are not received. Throughout the story there is no goal, no objective to his journey, and his rages and feelings of violence have no objects. The narrator continually emphasizes that the three days he relates are not necessarily significant; it is the telling itself that is crucial. He haphazardly moves to the general from the particular, neglecting even the most basic causal link: we never learn how or why the narrator came to this state. In *Molloy*, Moran's sentences and paragraphs disintegrate in direct proportion to the disintegration of his relationships with people and with his own mind. We can trace a motivated stylistic fragmentation that is regressive as we read from the beginning of Moran's report to the beginning of Molloy's. Also, it is easy to determine that (at one level) Moran's object is a search for self via the search for Molloy, and that Molloy's object is a quest for self via the journey toward his mother. But in *Abandoned Work* we can only guess—by making numerous interpretive connections—that the narrator's true object is himself.

The hero of *Abandoned Work* stands psychologically and stylistically intermediate between Moran and Molloy, between the Apollonian and the Dionysian mentality. Individual sentences are breaking up before our eyes, and because of awkward transitions and large gaps between sentences or ideas, his monologue continuously verges on non sequitur. Although the chronology of the piece is choppy at best, the potentially rigorous mind of the narrator strives to impose some order on his thoughts: he likes to qualify, to contrast, to pursue cause and effect. This man of conflicting motions and emotions appropriately lives in a verbal world of extreme opposites, and describes them with polar adjectives: "awful," "horrid," "worst," "violent," and "atrocious" are balanced by "remarkable," "pretty," "best," "lovely," and "extraordinary." A sentence beginning with "But" or "So" implies a logical connective, yet causal relationships often are thwarted because, practically and verbally, the narrator inhabits a terrain where occurrences may possess rhyme but no reason. Hence he cannot explain the impetus of his rage: ". . . some days I would be feeling violent all day and never have a rage, other days quite quiet for me and have four or five" (p. 41). These rational and stylistic discontinuities and other frustrating syntactic and tonal dislocations of the narrator are already prominent in the first several sentences of the text:

> Up bright and early that day, I was young then, feeling awful, and out, mother hanging out of the window in her nightdress weeping and waving. Nice fresh morning, bright too early as so often. Feeling really awful, very violent. The sky would soon darken and rain fall and go on falling, all day, till evening. Then blue and sun again a second, then night. Feeling all this, how violent and the kind of day, I stopped and turned. So back with bowed head on the look out for a snail, slug or worm. [P. 39]

It is strange that on a first reading this passage does *not* appear strange. (Perhaps, especially at the beginning of a Beckett story, readers are too willing to suspend their belief in coherence.) Tone is ambivalent throughout the passage and even oscillates within the space of one thought. Not only is there no logical connection between sentences; there is no logic within a single sentence. Initially we are flooded with the positive connotations of brightness, morning, and youth; yet such impressions jar shockingly with a weeping mother and feelings of violence. The phrase "and out" seems deliberately misplaced to leave open an ambiguity ("up and out" or "feeling out"). Of course, there is a natural association between being up early and going out, but what is the correspondence between youth and feeling awful? Between the mother's waving and the hero's feeling awful? Is feeling awful the given from which all consequents follow, or is leaving home the origin of his rage? Is our hero being expelled from home as so many other Beckett tramps have been—literally, kicked out? "And out" verbally echoes "mother hanging out of the window"; and our word-loving narrator goes on to play with alliteration in "window," "weeping," and "waving." The next sentence, presumably missing an initial "It was a," contradicts the positive "nice fresh morning" with a negative and petulant "bright too early as so often." Continuing to alternate statements about the character and about his environment, Beckett directly expresses the narrator's emotions ("Feeling really awful, very violent."), though minus the syntactic sign of his being ("I was"). Just as we never learn why he is feeling awful, we see no orderly sequence in the weather either, as the day shifts from dark rain to bright sun in a matter of seconds.

Then appears a sentence which tempts us with the key to meaning thus far: "Feeling all this, how violent and the kind of day, I stopped and turned." The intense feeling caused his stopping, but why and how? Again the reader is as thwarted in finding a missing link as is the narrator in seeking sense in his narrative. More puzzling is the next sentence beginning with "so," a word which usually implies some irrefutable, almost axiomatic logic—a logic which eludes one in the text. We do not know why he returns looking for snails; he simply does. This man, like the woman in *Enough*, never asks himself the right questions (*Enough*'s speaker admits that all questions come from her master), and at the moment when the reader first asks "Why?" the narrator begins to fragment his chronology. Only later do we learn that our hero hates quick action, which would explain his fondness for slow moving snails, slugs, and worms. As the narrator rants on for a page about his likes and dislikes, it is significant that in his first digression he dwells on a psychological problem. After a long tangent he resumes his random narration of the first day's events: "Then I raised my eyes and saw my mother still in the window waving . . ." (p. 40). Already, with this return to sentence one, we have revolved through one small cycle within the larger circle of the story.

Subverting the rules of the realistic novel (including episodic ones), Beckett refuses to link the vignettes of *Abandoned Work* as a coherent story, or to connect sentences into coherent paragraphs. Instead of stylistic and narrative units building some structure, they dart off in tangential directions or loop back to an unexplained event. In some instances the relationships between sentences seem merely associative, and in one case the correspondence is not even one of meaning but of sound, the phoneme /o/: "vero, oh vero. Oh but for those awful fidgets . . ." (p. 48). At the broadest level of coherence, a reader expects progression in the three days' events. With this triple structure day two is the essential connection, yet it is this day that breaks up the patterns that days one and three established. Beckett probably chose the number three to induce anticipations in the reader which he could then leave unfulfilled; and local frustrated expectations become the norm as we read clause by clause.

It is unwise for the reader of *Abandoned Work* to expect a rational series of causes and effects in a story whose narrator declares "breaking up I am," or in any post-*Unnamable* narrative. By the time of the monograph on Proust, Beckett had turned his back on realism in fiction and was influenced by the surrealist view of the world as alogical. Like the surrealists, Beckett used unmotivated violence to free his characters from space and time in the French stories.[28] This tradition of haphazard events, added to his analysis of Proust's treatment of character and action, helps account for the uncertainty of narrative progression in *Abandoned Work*. Beckett defines "impressionism" in Proust and applies it to characterization:

> By his impressionism I mean his non-logical statement of phenomena in the order and exactitude of their perception, before they have been distorted into intelligibility in order to be forced into a chain of cause and effect. . . . we are reminded of Schopenhauer's definition of the artistic procedure as 'the contemplation of the world independently of the principle of reason.' In this connection Proust can be related to Dostoievski, who states his characters without explaining them. It may be objected that Proust does little else but explain his characters. But his explanations are experimental

and not demonstrative. He explains them in order that they may appear as they are—inexplicable. He explains them away.[29]

Analogously, the style of *Abandoned Work* is as variable and unpredictable as are human emotions themselves. One rationale is that our narrator purposely denies linear progression because he wants to evade connections between the past and the present, between feelings toward mother and facets of his personality. If so, then his self-deceiving prose of alogic is a forerunner of the self-deluding language in *Enough*.

This abandoned narrator offers us anecdotes and observations sans analysis, always stopping short of conclusions and interpretations; he plays patient to our therapist, as his mind works associatively, seldom progressing to valid inductive or deductive reasoning. The gaps between sentences created by this kind of random and rambling fiction challenge the reader—to shape some narrative sense and then to formulate some thematic unity. Simultaneously, a Beckett reader is called upon to analyze the very process of reading, to be purposefully and self-consciously "on his way" through the prose. We can string together numerous clues and make some deductions, but after we have traced motifs and verbal echoes (about vision, for example), where does this ultimately lead us? Perhaps up against tortuous dead ends similar to those in the syntactic mazes of *The Lost Ones* (1971), in which Beckett presents an elaborate metafictional structure that is more directly about reader frustration. Thus, as early as the 1950's, Beckett was developing a prose style reflective of the reading process as well as imitative of the narrator's mental process. As a disjointed monologue with fragmented and uncertain language, another babel of silence, *From an Abandoned Work* achieves a suitable form for conveying physical, mental, and verbal disintegration. While the imagistic thrust for the later fictions may reside in *Texts for Nothing*, the impetus for a leaner, more jagged prose comes from *Abandoned Work*. Beckett's development of what some critics call his telegrammatic style (to describe the syntactic fragments of *How It Is*, his short but not abandoned novel of the 1960's) has its beginnings here. Indirectly, the spare language of *Ping* and the later fictions derives from the style of this truncated and orphaned "novel," further refined by the prose of paradox and revision Beckett devised for *Enough*.

4

Enough
Enough Reality Is Too Much

In the midst of several innovative pieces after *Texts for Nothing*, a small narrative called *Enough* (1966) appears. Coherent paragraphs, a tale of romance, a nostalgic tone—what is a reader of late Beckett prose to make of such apparently conventional fiction? Although *Enough* was written between *Imagination Dead Imagine* and *Ping* in the early sixties, stylistically (and in some ways thematically) it naturally follows *From an Abandoned Work* (1956). As in *Abandoned Work*, the setting is a recognizable nook of the natural world, and action is still possible. Beckett had yet to reach the "immobility of the infinitely small in which the narrative will soon be enclosed."[1] More important, the style of *Enough* lies somewhere between the meandering narrative of *Abandoned Work* and the fast-paced, extorted gasps of *How It Is*; between the long non-sequitur sentences of the former and the short fragmented phrases of the latter. Read as a story, this piece, besides appearing to be an anachronism in Beckett's fiction, initially seems one-dimensional; but heard as a dramatic monologue—it was delivered by his favorite actress, Billie Whitelaw[2]— it radiates a metafictional richness. A voice reciting the text aloud foregrounds the narrator as quintessential Beckettian writer, as speaker plus listener, as dictator and scribe. While not as experimental in language as Beckett's other late prose works, *Enough* is nonetheless written in a style that obliquely mirrors its meaning, that both describes fiction writing itself and comments on Beckett's career as fiction writer. For this aging narrator, Beckett chooses phrases that concurrently disclose her self-delusion about immortality and unfold an endless revision process that extends her life.

First, as a simple love story *Enough* makes a statement about the inevitable dissolution of human bonds, and the theme of union and division is brilliantly reflected in every facet of the text: the meeting and parting of the lovers, the holding of *gloved* hands, the alternation of communication with noncommunication, and the operations of multiplication and division.[3] What is missing from this preliminary interpretation is a focus beyond plot elements and motifs toward style and structure: inward to the level of the sentence, and outward to the broadest level of meaning. In this case the literary microscope and telescope converge on the same image, a human being avoiding the ultimate division—death—with her every phrase. One wonders if Beckett's characters since *The Unnamable* somehow sense that life after the grave is even more horrible than life before.

The protagonist of *Enough* begins her story abruptly and paradoxically:

> All that goes before forget. Too much at a time is too much. That gives the pen time to note. I don't see it but I hear it there behind me. Such is the silence. When the pen stops I go on. Sometimes it refuses. When it refuses I go on. Too much silence is too much. Or it's my voice too weak at times. The one that comes out of me. So much for the art and craft.[4]

As a character she wants to forget certain past events of her life. Ironically, though, the story consists solely of her reminiscing.[5] As narrator she wants to start the story afresh; while the phrase "All that goes before" is ambiguous, it most plausibly refers to a previous narration of the same events, and ultimately to all of Beckett's previous fiction. Locally the woman's voice is dictating to a pen she imagines as "behind" her, and so she is commanding the transcribers to delete whatever came immediately before this new first sentence. Even more ironically, at the end of the story the narrator decides to "Wipe out everything but the flowers" (p. 60), perhaps because this is the only meaningful memory left to her. Simultaneously, the reader is again instructed to wipe out, to forget all that came before, that is, this whole story. Given a self-negating beginning and ending, the "I" seems forced to retell her tale repeatedly like one of the women in Beckett's short drama *Play*. Echoing them, this narrator can never confront the truth about her past—or her present. Erasing her story at the conclusion, as does the narrator of *How It Is*, she denies that this is how it was. Too much reality at one time is more than enough.

I write "her" even though Beckett stresses the narrator's sexual ambiguity—stresses partly through contradictions. Even in the French version of the text in *Têtes-mortes*, where French suffix agreements could reveal gender, Beckett is careful to delete or obscure any grammatical clues.[6] This may be one more example of Beckett's concentration on the universal human condition rather than the particular,[7] or one last recollection, like Krapp's, of a male/female relationship. Also, in his drama of this period Beckett was turning to female characters who indulge in self-deluding stories: Winnie in *Happy Days*, and later Mouth in *Not I* and May in *Footfalls*. But whether female or male narrator, whether homosexual or heterosexual affair, the important element is the parting of the two lovers, and the significant issue is what this parting symbolizes. Molloy maintained a similar indifference about the issue of sex; wondering if Lousse perhaps had some masculine features, he finally decides, "Don't be tormenting yourself, Molloy, man or woman, what does it matter?" (*Molloy*, p. 75).

Enough concerns the narrator's meeting with "him," their years together (especially the ten between revelation of his "sacral ruins" and his order that she leave), her departure, and the aftermath. Although the narrator is a vague figure, the man, with his indolence and his bent body, climbing up gradients of one in one (p. 57), is none other than Dante's Belacqua, the lazy sinner who had waited until the last deathbed moment to repent his transgressions. Beckett was so fond of this creature, who had favored Dante with wan smiles, that he chose Belacqua as the protagonist for his first novel, *Dream of Fair to Middling Women*, still unpublished. In the early story "A Wet Night," Beckett's first published Belacqua doubles over with stomach pains "till finally he was creeping along with his poor trunk parallel to the horizon" (*More Pricks Than Kicks*, p. 83). Murphy creates the same image as he contemplates the peace of "Belacqua bliss": "Then he would have a long time lying there dreaming, watching the dayspring run through the zodiac, before the toil uphill to Paradise. The gradient was outrageous, one in less than one" (*Murphy*, p. 78). In *Enough*, Paradise is merely imagined, not promised; and the trip is a circular one, with the narrator becoming the reincarnation of her Belacqua, appropriating his old voice when it fades.

But are there actually two people involved, or as Brian Finney suggests, is one character "enough"?[8] As in other works, Beckett may be representing the human self as a Proustian series of various personalities fractured over time, as the Cartesian dualism of mind and body, or the artist as binary union of voice and hand. From the first paragraph the narrator displays a tendency to divide herself, using a method that combines the speaker/scribe dichotomy of the narrator in *How It Is* and the first-person/third-person tension of Mouth in *Not I*. Initially *Enough*'s narrator separates the pen from "the voice": "When the pen stops I go on." Malone felt a similar distance between his pencil and his creative self: "My little finger glides before my pencil across the page and gives warning, falling over the edge, that the end of the line is near. But in the other direction, I mean of course vertically, I have nothing to guide me" (*Malone Dies*, p. 32). The vertical guide would surely have to control the composition mentally, and in *Enough* this function is the province of "the master" who led the woman in her education—and who now directs her narration. Everything, particularly thought, springs from him, confirming that he represents the brain, a figurative rather than a literal "master."

Since the second paragraph demonstrates the narrator's utter dependency, her split-self dichotomy, the halting syntax of the piece, and the deadpan playful language, it deserves to be quoted in full:

I did all he desired. I desired it too. For him. Whenever he desired something so did I. He only had to say what thing. When he didn't desire anything neither did I. In this way I didn't live without desires. If he had desired something for me I would have desired it too. Happiness for example or fame. I only had the desires he manifested. But he must have manifested them all. All his desires and needs. When he was silent he must have been like me. When he told me to lick his penis I hastened to do so. I drew satisfaction from it. We must have had the same satisfactions. The same needs and the same satisfactions. [P. 53]

The "I" and the "he" are differentiated from this paragraph onward, but many indications convince the reader that their characteristics define one individual: the two characters share more than the same desires, needs, and satisfactions. That her calmness and all her knowledge derive "from him" further suggests that "he" symbolizes the mind. This odd couple seems compelled to act in unison, usually with "he" as the initiator and "I" as the passive follower: "I never asked myself any questions but his"; "Yet sometimes he took off his glove. Then I had to take off mine"; "Sooner or later *his* foot broke away from the flowers and *we* moved on" (pp. 56–57, my italics); "He loved to climb and therefore I too." At moments of closeness, the two heads and hands (minds and bodies) become one in a beautiful and rhythmically regular sentence: "Bent double heads touching silent hand in hand" (p. 56). Most explicitly, when they are "Wedged together bent in three"—curled side by side in sleep—they "turn over as one man when *he* manifests the desire" (p. 59, my emphasis). Beckett depicts this union with marginal doodles in *Enough's* manuscript (in the collection at Washington University in St. Louis), drawing the couple as double stick figures angled in three parts. All these details indicate that, as in the trilogy of novels, the Beckett writer is a binary creature—a speaker/scribe.

A pair of characters is one of the archetypes of Beckett's work, as all his readers and audiences realize. Nicklaus Gessner's formulation of this double motif also shows its paradoxical nature:

The pairs . . . never complement each other to form one whole. Even friendship seems to be what Beckett once calls in his *Murphy* 'l'amitié d'une paire de mains.' 'This is precisely . . . what unites Vladimir and Estragon: the friendship of two hands—thus no real friendship. The two had simply always been together—like two hands; they must help each other—like two hands; and, like two hands, they embrace meaninglessly. Like hands, they cannot move away from each other beyond a definite limit and are thus, without truly belonging to each other, inseparable.'[9]

The main delusion of the narrator in *Enough* is that love brings togetherness, but the reader recalls that a glove forms a barrier between the joined hands. Throughout his works Beckett rejects love as a solace for human misery. In the comic mode, Malone's matter-of-fact description of a romantic pair makes their striving for union appear animalistic and ridiculous:

For they cleave so fast together that they seem a single body. . . . But when they totter it is clear they are twain, and in vain they clasp with the energy of despair, it is clear we have here two distinct and separate bodies, each enclosed within its own frontiers, and having no need of each other come and go and sustain the flame of life. . . . Soon they will be able to part. Or perhaps they are just having a breather. . . . Back and forth, back and forth, that must be wonderful. They seem to be in pain. Enough, enough, goodbye. [*Malone Dies*, p. 65]

Merely thinking about another couple's incomplete fusion is "enough" for Malone. In a more serious mode, Beckett in *Proust* mocks man's penchant for self-deception about love, and quotes Proust on the isolation of the individual: "We are alone. We cannot know and we cannot be known. 'Man is the creature that cannot come forth from himself, who knows others only in himself, and who, if he asserts the contrary, lies'" (p. 49). The "I" of *Enough* lies continually, to convince herself that she was not actually alone in the past and that she will not die alone, lies in order to create a comfortable fiction.

In *Enough*, as in Proust's novel, time in general and the transience of desire work against any lasting happiness. Moll and Macmann in *Malone Dies* enjoy a relationship ruled by the law of conservation of affections: an increase of emotion in one person produces a decrease in the other. Similarly, as the narrator of *Enough* draws emotionally closer to her lover, he distances himself and then separates from her; yet this break ironically precipitates her assuming of the lover's characteristics. As she matures, he disintegrates; and by the time of his departure, she has acquired many of his proclivities. Now it is the narrator who scans the ground, as her lover did before her: "For I hardly raised my eyes from the flowers"; "Reluctantly I raised my eyes. . . ." During their relationship, she is forced to bend double, as he once did, in order to catch his mutterings. His voice had gotten regressively weaker; and by the time we hear the narrator, she is reduced to a faint voice apparently composing aloud. In the past the lover had murmured fragmented messages to the narrator; now it is she who speaks (like Mouth in *Not I* again), words "Spaced out. A bare million in all. Numerous repeats. Ejaculations. Too few for even a cursory survey" (p. 60). Peter Murphy hears in the alternating continuity yet discontinuity within her narrative a stylistic echo of her union yet division from the man.[10] Another analog for *Enough*'s style, and for Beckett's later styles in general, is also provided by the text itself: although the cotton gloves worn by the lover were tight, "[f]ar from blunting the shapes they sharpened them by simplifying" (p. 54). Beckett's tight sentences sharpen his metaphorical details by simplifying them.

In an imitative style close to that of *Abandoned Work*, the master's disjointed language (and that of the narrator) reflects a discontinuous universe; however, in *Enough*, sentences become drastically condensed, and the comma—still present in *Abandoned Work*—is abandoned here.[11] Instead of composing via long digressions, which necessitate commas for readability, *Enough*'s narrator thinks in short afterthoughts, each of which comprises a separate typographical sentence:

If the question were put to me suitably framed I would say yes indeed the end of this long outing was my life. Say about the last seven thousand miles. Counting from the day when alluding to his infirmity he said he thought it had reached its peak. [P. 56]

The conversational tone of her language makes the afterthought a natural means of expression. At times we can envision a woman chatting informally to a female friend: "With his upper hand he held and touched me where he wished. Up to a certain point" (pp. 59–60). Typically we find an independent clause followed by a grammatical fragment: "I desired it too. For him"; "Sudden pelting downpours overtook us. Without noticeable darkening of the sky." Much of the prose consists of simple declarative statements with some ellipses;[12] many of the typographical "sentences," as in *Abandoned Work*, technically are compressed sentence fragments lacking the crucial finite verb: subordinate clauses, parenthetical comments (for example, "I on the inside"), or prepositional phrases. Beckett's narrators typically talk and walk in the same manner, and thus we can see the halting quality of the speech echoed in the master's halting steps.

The jagged and hesitant pace—characteristic of speech in revision—is usually caused not merely by deleted verbs but by fragmentary, periodic punctuation used to divide a longer grammatical sentence into short segments, modifiers building upon modifiers. One variation is the construction of a "sentence" out of a noun phrase, which then introduces a description of some new item in the story: "Our meeting. Though very bowed already he looked like a giant to me" (pp. 54–55); "Night. As long as day in this endless equinox" (p. 59); "Attitude at rest. Wedged together bent in three" (p. 59). What could be called a grammar of afterthought traces the creative mind in process: imagining a story element and then expanding it, modifying it, revising it with the next phrase. A related reductive syntax appeared again in Beckett's fiction a few years later, used to preface the numerous descriptions in *The Lost Ones* (for example, "The light." or "The temperature."). The noun phrases give a scientific, "objective" tone, suggesting a lab report, to the prose of both stories—an objectivity which is one more delusion in *Enough*.

Self-delusion also manifests itself in the narrator's verb tenses in sentences that do contain true predicates. Maintaining the past tense for most of the piece, the melancholy lover chooses the present when she wants to recreate a stable history: "I see the flowers at my feet and it's the others I see" (p. 56). By the conclusion, her recollections of the past slide into consoling statements about a current romance; "[Night] falls and we go on. Before dawn we are gone" (p. 59). For the following paragraph, the first half of the passage develops in the present tense ("I can feel him at night . . .") while the second half returns to the past: "With his upper hand he held and touched me . . . (p. 59). Significantly, the last verb in the story is the present tense "feel" as the narrator strives to relive her memories linguistically by converting them into the continuous present: "[It is] Enough [that] my old breasts feel his old hand." One senses that, like Maddy Rooney in Beckett's radio play *All That Fall*, she would be satisfied with "twice daily love," and the life of the mind be damned.

While the nonintellectual speaker learns everything she knows from her lover, we in turn derive what little we know from the speaker; but our narrator is far from reliable, and her uncertainty and confusion confound the reader/audience. The very repetition of "I never asked myself the question" indicates that questions are in order. Often the narrator admits "I don't know" or "I cannot say," or concedes "seemed" and "perhaps." Instead of relying on simple past-tense verb forms throughout most of the story, she frequently employs the conditional mood: "must have had," "must have been," "cannot have been," and "could not have been." She begins several sentences with the word "if," twice starting "If the question were put to me. . . ."[13] Her very existence is conditional, dependent on the lover; and her life is fictional, dependent on her own narrative reconstruction. Also, since she represents the oral dimension of the artist, the voice that must precede the pen, this language of uncertainty reflects the inability of the writer to chart creative inspiration, or to explain the development of a text. Incompleteness in her memory and analysis compels her to rely on such constructions as "To those engulfed years it is reasonable to impute my education" (p. 58) and "How far this was not a delusion I cannot say" (p. 56). This last sentence—with its ironic mention of "delusion," its double negation, and convoluted structure—itself implies duplicity and evasion.

The "I" cannot say the truth, does not ask herself questions, because she is content with surface meanings, content to delude herself. She interprets "leave me" quite literally, and mentions that "[h]e was on his last legs" in language that unintentionally goes beyond (actually beneath) the figurative. Naïvely accepting pronouncements from the master at face value has humorous results: "He said I had Aquarius hands. It's a mansion above" (p. 54). *Enough*'s prose abounds in metaphors which become puns, or which reveal deeper meanings if the literal is exploited; for example, about the master's penis she innocently puns with "I drew satisfaction from it." Several comments when taken together outline a compressed version of evolution from plants to animals, from apes to man: "His trunk," "anatomy is a whole," "He gave me his hands like a tired ape," and "paternosters that he poured out to the flowers" (in the course of evolution, the flowers were, in a biological sense, "our fathers"). The lover, "on his last legs," with his bent knees and bent back, his "sacral ruins" causing him to bend double, his spine parallel to the ground, and his head nearly touching the earth on the slopes, conjures up the image of an old gorilla, an animal having the same common ancestor as homo erectus. More significant for the story as self-conscious reconstruction, by the phrasing of "I set the scene of my disgrace . . ." our narrator inadvertently discloses that she is not relating a biography, but is staging a drama, a fiction.

Even without the unintentional admission that life is being transposed into art, the reader notices that her story is full of gaps, paradoxes, contradictions, and backtracking. Despite this, and equally indicative of an artificial fabrication, the narration is in some places *too* carefully shaped, details falling neatly into dichotomies. "Contrary" emerges as one of the speaker's favorite words: "He must have been on his last legs. I on the contrary was far from on my last legs" (p. 53). The motif of opposites dominates her prose: the voice and the pen, I and he, the past and the present, youth and age, right and left, bent and erect, movement and stasis, speech and silence, mountains and plains, and ascending and descending the hills. Indeed, the master himself takes the form of opposite (vertical and horizontal) pieces joined at the sacrum: "His human frame broke down into two equal segments" (p. 57). His actions as well as his body divide into two parts: he performs the operation of raising to powers, and then "the converse operation"; and by looking in a mirror placed on the ground, he peers at the sky from the opposite direction. We hear the vacillation of the narrator's hope and despair about rediscovering her lover (like the mutually cancelling yeses and nos in *Texts for Nothing*), and the humorous permutation of opposites to describe the master's peripatetic methods:

"Immediate continuous communication with immediate redeparture. Same thing with delayed redeparture" (p. 57). Eight variations of this consume an entire paragraph, teasing the reader into calculating whether all possible combinations are listed.

Inconsistencies and apparent contradictions in the narrative make the reader hunger for fictional "truth." The speaker readily calls attention to the paradoxes in her relationship: "Though very bowed already he looked a giant to me. In the end . . . I had only to straighten up to be head and shoulders above him"; "Contrary to what I had long been pleased to imagine he was not blind"; "His talk was seldom of geodesy [the study of geodesics, straight lines on curved surfaces]. But we must have covered several times the equivalent of the terrestrial equator," that is, walking in a geodesic manner. Not only does the narrator include seeming discrepancies; she also adds blatant contradictions:

I cannot have been more than six when he took me by the hand. Barely emerging from childhood. But it didn't take me long to emerge altogether. [P. 54]

Mine [her glove] was naturally too loose for years. But it didn't take me long to fill it. [P. 54]

If I had looked back I would not have seen him. [P. 57] If I had looked back I would have seen him in the place where I had left him. [P. 58]

But in my life it was eternally mild. . . . Sudden pelting downpours overtook us. [P. 59]

Thus, rather than the narrator's being the victim of incomplete understanding, she is the perpetrator of inaccurate information: she lies to herself and to the reader. Instead of retelling her past, she recreates it—purposely retaining only the most romantic of memories and altering the most disturbing: "Contrary to what I had long been pleased to imagine he was not blind. Merely indolent. One day he halted and fumbling for his words described his vision. He concluded by saying he thought it would get no worse. How far this was not a delusion I cannot say" (p. 56). Here "been pleased to imagine" betrays the narrator's own addiction to self-delusion. It is *her* vision that is impaired, because she does not want to perceive the truth about her past. She will not even call a valley a valley:

We were not in the mountains however. There were times I discerned on the horizon a sea whose level seemed higher than ours.

Could it be the bed of some vast evaporated lake or drained of its waters from below? I never asked myself the question. The fact remains we often came upon this sort of mound some three hundred feet in height. Reluctantly I raised my eyes and discerned the nearest often on the horizon. [P. 58]

The narrator is making a Dantesque mountain out of a sea bed. Physical reality for her, as for many modern writers, becomes something to transform mentally or to dismiss: "It is only fair to say there was nothing to sweep away" (p. 59). This description of the sea bed recalls the Biblical quotation that Beckett alludes to in *Murphy*, a passage which may have given *Enough* its title:

The horseleech hath two daughters, crying, Give, give. There are three things that are never satisfied, yea, four things say not, it is enough:
The grave; and the barren womb; the earth that is not filled with water; and the fire that saieth not, It is enough. [Prov. 30.15–16]

The "earth that is not filled with water" (similar to the lake "drained of its waters from below" in the passage above) becomes a metaphor for the narrator's unfulfilled life; the woman will never be satisfied, will never have enough, because what she desires, besides true love and union, is immortality. One life before the grave is not enough, she complains: "Given three or four lives I might have accomplished something" (p. 54).

Later in the story, in a paragraph which appears in the French original, *Assez*, but is deleted in the English translation, she increases her request to four or five lives: "Toutes ces notions sont de lui. Je ne fais que les combiner à ma façon. Donné quatre ou cinq vies comme celle-là j'aurais pu laisser une trace."[14] The need to leave a trace connects this narrator with other Beckett creatures in *Imagination Dead Imagine* and *Ping* and suggests the process of writing, since words are "traces," marks of thoughts. In *Ping* the repeated phrase "traces blurs signs no meaning" refers to the very letters and words of a text; in *Enough* the woman's desire to leave a trace becomes the impetus to restart and finally finish the story she is narrating/scribing. The term "trace" also denotes a mathematical graph or a chemical residue—certainly appropriate for one of the "Residua," Beckett's collective title for these three 1960's pieces (*Enough, Imagination,* and *Ping*). It is as if, for Beckett's later fiction, all that remains after much literary and linguistic distillation are the precipitates of a story.

With terms like "donné" (given), Beckett places his characters in a world of logic and geometry (for analogy, consider the statement "Given X greater than zero, find a Y such that. . . ."). The art and craft of living and of writing is reduced to mathematics, as the French original underlines with an allusion to the field of combinatorics: "L'art de combiner ou combinatoire n'est pas ma faute" (*Assez*, p. 36). For "the minutes flew," the French has "les minutes s'ajoutaient aux minutes"; adding the instants of life, the couple takes flight from reality in arithmetic, even though later the woman realizes that she cannot "count" on the relationship. Since the lovers exist in imaginary space rather than realistic settings, all the numbers in the piece revolve around the magical three: the mountains are three hundred feet high, the average rate of travel is three miles per day, their pastime consists of raising ternary numbers to the third power and memorizing the cubes. Dwelling in a world of mental calculations, the narrator graphs their lives—like two functions—as overlapping curves, with a ten-year span delineated by two points in time. Similarly, Malone's exercise book is in fact a tablet of graph paper: "It is ruled in squares. The first pages are covered with ciphers and other symbols and diagrams, with here and there a brief phrase. Calculations, I reckon . . . [Beckett's pun intended]. Perhaps it is astronomy or astrology" (*Malone Dies*, p. 34). And curiously, Beckett himself often chooses graph paper notebooks on which to trace his fanciful fictions. This objective mapping of a life implies a certainty and accuracy at odds with the narrator's subjective and selective interpretation of the past: precise mathematical and geometrical terms artificially validate and solidify her imprecise fictions.

By the end of the piece, specific language alternates with sketchy prose in a schizophrenic style recalling Pozzo's speech about night in *Waiting for Godot*, for which Beckett's stage directions alternate between "Prosaic" and "Lyrical." This prose also anticipates the strange mixture of the scientific and the poetic in the styles of his later stories. Even at the end of *Enough*, the "I" appeals to more exact formulations as she deludes herself into believing that one can compute an existence by subtracting and dividing. She concludes by cancelling out everything but her favorite image: "Nothing but the two of us dragging through the flowers" (p. 60). If mathematical operations can distort space, then imagination (and self-deception) can warp time. Memory's method superimposes the present on the past, and when the mind forces these two states to appear identical, then time does not advance: "I see flowers at my feet and it's the others I see. Those we trod down with equal step. It is true they are the same" (p. 56). Throughout their wanderings, according to the master, "the sky seemed much the same"; and their last years together replay the first: "It veils those that went before and must have resembled it like blades of grass" (p. 58). But here the verb phrase "must have resembled" reveals the narrator's insistence on what might be yet another delusion. In fictional reality, the woman as character lives in the eternal present of literature, and as a self-conscious narrator, she exists within the cyclic process of revision.

Since the end of the story echoes its beginning, and since the tale is told and retold in fragments defying any chronological order, time is suspended, almost stalled. The lover's movement is compared to an equatorial path and becomes locally circular when the couple reascends the mountain they have just descended. In fact, the very structure of the narrative describes a circle analogous to a giant clock on which the hands of the couple join and separate. When holding hands, the lovers seem to transcend time, "While all about us fast on one another the minutes flew"—recalling Gessner's description of the "friendship of two hands." (Another Beckett couple, Mercier and Camier, finally manage to meet at ten minutes to ten, just as the hands of the clock meet.[15]) For the last paragraphs of *Enough*, present tense and past tense verbs become so jumbled that we are located in a state beyond time, in an outer limit of the fourth dimension where the lovers cannot coexist: "He murmured of things that for him were no more and for me could not have been" (p. 60). The hands of the broken watch remain forever apart.

Enlarge the clock to the earth's equator, and now enlarge that to form a circle around the sun where twelve constellations of the zodiac occupy the same plane, approximately evenly spaced like the numbers on a clock face. As the old man is astrologically fixated on the Lyre and the Swan, the astronomical time of the earth appears to be stuck—at least in the narrator's imagination: "But in my life it was eternally mild. As if the earth had come to rest in spring" (p. 59). The woman, perhaps subconsciously, wants to reverse the clock, frantically yearns to relive those past ten years. "It is then I shall have lived then or never," she says, using the future perfect tense, which matches Winnie's verbs in *Happy Days* ("This will have been another happy day"). A strong desire to crystallize instants makes sense here because time destroys. At the very least, history reduces recollection: "Graving themselves in his memory as best they could the ensuing cubes accumulated. In view of the converse operation at a later stage. When time would have done its work" (p. 56). Time diminishes both memory and love; and at its worst, time steals life.

"What do I know of man's destiny?" Enough. The narrator knows, although she deceives herself about it, that man's ultimate destiny is death. She asserts in answer, "I could tell you more about radishes"—that is, about radices (base numbers), about roots, about cube roots, about plants and flowers, about the roots of man. But to take cube roots is to diminish: from three dimensions to one dimension, from a human being in space to a speck in the void. It is because the "I" is dimly aware of all this that she is obsessed with the moment when her lover said "leave me," the moment of departure. Any separation foreshadows the final leaving—the separation of mind and body, the departure from the world of finite time and space. Far from *Enough* being a "hymn of adequacy and acceptance,"[16] it is a whistle in the dark of self-deception. A similar self-delusion motivates many of Beckett's dramatic characters who are fond of narrating long stories within the play, which returns us to the notion of *Enough* as spoken monologue. Most of Beckett's dramatic storytellers are masters of evasion, deception, disguise; they create fictions within fictions, peopled by alteregos which reveal yet conceal their true conditions.[17] That these speakers hide as much as they betray means that they never derive the purgative benefits of a full confessional release. They thus are condemned to retell the tale, yet the process of composing itself gradually becomes a comfort as well as a curse.

All that goes before, forget. Only the most consoling memories will remain, for this narrator as for the speaker of *How It Is.* One meaning of the word "flower," from Middle English, is "best" (as in love ballads: "She was the flower of them all"); therefore, wiping out all but the flowers is erasing all but the best in her life. The full reality of death is too much (the phrase "too much" is repeated four times in the short first paragraph); at least one sustaining illusion, one affirmation of life, is needed. And for Beckett as for Bishop Berkeley, the proof of existence lies in being perceived—in this case, being touched: "Enough my old breasts feel his old hand" (p. 60). But the self-assurance of sufficiency is only a memory, recalling the breasts and the separation of lovers "nel fior degli anni" in a section of Giacomo

Leopardi's "The Solitary Life."[18] Since Leopardi is one of Beckett's favorite poets, and since *Enough* shares some themes with this poem, several lines seem to echo back to the story:

> Love, love you have flown off so far
> From my heart: It once was warm for you,
> Not warm but ardent. With its cold hand
> Misfortune seized it, it is turned to ices
> In the flower of my years. My breast remembers
> The day you entered it. It was that dear,
> That unrecapturable time when youth
> Looks out at the unfolding scene of this
> Unlucky world and that world wears a smile
> Like paradise.

Less matter-of-fact than Leopardi's persona and more prone to create romantic illusions, Beckett's narrator attempts to avoid thoughts of the future, and the future of all men, as she approaches death with fear and loathing and with an absurd hope for another life. If she can make time stop, then there will be no aging, no suffering, no death. She does not objectively and realistically describe the old man because she sees herself, and her mortality, in him. While it is true that she will not accept the details of her past, this is largely to bury the final fact of death, which overwhelms her. Indeed her entire story is "an impossible fabrication, an invention to comfort the isolation of a human person, an invention to calm the terrors of lonely death."[19] Her insistence that she is calm is one last deception.

The self-deluding narrator is smarter than she seems, however; admitting to wanting four or five lives, she actually desires an infinite number of lifetimes, that is, immortality. If her avoidance of the reality of the lover's departure signifies an obsessive fear of death, then in the very telling of this story she is finding a solution. For the supreme work of art ensures the artist eternal life; the only way to evade death effectively is to produce a perfect artifact. This is a concept—and a theme—as old as the Greek poets, as romantic as Wordsworth, and as modern as Joyce in *Ulysses*. Stephen Dedalus, fixated on death for most of the novel, in "Proteus" recalls that as a boy he had self-consciously yearned for the immortality that only literature could promise:[20]

Books you were going to write. . . . Remember your epiphanies on green oval leaves, deeply deep, copies to be sent if you died to all the great libraries of the world, including Alexandria? Someone was to read them there after a few thousand years. . . . When one reads these strange pages of one long gone one feels that one is at one with one who once. . . . [P. 40]

Everlasting oneness, then, cannot survive between woman and lover, yet can endure between author and reader through Art. Only partially aware of this, Beckett's speaker continues to delude herself about departure and death, but in the process also continues to revise a fabrication that could live on.

This creation to disguise the realities of departure and death, and perhaps to achieve eternal life, is also a story *about* fabrication, about imagination. The relationship between the two lovers translates easily into the union yet division of brain and hand, idea and execution, fact and fancy. *Enough's* narrator creating a fiction from her life, exploiting the language of self-conscious revision, locates herself neatly in the tradition of metafiction. Like the narrator of John Barth's "Lost in the Funhouse," she is simultaneously writing a love story and a discourse about stories. Ambrose can never unite with Magda—not in the maze of the fun house, in the intricacies of the real world, or in the twists and halts of the story's plot. Also, in interviews Barth speaks of love and fiction with the same terms—emotion and technique—arguing that lovemaking and writing are analogous activities. Besides representing the internal and external processes of a writer, the metaphor of two lovers can suggest other dichotomies and liaisons in literature. Italo Calvino's recent novel *If on a Winter's Night a Traveller* uses a frame story of two lovers meeting as they seek the endings of incomplete novels. With these subplots about searching, Calvino mirrors the intimate relationship between Author and Reader and the pursuit of Reader for Text.

At yet another figurative level of *Enough*, the departure of the old man, the master, is Beckett's farewell to old fiction. Voice and world had been precariously joined in Beckett's fiction for at least ten years—the interval in the story metaphorically referring to the ten-year span of his greatest productivity, including *Godot* and his trilogy of novels—but with *Enough* they have parted company. During the time following this creative decade, Beckett departed from the mature characters in *Enough* and moved to the fetal creatures in *Imagination Dead Imagine*, *Ping*, and *Lessness*; he left the near-sentences of *Enough* for the verbless, staccato phrases of *Ping* and *Lessness*. When *Enough's* old voice "murmured of things that for him were no more and for me could not have been," he is speaking of the natural world, his old subject and thus material that was precluded for the narrator's (and Beckett's) new voice, new styles: "The wind in the overground stems. The shade and shelter of the forests" (p. 60). Finally, the death of older fiction is marked in *Ill Seen Ill Said* (1981), where Beckett's readers again encounter a wandering woman, here visiting a grave and visited by a shadowy, ghostly old man. In order to delineate the imaginative process even more minutely, Beckett in this recent metafiction perfects the syntax of afterthought he developed for *Enough*:

If only she could be pure figment. Unalloyed. This old so dying woman. So dead. In the madhouse of the skull and nowhere else. Where no more precautions to be taken. No precautions possible.

Even in his stories of the 1980's, character transcends pure imaginative construct; the woman still bears some taint of mimesis. Later in *Ill Seen Ill Said*, Beckett self-referentially offers the image of a zone of pasture and a wall of stones to portray his artistic reduction from nature to realistic fiction to a closed system of language. If enough reality is too much for the 1960's narrator, enough realism has become entirely too much for Beckett. Neither realistic fiction nor human love is enduring; nature, love, and art all deceive.

A much harsher story of loneliness and self-deception, *How It Is*, appears in language more fragmented and phrasal than that of *Enough* and more "ungrammatical" than any Beckett had developed before. Both fictions enact a dictating-scribe method of writing; the narrator of *How It Is* repeats "I say it as I hear it," just as *Enough*'s narrator claims to repeat ideas "from him." This hierarchy of master and apprentice in *Enough* represents the creative line of power from voice to hand, from author to narrator, and from narrator to character. In *How It Is*, though, not only is the narrator given dictation, provided words to utter by a sort of master; he is forced to speak—indeed tortured into speech—and his extorted language appropriately takes the form of truncated, disjointed phrases as if expelled with pain. One can understand why Beckett glanced back one more time toward the style of his earlier fiction for *Enough*, a prose too human for his later metafictions.

5

How It Is
Midget Grammar

The language of *How It Is* looked so strange, even to eyes already accustomed to Samuel Beckett's prose, that readers were perplexed and reviewers were peevish. In a review cleverly entitled "How How It Is Was," and written to imitate Beckett's new style, John Updike expressed the reaction of many readers in 1964:

the plays OKAY very the stage an altar anyway the radio plays EVEN BETTER the ear rebuilds the actors foist existence on the words I remember videlicet the wonderful lavender sandals of the messenger boy in a certain production of Godot and his mystical haircut BUT in how it is where Joyce and Kafka intersect one misses now the one and now the other compare The Burrow compare Nighttown compare The Penal Colony and deplore the relative thinness the sterile stridency[1]

In fact, *How It Is* is full and fertile, one of Beckett's most successful and beautiful fusions of style and content, a success apparent when we compare Beckett's haunting phrases with Updike's haughty parody. With *How It Is* the bits and scraps of a tortured life are spewed out in bits of sentences and scraps of paragraphs with contracted syntax that the narrator terms "midget grammar." Here the situation of all men, and in particular of the artist, is presented through an allegory of tormentors and victims either languishing in solitude or locked together in pain.

But the real "story" of *How It Is*, a statement about man's use of language, and the writer's relationship to language, is difficult to discern in a text experimenting with linguistic and narrative shapes, a novel for which a three-part structure is introduced but then abandoned. The three parts—before Pim, with Pim, and after Pim—are based on the protagonist's interactions with a similar creature in the mud, named Pim. But the divisions are merely artificial ordering devices for a narrator obsessed with order:

here then part one how it was before Pim we follow I quote the natural order more or less my life last state last version what remains bits and scraps I hear it my life natural order more or less I learn it I quote a given moment long past vast stretch of time on from there that moment and following not all a selection natural order vast tracts of time[2]

Besides reconstructing narrative order, the reader must decipher natural word order. Reading, even at the phrase level, presents a problem since there are no conventional sentences and no punctuation and since the fragmented clauses are almost impossible to parse. Should we read "bits and scraps/ I hear it, my life [in] natural order" or "bits and scraps, I hear it/ my life/ natural order." Does "it" refer to the last version, the bits and scraps, or my life? Or is the referent meant to be ambiguous? Rearranging phrases becomes a necessary prelude to a critical analysis of this bizarre novel, and in turn, an understanding of its imitative style and structure can help to unravel its jumble of condensed phrases and images. This shuttling back and forth between style and substance settles on two main linguistic units, word and phrase, and calls on the traditional critical concerns of repetition, imagery, and structure.

Piecing together phrases and images, we can envision a nameless narrator taking on the characteristics of Belacqua, of Christ, and of God. Beckett's wanderer in the dark becomes all men in the suffering of waiting, and all artists in the suffering of creation. What he creates is an intricate, mathematical system of mutual torture—a system with a fatal flaw, the missing part 4. In part 1 the narrator crawls in the mud toward Pim; in part 2 the narrator tortures Pim; in part 3 the narrator waits as his torturer crawls toward him. Symmetry demands that we then meet the first person protagonist as victim, yet he insists that it is not necessary to include a section about himself being tortured. Forced into speech, he creates the monologue we read, a monologue which accounts for the missing part 4. All this materializes on the page in blocks of prose variously labeled by scholars "poetic," "musical," "formal," "chaotic," and above all "repetitive."

For almost any novel, repeated phrases or ideas demand our attention because recurrent motifs obviously have thematic import. But *How It Is*, composed largely from about twenty repeated phrases,[3] is an absurd extension of Watt-like permutation. Within this network of repetition how does a reader determine patterns that are clues to meaning? David Lodge defines certain criteria for "significant repetition" which may be useful,[4] but while his method succeeds for analyses of traditional novels, Lodge himself admits that it becomes difficult to apply to experimental, highly repetitive fictions. Some linguists who work in the area of stylistics consider repetition as a deviation from the "norm" of a varied literary text; yet where repetition itself is the norm, it becomes the background for any "deviant" words. Other linguists search for foregrounded elements and then for correspondences between them: if foregrounded words or patterns of a text conjoin, they produce cohesion, another tool for interpretation. A "collocative set," a group of words which collate semantically, may form an image cluster in a poem, for example, and this set may also cohere with similar linguistic sets. In *How It Is*, where the same phrases are repeated numerous times to make up the body of the work ("vast tracts of time," "I say it as I hear it," "above in the light," "in the dark in the mud"), these become the background against which other phrases stand out. Thus the most foregrounded element in a text such as this would be an unusual word or phrase used only once.

"Belacqua" is just such a word and should not be foreign to Beckett readers. Belacqua is one of Dante's sinners, who as punishment for a last-minute conversion is detained outside of Purgatory, reviewing his life. He stars in the early fiction *More Pricks Than Kicks* and makes guest appearances elsewhere on Beckett's stage. The span of man's life, from dust to dust, is condensed into one night's dreaming for a creature like Belacqua. One of the narrator's refrains is "I have that in my life this time," indicating a recycling of his existence, or perhaps a recycling of Beckett's characters, as in the trilogy. Throughout *How It Is* an emphasis on waiting, sleeping, and dreaming—combined with obvious references to Dante's *Inferno* and *Purgatorio*—coheres in a cluster of images around Belacqua; as the narrator waits for rest he prays, like Dante's sinner, "in thy clemency now and then let the great damned sleep" (p. 36). His dream cycle moves from "hell to home to home to hell always at night Z to A divine forgetting enough," and playing on the cliché "there's no place like home," the narrator fantasizes about "ascending heaven at last no place like it in the end" (p. 104). Doubling and tripling his meanings, Beckett also implies that heaven may be a hoax; there may literally be no place like it at life's end.[5] Especially in part 1, characters relive experience through dreamlike images of the past, and the circularity of the novel's structure, of its content (a cyclical series of tormentors and victims), and of its language of recurring phrases makes Belacqua an ideal vehicle for Beckett's imitative style.

More generalized than a Belacqua figure, the narrator is also an Everyman analogous to HCE, Here Comes Everybody, in Joyce's *Finnegans Wake*. Repeated words like "family," "mankind," "species," and "humanity" form a collocative set which extends the implications of the character's life to all people. The phrase "that family" appears at least eight times in the text, first completely divorced from any logical context and only later in some plausible linguistic environment. In one instance "that family" breaks up a series of questions and thus becomes a foregrounded deviation from a local norm: "find something else to last a little more questions who were they what beings what point of the earth / that family / whence this dumb show" (p. 32).* This phrase also leaps out of the frantic questioning of a torture scene: "questions then DO YOU LOVE ME CUNT / that family / cut thrust" (p. 96). In part 3 "same family" becomes ambiguous instead of simply confusing; "before Pim long before with Pim vast tracts of time kinds of thoughts / same family / diverse doubts emotions too" (p. 103) can mean either that he and Pim are of the same family, that we are still concerned with the family of humans, or that although his thoughts may be diverse, they are in the same family, or phylum, in the biological sense.

Biological connotation converges with the narrator's frequent use of the word "species" and his tendency to speak in scientific and anatomical terms. He notices, for example, that the road outside his wife's hospital room was "lined with trees thousands all the same species." With the words "hanging on by the fingernails to one's species that of those who laugh too soon," Beckett alludes to a traditional definition of man as the only animal capable of laughter. Significantly, the narrator classifies animals according to their ability to experience happiness, and notes "the fragility of euphoria among the different orders of the animal kingdom beginning with the sponges. . . ." As long as the narrator can feel emotion, he can believe himself one of the species: "hanging on to humankind / a thousand and one last shifts / with emotions / laughter even / and tears to match / soon dried / in a word hanging on" (p. 94). By the end of the novel "that

---

*Beckett's text contains no phrase breaks, nor punctuation of any kind. The slashes added here and elsewhere in this chapter isolate significant phrases in a quotation. Two slashes (//) indicate a "paragraph" break.

family" becomes even more closely associated with the idea of laughter—humor of a very bitter, hopeless, and painful sort—and with the agony of time. Gradually the concept of "day" becomes ludicrous to the narrator as his life of torment stretches on forever: [6]

... until the day / hear day / say day / murmur it / don't be ashamed / as if there were an earth a sun / moments of less dark more dark / there laugh//dark bright / those words / each time they come / night day shadow light / that family / the wish to laugh each time . . . [P. 110]

Beckett implies that, given "how it is," man fools himself into thinking he is happy; man's only laughter must be a sarcastic or cynical snort. Thus the beastlike Willie in *Happy Days* has the correct attitude of detachment, while the self-deluded Winne cannot acknowledge the word "day."

Our narrator's obsession with the salvation of the human family is reflected in his vocabulary, especially the repetition of "loss of species." A drink ensures "humanity regained," but this is soon revealed as merely a temporary restorative. The true definition of man, suggests Beckett, classifies him as one who uses language. The baby's first word, usually "mama," earns him a place in the human family: "it comes / the word / we're talking of words / I have some still it would seem at my disposal / at this period one is enough / aha / signifying mamma / impossible with open mouth / it comes . . . the first to come and restore me to my [human] dignity" (p. 26). The sound /m/ in "mamma" is a labial (labials are explicitly mentioned later in the text) and requires the pursing of the lips; thus it is in fact "impossible with open mouth," so Beckett is linguistically accurate here. Like Hamm of *Endgame*, the narrator associates a frustrated need for parental communication with his present need for fiction: "the moment when I would need to say and could not / mamma papa / hear those sounds / slake my thirst for labials / and could not / from then on words for that moment and following" (p. 108). Man uses speech to define the self and to unify the self and others, so in two ways language distinguishes *homo sapiens* from other species.

Throughout *How It Is* the very murmur of the monologue separates man from beast, since "a word from me and I am again": I speak therefore I am. Thus "no sound" threatens a "loss of species": "part one before Pim the golden age the good moments the losses of the species . . . brief movements no sound" (p. 47). Almost invariably "loss of species" occurs in the linguistic environment of "no sound" thus reinforcing the association between man and language. Similarly, in *Wait*, Beckett uses the phrase "loss of species" to refer to Watt's condition after words begin to fail him, and after his world becomes literally "unspeakable." In the world of Pim, sound and language are bought only at the price of cruel torture, but the narrator remains "never quite fallen from my species" because he "hangs on" with his scraps of speech. Since in *How It Is* the alternative to hanging onto the human race is to become an animal, the narrator sometimes compares himself to a beast or takes on animalistic traits. He describes Pim's belly-down position: they are not face to face because the method of torture requires that one write on the other's back. Even animals have better communication than this, the narrator implies, in the phrase "even beasts observe each other" (p. 55). By the end of the novel he increasingly acquires nonhuman characteristics as his language disintegrates further: when his verbal pace quickens, "the panting [gets] wilder more and more animal"; "the panting [is] without pause the animal in want of air." Also, earlier in the novel the narrator was surrounded by equine metaphors. Obliquely he depicts himself as a horse when "through the jute the edge of the last tins rowel my ribs," where "rowel" means to prick with the jagged wheel of a horseman's spurs. He describes his lips as "very horsy," refers to his "forelegs," and says that he and Pim are "like two old jakes harnessed together." As in *Watt* where the picture of the old horse Joss becomes a picture of the human condition,[7] in *How It Is* the horse symbolizes Man as sufferer. Although human beings endure torture, their verbal expressions of that suffering effect a kind of salvation that raises them above the level of purely physical pain.

Through his vocabulary and his bits and scraps of remembered knowledge, the narrator of *How It Is* subsumes all humanity. His interest in etymology is demonstrated in his remark that the name "marguerite" derives from the Latin for "pearl," and his archaic phraseology sometimes surfaces in classical echoes like "Thalia for pity's sake a leaf of thine ivy" (p. 38). Although the voice moans, "I've lost my latin," Latinate and obscure words ("passim," "sparsim," "prepensely," "ad libitum," "idem," "farrago," and "speluncar") lend semantic and rhythmic variety to his monosyllabic murmurs. The narrator borrows "whelm" from Old English, "deasil" from Gaelic, "apostil" from French, "halm" from Old English, "oakum" from Middle English, "homer" from Hebrew. In fragments he pours out his academic background, claiming to have studied natural history, mathematics, humanities, anatomy, and geography. A study of the morphology of the text indeed reveals terms from all these disciplines, and the proper names mentioned (Malebranche, Erebus, Heraclitus, Haekel, and Klopstock) demonstrate considerable learning. Much of his erudite vocabulary is obviously scientific. Instead of saying that Pim's buttocks were of equal size he says they were "iso," a Greek word meaning "same" that is frequent in science and mathematics (as in "isotope" and "isomorphism"). He describes a romantic interlude with "we let go our hands and turn about I dextrogyre she sinistro," which becomes laughable since dextrogyration and sinistrogyration (meaning toward the right and toward the left) are technical terms from chemistry and optics. Words used chiefly in the field of botany ("introrse," "scissiparous," and "acervation") appear in the narrator's speech; and "macfarlane" shows that he is not unfamiliar with geology. But all this knowledge is worth nothing, and by part 3 a common refrain is "no knowing," an honest assessment contrasting with the delusion of "all known" in the later fiction *Ping*.

The narrator's scientific background is matched by his knowledge of the humanities. Many of his phrases echo the Bible in their language and style: "the earth must have been on fire when I see us we are already at hand," "this old kiln destroyed by fire and in all this tenement," "the same needs from age to age," and "long run fullness of time." Manna from heaven appears in the form of "celestial tin miraculous sardines sent down by God," and other passages also merge Bible history with humor: "had I only the little finger to raise to be wafted straight to Abraham's bosom I'd tell him to stick it up" (p. 38). In a more serious mood, the narrator ponders issues that theologians and exegetes have argued through the centuries; for example, when the Bible proclaims that God created the world in six days, does the author invoke the conventional meaning of "day" or does he mean a longer unit of time? The narrator reasons, "and the day so near its end at last if it is not compact of a thousand days good old question" (p. 39). This question permeates the novel—and indeed Beckett's entire canon: Is there ever any end, or does the last day continually recede?

Like Winnie with her fragments of misquoted poetry in *Happy Days*, the narrator of *How It Is* sprinkles his prose with classical allusions; and since these literary fragments span the centuries, our timeless narrator can represent all human beings and all writers. In fractured fashion the themes of seduction poetry (the carpe diem motif—"gather rosebuds while ye may") are alluded to with "profit while ye may silence gather while ye may" (p. 69). The narrator's large debt to Dante goes beyond the Belacqua imagery and the setting for his story (the muddy dark hell, of course, suggests the *Inferno*, cantos 5 and 6).[8] The sign above hell's gate, "Abandon hope all ye who enter here," is distorted in "abandon hope gleam of hope frantic departure" and "abandoned here effect of hope" (p. 46). The narrator comically refers to Dante's famous scene of lust where Paolo and Francesca admit that they were tempted by an erotic book, and so "that day [they] read no further," in his coupling scene with Pim: "in the rectum a redhot spike / that day we prayed no further" (p. 37).[9] But the most significant Dantean influence, on the structure and language of *How It Is*, derives from *Inferno*, canto 7. Dame Fortune (also called the Lady of Permutations), "whose charge is timely changing of vain wealth / Ever from folk to folk," decrees that "Wherefore one people rules, another serves" (see ll. 79–82), and she provides a model for the arbitrary "justice" meted out to Beckett's torturers and victims as their positions are permuted, turn and turn about.[10] Dante's angry sinners, a "muddy tribe" in the marshy Styx, are brawling, striking each other, and "rending with their teeth." Like Pim and Bom, they manage to spew out only bits and scraps of language:

> Fixed in the slime they say: 'Sullen we were
> In the sweet air cheered by the brightening sun
> Because of sulky vapors in our hearts;
> Now here in this black mulch we curse our luck.'
> This burden, though they cannot form in words,
> They gargle in their gullets. [vii, ll. 121–26][11]

Overwrought emotions in both texts produce verbal fragmentation. Beckett's narrator cannot express his anguish in a grammatical manner, cannot "form in words" of well-structured clauses and sentences his burden of pain, so he too gargles permuted phrases.

Allusions to Shakespeare as well as to Dante and the Bible permeate the language of *How It Is* and demonstrate cultural regression in the world of mud. Phrases out of context recall Hamlet's ravings, and like Hamlet (but with a sense of humor) the narrator debates with himself the alternatives of existence: "a little less of to be / present past future and conditional / of to be and not to be . . ." (p. 38). Hamlet declares that the air "appeareth nothing to me but a foul and pestilent congregation of vapors. What a piece of work is a man! . . . And yet to me what is this quintessence of dust?" (2.ii.298–305), and our narrator expresses similar feelings in his lament "my life as nothing man a vapour" (p. 80). Hinting at the title of another Shakespearean play, the narrator bemoans that feeding Pim out of love is "labour lost." The primary labor of the narrator is the creation of the fiction we read—a narrative phantasm that dissolves at its conclusion. With this creation, he resembles both Hamm in *Endgame* and Prospero in *The Tempest*:

> Our revels now are ended. These our actors,
> As I foretold you, were all spirits and
> Are melted into air, into thin air:
> And, like the baseless fabric of this vision,
> The cloud-capp'd towers, the gorgeous palaces,
> The solemn temples, the great globe itself,
> Yea, all which is inherit, shall dissolve
> And, like this insubstantial pageant faded,
> Leave not a rack behind. We are such stuff
> As dreams are made on, and our little life
> Is rounded with a sleep. [*The Tempest*, 4.i.147–58]

Many verbal echoes (for instance, the narrator's blending of "little life" and "sleep" into "little sleep") reverberate between *The Tempest* and *How It Is*, but an important difference is that Beckett's novel becomes one long dream-drama of how life is, in which the narrator simultaneously acts as producer, director, scriptwriter, and performer. With the magic of the imagination he calls forth his players, then lets them fade into nothing at the end. And this constitutes the entire story.

As in *Macbeth*, life in *How It Is* becomes "but a walking shadow, a poor player / That struts and frets his hour upon the stage" (5.v.24–25). *How It Is* contains a huge array of theatrical metaphors: the narrator announces "the big scene of the sack," "the little fables of above little scenes," "little scenes part one," "a few more little scenes . . . last scenes," "life little scenes," "start of little scene in the gloom," "little scenes in the mud or memories of scenes past," and "these perpetual . . . auditions." Very often "the curtains parted" signals a moment of insight for the narrator (pp. 53, 57) and occurs in linguistic conjunction with the verb "to see." Dramatizing his life permits the narrator to see it more vividly, but blinds him to its full significance. Minutely describing "little scenes" of the past—and finely calculating the mathematics of his future—allows him to evade the suffering of the present. (As ways of distancing truth, dramatizing and fictionalizing are practised by Hamm and also by the narrator of *Enough*, who says of her lover's desertion, "I set the scene of my disgrace just short of a crest.") A sudden turn of events in the mud and the darkness is equated with the turning point in a drama: "in viscissitudes and peripeteias the best in my life" (p. 56). The time has come for the narrator "to play at him who exists" as he questions Pim's life and his own, and even the wrist watch "will have its part to play." Thus his life and narrative become scripts: "training early days or heroic / prior to the script / the refinements difficult to describe / just the broad lines" (p. 61).

Much of *How It Is* consists of individual, not always integrated, tableaux ("clear picture of that / good"), the most stark but most compelling of which is the final "scene" of the narrator motionless and cruciform in the mud. Dialogue per se does not occur in the novel; in fact, we may consider the text to be one long monologue with the narrator answering his own questions, shouting his answers when the words are capitalized. But an imaginary dialogue between Krim and Kram, complete with stage directions, does take place.

Krim dead are you mad one doesn't die here / and with that with his long index claw / Kram shaken pierces the mud two little flues to the skins / then to Krim right for you they are warm / Krim to Kram roles reversed / it's the mud / Kram we'll leave them open and see one year two years / Kram's finger skins still warm

Kram I cannot credit it let us take their temperature / Kram no need the skin is rosy / Krim rosy are you mad / Kram they are warm and rosy / there it is we are nothing and we are rosy / good moments not a doubt [P. 93]

The narrator needs these dramatic metaphors to play out his existence because as a type of Belacqua he relives events in dream vignettes. After an image of animals, the producer of dramas remarks "with that I have lasted a moment"; he exists only through his words even more directly than does dying Malone.

Godlike, the narrator writes and directs the scenes he chooses to relive, and he creates Pim out of mere mud. But a simple identification between the narrator and the Creator is one of those overly neat critical pigeonholes that Beckett deplores, for the narrator is fallen man as much as divine being, a creature waiting for salvation. Paradoxically, he is also that very savior he awaits in his role as Christ. "God" is foregrounded in the text since it is one of the few proper names used besides Pim, Bem, Bom, Pam, Prim, Krim, and Kram (which recur often), and because it breaks the phonological pattern (a terminal /m/) established by these names. Very often "God" occurs in a colloquial expression not meant to be taken literally, as in "the humanities I had / my God." In other passages, however, God's existence becomes a most profound issue; and of course Beckett delights in combining the comic and the serious. The narrator displays a Woody Allen-like flippancy about religion as he wonders about Pim "if he talks to himself / no / thinks / no / believes in God / yes / every day / no" (p. 97). That temporary belief later dissolves into cynicism when the narrator curses God and uses a watch to time the slow response to a prayer.

But the autobiographical cynic cannot totally escape his youthful Christianity: references to the God of both the Old and the New Testament surface among the bits and scraps of his life, "even God that old favorite my rain and shine brief allusions not infrequent." His mother with her finger in the Bible points to "psalm one hundred and something," and many passages in the text point to the gospel according to Saint Matthew, for example "oh God man his days as grass flower of the field" (p. 78). Just as the flowers do not fret about their future, so the narrator should not worry about his sustenance, since there appears to be "an intelligence somewhere a love who all along the track at the right places according as we need them deposits our sacks" (pp. 137–38). The lonely creature's "intelligence" is the New Testament God who promises, "Therefore take no thought, saying, What shall we drink? or, Wherewithal shall we be clothed? For after all these things do the Gentiles seek: your heavenly Father knoweth that ye have need of all these things" (Matt. 6.31–32). Besides being a provider of food, Beckett's God must be a witness of existence: "he would need good eyes the witness if there were a witness good eyes a good lamp he would have them the witness the good eyes the good lamp" (p. 44). Mr. Knott provides this witnessing for Watt; for Winnie in *Happy Days* the blazing sun itself becomes her witness. Eyes and lamps are also linked in the gospels: "The light of the body is the eye: if therefore thine eye be single, thy whole body shall be full of light" (Matt. 6.22).

Much of *How It Is* parodies teachings on Christian love, particularly Saint Matthew's parables. The philosophy of an eye for an eye repudiated by Christ (Matt. 5.38) is made the essence of justice in this muddy hell. And Christ's "turn the other cheek" message (Matt. 5.39) is taken literally and scatologically in the torture/victim scenes, and as a forced necessity rather than as a sign of Christian meekness and nonviolence. Even though he is surrounded by darkness, the narrator sees a chance for light; the ever-present dark does not lead him "to conclude from that that no one will ever come again and shine his light on me" (p. 15). Is the creature in the mud waiting for a new Messiah, a new Light of the World? Perhaps. Meanwhile God is present in *How It Is* in several ways: as the possible party at the other end of the prayer line, through references (sometimes obscure) to the Old Testament, and through allusions to the New Testament. The strongest link between the Old Testament and *How It Is* occurs in one word, "tohubohu": "world for me from the murmurs of my mother shat into the incredible tohu-bohu" (p. 42). This term, derived from Hebrew, appears in Genesis i.2 as "emptiness and desolation" and is rendered in the King James version as "without form, and void"; the *Oxford English Dictionary* defines it as "that which is empty and formless; chaos; utter confusion." The latter phrase surfaces in Beckett's question and answer session between the narrator and Pim: "YOUR LIFE HERE BEFORE ME utter confusion" (pp. 73–74). Immediately after this, anxiety and despair, reminiscent of the tone in *Godot*, reaches a climax: "God on God desperation / utter confusion / did he believe / he believed / then not / couldn't any more / his reasons both cases / my God" (p. 74), implying that only God—and he himself as creator—can fill the tohubohu of mud.

The narrator attempts to play God as a self-effacing author who breathes life into his formless Adamic creatures: "Pim never be but for me anything but a dumb limp lump flat for ever in the mud but I'll quicken him you wait and see how I can efface myself behind my creature" (p. 52). Or, what is brought out of the mud, the raw material of the imagination, may be the novel itself. We are reading a rough draft written by a tentative creator, argues Frederik Smith: ". . . the many references to dark and light and the halting, laborious journeying through a primeval mud suggest a Genesis situation in which something—in this case a literary work—is being shaped out of the mud of one's own experience."[12] But by the end of *How It Is*, the narrator is left in nothingness, as his activities, creations, possessions, feelings, his whole life—all are cancelled out. God as Creator fills a void, but a Beckettian composer creates and maintains a void. Thus the repeated phrase in Genesis "and God saw that it was good" provides a reverse echo to the narrator's repeated "good," and contrasts significantly with his recurring "something wrong there."

Besides playing an ironic God the Father, the narrator also becomes an ironic Jesus; once Christ appears directly in a vivid dream image (p. 45). Also, the phrase "swaddling clothes" immediately evokes a picture of the Christ Child in the manger for so many Western readers that when Beckett includes the word "swaddle" at the beginning of *How It Is*, he inevitably calls forth the stable, the three wise men, and the life of Christ in miniature:

nor callers in my life this time no wish for callers hastening from all sides all sorts to talk to me about themselves life too and death . . . all sorts old men how they had dandled me on their knees little bundle of swaddle and lace then followed in my career

others knowing nothing of my beginnings save what they could glean by hearsay or in public records nothing of my beginnings in life [P. 12]

This passage sketches the span of Christ's life from the visit of the wise men to his thirty years of private life to his three years of public life.

Since Molloy sees each man's existence as a Via Dolorosa, a slow journey to Calvary, it is not surprising that in *How It Is*, Beckett should portray his Everyman who is on a path of torture as a Christ figure. His wanderer's "last meal the last journey" then becomes the Last Supper and the trip to Golgotha. The repetition of "nails," the torture of nails cutting skin, and a possible pun on the repeated "hanging on" together produce a metaphorical crucifixion: "sounds of hammers three or four at least hammers chisels crosses perhaps" (p. 89). (These crucifixion images appear again, even more condensed and more allusive, later in Beckett's fiction in the minimal text *Ping*.) Christ's burial in the vault and the prophetic tearing of the temple's veils at the instant of His death are suggested by "in the mouth of the

cave and the approaching veils." Whereas Veronica's veil wiped
Christ's face and miraculously retained its imprint, veils in *How
It Is* obliterate the face: "here come the veils most dear from left
and right they wipe us away" (p. 89). Just as the sacrificial Lamb
died on the cross, so the narrator describes himself comically as
"dead as mutton"; and his whole world amounts to "martyring
and being martyred." At the end of the novel we leave the narrator, who is dying, with his "arms spread yes like a cross" suffering the sacrifice of composition.

On one side of a moral spectrum we have Belacqua, and on the
other, Christ; man is in the middle, waiting and suffering—that
is how it is. In this fictional world where a god who probably
does not exist is alternately blessed and cursed, the narrator lives
in doubt (like the *Godot* tramps) midway between hope and despair. And this emotional oscillation echoes in the contradictory
and shifting phrases and tones: seriousness and humor, decision
and indecision. If there is no such thing as Divine Providence, at
least there must be some superhuman order; if there is no Being
to love the narrator, at least there must exist some force to rule
him. Order and certainty are sought in mathematics and in justice, two recurring motifs in *How It Is*.

Like earlier Beckett characters (and those to follow in *Enough*
and *Company*), this narrator counts on numerals to bring some
solace to his life. His favorite numbers, ten and fifteen, reappear
in many contexts, showing that he obviously delights in these
precise figures instead of a general word like "several." The most
trivial details are given importance through the application of
mathematics: "one buttock twice too big the other twice too small
unless an optical illusion . . . in other words the ratio four to
one / I always loved arithmetic / it has paid me back in full"
(p. 37). Arithmetic also produces a pun about the narrator's life
which, though humorous, is also meant to be taken quite seri-
ously: "Krim says his number's up / so is mine / we daren't leave
him / quick all numbers up / it's the only solution" (p. 81). His
journey can be traced on a number line or a line segment divided
into smaller units, as he graphs it in geometrical terms: "A to B /
B to C / home at last" (p. 78); "B to C / C to D / from hell to
home / hell to home to hell / always at night / Z to A / divine forgetting enough" (p. 79). "Z to A" implies circular travel; and this
cycle, extended to thousands and millions of beings, becomes
one of the mathematical equations in part 3 of *How It Is*. In the

manuscripts for *Comment c'est*, the French original, Beckett himself revels in numbers as he calculates—on the verso page of his draft—distances, speeds, and couplings.[13]

At the beginning of part 2 the narrator tries to develop a new, nonmathematical style, but finds it impossible. He promises "not the slightest figure henceforth all measures vague . . . and hence no more reckoning save possibly algebraical" (p. 51). Striving for literary order and structure, the narrator desires distinct techniques for each section of his story, but the three parts overlap in content and in style; contrary to his plan, it is part 1 that contains the "vague impressions"—the images from childhood and youth—and part 2 that emphasizes scientific accuracy. After the narrator's disavowal of figures in part 2, he describes in ludicrous detail his physical position relative to Pim's and performs an empirical test to determine their relative heights:

moving right my right foot encounters only the familiar mud with the result that while the knee bends to its full extent at the same time it rises my foot we're talking of my foot and rubs down one can see the movement all along Pim's straight stiff legs it's as I thought there's one

my head same movement it encounters his it's as I thought but I may be mistaken with the result it draws back again and launches right the expected shock ensues that clinches it I'm the taller [P. 57]

That this is one of the least precise passages (and one of the funniest) in part 2 is evidence that the narrator cannot forego his facts and figures; instead, language becomes more mathematical as we read, almost in geometrical progression.

With his anatomical terms, the narrator gives the descriptions of torture in part 2 the detached tone of a scientific treatise or medical journal; his cold depictions of Pim demean his own humanity. Words like "thenar and hypo balls," "meatus," and "piriform" (a variant of "pyriform" and only in technical use) render Pim a mere collection of bones and elements rather than a sensate human being. Therefore, the scientific style of the torture passages reinforces the hypothesis that these creatures fall midway between human and animal, and supplies a rationale for their cruel concept of justice. Actions in the mud become "mechanical":

the hand approaches under the mud comes up at a venture the index encounters the mouth it's vague it's well judged the thumb the cheek somewhere something wrong there dimple malar the anatomy all astir lips hairs buccinators it's as I thought he's singing that clinches it [P. 56]

Pim is sometimes reduced to an object obeying the laws of physics: as his limb is "released at last / the arm recoils sharp / a little way / then comes to rest" (p. 59). Little better, Pim resembles a phonograph device which produces sounds automatically: when "he stops / nails in armpit / he resumes / cheers done it / armpit / song / and this music as sure as if I pressed a button" (p. 64). At best Pim serves as a guinea pig used to test the narrator's "basic stimuli" theory, and since Pim is narrator—is ultimately all of mankind—the language of these scenes has a chilling effect on the reader.

Because his obsession with science and arithmetic increases, by part 3 Herr Narrator describes the pace of his journey in a paragraph composed almost solely of numerals; and Beckett teases the reader into jotting down the appropriate divisions and multiplications in the margin, as he himself did in composition (arriving at the exact figure of thirty-eight, rounded off to forty): [14]

four by twenty eighty twelve and a half by twelve one hundred and fifty by twenty three thousand divided by eighty thirty-seven and a half thirty-seven to thirty-eight say forty yards a year we advance [P. 125]

These calculations, meant to demonstrate the slowness of the couples' procession, actually slow the reader's progress down the page. But the numbers do more than characterize the narrator and reinforce imitative style. Mathematics is crucial because it embodies the ethical and metaphysical world of *How It Is*, a world in which "at the instant I reach Pim another reaches Bem we are regulated thus our justice wills it thus fifty thousand couples again at the same instant the same everywhere with the same space between them it's mathematical it's our justice." Henceforth the tormentor/victim couples become ordered pairs [15] in an infinite set; the total suffering is held constant, and justice demands that tormentors and victims come out equal.

In this precise hell, unequal bad luck is unjust: the narrator cannot fathom the possibility that Pim's sack is "not burst Pim's sack not burst there's no justice." A cry of pain causes infliction of more pain according to this legal system, "not that I should cry that is evident since when I do I am punished instanter"

(p. 63). Here the use of the term "instanter" (meaning instantly), derived from legal Latin, underscores the theme of punishment under these laws, and is an example of imitative style working at the morphological level. For a permutation of partners, it is not clear whether two people or three is the critical minimum; but well before the end the narrator has already admitted that he is speaking of "my imaginary journeys imaginary brothers," so the reader knows that these intricate fictional systems simply fill his void. In the darkness and mud, the concept of justice ultimately dictates the mathematics of his cosmos. A fair meting out of torture would necessitate a circular, rather than a linear, arrangement of couples, ensuring that the creatures at the two endpoints are not left without partners for the last tango of torment. But, after acknowledging this logic, the narrator asserts "we do not revolve." The only other mathematical solution is an infinite, instead of a finite, line of creatures, without end points so that no creatures are left "deprived." (In the manuscript of *Comment c'est*, Beckett planned the structure as "pas circulaire" and "progression sans fin.")[16] With a satiric twist Beckett suggests that ours—"above in the light"—is the world of true rotating suffering. Because his sense of justice demands an equal and instantaneous fate for all, the narrator argues that the question whether he is alone or surrounded by millions is irrelevant. But, of course, one solitary creature would contradict the procession of couples and thus the entire system. By the end, the mathematics, the justice, the intelligence, the other creatures—all are denied.

When other objects and concepts fade into uncertainty, the sack is the only belonging that the narrator maintains. Sacks mark the beginning and ending of the expedition and are the basic requirements for the journey itself. As "the first real sign of life," the sack comes to symbolize the embryonic sac, as critics have agreed. And because it contains "the opener that is my life," as well as the tins of food, the sack is the means of nourishment; it also lends comfort as a pillow and a companion. Beyond this, it transfers some of its characteristics to people: Pim's veins are said to be like the cords of a sack (p. 58). Finally, sacks metamorphose into cells, living creatures themselves, when the narrator employs the botanical term "acervate" meaning growing in heaps or clusters; he wonders "if all the sacks in position like us at the beginning that hypothesis such an acervation of sacks" (p. 137).

Sacks paradoxically represent both suffering and sustenance since the can openers they contain are instruments of torture as well as the means to food; the sack is the place "where saving your reverence I have all the suffering of all the ages." Life consists of one long journey of sadness in *How It Is*, with the sack around the neck weighing as much as an albatross curse. The rule of this muddy hell demands torture with an opener to produce screams of anguish; pain becomes the emotional source of life, given that "with it I may last a little more." Words sustain the narrator's existence as a man, and a scream from the victim demonstrates *his* existence: "the voice extorted a few words life because of a cry that's the proof good and deep no more is needed a little cry all is not dead" (p. 122). Hamm used the same test of vitality on Nell in *Endgame*, but the narrator of *How It Is* surpasses Hamm in sadism until cries of pain provide his real sustenance: "there is more nourishment in a cry nay a sigh torn from one whose only good is silence or in speech extorted from one at last delivered from its use than sardines can ever offer" (p. 143). Even a recounting of suffering revitalizes, as the narrator hints with the juxtaposition of "these perpetual revictuallings narrations and auditions."

Bags of food are not only the indirect means to words of pain (through the opener) but also are linguistically equated with words themselves. Usually the narrator speaks of his phrases being strung together, but at least once it is the sacks that are linked as he describes his method: "namely string them together last reasonings namely these sacks these sacks" (p. 136). Stringing words together—writing—can be tortuous or it can be comforting, and sacks represent both of these possibilities. While in *How It Is* sacks of words are mostly painful, in the later fiction *Company* word-sacks are more companionable, becoming the "pillow of old words for a head" that Watt had wished for.

Searching for morphological foregrounding and cohesion in *How It Is* provides one solution to the thematic problem of this enigmatic story, but only a clue about its style, since this method focuses mainly on the significant nouns and noun phrases of the text. Yet Beckett's exploitation of other parts of speech (pronouns and verbs) and larger syntactic units and their typographical and rhythmical features must be analyzed before we can answer more than the question, What does *How It Is* mean? As in the explication of a poem, the reader must ask precisely *how* it means. Marjorie Perloff interprets *How It Is* as a poem,[17] and other scholars term its blocks of prose "versets." While remembering that it is a narrative in monologue form, we must give *How It Is* the close attention usually devoted to poetry, pulling apart its phrases before resynthesizing them.

One way of dissecting the language is to isolate problematic parts of speech, and pronouns here are especially suspect. As in *Texts for Nothing*, finding the correct pronoun presents a grammatical concern for the narrator; his difficulty in turn raises the issue of point of view in the novel. Although at first the narrator purports to be telling the true story of his life, this story is dictated to him by "an ancient voice in me not mine," thus he continually stresses "I quote" and "I say it as I hear it." When the narrator contrasts himself with Pim, though, he argues that he does not have the power of speech at all (and hence cannot be saying anything): "he can speak then / that's the main thing / he has the use / without having really thought about it / I must have thought he hadn't / not having it personally" (p. 56). Still "quoting on" after Pim, he dwindles to merely a voice, for "that's all is left breath in a head nothing left but a head nothing in it almost nothing only breath" (pp. 104–105). But according to his system of torture, the narrator had to have been voiceless during part 2, "the tormentors being mute as we have seen." This rule implies the possibility that the narrator is actually the victim throughout *How It Is* and is thus trying to objectify and displace his suffering through the creation of Pim.

Only once is there a hint that a victim is more than the subject of a scientific experiment. Never does the narrator feel sympathy for Pim; rather, he loses heart only when he contemplates himself as sufferer. He argues that he need not write a fourth part of the book since this would merely be the reverse of part 2, so "it is sufficient for this episode to be announced." Many critics are taken in by the narrator's avowals, one stating that "part four is unnecessary to our narration because it is essentially a repetition of part two."[18] But the narrator/writer himself admits later that the story "is in danger of being incomplete," and as his tormentor, Bom, approaches, the narrator challenges the system's structure: "or emotions sensations / take a sudden interest in them / and even then / what the fuck / I quote / does it matter who suffers / faint waver here faint tremor" (p. 131). Apparently all is not mechanical; apparently it does matter if the narrator himself is being tortured, in the very act of speaking this monologue.

Is Pim the narrator's victim, his fantasy, or himself? Is the voice inside or outside of the narrator? Is he telling us of his own life or of another's? These questions are never completely answered, but rather are echoed in a self-deluding shifting of pronouns, here from "your" to "my" to "his": "I nothing only say this say that your life above YOUR LIFE pause my life ABOVE long pause above IN THE in the LIGHT pause light his life above in the light" (p. 72). In the context of the teacher-pupil situation of torturer and victim, changes in pronouns have the ring of declensions learned by rote: "YOU BOM me Bom ME BOM you Bom we Bom" (p. 76). And these two sentences jab into the reader's eyes since they contain such a high percentage of capital letters, capitals that are being carved into the victim's back. As in *Texts for Nothing*, a fumbling with pronouns reproduces stylistically the narrator's effort to affirm an identity through fantasies he creates. The narrator admits that "I talk like him / I do / we're talking of me like him," and because of the obsessive repetition of "we're talking of me," by the beginning of part 2 the reader suspects that only one being is present:

can't go on we're talking of me not Pim Pim is finished he has finished me now part three not Pim my voice not his saying this these words can't go on and Pim that Pim never was and Bom whose coming I await to finish be finished have finished me too that Bom will never be no Pim no Bom and this voice quaqua of us all never was only one voice my voice never any other [Pp. 86–87]

The same breathy phrasal rhythm and preoccupation with pronouns occurs in a later Beckett monologue, the play *Not I*. But the psychology has changed so that the speaker, Mouth, instead of complaining about solitude and suffering ("only one voice my voice"), denies identification with her horrified protagonist ("who? . . . no! . . . she!").

Not only does the speaker in *How It Is* find it difficult to define himself as character/narrator; he also has trouble beginning and concluding his narrative. Identity, position, and point of departure are still unknown after fourteen pages of text; and two pages later the narrator is ironically searching for a start, wondering "what to begin with ask myself that last a moment with that // what to begin my long day my life present formulation"

(p. 24). Gradually "begin" comes to mean not only the origin of the narrative but also the start of the narrator's day, the restart of his life. To end his story and his life (and these two are joined linguistically through ambiguity) is just as difficult as to begin them; yet he knows he must achieve an identity (as the Unnamable too realizes) before he can terminate it: "we'll end if we ever end by having been" (p. 108). He looks for the "blessed day last of the journey," but doomed to a life of circularity, he mocks himself as "the ancient without end me we're talking of me without end." Resembling the "I" of *From an Abandoned Work*, the narrator admires those with the sense to create an ending ("God knows I'm not intelligent / otherwise I'd be dead"—p. 63). Likewise, Kram becomes enviable in his apparent death throes: "can it be the end at last / the long calm agony / and me the happy witness" (p. 82). Like Pim, the narrator "wishes to die / yes / but doesn't expect to / no." The writing on Pim's back corresponds to the writing of the monologue: an *E* and an *N* are scored on his back but never a *D*.[19]

In *Malone Dies* the story perishes with its teller; in *The Unnamable* the narrative "goes on" with a self still seeking identity at the conclusion; in *Texts for Nothing* the "I" ends where he began—nowhere and nobody. Since Beckett shapes the style to the substance of his fictions, in *How It Is* (whose French title, *Comment c'est*, is a pun on circularity), the non-ending of the novel provides part of its meaning. For the Belacqua-like protagonist of *How It Is* circularity is his very life, in fact his punishment for life. Unlike his namesake in *More Pricks Than Kicks*, this latest Belacqua goes to the hospital not to die but to be reborn: "you are there again / alive again / it wasn't over / an error / you begin again / all over / more or less / in the same place or in another" (p. 22). A seeming contradiction to the doom of eternal earthly suffering, the end of the novel may offer some hope for an end to the narrator's life as he shifts from the tentative "I MAY DIE" to the grammatically more emphatic "I SHALL DIE." He rejoices that it is the finish "at last," but this is just fantasy wish fulfillment, since the final words in French snake back phonetically (*commencer*—*comment c'est*) to the first, and he is doomed to "go on."

Beckett employs phrasal style as well as global structure in the text to reflect and embody a fatal circularity. The narrator finds himself in the same paradoxical situation as the Unnamable: only through words can he attain silence and only by going on can he ever cease. His expression of the impossibility of continu-

ing ("one can't go on / one goes on as before / can one ever stop /
put a stop / that's more like it / one can't go on / one can't stop /
put a stop" [p. 90]) is itself a continuation; yet the only chance
for a real finish lies not merely in a long enough string of words
but in the *correct* concatenation—the ever-present Beckett pensum. Since new words to try must be found, the very repetitive-
ness of the narrator's monologue emphasizes and *causes* his failure; thus there is no hope in "listening to this unchanging drone
the faint sign for us of a change some day nay even of an end."
He would like to believe that voices continually vary ("never
twice the same"), but his obvious reiteration belies this; and too
many qualifications, signalled by "unless," occur to him:

unless recordings on ebonite or suchlike a whole life generations on
ebonite one can imagine it nothing to prevent one mix it all up
change the natural order play about with that

unless un-changing after all the voice we're talking of the voice and
all my fault lack of attention want of memory the various times
mixed in my head all the various times before during after vast
tracts of time [P. 107]

An image of Krapp with his tape recorder comes to mind, and
suddenly the monologue of *How It Is* sounds like a scratched
record or a rewinding and replaying spool.

The overwhelming repetition of the style mirrors the circularity
of the structure as it creates circular "paragraphs," passages,
and parts. Even though the narrator tries to "mix up all that"
and find a conclusion, he is limited to a finite set of phrases, bits
and scraps of life which he must permute endlessly.[20] For a narrator who cannot begin or end his story, Beckett has created a
timeless world; the narrator, like the creature in the later piece
Lessness, exists in a limitless, eternal now, stuck in the slime. He
realizes that the mud and the dark is "the same kingdom as before a moment before the same it always was I have never left it it
is boundless" (p. 43). Although a boundless world of infinite
time promises endless freedom, there is something terrifying,
paradoxically limiting or enclosing, about the very notion of infinity; hence the narrator's need to divide boundless time into
discrete units. Since temporality measured in eternities is difficult to envision, Beckett offers the reader a visual metaphor
transposing time into space: "no more time / vast figure / vast
stretch of time." A timeless world makes an ordered structure

impossible as the narrator tries vainly to "divide into three a single eternity for the sake of clarity"; but because the actual form is circular, his supposed three-part structure and (repeated) "natural order" are just two more self-delusions.

Himself timeless, the narrator is of "age unknown" and borrows from the recycling "I" of the thirteen *Texts for Nothing* to acquire "thirteen lives I say thirteen but long before who knows how long how many other dynasties" (p. 83). Time moves more quickly than normal for this narrator; aeons old, he boasts of having "not a wrinkle not one" presumably because "at the end of the myriads of hours / an hour / mine [is only] a quarter of an hour." While assuming that "when time ends you may end," the ageless wanderer in the mud must meanwhile, like Gogo and Didi, devise ways to pass the time; both eating (especially "gorging on [Pim's] fables") and questioning help him to "last a little more." Deluding himself, he projects onto Pim his anguished need to fill the empty hours, so that he wonders "what can I ask him now what on earth ask him further busy himself with that if only a few seconds." Most of the minutes are spent merely waiting, and as the possible actions decrease, mere words and thoughts amuse him. Only the absence of memory makes the eternity of repetition bearable. Having no past or future, the narrator lives in an eternal now—even though he denies this stasis—and obviously feels trapped in his present just as he is mired in the mud. In the following passages he singles out the word "now" as not belonging in his vocabulary: "but words like now before Pim no no that's not said only mine"; "but words like now not mine." As noted earlier, the narrator has a similar aversion to the word "day": "if daily ah to have to hear that word to have to murmur it" (p. 39). Henceforth in many occurrences "day" is followed by "that word again." This term inflicts pain because days do not mark off discrete temporal units as they pass, but rather prolong an indefinite lifetime.

The creator in the mud changes his pronouns to hide his true experience behind the pain of others; he gropes for nouns with which to express or evade his timeless state; and he searches for the correct verb tense in order to solve the problem of an eternal cycle.[21] While he yearns for fewer words in general, in particular he requests fewer verbs, particularly the verb "to be": "a little less of no matter what / no matter how / no matter when / a little less of to be / present past future and conditional / of to be and not to be" (p. 38). The text manifests (sometimes humorously, as here) this desire, enacting the goal of nonbeing that many Beckett characters seek, with a conspicuous lack of copulative verbs where one would ordinarily expect to find them, for example, "here then at last [is] part two," "in the sack then up to now [there are] the tins the opener the cord," "[there are] more sacks here then than souls," "words quaqua [were] then in me," "the people above whining about not living [is] strange at such a time." Beckett's discontinuous style in monologue form, composed largely of short noun and adjectival phrases punctuated with words clichéd through repetition, partly circumvents the narrator's problem of what verb tense to employ. Ideally, he would prefer the ordeal of his life and his story to be over, and with Pim "it goes on in the past ah if only all past all in the past" (p. 61). Logically, he should tell parts 1 and 2 (how it was before Pim and with Pim) in the past and only part 3 (how it is after Pim) in the present tense. But if the whole book consists of part 4, then the present tense (for how it is to *be* tortured) is the valid one for the entire monologue, but too painful to be sustained. Various hypotheses have been offered for the narrative strategy,[22] but in my view the novel is told from the vantage point of the missing part 4.

Quite explicitly, Beckett begins the novel "how it *was* I quote before Pim after Pim" and ends "that's how it was *end of quotation* after Pim how it *is*" (my italics). Thus the real human condition is the situation of the narrator after Pim, that is, the victim anticipating his tormentor. With doodles and notes in the *Comment c'est* manuscript, Beckett diagrammed and charted his plot in terms of "four cycles," and he refers to a "post III" section in his plans.[23] Earlier the narrator had asserted "part three it's there I have my life," but more accurately, it is in part 4, being victimized by the torture of having to write, that the true "present formulation" of his life takes place.

This is why a past formulation of his story provides such comfort. Failing to achieve a consistent past tense in part 1, the narrator hopes, for part 2 especially, to transport himself back in time; and using the verb "seemed" causes him to rejoice with "there's a past perhaps this part will work in the past part two with Pim how it was" (p. 52). After the clause on the next page "he must have heard them grate," the narrator congratulates himself with "there's a noble past." Present tense verbs resurface, however, in "his cries continue that clinches it / this won't work in the past either / I'll never have a past / *never had*" (p. 54, my italics). Ironically, in his discouragement the narrator uses a past-tense verb to deny his history. With the appearance of Pim's watch, past-tense verbs appear again, and the story is "off again in the past." But, lacking control, the narrator slides from the past to a present participle to the present tense [24] in one short string of words: "the day then when clawed in the armpit instead of crying he sings his song the song ascends in the present it's off again in the present" (p. 63). As in *The Unnamable* and *Texts for Nothing*, here the verbal shifts convey more than just a search for the grammatically "correct" verb tense; they trace a journey toward the psychologically, or even ontologically, appropriate time frame.

Thus stylistic revisions imitate changes in the narrator's concept of self. Towards the end of part 2 past-tense verbs gain the majority in some passages, only to be defeated ultimately by a future tense verb and all but demolished by a shifting of pronouns: "what then became of us him me flop back into the past in this position when the silence when Pim stopped past giving any more me permitting or thump on skull past taking any more I'll ask him but me me" (p. 91). His acute consciousness of this problem of temporally situating the self is shown in numerous alterations of tenses in mid-phrase or even in a trial of several tenses in a passage. Some revisions move him from the present to the past: "the kind I see sometimes see in the mud part one sometimes saw"; "I am right I was right"; "what else can I do could I do"; "I hear all understand all and live again have lived again." This same shift occurs with the imperative mood as well as the declarative when the narrator advises himself to hasten his story along and "be with Pim have been with Pim have him behind me" (p. 23). It is not surprising that by part 3 the three time frames commingle in "I had it all . . . knew it all did and suffered as the case may be in the present too and in the future that's sure" (pp. 127–28). The future tense appears more frequently in part 3 than in the other two sections, but it is a meaningless future. Indeed, any change in tense becomes ineffective when no change over time takes place, when "the life you had the life you have the life you'll have" are all the same life. Thus "this life how it was / how it is / how most certainly it will be" is efficiently compressed with the present tense "how it is" of the title. A humorous characterization of the voice as "refreshing alternations of history prophesy and latest news" announces Beckett's stylistic device of mixing the three verb tenses to portray a lingering limbo that is far from refreshing.

All this shifting of verb tenses is "the attempt, prolonged throughout the novel, to reveal the unrecounted fourth part of the story."[25] And the voice itself admits that "the essential would seem to be lacking." Given this interpretation, the repeated phrase "something wrong there," which other readers see as signalling the wrongness of past images,[26] or as a slight lapse in chronological order, also declares the wrongness of the entire structure. The "something wrong" is that the situation the narrator predicts for the future (his being tortured into speech by Bom) is actually occurring in the present, in the very composition of the novel. Thus repeated avoidance of the correct (present) tense speaks loudly of the writer's agony.

In other verbal choices Beckett is just as careful to mold style to content. A story told through dictation by an outside voice explains a large number of verbs in the passive voice. The narrator believes he is not relating a story but receiving one, is not remembering or creating words but mouthing and mimicking them. Perhaps the actual scenario is that the writer is being prompted by the tortured Bom, that is, by an alter ego, a compulsive inner creator. Naturally, passive voice appears in clauses describing the teller's supposed narrative passivity: "but the wish for something else no that doesn't seem to have been to me this time"; "that's the speech I've been given"; "I am given a fancy"; "scraps of an enormous tale as heard so murmured to this mud which is told to me"; "I shall pant on in abeyance in the dark the mud the voice being so ordered I quote." Passive voice governs the ordering of life (the system of sacks and couples) as well as the ordering of words; hence the repetition of "it's regulated thus" or "we're regulated thus." The responsibility for the system's cruelty, and for the tale's content and tone, is laid on someone else's shoulders, while Beckett allows the suffering narrator to hide behind the illusion of unemotional objectivity.

Another property of verbs in *How It Is* that reflects the hesitant and noncommittal nature of the narrator is the frequent use of conditional and subjunctive moods. Like the "I" in *Texts for Nothing*, this narrator feels that his very existence must be qualified with a large "if." Thus the conditional (or a prelude to it) occurs whenever he questions his own existence, his characteristics, or his location in time and space: "all I hear is that a witness I'd need a witness"; "if I was born it was not left-handed"; "if he wasn't me he was always the same cold comfort"; "what if I were he I would have said . . ."; "and if on the contrary I alone then no further problem." As is evident in this last example, Beckett's voice sometimes employs "if-then" statements in a logical, mathematical context. In the system of couples "if only four of us and so numbered only 1 to 4 // then two places only at the extremities of the greatest chord say A and B" (p. 117). While antecedent-consequent formulations of the system maintain their logic, conditional statements about the narrator's emotions break down, producing over-qualified "ifs" without "thens." Often in evocations of feelings, the antecedent of a statement is expressed in a retiring, even wistful, manner; and the consequent is either truncated or lost in futile tangents: "if I could lie down / never stir any more / [then] I feel I could / weakness for pity's sake / honour of the family / if I could move on a little further / if there is a further / we only know this little pool of light" (pp. 83–84). The same shade of despair tinged with uncertainty in "if there is a further" appears again as the narrator wonders if "all the Pims tormentors promoted victims past if it ever passes." Paradoxically, the precise logic of the "if-then" form jars with the indeterminacy of the narrator's existence: there can be few consequents if there is no movement in time.

For depicting action less conditional, the narrator's favorite tense is the present imperfect.[27] Statements frequently are variations on "I'm going," "we're talking of . . .," "the heart is going," "he's coming," "I'm listening," "we are looking at me," "he's singing," and "what else am I doing." The present participle appropriately embodies continuous action in a cyclical world; man is continually travelling, suffering, waiting, and speaking in a never-changing now. Beckett dramatizes the human predicament of waiting in the stasis and circularity of *Waiting for Godot,* and conveys it stylistically in the hesitant, cyclical, yet lyrical prose of *How It Is.* In addition to expressing activity in a timeless world, the present participle also connotes pretense and illusion; it is prevalent as the verb tense of children playing make-believe and of directors setting up a scene. Therefore it is the natural tense for a narrator actually alone and stationary in the darkness, spinning out a fantasy about billions of other beings engaged in complex rituals. It is significant, then, that when the fantasy breaks down in the last pages of *How It Is*, the number of present participle verbs shrinks to zero.

One must step back from counts of repeated nouns, analyses of shifting pronouns, and studies of verb tenses to find a more complex explanation of how the style imitates the content in *How It Is*. Hints from the narrator himself point us in the direction of syntax, rhythm, and the structure as a whole. In H. Porter Abbott's analysis, however, *How It Is* is seen as a repudiation of Beckett's earlier struggle for imitative form. Far from chaotic, *How It Is* is structurally and syntactically nothing but orderly and systematic, he argues. "Each prose stanza can be broken down into perfectly intelligible units each in turn containing what the transformational grammarian would call 'deep structure.' There is no direct attack on grammatical sense as there often is in *The Unnamable*." [28] But at least the long "sentences" in *The Unnamable* had their verbs still intact, and had commas and periods as clues for parsing. Also, the Unnamable had less of a tendency than this narrator has for practising free association. Finally, even Noam Chomsky himself would be unable to determine deletion transforms where so much of the Beckett "sentence" has been deleted. Beckett has taken a telegrammatic style to extremes—to a point where the prose sounds almost un-English, even when compared with the Unnamable's stream of language. He creates a new sort of English, an innovative type of syntactic order: we learn to extract meaning from series of cryptic and fragmented phrases because of rhythmic and stylistic consistency. Beckett, with this fictional entity that defies classification as poetry or prose, teaches us how to read in a new way.

The difference between middle and late Beckett fiction for Hugh Kenner is that *The Unnamable* is written in sentences, while *How It Is* definitely is not. "The official business of the Beckett sentence," says Kenner, "is to affirm a tidy control it cannot quite achieve." [29] This is an accurate description of the rambling prose of *The Unnamable*, but the condition of the voice in *How It Is* is that "he is trying to utter sentences, and seldom succeeding"; only the imagistic "[m]emories go into sentences that can be punctuated." [30] Although some qualification to this rule could be made (for example, very short, independent clauses, often containing the subject-verb contraction "it's," do occur in the "present formulation"), generally descriptions of how it was can be ordered into neat syntactic units, while the present how it is cannot be described grammatically. The reason is that the present situation actually is expressed as incoherent cries of anguish. Thus *How It Is*, in syntax also, succeeds in mirroring content with style, as its symmetry and order are merely fictions continually fading away to reveal scattered phrases of a solitary, suffering creature.

The narrator's account of extorting speech from Pim becomes the metaphor for the narrator's own tortured language. Forced by some other voice or higher power, the narrator as author recalls other Beckett characters compelled to write. A commanding voice "in me not mine" causes a split in the narrator's personality (like that in *Enough*) shown most obviously in the last pages of the novel where the prose in dialogue form reveals him as both tormentor and victim simultaneously. Language delivered as fragmentary answers to a tormentor accounts in part for the choppy syntax of the novel. This theory of the monologue as constrained speech is proposed by the narrator himself when he says, referring to Pim, "I talk like him . . . little blurts midget grammar" (p. 76). Pim's "extorted voice" is actually the voice of the narrator, and the style of writing on Pim's back corresponds to the style of *How It Is*, which is also "unbroken no paragraphs / no commas / not a second for reflection / with the nail of the index until it falls and the worn back bleeding passim" (p. 70). Even the use of the term "passim" links the words in blood to the words on the page, for while "passim" literally means "here and there," it is normally used to indicate the *repetition* of a phrase or an idea throughout a book. Finally, for Pim as for the narrator, in the telling of their lives "the proportion of invention [is] vast assuredly vast proportion a thing you don't know the threat the bleeding arse the cracking nerves you invent but real or imaginary no knowing" (p. 72). Thus, as in the play *Not I*, the description of the protagonist's streams of language also describes the text itself.

Pim above all is a clever invention, of course, used to embody a disjunction the narrator feels as writer—the dualism between the murmuring inner voice and the noting hand. After an outburst of words he clarifies "all that / not Pim / I who murmur all that / a voice / mine alone / and that bending over me / noting down one word every three / two words every five" (p. 87). As the narrator objectifies his anguish as victim in Pim, Beckett objectifies his anguish as writer in the narrator. (This interpretation would explain the many autobiographical touches in the novel, such as the scene of the flower-hatted mother watching over the praying child.)[31] Memory's faint murmur provides another reason for a syntax of incomplete fragments, for "bits and scraps barely audible certainly distorted." Only a fraction of the words are heard and recounted, "not the millionth part / all lost nearly all." In *Watt*, Sam has reconstructed the novel from his friend's barely intelligible bits and scraps; here we get Watt-like speech transcribed verbatim with no transitions or explanations. At first the narrator in the dark claims to miss nothing ("I say it as I hear it murmur it to the mud every word always"), but only some words heard are remembered, then chosen, then fewer recorded. Just as art is a selected reordering of life, so *How It Is* records "not all a selection." Adding to the stylistic fragmentation, the narrator's faulty memory in a timeless world causes temporal fractures and confused events, so that all is "discontinuous journey images torment even solitude . . . all discontinuous save the dark the mud" (p. 126). A similar ratio of words read to words deciphered holds for the reader as well: each fragmented cluster seems to be gone before he has the opportunity to register it. We too must "reread our notes pass the time . . . I lose the nine-tenths it starts so sudden comes so faint goes so fast ends so soon I'm on it in a flash it's over" (p. 81). This passage could serve as a critic's commentary on Beckett's more recent writings, as well as a frustrated response to *How It Is*. Also, just as the Beckett reader becomes one of the "searchers" in *The Lost Ones*, so the reader of *How It Is* is compelled to pant mentally in bits of phrases, to segment the prose into short strings, as the narrator does, if he is to interpret intelligibly.

The system of tortured and torturing beings which forms the substance of *How It Is* becomes embodied in its syntax, structure, and rhythm. In the world of *How It Is* one's voice becomes one's life; the circularity of the book is reflected in the circularity of the system; and the rhythm of the phrases themselves is a metaphor for the breathing, panting human voice. Beckett exploits the analogy of life as journey and makes the novel itself a difficult trip; the narrator's descriptions of physical motion also describe his style. During a conversation with Lawrence Harvey in 1961, Beckett spoke of writing as a "groping in the dark" which required the writer to "see with his fingers."[32] This image of the artist could have been the germ for *How It Is* (the French original was published in 1961), a creator crawling in the darkness and mud, hanging on with his fingernails. Describing another creature—who gets conflated with himself—the narrator says, "see it how it throws its four fingers forward like grapnels the ends sink pull and so with little horizontal hoists it moves away it's a help to go like that piecemeal it helps me" (p. 28). His own—and Beckett's—verbal travel is also piecemeal, seeing with his fingers, a painful grappling with the very stuff of syntax.

Repetitions of "ten" and "fifteen" for units of measure link the physical and verbal journeys, as the narrator travels, breathes, and talks all at the same rate. Envisioning his own chunks of prose as well as the victim's cries, the narrator sees "an image too of this voice ten words fifteen words long silence ten words fifteen words long silence" (p. 126). Obviously, blank spaces on the pages of *How It Is* visually represent the pauses between verbal outbursts; the narrator's pace consists of ten or fifteen yards and then a rest lasting the same number of seconds. Similarly he measures his breathing as "a hundred and ten fifteen to the minute when it abates ten seconds fifteen seconds" (pp. 132–33). With the comparison "ten words fifteen words like a fume of sighs," Beckett construes phrases as synonymous with exhalations, writing with living. Later the narrator asserts that all men tell the same story, "we exhale it pretty much the same," also implying that the urge to write is as inexorable as the need to breathe. If the narrator's sudden stops and starts are verbal as well as physical, he can incite himself onward in both journeys with the same phrase, "set forth again." Then, "when the panting stops," the bits and scraps of life continue but are broken by pauses in Pim's speech: "the gaps are the holes otherwise it flows more or less profound the hole we're talking of the holes not specified not possible no point I feel them and wait till he can out and on again" (p. 84). Thus the narrator uses Pim's supposed falterings as victim to justify his own discontinuous style. In fact, though, the gaps represent the narrator's own hesitations as Bom's victim, as victim of an inner compulsion.

How It Is describes the situation of man, alone, waiting to die, who creates a system of "justice" so that some order will elevate a meaningless existence. He pants out bits and scraps of his life using words to fill the void of the "tohu-bohu." In its pacing, incoherence, and repetition, the language of *How It Is* has its roots in the style of Lucky's monologue from *Godot*; and in fact many verbal echoes link the two pieces, notably "quaqua." In essence, the message is the same: man wastes and pines in the dark for an

Almighty who does not exist or does not care. Here, as in the Old Testament, men are divided into Cains and Abels, but since cyclical suffering replaces the finality of death, Pim/Abel becomes an "unbutcherable brother." Allusions to Dante's damned lovers and to seduction poetry sound an ironic note since the couples, "wooer and wooed," of *How It Is* unite only for mutual torture. Communication between men is reduced to a cruel sign language of jabs, and converse between man and God is reduced to a joke in the scene with Pim's watch: "curse God / no sound / make mental note of the hour and wait / midday midnight / curse God or bless him / and wait / watch in hand" (p. 40). By 1961 Beckett had narrowed the focus of his work from the situation of modern man as unredeemed to the predicament of modern artist as unredeemable. In *How It Is* he creates an allegory of suffering and a language of pain to convey this anguish of the narrator as futile writer.

Beckett's stylistic development is traceable from the feared linguistic dead end of *The Unnamable*, through the partly unsatisfactory experiment of *Texts for Nothing*, to a successful imitative style sustained throughout a novel (albeit a short one). Beckett uses *Comment c'est* after 1961 not just as a turning point in narrative technique but also as the stylistic catalyst for the fictional residua that he devises later. Even stranger physical environments and systems are explored with escalating precision and pseudoscientific language in *Imagination Dead Imagine* and *The Lost Ones*. More significant for Beckett's new styles and more demanding for the reader's response to them are the fictions *Ping* and *Lessness*, in which beings further diminished from the creature in *How It Is*, in a bleaker world still, are embodied in language further denuded and fragmented. From this point on, the phrase rather than the sentence becomes Beckett's minimal literary unit, a particle he will recombine to create larger elements. Beckett invents new language systems of "lessness" in which phrases more condensed and ambiguous than the bits in *How It Is* are permuted in a babel of repetition. Ironically, the styles of some of these later pieces make the prose of *How It Is* seem varied and conventional by contrast.

Imagination Dead Imagine
The Microcosm of the Mind

The little world of the mind has been the province of Beckett's fiction from the beginning, but whereas in his earlier novels he wrote *about* perception, imagination, and consciousness, in the later fiction—especially in *Imagination Dead Imagine*—he stylistically enacts these cognitive processes. This text begins with a white dome, and a white enclosure had suggested the inside of a head to the narrator of *How It Is*:[1]

the voice quaqua on all sides then within in the little vault empty closed eight planes bone-white if there were a light a tiny flame all would be white ten words fifteen words like a fume of sighs when the panting stops then the storm the breath token of life part three and last it must be nearly ended [P. 128]

In this passage we get a sneak preview of the oscillating storm in the tiny cosmos of *Imagination Dead Imagine*, and of its creatures barely breathing. While the "setting" and "characters" of *Imagination* at first seem strange, its white rotunda containing white bodies is actually one more contraction of familiar Beckettian images and preoccupations. The three-zone conception of Murphy's mind, the light and dark imagery of the plays, the skull-like set of *Endgame*, the womb and tomb imagery in the trilogy, and the obsession with white in *From an Abandoned Work* all merge here as Beckett explores some of his old concerns—perception, being, and the activity of composing—but with a new style.

In *Murphy*, Beckett analyzes the protagonist's mind in a detached way, and even as late as *The Unnamable*, although the reader witnesses consciousness, she does not experience it fully. In *Imagination Dead Imagine*, however, Beckett achieves a style evoking a journey into the imagination, and he gives the mental microcosm a suitable narrative enclosure. Providing exact directions for readers and employing the imperative mood, Beckett invites us to visualize an image and then dissect it. By describing his fantastic image (a vault within a rotunda housing two white beings lying within a circle three feet in diameter) in a matter-of-fact tone and with scientific precision, he makes it seem real—at least in the imagination. Beckett's narrator does not so much depict the image as create it, does not so much create it as urge the reader to create it, through consistent use of the second-person perspective and other linguistic stratagems. Since this image arises out of nothing, fades into nothing, and may represent the nothingness of the dead imagination, Beckett is faced with a problem similar to the one he surmounted in *Texts for Nothing*: he must develop a language of paradox that can picture a void.

Beckett had begun a novel in the early 1960's, but a scant residuum is all he produced. For this text he introduces a new detached tone that filters out both the ironic, omniscient voice of *Murphy* and the tortured, first-person voice of *How It Is*: "Lying on the ground two white bodies, each in its semicircle. White too the round wall eighteen inches high from which it springs." A white enclosure has appeared in many of Beckett's works, and a glance at those earlier images for the microcosm reveals how different is *Imagination*'s focus and presentation. Finally, Murphy's dream of "embryonic repose" is realized in the late fiction; his white garret has shrunk to a white vault barely able to contain two bodies in fetal position. The rotunda of *Imagination* may be classified as one of the items conceivable in the third zone of Murphy's mind, "a flux of forms" where "there was nothing but commotion and the pure forms of commotion" (*Murphy*, p. 112). Murphy withdraws from the real world and tries to live in his mind, which for him is a place. In this mental area of confusion, ordinary space and time are destroyed so that the two end points of a life span become one, and time is stopped. In *Imagination Dead Imagine* life and death are similarly fused: the rotunda's creatures may be either fetuses or dying bodies, or both. These figures in a comatose state, suffering alternations of heat and cold, light and dark, resemble Molloy when he "was virtually bereft of feeling, not to say of consciousness, and drowned in a deep and merciful torpor shot with brief abominable gleams . . ." (*Molloy*, p. 72). Malone thought he was "in a kind of vault" (*Malone Dies*, p. 44) and talked of coming "back to this foul little den all dirty white and vaulted" (p. 63). *Imagination*'s vault, when rapped, gives "a ring as in the imagination the ring of bone."[2] Similarly, Malone wonders if "these six planes that enclose me are of solid bone" (p. 47). Echoing this, and anticipating the still figures in *Imagination*, the Unnamable sees himself as "a head, but solid, solid bone, and you imbedded in it, like a fossil in the rock" (*The Unnamable*, p. 148).

Molloy seeks physical stasis and mental isolation comparable to Murphy's ideal and the Unnamable's achievement, and his image prepares for the setting of *Imagination*: "I listen and the voice is of a world collapsing endlessly, a frozen world. . . ." *Imagination*'s structure emerging from nothingness is white, the characters appear frozen, and their world compresses and expands endlessly in cycles. The Viconian cycles explored in Beckett's essay on *Finnegans Wake* suggest a model for this vibration in an environment of flux. Young Sam, interpreting Joyce, demonstrates how Vico devised his cyclic theory of history from Giordano Bruno's ideas on opposites:

> The maxima and minima of particular contraries are one and indifferent. Minimal heat equals minimal cold. Consequently transmutations are circular. The principle (minimum) of one contrary takes its movement from the principle (maximum) of another. Therefore not only do the minima coincide with the minima, the maxima with the maxima, but the minima with the maxima in the succession of transmutations. Maximal speed is a state of rest.[3]

Beckett's minimal characters in *Imagination Dead Imagine* are fetal mummies oscillating between the extremes of the white-hot calm of prebirth and the great cold dark of postmortem. But these two states actually become one, and the fluctuation between them constitutes the purgatory of human existence. Very often in Beckett a transition between two extremes (day and night, or land and sea) becomes a metaphor of the mental microcosm,[4] here representing not just the human condition but also the writer's predicament.

Within the text, the "absolute stillness" of the bodies jars with the "convulsive light" of the rotunda, and this disjunction is reflected in the style itself and its agitating effect on the reader. While the language appears static, the prose actually races ahead in some passages, impelled forward, and then is stalled by an aside. Similar linguistic movement—sometimes in quite long sentences—takes the form of repetitive clauses (naturally parallel to repeated physical states in the vault) so that the conclusion of a sentence cycles back to its beginning. In one seventy-one-

	Beckett Text (*parentheses added, enclosing modifiers*)	Activity
	It is possible too, (experience shows,)	
[1a]	for rise and fall to stop short (at any point) and mark a pause (more or less long) before resuming,	stasis
	or	
[2a]	(reversing) the rise now fall, the fall rise, (these in their turn to be completed),	movement
	or	
[1b]	to stop short and mark a pause (more or less long) before resuming,	stasis
	or	
[2b]	(again reversing) and so on,	movement
[1c]	till finally one or the other extreme is reached.	stasis

Fig. 2. Beckett's use of modifiers and qualifiers in one sentence in *Imagination Dead Imagine* to convey stasis and movement. Numbers in brackets indicate alternation between two states. (See original sentence in *First Love and Other Shorts*, p. 64.)

word sentence the modifiers and qualifiers (placed in parentheses in figure 2) slow the progression of the prose as they create temporary pauses in reading. The structure of the sentence (indicated with annotations in brackets) reveals an alternation, signalled by numerous "ors," between stasis and movement. And this same oscillation mirrors the writer's shifts between composing and thinking. By the time he arrives at the phrase "and so on," the narrator—simultaneously artist and scientist—has become tired of specifying the various permutations, and the description itself falters and winds down. Thus this one sentence, beginning with the speculative, imaginative "It is possible," stylistically encapsulates the world of the rotunda. (See Figure 2.)

Parallel to the oscillation between stasis and tremor, and within the convulsions between rise and fall, the sentences— both internally and sequentially—graph an alternation between certainty and uncertainty. In the following passage, through tone shifts and also through precise assertions undercut by modifiers and qualifiers, the narrator self-reflexively portrays his very hesitation about the imaginative construct he is creating:

> But on the whole, experience shows, such uncertain passage is not common. And most often, when the light begins to fail, and along with it the heat, the movement continues unbroken until, in the space of some twenty seconds, pitch black is reached and at the same instant say freezing-point. Same remark for the reverse movement, towards heat and whiteness. Next most frequent is the fall or rise with pauses of varying length in these feverish greys, without at any moment reversal of the movement. But whatever its uncertainties the return sooner or later to a temporary calm seems assured, for the moment, in the black dark or the great whiteness, with attendant temperature, world still proof against enduring tumult. [Pp. 64–65]

Despite assurances, doubt reigns even at the phrase level because of unsettling near-oxymorons like "temporary calm" and "enduring tumult" and the insistent repetition of "seems." Agitation and uncertainty lie in "these feverish greys," mergings of white and dark, black ink upon a white page; whereas either the pristine sheet or the page obliterated by blackened margins (that earlier Beckett narrators had welcomed) brings peace. Thus *Imagination Dead Imagine* can be read as a sequel to *From an Abandoned Work*, though it is delivered in an entirely new style, which allows one to discover within the ever-desired whiteness the potentially fertile, creative brain—in imagistic language, a male/female couple enclosed in embryonic space, the imaginative and imagined microcosm.

One possible property of the small world of the mind, especially in *Murphy*, is the absence of all things, or nothingness. After his infamous chess game, "Murphy began to see nothing, that colourlessness which is such a rare postnatal treat, being the absence (to abuse a nice distinction) not of *percipere* but of *percipi*" (p. 246). This lethargic protagonist receives his first direct contact with nothingness through his chess partner's eyes. "Mr. Murphy is a speck in Mr. Endon's unseen" (p. 250), just as *Imagination*'s rotunda is termed a "white speck lost in whiteness." Perception, real and imaginary, emerges as the challenge to both reader and narrator in *Imagination Dead Imagine*. The reader must alternately enter and exit the dome; and while symbolically this represents the movement into and out of one's mental world, literally the narrator is requesting an observer to view the rotunda and its contents from different perspectives. Beckett depicts this movement as repetitive and perhaps endless by revising the phrases "Go out" and "go in, knock" to "Go *back* out" and "go *back* in, knock" (my italics).[5] In order to visualize the creatures' positions, the reader must do precisely what the narrator recommends—actually draw a circle, with properly labeled diameter, and sketch the bodies inside. Beckett himself doodled some calculations and diagrams on the handwritten first draft of *Imagination Dead Imagine* (for which his habitual use of graph paper now becomes quite appropriate). Imitating the narrator, who is for the moment as concerned with geometry as he, we become active participants in the process of reconstructing.

The reader is granted one glimpse of a world full of places and things before it is erased; then he is instructed to distinguish the white rotunda against its white background: "Go back out, move back, the little fabric vanishes, ascend, it vanishes, all white in the whiteness, descend, go back in" (p. 63). It is curious to remember that in *Murphy*, Neary makes the general statement, "Murphy, all life is figure and ground" (p. 4).[6] In *Imagination* all life reduces to ambiguous figures against a monotone background. Next the reader must discern—through the guide's directions—the wall, the vault, and the bodies inside. But since vision depends on the presence of light, when "the light goes out, all vanishes." And when the light is vibrating, or oscillating with darkness randomly, then perusal becomes especially difficult: "In this agitated light, its great white calm now so rare and brief, inspection is not easy," says the narrator, not one given to overstatement.

By stressing the dichotomy between a distant shot of the rotunda and a close-up of the bodies inside, Beckett contrasts objective and subjective views, and opposes surface and inner reality. The narrator forces the reader to see through *his* eyes, implying that the only valid frame of reference is the *internal* view: "Rediscovered miraculously after what absence in perfect voids it is no longer quite the same, from this point of view, *but there is no other*. Externally all is as before. . . . But go in . . ." (p. 65, my italics). When inside, the reader must mentally project a three-dimensional reality from the two-dimensional one he is allowed to see. Our scientific narrator examines the creatures: "the bodies seem whole and in fairly good condition, to judge by the surfaces exposed to view. The faces too, assuming the two sides of a piece, seem to want nothing essential" (p. 66). This "assuming" (aided by the recurrent "seem") pushes perception to the brink of imagination.

Of course in English the word "vision" may refer to one's sight or to a fantastic delusion; it spans the spectrum from physical reality to imaginative fancy. In Beckett's work these various meanings are often conflated, and even more often the eye or visual perception becomes synonymous with the mental world. For example, one morning Murphy awakens realizing that he has forgotten what he dreamt, so "Nothing remained but to see what he wanted to see. Any fool can turn the blind eye, but who knows what the ostrich sees in the sand?" (p. 176). In the first part of the novel Murphy sees more clearly with his eyes closed (in his imagination) than with them opened: "In the days when Murphy was concerned with seeing Miss Counihan, he had had to close his eyes to do so" (p. 90). Hence his penchant for spending hours in his rocker dead to the world but alive to his own internal perceptions. In *Imagination Dead Imagine* the characters as well as the reader have difficulties with vision. It is as if two Murphys were tied back to back in two different rocking chairs and then commanded to view each other. Within the vault the left eyes of the creatures open and stare "at incalculable intervals," but because of their positions and their out-of-sync eye movements, mutual perception is impossible. Linguistically, their eyes are often nonexistent, thus the problem lies even deeper: "Piercing pale blue [eyes] the effect is striking, in the beginning" (p. 65). (In the original French version of the piece also, *Imagination morte imaginez*, the word for eyes is missing.)

Although they cannot perceive each other, the two creatures are brutally scrutinized by the narrator and the reader: "Only murmur ah, no more, in this silence, and at the same instant for the eye of prey the infinitesimal shudder instantaneously suppressed" (p. 66). This sentence, surrounded by relatively conventional sentences with straightforward syntax and shorter words, is stylistically foregrounded because it is difficult to parse, wonderfully ambiguous, and sonorous. With its accumulation of /s/ and /i/ sounds and its regular meter ("infinitesimal" and "instantaneously" with six syllables, "shudder" and "suppressed" with two), the sentence is poetically balanced and rich. Significantly, it also marks the dramatic climax of the piece. Like the lone character of *Film*, the two bodies experience the "agony of perceivedness," of being, when they are viewed. In *Film*, Beckett dramatizes Bishop Berkeley's motto (also used in *Murphy*), "To be is to be perceived." In *Imagination Dead Imagine*, Beckett shows that the reverse is also true: to be perceived is to be; perception of *A* by *B* brings *A* into existence. The opening shot of a huge orb in *Film* suggests that the eye of the camera is human,[7] and although ambiguity surrounds the phrase "the eye of prey" in *Imagination*,[8] the eye is unambiguously human here even if the reader is compelled to focus and refocus like a camera lens. As part of the introductory remarks for *Film*, Beckett provides: "Search of non-being in flight from extraneous perception breaking down in inescapability of self-perception. . . . It will not be clear until the end of the film that pursuing perceiver is not extraneous, but self."[9] This same confusion of perceiver and perceived occurs in *Imagination*, in which, argues John Grant, "the eye of the investigator takes what is, at bottom, a morbid interest in his subject. And how he sees reflects his character and, conceivably, what he sees produces *in him* the 'shudder' that is covered up as quickly as possible."[10]

Beckett said of an earlier version of *Imagination Dead Imagine*, entitled *All Strange Away* and composed during 1963–64, that it was written "I imagine on the way to *Imagination morte imaginez*."[11] At that time he had not yet exploited the possibilities of the narrator/observer. The self-conscious narrator of *All Strange Away*, revealing merely a bored tone, stops himself from a continued examination of the lower parts of a character's body, thinking "all this prying pointless."[12] He seems to share some characteristics with his two creatures (for all three characters "Fancy is [the] only hope"), but does not react to them emotionally. In *Imagination*, however, as the agony of being is transmitted from the two bodies to the narrator, the shudder instantaneously flows into the reader: "But if it is painful for the two archetypal victims of their environment to be made to face the truth about human existence, then it follows that it must be equally painful for the reader-cum-observer to face the same truth."[13] At this point in the story the reader realizes how unfeeling he has allowed himself to become, under the power of a clinical narrator. Released sympathy for the creatures becomes sympathy for self (after the shock of self-recognition), and the walls of delusion come tumbling down as they did finally for the narrator of *How It Is*.

Throughout Beckett's works the opening or closing of eyes has represented the acceptance or rejection of physical reality.[14] Murphy attempts to close his eyes and his mind and retreat to his blissful dark zone. Conversely, Krapp tries to stay in his "zone of light," the magic circle near his table, since in *Krapp's Last Tape* the movement from light to darkness symbolizes the movement from the self to the outside world, as well as from reason to emotion. Krapp has the illusion that he can completely separate the light from darkness, and (in James Knowlson's interpretation) he misses his one opportunity for unity—through the girl, the Other. The French for Krapp's romantically sexual "Let me in," "M'ont laissée entrer," indicates that the real subject here is "eyes,"[15] suggesting that the eyes of the girl contain everything, the whole world. Within some philosophical circles, of course, a similar proposition has been endlessly debated; and indeed one's perception may determine the "reality" of, or at least the quality of, the universe. As Bishop Berkeley argues, visual perception is crucial to both material existence and to the imagination. In his dialogues between Hylas and Philonous[16] he demonstrates that sight is relative and subjective, partly because clearer vision can be obtained through scientific extensions of the eye—the telescope and the microscope. Analogously, Beckett's scientific narrator recommends telescopic and microscopic views of the rotunda, its surroundings, and its contents; he speaks of things "to be observed" and of "sightings." In *Film* the eye functions as the symbol of separation between inner and outer worlds, and a similar boundary is drawn here. If to be perceived is to be, then also to be imagined (to be seen in the mind's eye) is to exist. Berkeley's Philonous would agree: "But are not things imagined as truly *in the mind* as things perceived?" (*Three Dialogues*, p. 52, his emphasis). Perhaps the white structure, the only physical reality given in *Imagination*, itself represents an eye—a huge eyeball as well as a mental world.

Besides suggesting first a skull and then a giant eye, the rotunda, of course, serves as a womb for the two fetal characters and also a tomb ("vault"). In Beckett's poetry both womb and tomb become recurrent images of the transforming imagination.[17] Extending this imagery, Beckett's poem "The Vulture" portrays the microcosm of the imagination as a place in which to live and do creative work; here the bird and its prey correspond to the poet and his poem.[18] Thus the rotunda is on one level the construct of an imagination to prove that it is not dead, and *Imagination Dead Imagine* as text becomes Samuel Beckett's written proof that he has not been permanently halted by the fictional impasse after *The Unnamable*. Once again arises the Beckettian paradox of a storyteller trying to narrate a story with nothing to express and no means of expression. This time the artist of failure has succeeded.

The first sentence of *Imagination* indicates that someone (the reader? an inner voice?) is daring the narrator to create a work of fiction in which there is no life: "No trace anywhere of life, you say, pah, no difficulty there, imagination not dead yet . . ." (p. 63). The narrator accepts the challenge, but then complicates the task: if there is no life anywhere, then there is no mental life, so even the imagination must be dead. But, paradoxically, there always remains a mind (the reader's?) to imagine the death of the imagination: ". . . imagination not dead yet, yes, dead, good, imagination dead imagine." Who performs this last imagining? For one answer, the second of John Mood's three expressive renderings of the title is helpful: "'Imagination dead. (Well, then,) imagine (something anyway)'—using the imperative." [19] But in general the title suggests that we recursively imagine the death of imagination itself. Either way, the title sets the syntactic pattern of the entire piece, since it introduces a style of ellipses and imperatives. [20] In terse, compelling language, Beckett makes the reader experience the process of the imagination, the creation of something out of nothing.

In *Murphy*, Beckett explores different levels of consciousness in a way reminiscent of Henri Bergson's *Creative Evolution*, [21] and we know from lecture notes of a Trinity College student that young Professor Beckett included Bergson in his course on the novel. [22] Layers of cognition in *Imagination Dead Imagine* also appear to be modeled on Bergsonian philosophy. Bergson continues Descartes's method and demonstrates that even if man can think himself out of existence, some awareness must remain to perceive the departing awareness:

I see myself annihilated only as I have already resuscitated myself by an act which is positive, however involuntary and unconscious. So, do what I will, I am always perceiving something, either from without or from within. When I no longer know anything of external objects, it is because I have taken refuge in the consciousness that I have of myself. If I abolish this inner self, its very abolition becomes an object for an imaginary self which now perceives as an external object the self that is dying away. Be it external or internal, some object there always is that my imagination is representing. My imagination, it is true, can go from one to the other. I can by turns imagine a nought of external perception or nought of internal perception, but not both at once, for the absence of one consists, at bottom, in the exclusive presence of the other . . . we cannot imagine a nought without perceiving, at least consequently, that we are acting, that we are thinking, and therefore that something still subsists.[23]

Beckett appears to borrow from Bergson again for his first attempt to imagine nothingness; the philosopher's recipe advises that we begin by imagining everything, and then destroy it all.[24] *Imagination*'s narrator calls up a world and then erases it: "Islands, waters, azure, verdure, one glimpse and vanished, endlessly, omit" (p. 63). The omitting continues until we are left with a perfectly blank slate on which we can mentally draw our white rotunda. Beckett achieved a sense of sudden transformation through some minor revisions to the original manuscript: "one look" became "one glimpse," and "gone" became "vanished." Also, the French original for "one glimpse and vanished, endlessly, omit" is "fixez, pff, muscade, une éternité, taisez."[25] Here the onomatopoetic "pff," and the choice of "muscade," which translates as "presto!," give the impression of a verbal magician manufacturing a world out of nothing.

   Then Beckett peoples his imaginary world with two imaginary creatures and through them represents inner and outer reality. That his rotunda exists in the mind only is continually emphasized, for in this fiction Beckett develops Schopenhauer's idea that if imagination is dead, then the external world disappears and only the internal remains.[26] After all is "vanished," the mental worlds of the narrator and of the reader still survive, and through an act of the imagination we must, together, construct a new world out of the void. Since the whiteness of the rotunda blends into the surrounding whiteness, it can be distinguished only by the eye of the imagination. The rotunda twice is termed "the little fabric"; it is a pure fabrication. This is an aspect missing in earlier English drafts—and in the French version of the piece, where the rotunda is referred to at first simply as "elle" (p. 52) and later as "le petit édifice" (p. 55). With a change to "fabric" in the English, Beckett is able to recall Shakespeare's magician, Prospero, and "the baseless fabric of this vision."

Bergson's thoughts on the process of fabrication elucidate the very narrative technique of *Imagination Dead Imagine*:

an intelligence which aims at fabricating is an intelligence which never stops at the actual form of things nor regards it as final, but, on the contrary, looks upon all matter as if it were carvable at will . . . it is this power [fabrication] that we affirm when we say that there is a *space*, that is to say, a homogeneous and empty medium, infinite and infinitely divisible, lending itself indifferently to any mode of decomposition whatsoever. A medium of this kind is never perceived, it is only conceived. What is perceived is extension colored, resistant, divided according to the lines which mark out the boundaries of real bodies or of their real elements. [*Creative Evolution*, p. 172]

As a multilevel description of the imaginative process, this helps account for the geometry, measurement, and boundaries in Beckett's text. Once the real world has disappeared, and planes and domes have been conjured up, the language of mathematics allows us—compels us—to "divide" newly created space, to fix the dimensions of an imaginary structure and the position of imaginary bodies. More precisely, after the neutral "islands, waters" and the poetic "azure, verdure" are "vanished," these four natural constituents are replaced by four points, A, B, C, D (perhaps representing the four points of the compass), which determine two lines at right angles, which in turn describe a circle. This schematic circle then creates a new miniature globe in the abstract language of geometry: its determiners, the four points "along the circumference, do not exist—they are only convenient means of making space imaginable."[27]

The narrator does not depict a preexistent, real rotunda; he conceives it, fabricates it and its world, as he proceeds. Molloy proclaims (although he retracts it later) that "saying is inventing" (*Molloy*, p. 38), and this equation typifies the speaker's technique in *Imagination*. Here a conversational usage of the word "say" (to mean "let us assume") implies that the narrator/inspector is devising the details of the vault's environment as he speaks—that he is imagining out loud: ". . . all grows dark together, ground, wall, vault, bodies, say twenty seconds . . ." (p. 63); "At the same time the temperature goes down, to reach its minimum, say freezing-point . . ." (p. 63). This is the same language Beckett himself employs in the stage directions for his plays. For example, before Winnie's opening scene in *Happy Days*, he has, "Long pause. A bell rings piercingly, say ten seconds, stops. She does not move. Pause. Bell more piercingly, say five seconds. She wakes." This is the language of a fabricator.

Inventing through saying is even more apparent in the prose of *All Strange Away*. Here all the strange and extraneous narrative embellishments are removed through self-conscious revision. Its narrator's motto is "Imagine what needed, no more"; any detail that he adds "always was," and any object that he deletes is "gone . . . never was." Thus the process of selection and deletion, which produces shifts in narration even within one sentence, graphs a kind of de-creation in prose. Similarly, *Imagination's* narrator wipes out the real world by destroying four elements—islands, waters, azure, verdure—yet in order to offer something for the imagination to grasp, he must supply other things, other nouns. By erasing certain verbs, omitting many articles, and rearranging some phrases, he places a great deal of stress on each noun. To supplant the four elements of nature that vanished at the beginning of the piece, he provides "emptiness, silence, heat, whiteness," and four other nouns that recur as a group throughout the piece: "ground, wall, vault, bodies." The natural world was represented by four constituents; the artificial world of the rotunda consists of an equal number of objects and properties.

Trying to impart an illusion of reality to this imaginary rotunda, the narrator exploits language and its magic tricks. Beckett's repeated use of the imperative forces the reader to take possession of the rotunda, to enter in and to explore.[28] The invitation (or the command) to measure the dome, coupled with Beckett's geometrical notation and accurate scientific language,[29] lends credibility to this object created out of nothing. Our scepticism is calmed with the recurrent qualification that "in the beginning" all this may "seem strange," but that "experience shows" (the French is even a bit stronger: "l'expérience le prouve") that not only the regularities of the rotunda's environment, but also certain irregularities, are "possible." More important, even the movement from "in the beginning" to "experience shows" grants the rotunda some illusory duration in time as well as reality in space.

Finally, Beckett uses the presence and absence of various verb forms (not just the imperative) to imitate his content linguistically. If imagination is dead and if nothing exists, then Beckett cannot portray any mind or body acting: he must erase actors, subjects of sentences; also he qualifies action with repeated uses of "if" or "seem" and by resorting increasingly to passive- voice verbs, such as "to be observed" and "as is stressed by," reminiscent of prose in scientific lab reports. Thus in the first English manuscript the temperatures "reach their initial level," but in the next version, the first typescript, "their initial level is reached." Use of the passive "rediscovered" at the beginning of the sentence that resurrects our vault begs the question of who is doing the rediscovering (the narrator? the reader?): "Rediscovered miraculously after what absence in perfect voids it is no longer quite the same, from this point of view, but there is no other" (p. 65). At times even a passive construction sounded too active, apparently, so that Beckett revised "a pause is made" to the more static and impersonal "a pause occurs" by the first typescript, obliterating an implied agent of the pause.

Agent and action, noun and verb, are equally problematic if imagination is dead. At the beginning of the piece there is a noticeable lack of copulative verbs, whereas ordinarily one would expect a description to contain many "there is's" and "there are's." Instead, Beckett writes otherwise grammatical sentences minus the finite verb. With this stylistic device, he avoids stating that anything exists just yet; only after he has engendered the rotunda in subtler ways does he employ the verb "to be" as other than a mere auxiliary. Thus at the start of *Imagination Dead Imagine* we read sentences like: "Till all white in the whiteness [there is] the rotunda. . . . Diameter [is] three feet, [there are] three feet from ground to summit of the vault. . . . Lying on the ground [are] two white bodies, each in its semicircle. White too [is] the vault . . ." (p. 63). Conversely, by the end of the piece, copulatives and verbs in general abound. Now "there is" grammatically affirms the probability of life itself as Beckett progresses from "there is better elsewhere" to "there is nothing elsewhere." The latter implies that this *is* something here—lost perhaps, but still existing. No trace of life has developed into at least a "white speck" with creatures inside. They have become real (or at least possible) through language, and the reader is able to wonder "if they still lie still in the stress of that storm, or of a worse storm, or in the black dark for good, or the great whiteness unchanging, and if not what they are doing" (p. 66). This structure of "if . . . and if not . . . ," supported by a proliferation of "ors," offers a wealth of possible events and a rich choice for reader speculations, arguing against a negative ending, a dead end.[30]

We have come to accept the rotunda as plausible if not probable even though its qualities and parameters contradict our assumptions and knowledge about the real world;[31] and the only way to reconcile these contradictions is through the phenomenon of the imagination. Entering the world of the dome is like going through Alice in Wonderland's looking glass. It is impossible to get in, but somehow we are there: "No way in, go in, measure" (p. 63). Paradoxical juxtaposition in Beckett occurs as early as *Godot*, where the tramps' gestures conflict with their intentions: "'Yes. Let's go.' *They do not move.*" In Beckett's recent wonderland the strong light has "no visible source" and creates "no shadow"; unlike the rational universe, this is a place where causes have illogical effects, where bodies can be "sweating *and* icy" (my italics). Temporality as well as causality is warped in this world with its "pauses of varying length, from the fraction of the second to what would have seemed, in other times, other places, an eternity" (p. 64). Instants of time are as "unimaginable" as infinities, and equally hard to imagine is the interval of time between the "murmur" and the "infinitesimal shudder." This action and reaction, supposedly occurring "at the same instant," is impossible to convey as simultaneous since written phrases are always sequential.[32] Other temporal incongruities appear not just once but throughout the piece: contrary to the laws of physics, in the rotunda there is no time lag between changes in light and changes in temperature.[33] In addition, duration is stretched and human capability exceeded: the left eyes of the creatures "gaze in unblinking exposure long beyond what is humanly possible" (p. 65).

Attempting the impossible becomes a goal for the reader as well, even with the smallest details: we are challenged to perceive the woman's long hair "of strangely imperfect whiteness" against a background of pure white. In fact, the narrator admits that he had been requiring the reader to imagine this world cumulatively by inserting a revealing qualification about the immobile creatures toward the end of the piece: "It is clear however, from a thousand little signs *too long to imagine,* that they are not sleeping" (p. 66, italics added). Through the paradoxes and the contradictions of *Imagination Dead Imagine,* Beckett has managed to write about the inexpressible and, in a sense, about nothing. By the end of the piece the white rotunda and the two creatures

possess being, and the only questions concern their where-
abouts and condition. Ironically, the narrative which began "No
trace anywhere of life" ends with "what they are doing," that is,
with beings and activity, the essential constituents for life—and
most types of fiction.

Henri Bergson's image of Nothing offers an elaborate analysis
that prompts analogies for the narrating process and for reader
response in *Imagination*:

> The image, then, properly so called, of a suppression of every-
> thing is never formed by thought. The effort by which we strive to
> create this image simply ends in making us swing to and fro be-
> tween the vision of an outer and that of an inner reality. In this com-
> ing and going of our mind between the without and the within,
> there is a point, at equal distance from both, in which it seems to us
> that we no longer perceive the one, and that we do not yet perceive
> the other: it is there that the image of "Nothing" is formed. In reality
> we then perceive both, having reached the point where the terms
> come together, and the image of Nothing, so defined, is an image
> full of things, an image that includes at once that of the subject and
> that of the object and, besides, a perpetual leaping from one to the
> other and the refusal ever to come to rest finally on either. [*Creative
> Evolution*, pp. 303–304]

The reader's attention in *Imagination Dead Imagine* swings from
the narrator himself (as object) to the creatures in the dome (who
in turn become the objects of the narrator-subject's attention).
This oscillating movement is mirrored in the flux of the vault's
atmospheric conditions—which may determine the ebb and
flow of consciousness within the creatures—and in the oscillating rhythm of the prose itself, including the blend of third person and second person narration. Just as the reader's eye must
look within and without the rotunda, so his imagination must
travel to and fro according to Bergson's directions, in order to
perceive the rotunda and his own act of imagining. By the conclusion of the text, this dead world seems abundantly alive and
complex.

Indeed, the fabricated rotunda has gradually become *too* real,
and this is why it must disappear at the end of the piece, never
to be discovered again. "Leave them there, sweating and icy,
there is better elsewhere. No, life ends and no, there is nothing
elsewhere . . ." (p. 66). Perhaps there is *better* elsewhere because
there is *nothing* elsewhere. Beckett's earliest protagonist, Belac-

qua, began the search for absence which translates as the search for the mental microcosm.[34] The early unpublished novel "Dream of Fair to Middling Women," despite its humor, is quite serious about Belacqua's philosophical quest for the void:

—The real presence was a pest because it did not give the imagination a break. Without going as far as Stendhal, who said . . . that the best music . . . was the music that became inaudible after a few bars, we do declare and maintain stiffly . . . that the object that becomes invisible before your eyes is, so to speak, the brightest and best.[35]

Beckett filled the empty space created by the destruction of the real world and the death of the imagination with mere words, and his stylistic problem in this piece was to use language that would conjure up something and yet create nothing simultaneously. Watt asserts that "the only way one can speak of nothing is to speak of it as if it were something." The prose of *Imagination Dead Imagine* is modeled on Watt's advice, and the work as a whole serves as evidence for Beckett's favorite statement by Democritus (also used in *Murphy*), "Nothing is more real than nothing." Another formulation of this inverts the paradox of artistic representation "that the more one tries to grasp the elusiveness of an object, the more convincing its representation would appear."[36] The fantastic creatures in the imaginary dome—because of their verbal embodiment and their enchanting elusiveness—materialize and reverberate on the page and in the microcosm of the reader's mind.

These "ashen or leaden" bodies, white or grey against the whiteness, and vibrating in extreme light or darkness, visually suggest white pages, blank or with emerging bodies of prose; thus the transition stage of "feverish greys" describes the agony of writing, of placing dark figures on white grounds. With the undulating rise and fall of temperature and light, Beckett suggests the rises and falls in the very prose rhythms he sets flowing within the text. In more specific ways, the linguistic behavior of *Imagination*'s narrator traces the process of writing: imagination, creation, reconsideration, revision. By changing "at the same time" to "at the same instant" the writer exercises control over his material, but in other passages words get out of hand, and repeated qualifications—which have the ring of in-process revisions—undermine the original narrative statement: "But whatever its uncertainties the return sooner or later to a temporary calm seems assured, for the moment, in the black dark or the great whiteness, with attendant temperature, world still proof against enduring tumult" (pp. 64–65). Here is composition alternating with what Bergson so prophetically termed "decomposition"—achieved in this case by modifiers that qualify and unwrite so that gaps are created which the reader must fill.

Describing an imaginary rotunda, the narrator concurrently presents the process of fictional composition and prompts active reading, that is, the reader's imaginative reconstruction. Rather than beginning his story with a sentence of the form "Once upon a time there was *a* strange couple who lived in *a* magic dome . . . ," the narrator initially employs definite articles instead of indefinite ones to make us immediately accept *the* rotunda, *the* vault, *the* white ground, *the* round wall, *the* light. These objects are descriptive givens that the writer—and the observer—must elaborate on. For many details, the narrator abdicates authorial responsibility, so that the reader is forced to take charge. With recurrent phrases like "more or less long" and "sooner or later," Beckett implies that lapses in the writer's creation are challenges to the reader's imagination. Our narrator creates the pauses within the rotunda, but we must determine their duration; he envisions the rotunda, but we must imagine the timing and manner of its reemergence. Despite the narrator's meticulous geometric rendering of the bodies' positions, he withholds any further information on their appearance, remarking (in the negative) only that they are "neither fat nor thin, big nor small," and that they "*seem* to want nothing essential" (negative phrasing again). What a perfect nondescription of noncharacters for this residuum of a novel, directly opposed to a traditional novel that begins with pages of background about the characters' lineage, stature, facial features, mannerisms, dress, and gestures.

Thus *Imagination Dead Imagine* comments on the reader's mental processes as well as the writer's—on regression from a definitive image and one's frustration in imagining. Beckett uses imitative syntax—sentence structure imitating the ideas of the discourse—by exploiting inversion and multiple modifiers to produce (among other effects) pauses in a reader's interpretation of a sentence, once, for example, in a statement that is itself about pausing: "Wait, more or less long. . . . More or less long, for there may intervene, experience shows, between end of fall and beginning of rise, pauses of varying length, from the fraction of the second to what would have seemed, in other times, other places, an eternity" (pp. 63–64). Ironically and humorously, ten words intervene between "there may intervene" and "pauses"; and by the period, delays in the sentence do seem to last "an eternity." Reader perception is held in suspension for another eon in a Germanic sentence that interposes sixty-six modifying words before we learn, "finally," what it is that is "still on the ground":

Still on the ground, bent in three, the head against the wall at B, the arse against the wall at A, the knees against the wall between B and C, the feet against the wall between C and A, that is to say inscribed in the semicircle ACB, merging in the white ground were it not for the long hair of strangely imperfect whiteness, the white body of a woman finally. [P. 65]

This waiting until the end of a sentence for the subject of a clause, or for further description, is literalized, dramatized, in the repeated imperative to "wait." We must "wait," "more or less long" for the author/narrator to provide fabrications, enclosures for us to enter. Besides the frustration of syntactic delay, and of incomplete or vague information, the mental puzzle of paradox compounds all interpretive problems. Similar stylistic hurdles, plus the challenge—and sometimes the agony—of circular, fruitless syntactic journeys, await the reader who continues through the metafictional maze of *The Lost Ones*.

The Lost Ones
The Reader as Searcher

For *The Lost Ones* Beckett advances from a small imagined dome with two still figures to a complex cylinder with hundreds of roving bodies moving according to intricate rules. This fiction at first seems to demand an allegorical interpretation: the cylinder is hell; the cylinder is the Tower of Babel. But one can almost hear Beckett echoing his warning in *Watt*, "No allegories where none intended." Instead, it is more appropriate to view *The Lost Ones* as Beckett interpreted *Finnegans Wake* and *Remembrance of Things Past*, as a work in which the form is a metaphor of its content; so that syntax and structure themselves here are indications of meaning. While the technique of imitative style has been noted in some passages of *The Lost Ones*,[1] and although there is some critical agreement on its theme of frustrated hope, neither the stylistic nor the thematic elements of this piece have been explored deeply enough. Nor have they been linked. The style of the story, from the morphological to the structural level, suggests fruitless waiting, futile searching, and unsatisfied hoping. Beyond the text being a perfectly self-contained "cylinder of fiction [which] does not represent anything exterior to itself,"[2] it is a cylinder of syntax which represents its own interior structure. If *The Lost Ones* presents a statement about humanity's unfulfilled search for order and meaning in the world, this translates into a comment on the reader's futile search for order and meaning in the piece itself and more generally in literature as a whole. Thus the reader becomes one of the searchers trying to find a (critical) "way out" of the enclosure.

Creatures in the story, apparently seeking an escape from their container, are of four types (in order of decreasing activity): climbers, sedentary-searchers, the sedentary, and the vanquished. Using ladders, the searchers, a general term for the first three types, climb to niches in the inner surface of the cylinder and explore tunnels in its walls. Meanwhile, the vanquished, who have—at least for the moment—given up the search, sit motionless. The physical environment in *The Lost*

Ones varies only slightly from that of *Imagination Dead Imagine*, consisting of periods of light and heat alternating with periods of darkness and cold. At the hypothetical final state of this cosmos, the conditions will be halted at the extreme end of the cold/dark cycle and all motion of the creatures will cease.

This narrative about a quest ironically begins with the word "abode," derived from the Middle English "abode" meaning "a waiting, delay, stay"; and with this allusion Beckett circles around the themes of *Waiting for Godot*. The setting for *The Lost Ones* recalls Lucky's speech about "the earth in the great cold the great dark the air and the earth abode of stones in the great cold."[3] In similar terms the narrator of *The Lost Ones* describes the end point of this later abode: "In cold darkness motionless flesh."[4] When Beckett was asked for the meaning of Lucky's name, he is reported to have replied, "I suppose he is lucky to have no more expectations."[5] Similarly, the vanquished in the abode are lucky enough to be resigned to their imprisonment, acting out a dictum of the philosopher Arnold Geulincx, often quoted by Beckett, "*Ubi nihil vales, ibi nihil velis*" (Where I can do nothing, I ought not to will anything), and used in *Murphy* (p. 178). That man can be at peace only when all expectations have died is an idea that surfaces in nearly all of Beckett's works, and it appears with special force in *The Lost Ones*.

While citizens of the abode suffer extremes in temperature and light, their most excruciating torment is the rekindling of hope. There are lulls in this pattern of oscillation from blazing heat to freezing darkness and back again, and "Then all go dead still. It is perhaps the end of their abode" (p. 7). It is not actually the end of their abode (their waiting), however, only a temptation to believe so. "A few seconds and all begins again" (pp. 7, 8). With this very repetition Beckett stylistically imitates a condition of oscillation punctuated with periods of stillness. Lulls provide a temporary release from torment only at the expense of greater shock and tension when the vibration begins again. Since there is no temporal continuity and therefore no memory in the cylinder, each pause seems the first, "Whence invariably the same vivacity of reaction as to the end of a world and the same brief amaze when the twofold storm resumes and they start to search again neither glad nor even sorry" (pp. 54–55). Every searcher is a Sisyphus, condemned to meaningless, repetitive activity, forgetting the failures of past attempts. Beckett used this image for futile human existence earlier: Moran analyzes Sisyphus and decides that "perhaps he thinks each journey is the first. This would keep hope alive, would it not, hellish hope" (*Molloy*, p. 182). Relentless hope prevents the searchers from attaining the stasis that should be their aim.

Like the Unnamable, like Hamm and Clov in *Endgame*, like Winnie in *Happy Days*, the inhabitants of *The Lost Ones* are all approaching stasis, or death. Light itself in the cylinder becomes a dying person: "Its restlessness at long intervals suddenly stilled like panting at the last" (p. 7). Movement toward the search's inevitable end, toward universal stillness, continues gradually: "Even so a great heap of sand sheltered from the wind lessened by three grains every second year and every following increased by two . . ." (p. 32). This analogy recalls the image of Zeno's grains of sand that Beckett used in *Endgame*, and in both works the diminishing heaps of sand are metaphors for an infinitely long process and the frustration it produces.

The gradual, almost imperceptible decline of life in *The Lost Ones* proceeds with a pace as slow but as inexorable as that in *Endgame*, and this incremental change is reflected in the style. Little by little the desire to climb is extinguished, but this is "[a] languishing happily unperceived because of its slowness and the resurgences that make up for it in part . . ." (p. 15). Just as hesitant is the shift from belief in an escape via the tunnels to belief in escape via an upper trapdoor, a shift "so desultory and slow and of course with so little effect on the comportment of either sect that to perceive it one must be in the secret of the gods" (p. 19). The cylinder's strong light destroys the eyes "by such slow and insensible degrees to be sure as to pass unperceived even by those most concerned," so that at each instant creatures appear unchanged. In short, the narrative is based on the premise that "here all should die but with so gradual and to put it plainly so fluctuant a death as to escape the notice even of a visitor" (p. 18). Of course this idea describes human life on earth, and it also determines the story's fluctuant form: the fifteen sections of the text at first seem highly repetititve and retrogressive, but by moving three steps forward and two steps backwards, Beckett, by "insensible degrees," adds more information to the description of the cylinder's civilization as it approaches its conclusion of stasis.

Time moves so slowly in the cylinder, and in the narration of *The Lost Ones*, that it seems stopped. When the narrator begins to relate a short history of the cylinder's citizens, he soon forces himself back to the present: "But as to at this moment of time and there will be no other . . ." (p. 35). Since time is infinitely slow, past and future stretch out infinitely in opposing directions so that both end points fade away: "In the beginning then unthinkable as the end all roamed without respite . . . and so roamed a vast space of time impossible to measure until a first [being] came to standstill followed by a second and so on" (pp. 34–35). Beckett suggests this gradual regression to a total "standstill" with a style imitative of an arrested world; his narrator uses a series of tableaux and vignettes, sometimes prefacing them self-consciously with such painterly phrases as "picturesque detail":

No other shadows then than those cast by the bodies pressing on one another willfully or from necessity as when for example on a breast to prevent its being lit or on some private part the hand descends with vanished palm. Whereas the skin of a climber alone on his ladder or in the depths of a tunnel glistens all over with the same red-yellow glister and even some of its folds and recesses in so far as the air enters in. [P. 40]

During sections one through fourteen, the reader gets no sense of chronological progression, but rather a static description of the abode's state at a moment when there are five vanquished and one hundred and eighty-five searchers. So the reader is as trapped in the present as are the searchers. The climbers' saga could have continued almost indefinitely as the narrative "consequences" of earlier sections were developed. The closed system of language, which Beckett used later in *Ill Seen Ill Said* (1981), accumulates detail in a similar nonchronological way: beginning with a few propositions, the narrator then adds logical results of these givens, as corollaries follow from axioms in mathematics. The manuscripts of the French version of *The Lost Ones* (called *Le Dépeupleur*) reveal that accumulated consequences building geometrically section by section from initial fictional premises were getting artistically out of control, so that after working on the text in 1965 and 1966, Beckett put it aside with a note about its "intractable complexities."[6] He did not finish the story until 1970,[7] when he appended a fifteenth section that discontinuously leaps in time to the last instant of life in the abode: "So on infinitely until towards the unthinkable end if this notion is maintained a last body of all by feeble fits and starts is searching still" (p. 60). Something has taken its course in the cylinder as in *Endgame*'s shelter, and at this end point all the beings are motionless and blind like Hamm: "every body will be still and every eye vacant." Then light will be "extinguished as purposeless."

In the harsh environment of the abode, although light makes vision possible, the extreme light ultimately destroys vision: since the eyes never adapt, sight is "ruined by this fiery flickering." Earlier in Beckett's fiction, *Murphy*'s solipsistic Mr. Endon, living in his self-contained system like the vanquished in *The Lost Ones*, has pupils which are dilated "as though by permanent excess of light" (*Murphy*, p. 249). Blue eyes, we are told, are the most fragile in the abode: the eye literally destroys itself as the constantly dilating pupil overtakes the orb and the white. The state of one's eyes in the cylinder becomes an indication of one's state of being: although some vanquished are "indistinguishable to the eye of flesh from the still unrelenting," a close observer will examine the eye for vital signs. It is logical that the vanquished have gone blind and that the sedentary, though their heads may be "dead still," have "devouring" eyes. Indeed, some sedentary searchers move only "the unceasing eyes," while some vanquished (the only bodies with bowed heads) no longer open their eyes at all, staring only within and seeing only mentally. Conversely, the first searchers of the cylinder are described as being "all eyes," and searchers are also named "watchers." Finally, the last action of the last man in the cylinder is to peruse the face of the (vanquished) North woman and to search the "calm wastes" of her blind eyes. When his eyes close, all vision—and all life—in the cylinder ends.

The reader's perspective is given as much consideration as a searcher's vision when the narrator provides a general overview of the abode first and then moves us closer for a detailed examination. His visual descriptions are introduced with such phrases as "at first sight," and "first impression"; and the reader is referred to as "an observer." A recurring sentence in the text is "so much for a first aperçu of ————," and Beckett significantly retains the French term "aperçu" for *Le Dépeupleur*,[8] probably because this word has a broad spectrum of meanings from "a hasty glance, a glimpse," to "an outline" and "an insight." Obviously Beckett has all three definitions in mind as his narrator progresses from a quick panorama of the abode in section one, to an outline of particulars, to a summary of the description, then to a fuller explanation of the environment's characteristics and their "consequences" for the beings. Concern with visual impressions makes the text dramatic and cinematic, so a description of *Imagination Dead Imagine*'s style applies to the style of *The Lost Ones* as well: "The writing is like stage directions, tight-lipped, condensed, and to the point, meticulously detailed as to measurements, the duration of the changes of light and heat and the positions of the bodies. . . ."[9] We can speculate that Beckett was working on *Film* (1967) concurrently, and that he merged the form of a film script with that of a short story. *The Lost Ones* opens with language sounding like instructions to a cameraman, and the clipped noun phrases for each element of the cylinder make the reader shift his focus and attention. As the camera eye roams, the narrator defends the system of ladders in prose that recalls again the style of *Imagination Dead Imagine*: "This at first sight is strange" (p. 21). The narrator snidely criticizes the observer's deficient vision, his "eye of flesh"; in particular, an observer ("some visitor") will not be able to distinguish the last man, still stirring among the others who seem dead, "at first sight." In these instances a television camera close-up is needed, since the reader/observer's first impressions are suspect. The narrator realizes that what "first impresses" the observer in this gloom is the yellowish light, and he acknowledges its strangeness by saying, "Once the first shocks of surprise are finally past this light is further unusual . . ." (p. 39). Cautioning the reader, our guide describes the light's vibration and predicts that it may "disturb" us. Then he promotes rational solutions to all mysteries: "But this is a disturbance analysis makes short work of. For on due reflection . . . [Here the narrator speaks in prose reminiscent of mathematical proofs]. . . . So all is for the best" (p. 42). He compliments the observer in a backhand way for having a reasonable, empirical mind: "An intelligence would be tempted to see [a logical and continuous regression from the searchers to the vanquished] . . ." (p. 33). Finally, the reader is cast in the negative stereotype of a scientific experimenter, "the thinking being coldly intent on all these data and evidences." Throughout all of these descriptions of the observer, the sardonic tone mocks, taunts, and distorts.

Yet, ironically, the narrator himself appears as a cold tabulator, partly because of his numerous qualifications. When he lapses into inexact statements he is careful to add the disclaimer "roughly speaking," and he modifies his computation of the cylinder's area with "Not counting the niches and tunnels." After a series of numbers he admits, "That is not quite accurate"; and he takes great pains with his description of the temperature: "Does this mean that with every passing second there is a rise or fall of five degrees exactly neither more or less? Not quite" (p. 41). Always self-conscious about his language, the narrator—sometimes with comical results—revises his prose in midsentence: "From time immemorial rumour has it or better still the notion is abroad that there exists a way out" (pp. 17–18). (In this case the revision may not be "better," because both "rumour has it" and "the notion is abroad" are equally well-worn clichés.) The repeated phrase "or better still" may serve to introduce a more exact restatement of a remark, as in "There does none the less exist a north in the guise of one of the vanquished or better one of the women vanquished or better still the woman vanquished" (p. 56). But the same phrase also effects more radical revision, in fact, a contradiction, with "addition or better still division." Enhancing the aura of exactitude, the narrator's repeated phrase "there does exist a . . ." takes the form of a mathematician's statement of a theorem to be proved, for example, "There exists an X such that, for all Y not equal to zero. . . ." All these humorless statements demonstrate Beckett's wonderful sense of humor; they are verbal practical jokes played on the reader, little buzzers in a literary handshake that nonetheless never cause us to distrust the narrator entirely.

His absurd obsession with precision causes the narrator to qualify some of his remarks out of existence, as when he says that light seems to emanate from all surfaces "[t]o the point that the ladders themselves seem rather to shed than to receive light with this slight reserve that light is not the word" (p. 40). This Molloy-like searching for the correct word, this fluctuation of language between the exact and the approximate, enacts a creator in the process of composing, of revising. Another stylistic feature of *The Lost Ones* that chronicles the creative process is the narrator's tendency (especially in section one) to announce a new aspect of the cylinder and then to subdivide and define it: "The light. Its dimness. Its yellowness." (p. 7); "The niches or alcoves. These are cavities . . ." (p. 11). It is almost as if the voice were imagining and outlining aloud. Ludovic Janvier notices a similar stylistic pattern in the first fifty pages of *Malone meurt*— "Situation présente. Cette chambre . . . Le marché . . . Les paysans . . . La ferme . . ."—and he christens these phrases "formules maieutiques." [10] According to the *Oxford English Dic-*

tionary, "maieutic" means "pertaining to (intellectual) midwifery, i.e., to the Socratic process of assisting a person to bring out into clear consciousness conceptions previously latent in his mind." Like Malone, the narrator of *The Lost Ones* gives birth to the story as he writes, clarifying the rules of the climbers' code for himself as he articulates them for the reader. Thus the form of *The Lost Ones* as a whole becomes one of the fetal creatures, one of the forms not able to stand upright, that is embodied in *Lessness*.

At the phrase level too, structure is immature, groping. The isolated noun phrases mentioned above, along with misplaced modifiers and convoluted and strained syntax, make the style of this narrator a variation of Watt's style. Lawrence Harvey argues that "Watt's excessive yet ineffectual efforts to organize his information show through in his linguistic ineptitude, in the gross way in which he disrupts the conventions of the language. . . ."[11] We must qualify our comparison by noting that the narrator of *The Lost Ones* is not so much linguistically inept (he knows his grammar) as syntactically awkward (e.g., "But never again will they ceaselessly come and go who now at long intervals come to rest without ceasing to search with their eyes," p. 34), and stylistically inappropriate. One element of linguistic good manners he ignores is the convention to choose a rhetorically correct speech register or level of diction and to maintain it consistently. Instead, the narrator playfully mixes the high and the low, the exotic and the common, in language. He indulges in Latin terms: "in camera," a legal term meaning "privately"; and "quidam" for "someone." But with equal frequency he descends to clichés ("roughly speaking," "to put it mildly," "for some reason or another"), reaching a low point in the sentence "Light in a word that not only dims but blurs into the bargain" (p. 38). While he can impersonate a philosopher with phrases like "in theory" or "a priori," and with repeated "therefores," he also echoes the vernacular of the man in the street. Proud of a large vocabulary with a scientific flavor, the narrator strives for precision, though at times hackneyed commonplaces undercut his accuracy: the lulls are "of varying duration but never exceeding ten seconds or thereabouts" (p. 17). Here the "or thereabouts" contradicts the finality of "never," making the sentence as a whole laughable. Oscillations of diction and cancellations of meaning within a sentence approach absurdity and flout the narrator's disregard of verbal rules.

Throughout his description, the narrator is having fun toying with language, most notably in the sally "The situation of this latter having lost his ladder is delicate indeed . . . ," which recalls the nursery rhyme about kittens having lost their mittens. Thus this narrator fits Raymond Federman's characterization of the Beckett voice since *Comment c'est*: he is able to "LAUGH at his own activity." [12] Donald Davie extends this to the whole canon; Beckett is surely a comic writer, he maintains, and by way of illustration he analyzes some speeches in the play *All That Fall*:

Mrs. Rooney: . . . It's like the sparrows, than many of which we are of more value, they weren't sparrows at all.

Mr. Rooney: Than many of which . . . You exaggerate, Maddy.

The narrator of *The Lost Ones* seems to have taken rhetoric and elocution lessons from Maddy Rooney; both abuse a convoluted syntax which parodies itself. Davie's description of Maddy's style characterizes the language of *The Lost Ones* as well: "By the meticulousness of her syntax ('than many of which') she achieves an elegance so conscious of itself that it becomes absurd, a parody of all stylistic elegance whatever, insinuating the suspicion that all the elegances of language, which seem so superbly to articulate experience, in fact articulate nothing but themselves." [13] Since *The Lost Ones* is not so much a story as a verbal system feeding on itself, its style is imitative of man's delusions, which are perpetrated through language. So if we are concerned with allegory at all in *The Lost Ones*, it is not at the plot level but at the level of style; and rather than speaking of the microcosm of the cylinder, we should speak of the microcosm of the sentence. Davie shows that in *All That Fall*, as in the rest of Beckett, the comic playing with prose is highly serious: "A concern with the dignity or decrepitude of language is, after all, a concern for the dignity or decrepitude of man" (p. 29). Therefore in the exaggerated pomposity, in the ludicrous order of the sentences of *The Lost Ones* is written an elusive human search—for meaning, for dignity.

All the while, Beckett laughs at his verbal creation, at the conventions of fiction, and at the assumptions of readers. He openly manipulates then mocks literary responses: "What first impresses in this gloom is the sensation of yellow it imparts not to say of sulphur in view of the associations" (p. 36). Ridiculing novelistic form an conventions of reading, Beckett periodically stresses the artificiality of his cylindrical creation. The frequent recurrence of the phrase "if this notion be maintained" undermines any authority the narrative may have had. While depicting a society approaching its end, the narrator emphasizes the hypothetical nature of his conclusion, and even questions the searchers' belief in escape: "Its fatuous little light will be assuredly the last to leave them always assuming they are darkward bound" (p. 20). This "assuming" calls on the reader's continuous suspension of disbelief. Thus the narrator of *The Lost Ones* operates in the tradition of the trilogy: like Molloy, Moran, Malone, and the Unnamable, he reminds the reader that his self-conscious words fabricate a self-reflexive fiction. If his notion is to be maintained at all, it must be in the reader's imagination. The paradox here is that we have a narrator (similar to the voice in *Imagination Dead Imagine* or *How It Is*) who is precise on each minute detail and yet vague and insecure about the validity of his story as a whole. Once again the reader is put in the same position as the searcher: just as the searcher must follow intricate, exact rules for climbing the ladders with little hope for a way out to the stars, so the reader must follow intricate, exact sentences with little hope of a way out to critical meaning.

The narrator repeatedly concedes crucial reservations about his own fictional creation: are the rules workable, are the zones viable, is the future of the cylinder assured? "To these questions and many more the answers are clear and easy to give. It only remains to dare" (p. 52). However, the searchers do not dare to question the consequences of their absurd system; and Beckett's challenge for the reader becomes, Do you dare to face the real conditions of your physical and mental world? The elaborate and precise rules for climbing in the cylinder become ridiculous evasions of reality,[14] since the futile quest for a physical escape is governed by a procedure far more orderly than the search deserves. To compensate for forces over which they have no control (the oscillations of light and temperature, the random and unpredictable lulls, and the gradual shift to frozen darkness) the citizens devise and enforce a ludicrous climbers' code which parodies a legal system. Beckett reveals, by applying legalistic terms to the physical environment, that the real power to convict or to acquit is out of their jurisdiction. A lull provides "remission," and the changes in light and temperature cease as if by "a single commutator." The murmur in the cylinder is "cut off as though by a switch" in the English version of the piece (pp. 37–

38), but "comme coupée au commutateur" in the French version (p. 33). Although "commutator" is a technical word meaning "switch," it also carries the connotation of one who commutes a sentence. Searchers do not risk seeking the truth about their imprisonment, but are complacent in their illusion of order, "For in the cylinder alone are certitudes to be found and without nothing but mystery" (p. 42). Of course, this "certitude" is one more delusion accepted by the naïve climbers, a false sense of security that (paradoxically) keeps them trapped.

Opposition between these two extremes of certainty and mystery extends to most elements of the cylinder; like other Beckett works, *The Lost Ones* depicts a binary world. Here the light and temperature swing between two poles, and analogously, strategy theorists belong to opposing schools—those who believe in escape through the top, and those who search for escape through the tunnels. Very often in the abode a situation involves not only two extremes but a paradoxical relationship between two incompatible states. An analogous predicament is inherent in the very activity of writing: "The work of art is by definition paradoxical and Beckett not only recognizes this but flaunts it in the face of the reader. Again and again he resorts to paradox in his attempts to describe the indescribable."[15] Paradox is obviously nothing new for Beckett; in almost all his fiction the narrator is placed in an impossible situation, and by the late texts the reader has joined the narrator there. In *Imagination Dead Imagine*, the reader must imagine the death of the imagination; in *The Lost Ones* and *Ping* he is invited to view objects that are invisible. Since the cylinder represents a closed system of language, is a self-contained structure of metafiction, it makes sense that the structure itself (as well as its rules) is founded on paradox.

Beckett begins *The Lost Ones* with a description of the cylinder as a "catch-22" prison: "Vast enough for search to be in vain. Narrow [tall] enough for flight to be in vain" (p. 7). While the searcher is trapped in a physical predicament, the reader is hemmed in by verbal paradoxes, illusive patterns that taunt him to continue his critical search for meaning. Some apparent contradictions result from the traditional appearance/reality dichotomy: "Seen from below the wall presents an unbroken surface all the way round and up to the ceiling. And yet its upper half is riddled with niches. This paradox is explained by the levelling effect of the dim omnipresent light" (p. 55). Logical conundrums further cloud the hellish atmosphere of the abode, and paradoxical language stylistically reinforces the theme of futile hope; even the "lulls," which should prove a relief, become a greater torment. Though one would expect the sedentary to be among the most peaceful beings, ironically it is the sedentary's violent acts that most disrupt the cylinder's quiet (p. 14). Instead of pitying the "vanquished," we should envy them: they come nearest to complete repose. The abode's citizens are victims of inconsistent behavior: although they maintain a Byzantine system of laws for governing the use of the ladders (and these rules are enforced rigidly through eternal vigilance on the part of every inhabitant), these same beings cannot cooperate for their universal benefit. There does not exist that "one instant of fraternity" to put the tallest man on the tallest ladder in order to reach the top of the enclosure. Ironically, they maintain harmony in the details of the search but not in its apparent goal, the escape; they cooperate for "collective fury" but not for collective release.

Other aspects of the abode combine opposing elements of harmony and disharmony. The cylinder's dimensions are "fifty metres round and eighteen high for the sake of harmony," but the ladders positioned against the walls are "without regard to harmony," and ladder rungs are missing "without regard to harmony." Niches may be found only in the upper one-half of the cylinder, "disposed quincuncially for the sake of harmony"; yet they are arranged in *"irregular* quincunxes"—almost an oxymoron—and are "so cunningly out of line" that only climbers with a mental picture of the entire system can appreciate "such harmony." Three concentric zones on the cylinder's floor suggest a combination of structure and chaos: the two outer zones, when lit, give the impression of "two narrow rings turning in opposite directions about the teeming precinct" (p. 29). These geometrical and visual oppositions find their stylistic counterpart in some of the narrator's sentences, which cancel themselves out: "Some [searchers] could thus revolve through thousands of degrees before settling down to wait were it not for the rule forbidding them to exceed a single circuit" (p. 48). Verbal structures like "were it not" pivot the sentence and force the second half to strike out the first.

Modes of movement also balance order with disorder. The main rule of climbing states that only one person at a time may stand on a ladder, and that descending has priority over ascending. Then, one may enter the climbers' circle only if another departs, "One example among a thousand of the harmony that reigns in the cylinder between order and license" (p. 44). Bodies may roam as they like as long as they obey the rules of the various zones. There is a wildly absurd quality about all this precision in the midst of chaos that is worthy of Kafka.[16] Beckett's climbers are free to line up for a ladder, but then are required to stay there; they may choose their preferred queue provided that they move to the right on entering the climbers' zone and do not exceed one circuit. "That a full round should be authorized is eloquent of the tolerant spirit which in the cylinder tempers discipline" (p. 49). In short, order and randomness in the cylinder remain in a state of stable equilibrium, threatened by only one problem: there is no regulation preventing a climber from remaining in the climbers' zone indefinitely. Because of this, the narrator himself doubts the continuing general harmony of the abode, and predicts "a state of anarchy." He admits that multiple transgressions against the climbers' code "would soon transform the abode into a pandemonium," but the irony here is that the cylinder is already a kind of hell.

In Dante's *Inferno* the pleasures of earth are exaggerated or reversed to become torments. In Beckett's world any tactile communication becomes excruciatingly painful because of the charred skin of bodies, and dry "mucous membranes" make the act of love an act of assault. One is tempted to view the other consequence of the bright light, blindness, as an added punishment; but the narrator has characterized the blind vanquished state as preferable, or at the very least, neutral. No, the main torment of the abode is the fevered need to search. Most Beckett characters are engaged in some sort of quest: Watt seeks out Mr. Knott; Molloy journeys to find his mother, as Moran searches for Molloy; Malone longs for death, and the Unnamable pursues silence. The questing behavior in the cylinder is summarized in *Lost Ones'* first sentence, but the quest's goal is ambiguous: "Abode where lost bodies roam each searching for its lost one." This recalls the famous Platonic myth about humans originally containing both male and female; after the whole being was split in two, each person on earth sought his other half. Critics have been lured by the possible allusion to this myth in *The Lost Ones*,[17] but in Beckett's story, when husbands and wives meet by chance in the arena of the cylinder, they pass each other with little or no recognition. The lost ones, then, are not searching for their other selves; or if they are, they do not realize the object of their quest when they find it. Like the narrator of *From an Abandoned Work*, they seem simply on their way.

The reader/searcher abandons this dead-end interpretation to look in another direction. Ostensibly the beings' search is for a way out of the cylinder, but the "instant of fraternity" necessary for escape is deemed impossible because of "the ideal preying on one and all," as if this "ideal" did not involve a physical escape. These lost ones show a "general indifference" to each other "apart from the grand affair," but we know that this grand affair cannot be a plan of escape, since the inhabitants do not cooperate in such a plan. From what we can observe, the only time the bodies are not indifferent to each other occurs when they carefully scrutinize one of the vanquished. Most often the searchers move endlessly in order to find peace, just as the Unnamable talks nonstop to achieve silence; the goal of the search then becomes the state which the vanquished have reached. Paradoxically, though, the way to attain this static condition is to relinquish the desire to search, to cease hoping for a way out, and to demonstrate the death of hope by ceasing to move. As early as *Murphy*, Beckett had expressed his view of hope as a curse in the phrase "doomed to hope unending." And, like Murphy, Watt learns that "when you cease to seek you start to find."

Murphy's goal of mental peace, of "Belacqua bliss," probably derives from Schopenhauer's concept of "the self-consciousness of the knowing person."[18] His description of "pure will-less subject of knowledge" in *The World as Will and Idea* helps explain Beckett's latest vanquished, who, significantly, are in the same posture as Belacqua (p. 14), Dante's slothful character who waits hopelessly in the anteroom of Purgatory. Schopenhauer maintains that

. . . if we turn our glance from our own needy and embarrassed condition to those who have overcome the world, in whom the will, having attained to perfect self-knowledge, found itself again in all, and then freely denied itself, and who then merely wait to see the last trace of it vanish with the body it animates; then instead of the restless striving and effort, instead of the constant transition from wish to fruition, and from joy to sorrow, instead of the never-satisfied and never-dying hope which constitutes the life of the man who wills, we shall see that peace which is above all reason, that perfect calm of the spirit.[19]

This spiritual calm is achieved by Belacqua, who had quoted Aristotle's dictum to Dante: *"sedendo et quiescendo anima efficitur sapiens"* (by sitting and remaining quiet the mind is made wise).[20] The Belacqua-like vanquished have found a similar wisdom.

Conversely, the searchers in the cylinder resemble the lone character in Beckett's short mime *Act Without Words I* (1957), whose every desire is frustrated. As all the movements of the creature (toward water, toward escape, toward suicide) are thwarted, he gradually learns to relinquish hope, to cease responding to temptations for release dangled in front of him. A final tableau shows him lying, motionless, on his side, staring first straight ahead and then at his hands. More recently (1973) Beckett has again expressed his position on the futility of hope. When asked to contribute a piece to the centenary issue of *Hermathena*, he submitted a rhymed translation of one of Chamfort's *Maxims*:

> Hope is a knave befools us evermore,
> Which till I lost no happiness was mine.
> I strike from Hell's to grave on Heaven's door:
> All hope abandon ye who enter in.[21]

While the searchers cannot part with hope, they remain "amateurs of myth" dreaming of a hidden "way out to earth and sky"; and readers in turn are tempted to search for an interpretative framework or allegory. Beckett mocks believers in religious myths, and (as shown in *Proust*) he scorns all those who impose an artifical order, or hope for order, on chaos. His opinions echo loudly in the narrator's tone of *The Lost Ones*, especially in the undercutting and biting satire of "in the words of the poet": "One school swears by a secret passage branching from one of the tunnels and leading in the words of the poet to nature's sanctuaries" (p. 18). Here, as in his other works, Beckett derides the escapist notions of Romantic poets; the only possible escape is through the disembodied mind.

Solely the "vanquished," those who have given up the search, can attain physical and mental rest and thus a way out of sorts. This ideal of a vanquished state has also appealed to many of Beckett's earlier characters. Murphy yearns for a life inside his head, possible for him only when the body is tied to a rocking chair or otherwise constrained. After Molloy fails to recognize a mysterious object (which is actually a knife rest), he decides that "to be beyond knowing anything, to know you are beyond knowing anything, that is when peace enters in, to the soul of the incurious seeker" (*Molloy*, p. 86). Trying to reconcile body and mind, Sapo in *Malone Dies* broods about "the babel raging in his head," and wonders "how he was going to live, and lived *vanquished*, blindly, in a mad world, in the midst of strangers" (p. 16, my emphasis). Similarly, the lost ones require physical stasis as a means to mental transcendence. Hence those climbers who lapse into a semiconscious state while standing on a ladder are tolerated; the sedentary searchers are admired as "semi-sages"; and the vanquished, despite their negative appelation, are objects of curiosity and envy. Searchers spend their time examining the vanquished as well as exploring the tunnels, and this examination includes a long look at the eyes. Thus the visual confrontation between the last man and the blissful North woman at the end of the story replays the scene in *Murphy* in which the hero tries to steal peace from the lapsed-out eyes of Mr. Endon.[22] Analogously, the protagonist of *Film* is made to view himself at the end of the film, to come face to face with his own being. In the cylinder, when the last man goes blind, all the creatures are then unable to perceive; then all bodies are unable to *be* perceived, and this state of implied nonbeing is the unconscious goal of searchers.

But even this interpretation is an acrobatic act on logical ladders with some rungs missing; this reader/searcher may be finding more structure in the text than is actually present. As one case of Beckett's tantalizing the reader's appetite for order, consider the repetition of "So much for a first aperçu of ———." The phrasal motif seems to have structural import on first reading, as we learn to expect it at the end of each section; but such a pseudopattern soon becomes a frustration for the reader/searcher. Section one ends with "So much for a first aperçu of the abode." Section two, a description of the four different types of lost ones, ends "So much roughly speaking for these bodies seen from a certain angle and for this notion and its consequences if it is maintained." The conclusion of section three already breaks the pattern thus far established, although it resumes at the end of section four, which concerns the notion of escape: "So much for a first aperçu of this credence . . ." (this sentence is the penultimate, not the ultimate one, of the section, however.) Section five ends "So much for this inviolable zenith where for amateurs of myth lies hidden a way out to earth and sky." The ending of section six reinforces the reader's expectation of this repetition because its form matches the ending of section one: "So much for a first aperçu of the climbers' code." Sections seven through eleven frustrate the reader's desire for consistent structure by omitting any sentence of the form "So much for ———." When the pattern recurs again in section twelve, it does not appear as the final sentence of the section, as the reader has come to expect. Instead, the recurring phrase presents itself at the beginning and middle of the section: "So much for access to the ladders," and "So much roughly speaking for the main ground divisions. . . ." Sections thirteen and fourteen destroy expectations again, but fifteen brings the inconsistent pattern full circle with the concluding sentence: "So much roughly speaking for the last state of the cylinder. . . ."

The fifteen sections of this piece deceptively promise fifteen ladders to meaning, but nothing in the abode fits together exactly. Population density is given as one body per square meter in 200 square meters of space; yet there are actually 205 people and only 199 square meters of area. Mathematical calculations, like the allusions in the text, do not result in precise equations. If each "fact" contains a measure of uncertainty and incompleteness, the same may be said of each sentence, as strained and disordered syntax reflects the tension and disorder of the environment in the abode. Tunnels are dead ends, and some sentences are fragmentary, like the syntax of afterthought in *Enough*: for example, "This is a rule no less strict than the prohibition to climb more than one at a time and not lightly to be broken. Nothing more natural" (p. 27). What could have been a long clause is reduced to a long phrase; the description of the abode's end lacks a finite main verb—the source of action and an essential element in an independent clause: "A languishing happily unperceived because of its slowness and the resurgences that make up for it in part and the inattention of those concerned dazed by the passion preying on them still or by the state of langour into which imperceptibly they are already fallen" (p. 15). This "sentence" languishes grammatically and stylistically, and also turns back on itself in a paradox: the bodies cannot perceive their weakness because they are already too weak. Many sentences, then, resemble broken ladders leading to elusive trapdoors.

Articles and copulative and auxiliary verbs are lost ones in this text, producing a linguistic shorthand sounding like prose in a scientific lab report or a literate movie script: "Omnipresence of a dim yellow light shaken by a vertiginous tremolo between contiguous extremes. Temperature agitated by a like oscillation . . ." (p. 16). Like the incomplete and nested sentences of John Barth's story "Lost in the Funhouse," which reflect the dead ends and mazes within a carnival structure, *Lost Ones* sentences with involuted syntax describe involuted niches and tunnels: "Such harmony only he can relish whose long experience and detailed knowledge of the niches are such as to permit a perfect mental image of the entire system" (pp. 11–12). When unravelled, this sentence (as "cunningly out of line" as the "irregular quincunxes") would read: "Only he [,] whose long experience and detailed knowledge of the niches are such as to permit a perfect mental image of the entire system [,] can relish such harmony." Here imitative style operates quite precisely at the sentence level.

In general, when the cylinder's laws break down, so does the syntax, and large gaps appear between a subject and its verb, or between a verb and its object: "Thus the prostration of those withered ones filled with the horror of contact and compelled to brush together without ceasing is denied its natural end" (p. 61). Many modifiers separate "prostration" and "is denied," delaying the natural end of the sentence. Similarly, in one long, rambling utterance the main point becomes lost in digressions as well as in modifiers: "But as to at this moment of time and there will be no other numbering the faithful who endlessly come and go impatient of the least repose and those who every now and then stand still and the sedentary and the so-called vanquished may it suffice to state that at this moment of time to the nearest body in spite of the press and gloom the first are twice as many as the second who are three times as many as the third who are four times as many as the fourth namely five vanquished in all" (p. 35). Here Beckett frustrates the reader with three consecutive tangential qualifiers, and teases him into searching for the solution to this word problem by recourse to a little arithmetic. At times subject and verb are not only separated but inverted as well: "Cleave also to the wall both sitting and standing four vanquished out of five" (p. 29). In some cases, the object precedes both subject and verb: "Some searchers there are who join the climbers with no thought of climbing . . ." (p. 58); this unusual construction reflects the unusual searchers who examine people rather than niches.

Negation compounds inversion to multiply paradox and am-

biguity. As an apt definition of the vanquished, the narrator remarks, "None looks within himself where none can be" (p. 30).
Somewhere among these negatives resides a positive statement:
the vanquished have found their lost minds within themselves;
or anyone who is empty looks within. In short, only the vanquished look inward because only they are locating their lost
ones. Beckett forces the reader to add and subtract a series of
negatives: "So true it is that when in the cylinder what little is
possible is not so it is merely no longer so and in the least less
the all of nothing if this notion is maintained" (p. 32). Translated,
this means that the sedentary searchers may become searchers
again for a while; and "the least" refers to the vanquished: even
they have not reached the "all of nothing," that is, perfect stasis
and transcendence. The reader must continuously find his way
out of grammatically or logically involved sentences. A similar
syntactic maze is built into "And the thinking being coldy intent
on all these data and evidences could scarcely escape at the close
of his analysis the mistaken conclusion that instead of speaking
of the vanquished with the slight taint of pathos attaching to the
term it would be more correct to speak of the blind and leave it at
that" (p. 39). Here the adjective "mistaken" negates the whole
"conclusion." Even the Golden Rule of ethical behavior is rendered by its obverse: "It is enjoined by a certain ethics not to do
unto others what coming from them might give offense" (p. 58).
At the story's close, grammar as well as movement is running
down, and what starts out as an assertion ends up as a negation:
"At the foot of the ladders propped against the wall with scant
regard to harmony no climber waits his turn" (p. 61). The first
fifteen words of this self-destructive sentence present the ladders, while its last five words then give us the *absence* of climbers.
We are brought to the foot of the ladders with a false promise,
duped like the searchers.

The cylinder is devised to tempt and frustrate hope; the language of the text is devised with a similar intent. While regular
fluctuation of the light appears to promise some order, some indication of predictability, its oscillation never becomes bearable:
"Then how it throbs with constant unchanging beat and fast but
not so fast that the pulse is no longer felt" (p. 36). One would
hope that, in an environment of constant pain, habit would dull
suffering; but this does not happen: "It might safely be maintained that the eye grows used to these conditions and in the end
adapts to them were it not that just the contrary is to be ob-

served . . ." (p. 38). In many aspects the lost one's cylinder becomes a metaphor for *The Lost Ones'* style as it taunts and teases the reader: repetition, overly precise language, convoluted sentences, pseudopatterns, and an arbitrary ending involve the reader in hopeless mental activity analagous to the futile physical movement of the searchers. Just as the niches terminate in dead ends, and the tunnels lead back into the cylinder, so structural patterns lead to frustrating dead ends for the critic, and the "plot" circles back on itself. The story winds down with "if this notion be maintained," thus calling into question all that came before; a conclusive ending to *The Lost Ones* is lost, as the story is declared not how it was at the end of *How It Is.* Present-day readers, like the ancestors of the inhabitants, manage only partial paths through the cylinder: "It is as though at a certain stage discouragement had prevailed" (p. 12). The reader's experience of interpreting the story, including his futile search for a traditional allegory, imitates the searchers' adventures, and in each case "discouragement" stems from a higher paradox about language—that it indicts itself. The philosopher Fritz Mauthner, whose *Critique of Language* much influenced Beckett (as we know from Linda Ben-Zvi), curiously enough used the images of steps and ladders at the beginning of his study:

I must destroy language within me, in front of me, and behind me step for step if I want to ascend in the critique of language, which is the most pressing task for thinking man; I must shatter each rung of the ladder by stepping upon it. He who wishes to follow me must reconstitute the rungs in order to shatter them once again.[23]

Beckett does seem to follow him by enacting a ladder image in his impossible story, by ascending in his own search for "liberation from language," and by deciding to "publish these fragments as fragments" (Mauthner's defense of his philosophical work).

With the prose fragments of the late 1960's, Beckett simultaneously built two very different houses of fiction—*The Lost Ones'* vast and intricate cylinder and *Ping's* small and simple oblong box—and these structures are depicted in correspondingly contrasting styles. Besides leading his readers through the mazelike sentences of *The Lost Ones,* with their elaborate and convoluted syntax, Beckett was also pinning them within the confines of *Ping's* minimal and recycling phrases, which lack most syntactic links. Although Beckett's new styles through the 1970's continued to develop in two opposite directions, the technique of placing readers in the same position as the character or narrator remained constant. We enact the process of interpretation as we search with the climbers; we share the process of composition if we enter the mental microcosm of *Ping*.

8

Ping
An Experiment in Fiction

In 1965 and 1966, Beckett was working on the French versions of *The Lost Ones* and of *Ping* simultaneously; in fact, he labeled the notebooks and manuscripts of this period "MSS *Le Dépeupleur-Bing*,"[1] as if they represented a single work. While there may seem little connection between *The Lost Ones'* extended tale of bodies roaming a vast cylinder and *Ping's* brief static image of a lone body fixed in a small oblong box, it is possible to trace the development from the longer piece to the shorter through the ten versions of *Bing*.[2] Parallel to compression of "character," "setting," and "plot" in *Ping* is a compacting of language: from the large vocabulary and syntactic variety of *The Lost Ones*, Beckett retreats to a style recalling that of *How It Is*—a "midget grammar" of repeated phrases, here separated by periods rather than by blank spaces—but more redundant, condensed, and ambiguous, and therefore more difficult to read. This fiction in yet a new way continues Beckett's statement on the difficulty of writing; now the artist is trapped within the very linguistic devices that were to have freed him:

Bare white body fixed only the eyes only just. Traces blurs light grey almost white on white. Hands hanging palms front white feet heels together right angle. Light heat white planes shining white bare white body fixed ping fixed elsewhere.[3]

What sense can one derive from a piece of fiction which (1) consists of relatively few words arranged in some sort of repetitive permutation, (2) rebels against orthodox English syntax, (3) is entirely devoid of finite verbs, and (4) includes the enigmatic title word, "ping," at irregular intervals? Edith Kern finds other discouraging obstacles—the lack of a clear narrator, the absence of personal pronouns, and the fact that "ping" (the English translation of "hop" and "bing" in the original French) is an ejaculation, a mere sound. She sees *Ping* as the climax of Beckett's innovations thus far: "As the work's title implies, language here is further essentialised and has come to be that 'single noise' and 'vast continuous buzzing' into which language started to merge for Malone."[4] One temptation is to take a hint from the text itself and to exclaim in despair, "Traces blurs signs no meaning." But at least two avenues are open for readers of *Ping*. First, they can view it as the culmination, thematically and stylistically, of Beckett's previous works and, in particular, as an artistic experiment testing a hypothesis first proposed in *The Unnamable*. Second, they can explicate a fuller meaning of the text itself through linguistic description and stylistic analysis. Both of these critical routes lead a reader down numerous dead ends and culs-de-sac; since like any good poem, *Ping* holds not one or two valid interpretations but several. And the very diversity of the readings collected, inspected, and projected here conveys part of *Ping's* purpose and message, which is that the reader's imagination must connect the dots of an enigmatic picture, tracing the blurs provided by Beckett.

In *Ping*, a nameless character, a bare white body with pale blue eyes, is fixed cruciform in a rectangular enclosure. The only other narrative certainty is an imploring black eye, which apparently is a minimal representation of a female character and by extrapolation a minimal suggestion of romance or its memories. Beyond this, the reader is left merely with hints of possibilities: some color within the whiteness, a "way out" of the enclosure, and murmurs within the silence. Images as well as phrases here are so condensed and allusive that the reader can interpret them only through the matrix of previous Beckett works, making *Ping* a prime case of intertextuality.[5] Perhaps we must travel all the way back to one of Beckett's first texts, his critical study *Proust*, in order to place this fiction of the 1960's: the little consciousness in *Ping* may represent man caught between the repetition of habit and the jolt of memory. If so, then the "pings" enact transitional periods, "the perilous zones in the life of the individual, dangerous, precarious, painful, mysterious and fertile, when for a moment the boredom of living is replaced by the sufferings of being" (*Proust*, p. 8). In this respect, the baffling word "ping" perhaps serves as Beckett's madeleine, which calls up the image of a black eye. Even the sound of "ping" ("bing" in the French) suggests a sudden flash of recollection, and as Beckett remarks, "if by some miracle of analogy the central impression of a past sensation recurs as an immediate stimulus which can be instinctively identified by the subject with the model of duplication . . . then the total past sensation, not its echo or copy, but the sensation itself, annihilating every spatial and temporal restriction, comes in a rush to engulf the subject in all the beauty of its infallible proportion" (*Proust*, p. 54). Simply the memory of another's eye would be enough to conquer loneliness for "one second."

A remembrance of things past is also a crucial element in *Waiting for Godot*, in which the tramps appear ill adapted for the present because of vague memories of happier events; their current emptiness seems worse as a remnant of a productive past.[6] In *Ping* memory, the vestige of hope, appears in the form of the dominant image: "one second perhaps not alone eye unlustrous black and white half closed long lashes imploring ping silence ping over" (p. 72). Lucky's "think" provides another obvious connection between *Ping* and *Waiting for Godot*, since the bare white body with white hair recalls Lucky's aged apppearance, and since Lucky's fragmented phrases figure again in *Ping*. Lucky's "for reasons unknown" is in *Ping* transformed into its opposite, the delusion of "all known"; and in each work "given" is used in a mathematical-philosophical sense to begin a proposition. Yet both the long stream of Lucky's speech and the short phrases which comprise *Ping* are "unfinished"; one never learns precisely the consequences of the given. One analysis of Lucky's style serves for *Ping* as well:

> Here a loss of faith in the adequacy of language is accomplished by an equal mistrust of axiomatic procedures used to establish a chain of meaning. If man's place in the universe is a matter of syntax, then the amorphous, incomplete sentence which trickles out of Lucky, like the sawdust blood of a stuffed doll, reflects the fact that man has been unable to make a place for himself.[7]

With his stasis and his arms and legs "joined like sewn," *Ping*'s creature resembles a large Raggedy Andy doll, just as Lucky resembles a puppet; he shares Lucky's enslaved, uncertain, and constrained situation. From his early fiction to his later plays, Beckett has been creating characters who are physically confined yet mentally roaming. Murphy in his "cage" is another prototype for the figure in *Ping*, as he fixes his bare white body to his rocking chair and there seeks the pure white colorlessness of nonbeing. *Murphy*'s climax also involves the protagonist's being seen by another, Mr. Endon; and Hamm in *Endgame* fits this pattern as well. Fixed in a chair within a small room, Hamm demands to be placed precisely at the center of his shelter, and to have a witness. Similar in physical condition to the body in

Ping are the characters in *Play*, embedded in greyish urns and flooded with light. In the second typescript of *Play* the stage direction calls for the actors to be in white boxes,[8] which prepares for the white oblong in *Ping*. And in *Play*, as in *Ping*, recollection—in the form of constant reiteration of the past—becomes the characters' curse.

For the Beckett character in general, "[i]t is in the memory of what he was that he must find himself."[9] The Unnamable declares that he is "buried under seconds" (p. 43), and the hero of *How It Is* tries to recall and recapture his good moments from the past in order to experience time and escape eternity. *Ping* is the next stage in this nightmare, since the language and preoccupations of Pim's torturer are echoed—further condensed—in this later piece:

all that almost blank that was so adorned a few traces that's all seeing who I always more or less so little so little there but there little there but there no alternative [*How It Is*, p. 103]

there then more or less more of old less of late very little these last tracts they are the last extremely little hardly at all a few seconds on and off enough to mark a life several lives crosses everywhere indelible traces [Pp. 103–104]

In *How It Is* "a few seconds" are "enough to mark a life," whereas in *Ping* only "one second" is needed to recreate "perhaps a nature." The "indelible traces" in the mud now diminish to the fainter "traces blurs signs" in the white oblong. Thus the "bare white body" in *Ping*—which is perhaps a variation of "Pim"—is probably Pim's descendant. He has another literary ancestor in the Unnamable, who fears that his location is "merely the inside of my distant skull where once I wandered, now am fixed, lost for tininess, or straining against the walls, with my head, my hands, my feet, my back, and ever murmuring my old stories . . ." (p. 20). Also fixed and with "head haught," the figure in *Ping* recalls some proud god being punished. In fact, "flesh torn of old" in *Ping* may refer to the flesh of Prometheus, since both Shelley and his protagonist are alluded to by the Unnamable, who hopes that "the torn flesh [would] have time to knit, as in the Caucasus, before being torn again" (p. 20). Further echoes of Prometheus sound in the "nails" which apparently fasten *Ping*'s protagonist in his box.

Like the consciousness in *Ping*, who begins by calculating his location, the Unnamable, whose first words are "Where now?"

and whose last sentence begins "The place," feels that "[i]t is well to establish the position of the body from the outset, before passing on to more important matters" (p. 22). The bare white creature in *Ping* is sexless; with his "long hair fallen," he again resembles the Unnamable, who reasons, "Why should I have a sex, who have no longer a nose? All those things have fallen, all the things that stick out, with my eyes my hair, without leaving a trace . . ." (p. 23). As the creature in *Ping* becomes "white on white" and "white invisible," all that remains are "traces blurs signs." The deteriorating body of the Unnamable still retains eyes, and thoughts in a head—"There I am in any case equipped with eyes, which I open and shut, two, perhaps blue, knowing it avails nothing, for I have a head now too, where all manner of things are known . . ." (p. 147)—and similarly the creature's brain in *Ping* is full of the "vile certainty" that things are "all known." These earlier passages from Beckett's trilogy seem to have been written with the germ for *Ping* already conceived; or perhaps *Ping* is one of the "residua" from a possible post-*Unnamable* novel in an impossible quartet. There is a gigantic stylistic leap between *The Unnamable* and *Ping*, however, in which the "I" has disappeared, syntax has revolted, and there is no more "going on." [10] In *The Unnamable* the main consciousness communicates his experience, with wide erudition and an immense vocabulary, to the length of a novel. In *How It Is* a more limited voice pants about his past learning in fits and starts, with isolated paragraphs of discontinuous "midget grammar"; but while his utterances may be fragmentary, his logic is still complete. In *Ping* the condensed, non-sequitur phrases lack even associative logic. Thus Beckett's works approximate syntactic regression (with a few anomalies) from *The Unnamable* to *Texts for Nothing*, *How It Is*, *Ping*, and *Lessness*.

Although *From an Abandoned Work* is written in a style that is traditional by contrast, its imagery bears on a discussion of *Ping*. Its narrator confesses, "White I must say has always affected me strongly, all white things, sheets, walls, and so on, even flowers, and then just white, without more"; in the one thousand or so words of *Ping*, "white" occurs ninety times. The narrator of *Abandoned Work* longs for death and imagines his body as being "all over" the earth: "Over, over, there is a soft place in my heart for all that is over, no for the being over, I love the word." Achieving the closure that has eluded other Beckett voices, *Ping*'s consciousness concludes with finality "ping finished ping over."

Abandoned's narrator offers a key to the atmosphere in *Ping* as he anticipates a mental state analogous to that of the isolated, white figure:

. . . a long unbroken time without before or after, light or dark, from or towards or at, the old half knowledge of when and where gone, and of what, but kinds of things still, all at once, all going, until nothing, there was never anything, never can be, life and death all nothing, that kind of thing, only a voice dreaming and droning on all around, that is something, the voice that once was in your mouth. [*Abandoned Work*, p. 49]

Despite *Ping's* repeated "all known," the "when and where" (the time and space of its setting) are not known; only "kinds of things" ("traces blurs signs") are left, and a voice droning on ("murmur") seems to come from outside the white body. More important, synthesizing the whiteness, the love of being "over," and the droning (or murmurs) of the two pieces suggests that, like *Abandoned Work*, *Ping* is concerned with the activity of writing. This indication of self-reflexive fiction comes into sharper focus when *Ping* is viewed against the background of other Beckett narratives, through other readings of the text, and with the critical frame of stylistic analysis.

Beyond *Ping's* correspondences with *Abandoned Work*, even stronger resemblances link it to *Imagination Dead Imagine*; it is no accident that *Ping* follows *Imagination* in the triad of stories called *Residua*. In *Imagination Dead Imagine*, a man and a woman are curled in two adjoining semicircles in fetal positions within a closed white rotunda that is suspended in a white vacuum. The reduction of this situation in *Ping's* lone white body contained in a white box provides Beckett an even greater narrative challenge. While the details of environments and characters' physical positions in the two pieces differ, in both texts the creatures are fixed in an area one yard (three feet) wide. *Imagination's* "Hold a mirror to their lips, it mists" is echoed in *Ping's* "heart breath no sound," in both cases indicating some evidence of life. Other similarities overshadow differences: the "light heat," the "white on white" images, the silence broken only occasionally by pinglike vibrations, the fixity of the bodies, the suggestion of dual characters in each piece, the oscillation between two states of being, and above all, the emphasis on sight.

Imagination's partners in white are distinguishable because of the woman's long hair, and similar "long hair fallen white visible over" appears in *Ping*; also at least one pair of the "piercing pale blue" eyes from *Imagination* recurs here. The perceptual problem in *Imagination* is that the two characters are almost invisible to each other, and their white rotunda is almost imperceptible against a white background. *Imagination*'s emphasis on seeing, knowing the interior and the exterior, is a concern in *Ping* as well (although now these motifs are even more condensed stylistically); twice "all known" is followed by "within without." Problems of vision are linguistically foregrounded: "never seen" occurs five times, and "invisible" is repeated thirteen times. While it is difficult to say who or what is "invisible" in *Ping* because of the lack of subjects, it becomes clear that (1) certain areas of the environment (e.g., the planes) converge in whiteness, (2) parts of the character's white body merge indistinguishably, and (3) the white body itself is lost against the white walls. No scheme emerges that accounts for the placement of the word "invisible" (except that "white" is always in the immediate linguistic neighborhood), but it is appropriate that "invisible" disappears for several lines before and after the "eye black and white." During this time the character is seen, if only for one second, by the imploring eye. As in *Ping*, there is a hint of communication in *Imagination* only once: "Never the two gazes together except once, when the beginning of one overlapped the end of the other, for about ten seconds." Thus *Ping* may be read as a dramatization, in altered form and from one perspective, of the lone instance of eye contact in *Imagination*. One moment of being seen, of being, is granted before the plunge back into nonbeing; this would explain the phrases "perhaps a meaning" and "perhaps a nature."

Changes in temperature and light within *Imagination*'s rotunda are fairly regular except for the periods of calm which ironically cause the bodies to vibrate. One consequence is that "ping" corresponds to the phenomenon experienced by the couple in the rotunda when the "eye of prey" invades their world: "an infinitesimal shudder instantaneously suppressed." Beckett places the reader of *Ping* intellectually in a limbo state similar to that of the white body, in that the piercing "ping" disturbs him as it agitates the central consciousness. Gradually we shift from the role of observer to that of fellow sufferer, as we did in reading *Imagination*.

For the creature, the "ping" effects some sort of change, since "ping" leads from "fixed" to "fixed elsewhere" and from "murmur" to "silence." Hugh Kenner finds it significant that Beckett was scanning strips of film in 1964, during the shooting of *Film*, the year before the fictions including *Ping* were begun:

This prompts a guess about *Ping*'s origins, maybe a helpful guess. It is pertinent to the emphasis on lighting, the absence of details as though in over-exposure, and does help to explain what became of the verbs. Each frame of a film is so, like a noun, and the action, normally specified by verbs, is an illusion generated by the frames' successiveness.[11]

One need not go outside the text of *Ping* to account for the lack of verbs, however. In an environment in which no movement, no progression in time occurs—a world of "one second" or "same time"—no description of movement or change is required. A world of stasis, a *tableau vivant*, can be depicted with nothing but nouns and participles (for example, "people dancing"). These participles are, technically, adjectival, as in "dancing people," so that "legs joined like sewn" contains "joined" acting as an adjective, not as a verb. Also a shift can be conveyed through a different modifier applied to the same noun (as when, "no meaning" becomes "perhaps a meaning") or a sudden change in nouns (for example, from "murmur" to "silence"). Kenner's hypothesis that these kinds of shifts are stimulated by "ping" are valid for most "ping" phrases, but this does not fully explain the meaning of the word, nor of course interpret the text as a whole.

Henri Bergson's work also offers the analogy of a series of snapshots for the processes of thought and language, and we do know from a notebook kept by one of Beckett's students at Trinity that Beckett discussed the philosopher in his lectures there.[12] This helps explain the stylistic stasis of *Ping*, since Bergson's theories on time, knowledge, and becoming could have influenced Beckett's depiction of human perception in his later fiction:

It is because the film of the cinematograph unrolls, bringing in turn the different photographs of the scene to continue each other, that each actor of the scene recovers his mobility. . . . Such is the contrivance of the cinematograph. And such is also that of our knowledge. . . . We take snapshots, as it were, of the passing reality, and, as these are characteristic of the reality, we have only to string them on a becoming, abstract, uniform and invisible, situated at the back of the apparatus of knowledge, in order to imitate what there is that is characteristic in this becoming itself. Perception, intellection, language so proceed in general. Whether we would think becoming, or express it, or even perceive it, we hardly do anything else than set going a kind of cinematograph inside us.[13]

If Bergson is correct, then Beckett's new style for *Ping*, a series or string of phrases projecting a series of images, perfectly imitates the process (be it perception, imagination, or composition) taking place in the character's mind. Again *Film*, and particularly the scene of O (Object) destroying his "becoming" through his past by tearing up old snapshots, becomes a dramatic parallel.

Logically associated with the interpretation of *Ping* as a chronological series of images or memories is the notion of "ping" as some type of time marker or bell, and critics have speculated about this meaning for the syllable. Ruby Cohn calls "ping" an onomatopoetic announcement of "sudden motion,"[14] and implies a connection with time as she recalls the narrator of *From an Abandoned Work*, who laments, "Oh but for these awful fidgets I have always had I would have lived my life in a big empty echoing room with a big old pendulum clock." In other Beckett texts, short syllables containing the phonemes /p/ or /b/ signify a temporal unit. Pozzo, in his set speech on time, uses "ppfff!" and "pop!" to indicate the sudden appearance of night (*Godot*, pp. 25–26). An earlier manuscript version of *Ping* was called *Pfft*, with "pfft" replacing each "ping" in the text. Beckett uses "hop" in the French *Bing*, and an early draft of the same work contains "paf." In *The Unnamable* each unit of time is a "bang": ". . . it's every second that is the worst, it's a chronicle, the seconds pass, one after another, jerkily, no flow, they don't pass, they arrive, bang, bang, they bang into you, bounce off, fall and never move again, when you have nothing left to say you talk of time, seconds of time . . ." (p. 151). Of the sentences that begin with "ping," ten contain "one second," two "always," and one "last"; if "ping" is not a marker of time, it is surely a temporal suggestion. Beyond this, ping/bing may measure amounts of pain, as when the Unnamable converts his one-second unit "bang" to "bing" and extends his image until "bing" comes to represent individual blows: ". . . I'll laugh, that's how it will end, in a chuckle, chuck chuck, ow, ha, pa, I'll practise, nyum, how, plop, psss, nothing but emotion, bing bang, that's blows . . ." (p. 170). In *Malone Dies*, Mrs. Lambert stares at an alarm clock and a crucifix on a nail, significantly side by side above her mantel (p. 39). These earlier Beckett works reinforce an association between "nails" and "ping" in *Ping*, implying that time is to be endured, suffered.

In *Film* a nail in the wall by the protagonist's head suggests that another torture is the pain of being perceived. Paradoxically, Beckett's characters have a desperate need to be seen and yet a dread of the observer's eye, as James Knowlson has shown with numerous examples of this pattern of perception from the Beckett world:

The eye stands at the meeting point between two worlds. It projects outwards and it registers inwards. Closing the eyes can then shut out, if only momentarily, the outer world and facilitate that plunge into darkness that, since *Murphy*, has both haunted and terrified Beckett's major characters. Yet, just as the voices echoing in the inner world fiercely resist this descent into silence and darkness, so the eye, regarded either as the observer or as the observed, (or at the end of *Film* as both) cannot easily be eradicated. For to do this would mean that one was succumbing to total extinction, failure and insignificance.[15]

Eyes are the last to go: the eye must remain to observe its own departure. In fact, in *Ping* a black eye is all that is left of one creature, like the suspended smile of Lewis Carroll's vanishing Cheshire cat. *Imagination Dead Imagine* and *Ping* emerge as Beckett's most explicit statements on perception, as their styles imitate the processes of imagination and vision.

The eyes in *Imagination* open at random intervals and "gaze in *unblinking* exposure long beyond what is humanly possible" (my italics). In *Bing* the recurring "bing" sound phonetically suggests in English the blink of the human eye, so that the English phrase "fixed ping fixed elsewhere" might be translated, with *Finnegans Wake*-like license, "eyes fixed on one thing, blink, eyes fixed elsewhere." The placement of pings (blinks) seems random—naturally so, as they mimic human behavior. In French "clin" means a wink of the eye, and Beckett may have had this word in mind when he chose "bing" and "ping." The noun "clin" appears frequently in *Textes pour rien*, and in Text 5 of the English *Texts for Nothing* we find: "It's an image . . . before my eyes, they see the scene, the lids flicker and it's in. An instant and then they close again, to look inside the head, to try and see inside, to look for me there, to look for someone there . . ."

(p. 95). *Ping*'s image of the imploring black eye may be "without," that is, may represent a lover or an observer; alternatively, the other (black) eye may be "within" (behind the blue ones) representing a search for the inner self, or a separate creation of the imagination. This third possibility returns us to *Ping* as the activity of composing.

Comparison between this text and Beckett's other fiction, early and recent, takes us only so far; *Ping* also can be seen independently as a pure experiment, as a test case for the ultimate work of minimal art. One of the fictions that make up what Beckett calls *Residua*, *Ping* may be his answer to the question, How many elements of the narrative can one syphon off while still retaining the residuals of a story? This issue is considered, in another context, by the Unnamable: "Even if there were things, a thing somewhere, a scrap of nature, to talk about, you might be reconciled to having no one left, to being yourself the talker, if only there were a thing somewhere, to talk about . . ." (pp. 150–51). Presumably a second character is expendable as long as there remains a voice and a scrap of nature ("blue and white in the wind" perhaps) or some thing ("eye black and white" perhaps) to discuss. In another attempt, the Unnamable as creator starts with a setting and determines how much he will have to accumulate in order to compose a story:

make a place, a little world . . . try and find out what it's like, try and guess, put someone in it, seek someone in it, and what he's like, and how he manages, it won't be I, no matter, perhaps it will . . . we must have eyelids, we must have eyeballs, it's preferable . . . you must go on thinking too, the old thoughts, they call that thinking, it's visions, shreds of old visions. . . . [P. 166]

Remnants of old visions are all that is left for "ping of old." The Unnamable concludes that "just one space and someone within" (p. 167) will suffice for a piece of fiction. Beckett, in creating *Ping*, operates in just this way: "All known all white bare white body fixed one yard legs joined like sewn. Light heat white floor one square yard never seen. White walls one yard by two white ceiling one square yard never seen." He begins here with a general description of a place and elaborates from the vague "all white" to the more exact "white walls," "white ceiling," and "white floors"; starts with "one yard" and then expands it to "one square yard" and then to "one yard by two."

This building by accretion explains why the novelist William Gass sees in *Ping* a literary reenactment of Genesis:

> For the purposes of analysis we can regard the sentences of fiction as separate acts of creation. . . . An audacious first term: all. The sentence isolates its words; they slowly fall, slowly revolve, slowly begin to group themselves. We are in the hands of an ancient atomist.[16]

He argues that the monosyllables of *Ping*'s first sentence spontaneously engender themselves and then give birth to the next units: "Stately monotonous strokes, like measured beats of a gong, occur within, but do not fill this void. . . . Truly, nothing is previous. Groups first formed form the first connections, and are repeated."[17] Similar to God constructing the world from nothing, the Beckettian artist challenges himself to write with one hand tied behind his back, with only a few phrases instead of the novelist's traditional verbal storehouse. But essentially how many words would the writer need in order to depict an instant of life? The Unnamable answers,

> and this word man which is perhaps not the right one for the thing I see when I hear it, but an instant, an hour, and so on, how can they be represented . . . blank words, but I use them, they keep coming back, all those they showed me, all those I remember, I need them all, to be able to go on, it's a lie, a score would be plenty, tried and trusty, unforgettable, nicely varied, that would be palette enough . . . that's how it will end, in heart-rending cries, inarticulate murmurs, to be invented, as I go along . . . [Pp. 169–70]

This is exactly what Beckett has attempted in *Ping*: narrating a minimal story (troubled by self-reflexive "murmurs") with a small number of repeated words in varied combinations. Beckett invents, as he goes along, four planes and from there a body; one eye, and from there a memory image. While the Unnamable begins simply enough with a place and a person, before he can control the stereotypical formulas of fiction, he is imagining, "They love each other, marry . . ." (p. 167), and he is off on plots of love and war which he extends to melodramatic multiplicity. Failing to construct anything resembling a minimal plot, he concludes sarcastically "there's a story for you" (p. 169).

By contrast, Beckett has succeeded in creating in *Ping* an intriguing fragment of fiction based on a static situation and a fleeting image. What *Ping* lacks in plot it supplies in rhythm, mu-

sical sound, visual effect, and mathematical complexity. Whether
Ping is treated as a poem, as an incantation, as a fugue in seven
parts, as a picture, or as a problem to be solved and graphed—
and scholars have explored each of these approaches—all critical roads lead to the phrase, *Ping*'s minimal unit. Linguistically,
Ping is a text of 1,030 words, composed of 120 words recurring in
about 100 different phrases. These phrases can be considered
discrete and countable because their constituent parts are found
only in the linguistic vicinity of certain other words. For example, "unover" is always preceded by "alone," so that these
two terms determine a unit. "Haught" is always preceded by
"head"; "known" occurs either in "all known" or in "but that
known not"; "given" is always followed by a color; and "within
without" travels together as a pair. Limbs are either "joined like
sewn" or "seam like sewn." Most words and sometimes whole
"sentences" are used repeatedly; for example, "bare white body"
occurs nine times. The frequent expression "ping" surfaces in
varied linguistic environments, at the beginnings, middles, or
endings of sentences, and between many different phrases. It is
the only word in the text that is not "fixed" in position, function,
or meaning. These statistics suggest that Beckett started with a
small set of words and then further restricted his artistic freedom by allowing himself only certain combinations of these stylistic units. This hypothesis is supported by one of Beckett's work-
sheets for *Ping* which lists phrases that have been checked off.[18]
Thus the artist is intentionally as "fixed" as the bare white body
of the piece, pinned within a scheme for verbal permutation.

As with *How It Is*, analysis of repetition can sometimes be
used to wrest meaning from chaotic literary works, but in *Ping*
the repetition overwhelms the reader and becomes the pattern—
not the significant variation.[19] Perhaps, then, the nonrepeated
words offer clues to meaning. In *Ping* the word "nails" is foregrounded linguistically, and combined with other details, it recalls the Crucifixion. David Lodge and his students noticed a
collocative set consisting of "nail," "hair," "scars," "flesh," and
"torn," all appearing only once in the text. When clustered,
these words implied "that the whole piece might be a bleakly
anti-metaphysical rendering of the consciousness of the dying
Christ—Christ in the tomb rather than Christ on the Cross."[20]
Certainly a case for the suffering creature of *Ping* as Jesus could
be advanced: "legs joined like sewn," "heels together right
angle," and "hands hanging palms front" could describe the sav-

ior's position on the cross, which may have been approximately "one yard by two." Further, "White scars invisible same white as flesh torn of old given rose" obliquely recalls the gash in the victim's side. In this reading, "ping" becomes Beckett's onomatopoetic signal for the nails being driven into Christ's hand and feet. A Christian interpretation of *Ping* has limitations, though, and in pursuing only one series of images, reduces the richness of the text. A more general interpretation, which subsumes Lodge's ultimate conclusion, has emerged as the standard one: that *Ping* portrays an agitated consciousness seemingly in the last moments of life. The body is "fixed," with only the eyes movable; his seeing, hearing, thinking, and remembering are all constricted. Most colors become white, causing objects to become invisible against a white background. The movement from color to noncolor reinforces the overall pattern of the piece, from "unover" to "over."[21] In addition, a large percentage of the text is composed of qualifiers, quantifiers, and delimiters, so that the vacillation between "tentative assertion and collapse," which Lodge notes as an occasional refrain, is actually demonstrable throughout the entire piece. Analyzing pairs of opposites reveals this pattern: "all" and "no," "never" and "always," "over" and "unover," "all" and "almost." The tentative words dominate the absolutes in *Ping*, though; there is no balancing out. "Perhaps" undercuts "all known," and "only just almost" destroys the force of the following word, "never."

A similar vacillation of opposites is uncovered by John Mood when he examines patterns of phrases containing key words,[22] but he too may be giving his data short shrift. With "meaning," for example, he counts

> 4 "signs no meaning"
> then 1 "perhaps a meaning"
> then 1 "signs no meaning" again
> then 1 "a meaning only just"
> then concluding with "perhaps a meaning"

Tracking the placement of the word "known" in the text discloses an alternation of "all known" and "but that known not" ending with "all known." Then observing that "image" always occurs in a sentence beginning with "ping," Mood mysteriously concludes that the structure of *Ping* approaches but never reaches zero. While it is true that all colors in the piece become white, a movement from "signs no meaning" to "perhaps a meaning" surely progresses from zero to some positive number. A more significant pattern may be found in the set of phrases beginning with "perhaps":

perhaps not alone
perhaps a way out
perhaps a nature
perhaps a meaning
perhaps a nature
perhaps way out there
perhaps not alone [occurs twice, the second time just before the black eye]
perhaps a meaning a nature
perhaps not alone

This sequence suggests that the presence of another creature was a possibility from the start of the piece. The black eye of another (or of the imagination) brings purpose or meaning to the existence of the white body, shows him his own nature, and affords a ways out of the self—perhaps.

More rigorous in methodology than Mood's analysis is Elisabeth Segrè's linguistic study, complete with graphs of word frequencies.[23] She argues that the form as a whole reflects its subject, a creature on the verge between being and nonbeing, and that sentence 63 is the stylistic highpoint of the piece. However, sentence 63 ("Ping fixed last elsewhere legs joined like sewn heels together right angle hands hanging palms front head haught eyes white invisible fixed front over") does not intuitively strike the reader as the lyrical or dramatic center of the text. Segrè's meticulous attention to each phrase, although empirical and precise, slights the resonances between the phrases that produce a minimal story. If there is any intellectual action or dramatic progression in *Ping*, it certainly concerns the effort of the consciousness to recall a human image. The black eye, different from the creature's blue eyes, by synecdoche implies an entire person—presumably a woman.

Thus "Ping perhaps not alone one second with image same time a little less dim eye black and white half closed long lashes imploring . . ." (sentence 61) marks the climax of the piece, since "long lashes imploring" introduces a human, emotional element for the first time, and the black of the other's eye is the only color saved from whiteness. A shift from "that much memory almost never" to "that much memory henceforth never" must indicate that the vision is over; and after the "long lashes imploring," other linguistic changes also take place in the text. "Unover" no longer occurs; there is one instance of "all over" and later some occurrences of "over" not introduced earlier. The word "last," which had been absent at the beginning of the text, appears three times after the vision: "last colour" (formerly "only colour"—referring to blue), "last elsewhere," and "last murmur." "Traces" gives way to "no trace," and specificity diminishes and description condenses from "perhaps a way out" to "perhaps way out there" to (after the vision) "perhaps there." A phrase foregrounded in the text because it is used only once, "afar flash of time," directly follows the vision and thus helps to highlight it. Finally, Beckett places the phrase "ping of old," which is new to the text, three times in succession after the climactic vision of the black eye. *Ping*'s consciousness has, in a condensed Proustian process, recaptured a past self through the involuntary memory of a previous relationship, recalling Krapp's recollections of black eyes.

Some elements in the French original[24] imply a different interpretation from the romantic one above, as they provide verbal echoes between *Ping* and *The Lost Ones*. In place of the adjective "unlustrous" to describe the black and white eye, *Bing* has "embu," a term used for paints meaning that the colors are soaked or dried in, which recalls the drying effects on human skin under the cylinder's harsh light (as a noun applied to pictures, "embu" means "dullness" or "flatness"). In the French, "rose," as in "flesh torn of old given rose only just," receives more emphasis than in the English translation (partly because of increased ambiguity) and suggests the pink flesh which turns grey in the strong light and heat of *Le Dépeupleur* (and *The Lost Ones*). Also, "sidéral" in "temps sidéral" (the French original of "light time") means "determined by or pertaining to the stars," and thus calls to mind the "way out" to the stars desired by the searchers trapped in the cylinder. Escape may also be promised by the "blue and white in the wind" appearing throughout *Ping*. If so, the body fixed in the oblong resembles one of the ultimate vanquished of *The Lost Ones*' cylinder, confined to its one square meter of space. (One of the early versions of *Bing* was called *Dans le cylindre*.) With this association, the moment of eye contact becomes an encapsulation of the last section of *The Lost Ones* where the final lost body studies the eyes of the female vanquished. This scenario would explain why the *Ping* woman's eye is black and white, if she is one of the lost creatures: the cylinder's fierce light would dilate the pupil until it overook the orb, so all that would be left is a large pupil and the white of the eye.

Beckett as blue-eyed artist/victim has found with *Ping* another "way out" of a stylistic impasse. A frequent word in the French version, "blanc" for white, also hints that *Ping* should be considered as a text about the writer. With its connotations of blankness, "blanc" represents the whiteness of an endpaper, the whiteness of a work that is "over," "achêvé," silent. Another early title of *Bing* was *Blanc*. "Traces alone unover given black . . ." may thus be expanded to "The traces alone are unfinished given that they are still black." It is hoped that the traces will fade from black to "light gray" to "almost white on white," that is, to a blank sheet of paper. Since Beckett uses "fouillis" for "blurs," a term which means a medley (of sounds) or a jumble (of words), his traces, blurs, and signs could represent the lines, phrases, and letters of words. In Beckett's early play, *Human Wishes*, the blind heroine wonders if she can feel "the trace of ink" on a sheet of paper. And in his first (unpublished) novel, "Dream of Fair to Middling Women," where Beckett had associated language and music, curiously he had used "ping!" several times to mean "word" or "note."[25] In "Dream" the narrator defines a novel as a linear progression of sounds forming orderly and pleasing music. Playing on Samuel Johnson's definition of good style as "the right word in the right place," Belacqua argues that what is needed for good fiction is

someone who could always be relied on for just the one little squawk, ping!, just right, the right squawk in the right place . . . only one, tuning-fork charlatan to move among the notes and size 'em up and steady 'em down and chain 'em together in some kind of a nice little cantilena. . . . [P. 112]

The "voices" in *Texts for Nothing* trying to find the proper harmony, the correct aggregate of words, have become disembodied thought in *Ping*. Beckett's later little prose songs like *Ping* and *Lessness* are rearrangements of phrases, notes loosely chained together with the right ping in the right place—or, in *Lessness*, in a random place. Now the artist, instead of being a "tuning-fork charlatan," becomes a pathetic creature fixed in an enclosure (*Ping*) or fallen over and trying vainly to stand (*Lessness*). Language in Beckett's new worlds either traps the writer or overwhelms him: as he chains words together, they also chain him, until by the most recent text he is bound *Worstward Ho*, putting the wrong word in the wrong place.

Since *Ping* is clearly one more Beckett piece of fiction about composing, the nails and scars become burdens of the suffering artist, a common theme in Beckett, and the central metaphor in *How It Is*. At the end of his monologue, Pim's torturer/victim finds himself in the same position as the consciousness of *Ping*, "the arms spread yes like a cross no answer LIKE A CROSS" (p. 146). Both works depict a lonely creator/martyr tortured or compelled to compose—perhaps urged on by each "ping" in the text. The *Oxford English Dictionary* lists as an obsolete meaning of ping "to prick, poke, push, urge," so that the repetitions of this nonsense word express an inner or outer voice spurring the writer toward further composition (like the repeated command "On" in Beckett's more recent fiction *Ill Seen Ill Said*). Thus the single word "ping," like the entire text, resonates with varied but related meanings—about perception, memory, imagination, and creative motivation.

Any linguistic study or close textual analysis of *Ping* encounters two large stumbling blocks, repetition and ambiguity, yet these two properties of the text have thematic import and in fact are essential to this fiction's imitative style. A small body of words linguistically constrained in a limited number of phrases—which in turn are permitted only a stipulated number of patterns and positions in the text—is the natural medium for a small body fixed in a minimal space. In addition, phrases reverberating in an enclosed area aurally produce a repetitive style; Ludovic Janvier argues that the phrases of the piece, elementary units one breath long, obey a law of echoes: "La répétition-refrain qui à la lettre constitue le texte ne peut s'être déclenchée qu'en fonction d'un certain vide, obsessionnel, comme la resonnance de l'echo ne peut se faire entendre qu'appuyée par le vide de l'espace."[26] Ambiguity also determines the imitative style of *Ping*: because of absent verbs and missing punctuation within and between clauses, the syntax of *Ping* is impossible to parse definitively. Since divisions between phrases are "invisible," stylistic and narrative boundaries forever shift and sway, and the text threatens to offer "no meaning." Yet the "traces blurs signs" become metaphors for the phrases themselves as the separations between units of meaning are blurred.

If we were to list the phrases of *Ping* alphabetically, the result would obviously be . . . no story. With the absence of verbs and

of syntactic connectives, the minimal narrative is written between the phrases, that is, in their careful arrangement. In *How
It Is*, Beckett's virtuoso text of phrasal structure, he had already
experimented with permitting the meaning to emerge not logically but associatively, through "the silences, the empty spaces
in the interstices of form."[27] In "Dream of Fair to Middling
Women," the main character, Belacqua, predicts that the "The
experience of my reader shall be between the phrases, in the silence, communicated by the intervals, not the terms, of the statement . . . his experience shall be the menace, the miracle, the
memory, of an unspeakable trajectory" (p. 123).[28] This is precisely the experience of the reader of *Ping* and *Lessness*, since
Beckett has created new fictional styles in which the silences between the phrases are just as full as the pauses between lines of
dialogue in *Waiting for Godot*. By eradicating the sentence as we
know it (with logical connections among subject, verb, and object), Beckett graphs only the two end points for each idea, leaving the trajectory to be traced by the reader. While denied anything resembling a conventional narrative here, at least observers
are granted the "traces blurs signs" of an image, which we ourselves must create, becoming co-authors as we too suffer the
pings and pangs of composition.

When *Ping* appeared, scholars wondered how Beckett could
do any less with minimal stories and condensed syntax, and
then—almost on cue—came *Lessness*. Because of the haphazard
arrangement of its sentences, trajectories can no longer be traced
consecutively through their constituent phrases. Rather, the
phrases recurring in scattered sentences set up resonances vertically among one another. For a full understanding of the piece,
as for *Ping*, the reader must measure the arcs of the linguistic
intervals, not the terms.

9

Lessness
Syntax of Weakness

Lessness originally appeared in French as *Sans* ("Without") in 1969; and "Sans" is a more appropriate title for this piece, which is without traditional syntax and without several common parts of speech.[1] Verbs are infrequent (with present tense verbs entirely absent), and the sparsely used pronoun "he" has no apparent antecedent. Can a writer who restricts himself mostly to nouns and adjectives still convey meaning or—harder still—produce a story? This was a question posed for *How It Is* and *Ping* as well, but with *Lessness* repetition is so pervasive that no new elements appear in the second half of the text, thus obviating any sort of narrative progression. How does a reader overwhelmed by repetition within and between sentences assimilate the piece as fiction? Here is prose which, like the language of *How It Is*, sounds as if it is being dictated by an external voice: "Little body same grey as the earth sky ruins only upright. No sound not a breath same grey all sides earth sky body ruins. Blacked out fallen open four walls over backwards true refuge issueless."

The construction of *Lessness* is even more intricate and formal than that of *Ping*. Its twenty-four paragraphs are composed of 120 sentences (actually 60, each used twice), the number of sentences in a paragraph and their order within a paragraph chosen at random. The manuscripts and typescripts of *Lessness* reaffirm its chance sequencing of sentences. Beckett began with six lists labeled A through F of ten sentences each, and then twice checked off each of the sixty (six times ten) sentences as he used them. He also typed out two linear orderings, one for each half of the piece, using a letter/number notation for each sentence: "A3 B9 C9 . . . ," meaning to select the third sentence from group A, then the ninth from group C, and so on. Finally, he noted the random "paragraph structure" for each half, indicating the number of sentences per paragraph by "4/5/3. . . ." Viewing irrefutable evidence of this mechanical art is disturbing to a reader, but it is a relief that the manuscripts also provide

179

proof of Beckett's conscious and careful creation of the initial sentences out of beautifully wrought phrases.

The six categories of sentences may be characterized by symbols or "signatures":[2]

Ruin—Collapse of refuge	'true refuge'
Exposure—Outer world	'earth . . . sky'
Wilderness—Body exposed	'little body'
Mindlessness—Refuge forgotten	'all gone from mind'
Past and future denied	'never'
Past and future affirmed	future tense

Edith Fournier analyzes the same six groups, which she calls "families,"[3] and finds that the ten sentences which make up each one are in turn composed of a related set of words, and that sometimes the sentences differ by only one phrase. As in *Ping*, the minimal unit of composition in *Lessness* is the phrase. J. M. Coetzee, adopting a mathematical approach, achieves "an unambiguous segmentation of the text into 106 different phrases varying in length from 1 to 12 words and occurring, on an average, 5.7 times each."[4] Using computational analysis, Coetzee then establishes a number of linguistic rules about the text, one of which is that each sentence of *Lessness* can be composed from the phrasal elements of at most three other sentences (and often from only two other sentences). This gives a precise measure of the redundancy of the text, but no measure of its poetic richness. While Coetzee shows statistically that the arrangement of sentences may be entirely random (as, in fact, it is), it would be an injustice to view Beckett as a mere random number generator.

When interpreting *Lessness*, readers should keep two things in mind: (1) however haphazard the order of sentences, the phrases themselves were carefully composed by Beckett and purposefully arranged in sentences according to the six categories listed above; (2) *Lessness* does not exist in a verbal vacuum, as a mere collection of words whose orderings have certain properties. Rather, *Lessness* can be interpreted as a variation (in style and substance) of *Ping*, and must be viewed against a backdrop of other Beckett works. Thus an initial impression of the author simply as stylistic juggler is too limited; *Lessness* reveals him, as Edith Fournier puts it, as both a mathematiciam and a poet. With these two aspects of the writer in mind, we can first linguistically describe the sentences of *Lessness*, then determine how its imitative style operates. Next, placing this fiction in the context of Beckett's earlier works (especially *Endgame*) and of his critical statements allows us to perceive the images of *Lessness* as a commentary on his philosophy of art and as a self-reflexive comment on his new styles.

A literary analysis of *Lessness*, even at the surface level, is only possible after some sort of linguistic analysis, but here the stylistician encounters the same initial problem that one faces with other late Beckett fictions: although the sentence is usually considered as a linguistic and narrative unit, the *Lessness* sentence is incomplete and not able to be expanded by the reader. In other elliptical prose, for example D. H. Lawrence's fiction, deletions of subjects and sometimes verbs are quite common (even becoming a writer's stylistic fingerprint), but there the deleted words appear in one or two preceding sentences, so that their substitution is "understood." In Beckett's sentences too much has been condensed, and we cannot retrieve the deleted segments by working back to earlier sentences. Without verbs we may only hypothesize about the link between potential subjects and objects; without commas we guess where phrase breaks are, how to parse the "sentence," and to which nouns or phrases a modifier attaches.

Thus each individual *Lessness* sentence lies open to many interpretations. The first one, for example, reads "Ruins true refuge long last towards which so many false time out of mind." One critic unfolds this into "Ruins are his true refuge at long last—the refuge towards which there have been so many false starts for time out of mind," and he justifies his addition of "starts" by noting that Beckett called two of his unpublished works "Faux départs."[5] This expansion seems reasonable enough, but because of the ambiguity inherent in such an elliptical and unpunctuated text, the "so many" could easily refer to people instead of to "false starts." If one uncompacts the fourth sentence and separates its phrases, the ambiguity problem multiplies: "Blacked out / fallen open / four walls / over backwards / true refuge [/ ?] issueless" (phrase divisions are mine). Here it becomes apparent that readers of *Lessness* experience most of the nouns they are given as objects (and most of the participles as predicate nominatives) for which he must supply both the subject and the verb. But is it the little body that has blacked out, or are the walls, usually white, blacked out? In the French, "éteint," the original of "blacked out," connotes colors (since "s'éteindre" means to fade), so that besides meaning that the walls are destroyed, this sentence can suggest that the white walls are turn-ing to grey. Looking forward in the text, we might judge that it is the light that is "blacked out," since "éteindre" also refers to the extinguishing of a light or the turning off of an electric switch. (This interpretation would link *Lessness* to the commutator in *The Lost Ones*.) If the walls have fallen over, then this provides a way out for the body. What, if not the enclosure, is issueless? Much depends on where the reader pauses between the words: if he reads "true refuge issueless" as a unit, then either the only true refuge is (paradoxically) one with no escape, or there is no true refuge; if he reads "true refuge / issueless" then "issueless" can refer back to some earlier noun. Maybe the body itself is issueless, having no children.

Reconstructing the sentences of *Lessness* is more difficult than paraphrasing a poem; indeed, many Beckett scholars interpret the language of *Lessness* as a strange form of poetry or music.[6] Working with the French texts, John Fletcher detects a "poetic and incantatory flavour" in *Bing* and *Sans*, "with their marked rhythms and steady beat in the diction," and he argues that "Beckett is evolving a new kind of French for his purposes."[7] Be-cause the same may be said of the English translations, a fruitful approach is to consider *Lessness* as a sample of another dialect, and to describe in linguistic detail the structure of this new lan-guage. The goal then becomes to discover how its grammar dif-fers from a grammar of English.[8] Moving far from English—away from Romance and Germanic languages—we find a parallel to the nominalized language of *Lessness* in the grammar of Sanskrit, in which the verb "to be" can always be omitted even when it means "exists." Understandably, Sanskrit compensates for this deletion with an abundance of nouns with the suffix "-ness";[9] similarly, many parts of speech in *Lessness* reduce to nouns, and many of its nouns end in -ness. This comparison with a Sanskrit feature raises a broader question: Which rules of standard English does Beckett break or bend, and why?

The obvious rules he ignores are the ones that govern stan-dard syntax: since most of the "sentences" in *Lessness* lack finite verbs, competent speakers of English would judge them to be grammatically incomplete (issueless). However, because Beckett clearly marks off syntactic units with capital letters and periods, we can examine the text at this pseudosentence level. Since the sentences were sequenced randomly, intentional unity and di-versity manifest themselves within and among the phrases instead. In particular, do the deletions, fragments, and unorthodox diction form any patterns? Do the anomalies of the prose together create a new syntax, a micro-grammar of their own? The most useful method of linguistic description for this piece (as for *Ping*) is to determine if at the phrase level a sample text demonstrates cohesion (lexical and syntactic), foregrounding, and cohesion of foregrounding.[10] Searching for patterns, words, or ideas that cohere, the stylistician notices immediately that in this piece Beckett exploits an unusual class of "lessness" words, that is, words containing the suffixes "-less" or "-lessness." These are "endless," "timeless," "issueless," "endlessness," and "changelessness," with "endlessness" appearing the most frequently (twenty-two times) and "changelessness" the least (twice). As a measure of the pervasiveness of "-less" visually, we can note that only two paragraphs out of twenty-four do not contain the bound morph "-less," and all the other paragraphs contain from one to four occurrences of "-less" or "-ness," in no apparent order except that paragraph seven with three usages of "endlessness" is followed by a paragraph in which "issueless" appears three times. This coherence of "issueless" in paragraph eight at first seems to correlate semantically with the sentence "Little body little block genitals overrun arse a single block grey crack overrun," since two of the sentences containing "issueless" frame this description of some destruction of procreative powers.

Yet we have just been making interpretive judgments while assuming a linear progression, even though we realize that the deceptive cohesion around "issueless" is accidental. Here and elsewhere in *Lessness*, the human mind manufactures logical connections when all it receives between sentences are random juxtapositions. Thus the reasoning in the paragraph above demonstrates the strong tendency of the reader to process a narrative sequentially, a reading behavior that Beckett is forcing us to suspend and a characteristic of narrative fiction that he is asking us to suspect. Instead, we are compelled to move back and forth, up and down, over and through the words in this text—visually, imagistically, linguistically—as we do when immersing ourselves in a poem.

Although haphazard sentence and paragraph juxtapositions allow for different reader reconstructions, we must remain within sentences and phrases to analyze conscious artistry—and therefore intentional meaning.[11] In the scope of a sentence, certain "lessness" words cohere with particular verbs in a regular pattern. While *Lessness* lacks present-tense verbs, it does contain past participles, such as "fallen," and present participles, such as "beating." The only past-tense verb is "was," and the few future-tense predicates all include the correct auxiliary "will." Precise grammar rules may be formulated for the verbal structures of *Lessness*, and more detailed stylistic description begins to approximate an interpretation. The word "was" in a sentence is usually preceded by "never" and followed (within a few words) by "timeless"; "never was *but* . . . timeless" implies that the environment was never anything except timeless, that is, was always timeless. We read: "Never was but grey air timeless no sound figment the passing light" (paragraphs 2 and 16); "Figment light never was but grey air timeless no sound" (paragraphs 4 and 15); and "Never was but grey air timeless no stir not a breath" (12 and 19). Based on these three samples, we can further generalize that "timeless" occurs after "grey air"; a grey atmosphere would be an atemporal zone, a "figment," like dawn and dusk, neither bright nor dark. Also, "timeless" always precedes a phrase of the form "no ———," and these phrasal constructions promote an accumulated sense of absence: no color, light, time, sound, or motion. That the first two sentences quoted differ by only the words "the passing" demonstrates "changelessness" in the vocabulary itself.

The future auxiliary "will" is linguistically bound to "endlessness"; that is, a sentence containing "will" usually contains "endlessness," for example: "In the sand no hold one step more in the endlessness he will make it" (paragraphs 6 and 14); and "It will be a day and night again over him the endlessness the air heart will beat again" (11 and 14). The word "again" with to "will" and "endless" forms a grammatical collocative set (a collection of items that are similar, such as bank, interest, and funds) since the notion of living anew ("heart will beat again") coheres semantically and syntactically with the expression of futurity. Some future tense sentences contain "again" but not "endlessness": "On him will rain again as in the blessed days of blue the passing cloud" (4 and 15); and "He will curse God again as in the blessed days face to the open sky the passing deluge" (3 and 24). In these two examples, the distant past is superimposed on the future with the phrase "as in the blessed days," and hence an infinite cycle results. Neither the deluge nor the cloud will pass, nor have they passed; rather, the present participle "passing" creates an action suspended in time, frozen in endlessness.

Paradoxically, Beckett describes the hours as passing in some sentences beginning with "never"; the hours pass only in a dream world, and thus "never" coheres with lexical items relating to a never-never land of the mind. Several sentences beginning "Never but" contain the word "dream": "Never but this changelessness dream the passing hour" (2 and 16); "Never but in dream the happy dream only one time to serve" (6 and 20); "Never but in vanished dream the passing hour long short" (7 and 19); and "Never but dream the days and nights made of dreams of other nights better days" (7 and 18). Also, two other sentences in this class link "never" to the general area of the imagination: "Never but silence such that in imagination this wild laughter these cries" (10 and 18), and "Never but imagined the blue in a wild imagining the blue celeste of poesy" (12 and 21). These linguistic associations are appropriate, and they constitute an important facet of imitative style in *Lessness*, since the cosmos of dreams and imagination exists outside time. By pairing particular verb tenses and words implying tense (like "never") with selected noun phrases, Beckett devises a syntactic/semantic pattern to undercut the effect of the verb tenses themselves. The past exists in an environment of "timeless," and the future occurs surrounded by "endlessness." Also, the construction "never but" is a self-contradiction: in most circumstances (for example, "Never [anything] but this changelessness . . ."), "never but" actually means "always." Locally the temporal aspects of the phrases cancel each other out; analogously, in the original sixty sentences Beckett alternates past- and future-tense expressions. Combined with numerous uses of "timeless," this creates a verbal situation in which chronological (and narrative) time freezes; the foregrounded word "changelessness" thus describes the text as a whole. Stasis without even the continuous present-tense marker of an on-going state suggests an analogy from physics, the distinction between potential and kinetic energy: the "little body" is a fetus, only a potential being, poised on the verge of action.

The binary nature of *Lessness'* temporal world of past and future tenses, of specific tenses paired with "timeless" or "endlessness," extends to almost every lexical and syntactic element of the piece. In fact, the key to the major cohesive pattern of *Lessness* may be found in the title itself: "less" signifies the negation of a quality (as in "colorless"), while the suffix "-ness" usually denotes the property or the quality of a preceding morpheme (as in "quickness"). "Lessness," then, means the quality of being less, or ultimately the condition of not being—the goal toward which so many Beckett characters struggle, in both their physical and verbal journeys. This extreme combination of opposites, the less-ness of the title, introduces a large set of oppositions throughout *Lessness*, including ultimately the tension between existence and death.

We first encounter the contradiction between ruins and refuge, and "all sides" and "endlessness," then visually, "blacked out" and "grey" contrast with "white" and "light." In "day and night," "long short," "old love new love," and "little void mighty light," the words of the phrases war against each other. "This wild laughter these cries" undercuts "no sound." In "He will curse God again as in the blessed days," "curse" tends to negate "blessed"; and later "blessed" incongruously occurs in the same sentence as "unhappiness." Imagistically and semantically, the "light of reason" contrasts with the "blue of poesy," setting up a dichotomy between rational thought and imaginative creation. In both *Ping* and *Lessness* the real (the actual setting and condition of the body) is further distinguished from the illusory (memories and dreams) by the absence of articles, "all the definite and indefinite articles being omitted in both works except for the incursions of past memories and dreams."[12] Thus, in *Lessness*, the dream of a future step is expressed by "He will stir in *the* sand there will be stir in *the* sky *the* air *the* sand" (my emphases), while a verbless (pseudopresent) sentence contains no "the"'s: "Grey sky no cloud no sound no stir earth ash grey sand."

Grammatically, besides the alternation of past tense and future tense, and the paradoxical construction "never but," Beckett chooses the equally self-cancelling phrase "all gone," and frequently goes to opposite extremes in quantifiers. The text repeats "all sides," "all white," "all light," but also "no sound," "no stir," "no cloud," Absolutes outnumber qualified statements: there are thirty-four "no"'s and thirty-eight "all"'s If we include and classify words like "only" and constructions like "not a ———," again the everythings and the nothings erase each other—even the two opposite temporal "figments," dawn and dusk. Equipped with linguistic tools for determining cohesion, the reader of *Lessness* is able to discover how certain aspects of the lexicon and the syntax operate together to convey the dominant preoccupations (we are not ready to say "themes" yet) of the piece. A next step in stylistic analysis is to identify fore-grounding, where the distinctive features of the author's style stand out against the verbal background, the norms of the language. But since in *Lessness* the norm means incomplete sentences, nominalization, and repetition, then any full sentence, verb phrase, or unique word immediately attracts the reader's attention. Usually all three conditions are met by the same structures, partly because an infrequent verb provides the only action in this otherwise static piece.

Of the few actions, the most prominent is the cursing of God, and of the lexical items the most shocking (and therefore the most memorable) is the overrun genitals, which implies infertility. (In the English, "genitals overrun arse a single block," "overrun" is ambiguous, but in the French, "parties envahies cul un seul bloc," "envahies" clearly modifies "parties.") The sentence beginning "He will curse God again" ends with "the passing deluge," and a lexically similar sentence starts "On him will rain again." Mentally gathering all these foregrounded elements, one cannot help but remember the story of Noah and the ark, which Beckett also incorporated into *Endgame*'s symbolic structure.[13] Beckett's language in *Lessness* faintly echoes the Biblical flood myth:

He will curse God again as in the blessed days face to the open sky the passing deluge. Little body grey face features crack and little holes two pale blue. Blank planes sheer white eye calm long last all gone from mind.

Figment light never was but grey air timeless no sound. Blank planes touch close sheer white all gone from mind. Little body ash grey locked rigid heart beating face to endlessness. On him will rain again as in the blessed days of blue the passing cloud. Four square true refuge long last four walls over backwards no sound. [Paragraphs 3 and 4]

The Old Testament God threatens a like desolation: "Behold I will bring the waters of a great flood upon the earth, to destroy all flesh, wherein is the breath of life, under heaven" (Gen. 6.17). In *Lessness* there is "No sound not a breath same grey all sides earth sky body ruins," a mythological disaster area similar to the devastation visited upon the Old Testament world: "And the rain fell upon the earth forty days and forty nights" (Gen. 7.12); "And all flesh was destroyed that moved upon the earth: and all men. And all things wherein there is the breath of life on the earth, died" (Gen. 7.21–22). The little body in *Lessness* is incapable of stirring, of taking one step, thus he suggests one of the unfortunate sinners left issueless after the flood, when the world becomes "mirrored earth mirrored sky" and earth and sky are as one (paragraph 1). If we construe "issueless" to mean without progeny, we may discern in the "he" an allusive reference to Canaan (the son of Ham) who was cursed by God because Ham saw his own father, Noah, naked. Noah's other two sons, Shem and Japheth, are blessed and told to increase and multiply, whereas Canaan is damned: "a servant shall he be unto his brethren" (Gen. 9.25). The "overrun genitals" results in the lessness of this character who may have "only one time to serve" (paragraph 6), and who will never produce issue. Also, if he himself cannot issue forth from the womb, then he is cursed by Beckett's unnamable god with the inability to end since he has not been truly born ("never was"). That all of Genesis concerns cyclic birth and death—a void, creation, destruction, rebirth, and renewal—makes it a perfect mythological home for Beckett's little body caught between nonbeing and being.

Helpful as it is, the Bible hardly explains all the foregrounded elements in Beckett's text. As we search for larger internal patterns, we find that besides the presence of an unusual or infrequent word like "genitals" in the foreground, the *absence* of a common word may be foregrounded and therefore significant. Many of the sentences' constituent noun phrases are minimal, and typically the grammatical units divide into rhythmic strings of discrete phrases stripped down to one adjective or quantifier paired with one noun, for example, "Grey sky / no cloud / no sound / no stir / earth ash / grey sand." Longer phrases may consist of a noun modified by an appositive or by a prepositional phrase (for example, "Legs a single block / arms fast to sides / little body / face to endlessness."), but in this condensed grammar sans articles and personal or possessive pronouns, the adjective-noun combination is most common. Within such a paradigm, one deviant construction (and therefore a foregrounded one) is the fragment "two pale blue." In every context, the noun "eyes" should logically follow, but the "eyes" have been deleted, as in for example, "Little body grey face features crack and little holes two pale blue" (3 and 20). Because of repetitious phrases, the missing eyes are never far from a singular "eye," so that immediately following this sentence we read: "Blank planes sheer white *eye* calm long last all gone from mind."

Since correspondences between adjacent sentences are purely the result of chance, however, it is more significant (again we remind ourselves) to look for associations among the phrases of individual sentences. There seems to be a correlation between touching and eyes in such clauses as "Face to white calm *touch close eye calm* long last all gone from mind" (9 and 17), and "Face to *calm eye touch close* all calm all white all gone from mind" (12 and 23, emphases mine). These sentences suggest the calm eye of another—different from the pale blue eyes of the little body—and therefore recall the black eye of *Ping* and look forward to the serene eyes of the vanquished in *The Lost Ones*.

An instance of what we might paradoxically call random foregrounding occurs in the last paragraph of *Lessness*: three consecutive sentences begin "little body." This visual and verbal parallelism encourages a comparison of the second segments in each sentence—"little block heart beating," "ash grey locked rigid heart beating," and "little block genitals"—which tend to associate the heart and the genitals as sources of life. Because of many-sided ambiguity, it is difficult to parse "grey crack overrun," but, however we interpret these phrases, a contrast between "beating" and "overrun" (and between strength and weakness) arises. These three very similarly constructed sentences form the prelude for the terminal sentence of the piece. Although the manuscripts and typescripts reveal no tampering with the ending, the final sentence appears to have been consciously chosen by a poet fully aware of emphatically conclusive sounds and senses. The word "dusk" is, semantically and phonetically, an ideal term for poetic closure: "Figment dawn dispeller of figments and the other called dusk."

The last step in a stylistic search is to look for cohesion of foregrounding, which elevates the reader to a higher level of linguistic description that seeks to correlate foregrounded elements and to align cohesive structures with the meaning of the whole. One frequent word in the text, "refuge," rhymes with, yet semantically opposes, the relatively rare word "deluge"; and two other infrequent words, "rain" and "reign," form an interesting phonetic pair. Hovering around the text's edges is the hope that it will rain again and that "unhappiness will reign again," as if the deluge *is* a refuge. As in Eliot's *Waste Land*, water in *Lessness* can both destroy and save, both drown and purify. By recalling the more general pattern of cohesion (binary opposition) and the most foregrounded element, the eyes—both present and absent—and then combining cohesion and fore-grounding, we can reach further strata of interpretation. Invoking the traditional eye/I pun spans the gap between linguistic description and critical analysis, and now the eye and the eyeless images translate into the oldest of universal dichotomies, life and death.

As in *Imagination Dead Imagine* and much of his other recent fiction, Beckett depicts in *Lessness* the timeless, changeless, endless world of man both before birth and after death. This extreme past and extreme future are symmetrical enough that the same descriptions portray the two states. In this double linguistic and physical environment a "little body" is both a fetus and a corpse; "four sides" determine a womb and a coffin. The calm eye defines the barrier between the self and the outside world, but the being in *Lessness* may never see this world: with his "legs a single block arms fast to sides" he may represent a fetus dying in the womb. To him birth and death are truly one, and he dies issueless because never born. Or Beckett may refer to the "lessness" of a being who "never was" because born dead—"Blacked out fallen open four walls over backwards true refuge issueless"—for whom the only true refuge is the mother. Beckett's earlier wanderer, Molloy, seeks the solace of his mother's room/womb, and the narrator of *Abandoned Work* expresses anger at the mother after she expels him from the shelter of her home. Beckett's more recent, lesser creature may be forced out from the mother before he is even ready to be born. Analogously, Beckett's language in his later styles is forced out as phrases, not ready to be delivered as mature sentences, expiring on the page before the sense fully lives.

Closed systems and confining structures have appeared throughout Beckett's works and with special emphasis in the late fiction. Besides symbolizing the womb and the grave simultaneously, these containers can represent the hermetically sealed mind, the isolated voice, and a microcosm within the macrocosm. In *Lessness* the "true refuge" continues the symbolism of Beckett's earlier enclosures, and the compacted language itself becomes both a haven and a prison. Discussing *Watt*, Lawrence Harvey notes that Knott's home is a "refuge" (*Watt*, p. 39), and that because of the etymology of the word (*re* means back and *fugere* means to flee] it implies a "retreat or flight back to the source. We are therefore hardly surprised to find figures of a return to the womb along with related images incorporating softness, warmth, darkness, or enclosure." [14] Of course, similar language may apply to a coffin. In Beckett's poem "Echo's Bones" the grave is the only real "asylum" (the first word of the lyric), and the opening sentences of *Lessness* introduce the same thought: [15] "Ruins [make up the?] true refuge long last. . . ." Between these two shelters is man's journey through the sands of time, an image used by Beckett in *Endgame*. The journey as a basic struggle for locomotion is inherent in the very phrases of *Lessness*.

Sooner or later many imagistic paths from *Lessness* and the other recent fictions converge in *Endgame*. Clov calls Hamm's shelter "the Refuge," sensing that it simultaneously serves as the beginning of life, the end of life, and man's shield from the outside world. Hamm predicts that in the future Clov will be a tiny figure in the void—a creature foreshadowing the little body in *Lessness*: "Infinite emptiness will be all around you, all the resurrected dead of all the ages wouldn't fill it, and there you'll be like a little bit of grit in the middle of the steppe" (*Endgame*, p. 36). This focus on the mind without dimension occurs in Beckett from *Murphy* to *Endgame*:

A mote in the dark of absolute freedom, a pebble in the steppe, a tiny plenum in the immensity of the void, something autonomous and separate from the void (as blind Hamm is a separate mote in the visual world), but *not separated from it by a wall*—such is the self in Beckett: something undefinable in space, something dimensionless, but *something* (we can call it consciousness), and something which, because it is dimensionless, exists outside the world of space and time and is by definition unattainable within that world. [16]

With his four walls falling over, and his world of endless greyness in a timeless state, the little body of *Lessness* reaches the end of life's game that Hamm could not attain. He also resembles the painter and engraver Hamm describes who looks out the window and sees only ashes (*Endgame*, p. 44), and this image explains the pervasiveness of "ash grey" in *Lessness*.

Considering the interpretation of *Lessness* possible from a stylistic analysis alone, plus the obvious associations between *Lessness* and *Endgame*, one is not surprised at Jerry Tallmer's review of the Cherry Lane production of the play. Recalling Hamm's line "something dripping in my head, ever since the fontanelles," he gives his vision of *Endgame*'s stage: "Imagine a foetus, doomed to be still-born, suspended in darkness in the amniotic fluid, its life not-to-be leaking away through the fontanelle—the membranous gap at the top of the skull of every human embryo."[17] Thus the analogous deluge, the literal set in *Lessness*, is microcosmic as well as macrocosmic; and the little body is cursing God for the "gift" of life just as Hamm condemns his parents. In this he recalls the narrator of *From an Abandoned Work* who also curses the deity, and who predicts that he will perish either by fire or by drowning. The world of *Lessness* already seems to have been destroyed by fire and to be awaiting destruction by water, returning us to the Noah story and its aftermath.

Lessness's creature is a later diminishment of Beckett's trilogy hero, a smaller Moran who, finding the fetal position intolerable, wants to lie supine: "When you can neither stand nor sit with comfort, you take refuge in the horizontal, like a child in its mother's lap" (*Molloy*, p. 192, my italics). In his cube, trying to stir, the little body shares the predicament of the Unnamable, whose protestations that he "can't stir" resound throughout that novel's ending. Preceding the Unnamable's physical disintegration and regression, Malone declares that he is "an old foetus, that's what I am now, hoar and impotent . . ." (*Malone Dies*, p. 51). Like Malone, the fetal character in *Lessness* will "never get born and therefore never get dead" (pp. 51–52). Molloy, in his journey toward lessness, is a comic precursor of the "issueless" little grey body with "genitals overrun": "I had so to speak only one leg at my disposal, I was virtually onelegged, and I would have been happier, livelier, amputated at the groin. And if they had removed a few testicles into the bargain I wouldn't have objected" (p. 47). Another passage in *Molloy* (significantly, with Biblical syntax and rhythms) contains verbal foreshadowings of *Lessness*'s language: "For what possible end to these wastes where true light never was, *nor any upright thing*, nor any true foundation, but only these leaning things, forever lapsing and crumbling away, beneath a sky without memory of morning or hope of night . . . (p. 53, my emphasis). Underneath a sky with only figments of dawn and dusk, the fallen over, issueless little body becomes Beckett's metaphor for the impotent artist—not able to issue forth more words. Voicing a desire for lessness, Molloy (speaking as character but also accurate as author) remarks, "The fact is, it seems, that the most you can hope is to be a little less, in the end, the creature you were in the beginning, and the middle" (p. 42).

Molloy and the "little body" find happiness only as constricted beings, like the static vanquished in *The Lost Ones*. One critical interpretation of the first sentence of *Lessness* ("Ruins true refuge long last towards which so many false time out of mind.") echoes the "abandon hope" theme pervasive in *The Lost Ones*: "The human being has lost himself time out of mind along false paths in pursuit of a calm haven. His greatest happiness comes with the greatest destitution."[18] The *Lessness* creature is without hope for a way out, and without the delusion that all is known; in this he is more fortunate than the searchers in *The Lost Ones*, less ignorant than the little body in *Ping*. He is blessed and yet cursed, unable to reach the absolute lessness of silence because he—like the "I" in *Texts for Nothing*—has no current existence.

Some Beckett readers lament that in *Ping* and *Lessness*, content has totally disappeared, leaving only repetition, rhythm, and word games; but instead, once again, in *Lessness* form *is* content. For a timeless world, Beckett has chosen a timeless zone between future verbs and past participles, where a still creature remembers and dreams but never lives in the present tense. Molloy, as self-conscious narrator, analyzes a similar stylistic problem: "My life, my life, now I speak of it as something over, now as of a joke which still goes on, and it is neither, for at the same time it is over and it goes on, and is there any tense for that?" (p. 47). For a changeless world Beckett repeats monotone greys for all objects, appropriately expressed in permutations of the form "X same grey as the Y" where X and Y are sand, earth, ruins, sky, air, or body; this interchangeability of nouns conveys linguistically the sameness of every natural feature. For an endless world Beckett exploits a pattern of repetition which could be extended, if not to infinity, then to an extremely large number. In a discussion of *Endgame* and the terror of endlessness in space and time, Colin Duckworth notes that "[t]he phenomenon of the sense of infinitude was studied by Freud under the term repetition: it has no boundaries (or is purely repetitive), moving nowhere."[19] This is precisely the situation of the creature in *Lessness*, with boundless freedom causing infinite fear. In a more recent play, *Footfalls*, May (a woman who hovers between being and nonbeing) repeatedly revolves "it all" in her cyclical speeches. Similar to the lesser, aborted body of *Lessness*, May asserts at the end of the play that she was "never there."

The frozen, nonlinear text of *Lessness* moves to no conclusion, the body trying to stir moves nowhere, and the reader decipher-ing repetitive sentences moves in circles. In one interpretation the creature is stymied by paradox just as the text is slowed by repetition.[20] With his "arms fast to sides" and "legs a single block," with "no hold" in the sand, and "on his back," the body tries vainly, ludicrously to take a step. This predicament, simi-lar to the "No way in go in" paradox of *Imagination Dead Imagine*, embodies the writer's situation, specifically Beckett's tests, trials, and challenges for himself as artist. By *Company* (1980), Beckett's narrator-as-writer is also lying "on his back," motionless in the dark, passively waiting for voices to speak to him. Beckett him-self in these recent texts increasingly becomes the helpless crea-ture with his arms fast to his sides who must paradoxically pick up his pen and write, who must go one pace further in the direc-tion of contemporary fiction. Like *Ping*, *Lessness* comments on its own composition: "One step more / one alone / all alone / in the sand / he will make it."

In many of Beckett's statements about himself as a writer, about creating, and about being in general, one image that re-curs evokes the fetal figure in *Lessness*. When asked, for ex-ample, why he turned to French, Beckett said to Lawrence Harvey, that "for him, an Irishman, French represented a form of weakness by comparison with his mother tongue. . . . The relative asceticism of French seemed more appropriate to the ex-pression of being, undeveloped, unsupported somewhere in the depths of the microcosm."[21] The four walls of the writer have fallen over in *Lessness*, leaving the little, undeveloped, "only up-right" body unsupported. More significantly, during interviews in 1961 and 1962 (the same time he was beginning these residual fictions in French), Beckett spoke of a sense of "being absent"; besides this feeling of "existence by proxy," there persisted "an unconquerable intuition that being is so unlike what one is standing up," an impression of "a presence, embryonic, un-developed, or a self that might have been but never got born, an *être manqué*."[22] In addition to the imagery of *Lessness*, images in two recent Beckett fictions derive from these recurrent personal metaphors: in *Company* the creature lying down is dependent on other creatures, on "devised devisers devising it all," to lend him existence; in *Ill Seen Ill Said* an undeveloped female protagonist is narratively born and vanished in repeated succession, and a potential male character is never fully formed. Beckett uses the same language to discuss writing that he uses to analyze existence; just as the self is an aborted being, so "the writer is like a foetus trying to do gymnastics."[23]

More than once Beckett has described the paradoxical situation of the modern artist: his problem is usually to find an adequate form in which to embody a subject as formless as consciousness. Beckett insisted in interviews that "there is a form, but it doesn't move, *stand upright*, have hands. Yet it must have its form. . . . It is a form that has been abandoned, left behind, a proxy in its place" (my emphasis).[24] He predicted that in the future some writer would conceive an appropriate form, a new "syntax of weakness." Both the author and his language have "fallen over," away from realism and from standard syntax. Fetal creatures crawling in the primeval mud of *How It Is* speak in spurts of "midget grammar," a related language of lessness. Thus the embryonic figure in *Lessness* serves as a metaphor for both the helpless writer, unable to "stand upright," and for his new "overrun" forms and styles.

After *The Unnamable*, Beckett spoke of having no way out to other kinds of fiction, of being issueless, impotent as a writer. He could not go on, could not stir, could not create:

> The kind of work I do is one in which I'm not master of my material. The more Joyce knew the more he could. He's tending toward omniscience and omnipotence as an artist. I'm working with impotence, ignorance. I don't think impotence has been exploited in the past. [. . .] My little exploration is that whole zone of being that has always been set aside by artists as something unusable—as something by definition incompatible with art.[25]

In earlier essays Beckett referred to the "issueless predicament of existence" as the only province of literature. Harvey takes this predicament to mean "man's need, which can never be abolished. He is a creature of voids that ache to be filled, of nothingness that yearns to be something."[26] Since human needs defy fulfillment, the best refuge is a situation of lessness—perhaps the lessness of not being born or, at most, the lessness of fewer desires, fewer possible notions, fewer expectations (like the vanquished in *The Lost Ones*). For *Lessness*, Beckett has found a new "syntax of weakness," and with it he has metaphorically described the condition of the writer in terms of the properties of language. Naturally, for many of the later fictions, Beckett has turned away from overweening Joycean sentence structure and toward the simple noun phrase as a minimal unit of composition: verbless, unattached, undeveloped, falling over ambiguously onto the next segment, the phrase marks the perfect compositional element with which to express the rudiments of being, from a writer who himself feels impotent and aborted in his expression. By writing about the impossibility of writing, with a syntax of weakness that becomes his new stylistic strength, he has again written himself out of an impasse.

10

Fizzles
Collapsing Language

Even after such a radical anti-narrative as *Lessness*, after many minimal stories and more condensed prose, Beckett had not yet reached a fictional end point. In 1972 he composed an innovative piece called "Still," which, like other experiments, produced a new temporary artistic impasse. One senses Beckett's exasperation with his own prose in his title for a project he had worked on through the 1960's, six short sketches called in French "Foirades" ("little farts"), translated between 1973 and 1975 as *Fizzles*. By 1975, Beckett stoically was trying "For to End Yet Again," which is the title of the last story in the *Fizzles* collection in English,[1] a piece that can serve as a coda to the "Foirades." Together these eight prose fragments (the six fizzles framed by "Still" and "For to End") demonstrate no clear stylistic progression—or regression; in fact, the series of texts as published does not reflect their order of composition, and the sequence varies in the French and in different English editions (see figure 3). From dates on the English manuscripts we learn that they were translated in the order Fizzles 7, 1, 4, 2, 6, 5, 3, 8; and if they are read in that sequence, which nearly parallels the order of the six original "Foirades," a vague outline emerges. Language collapses upon itself and upon the little creatures still struggling to make their paths through prose.

Fizzles combines imagistic and stylistic elements from early to more recent Beckett fiction, from *Murphy* to *Lessness* and *The Lost Ones*. Beckett began his career with the poem "Whoroscope," and the motions of the heavenly bodies also rule in *Murphy*,[2] showing that he was well read in both astrology and astronomy. Even in his unpublished first novel, "Dream of Fair to Middling Women," Beckett explored astral metaphors:

Much of what has been written concerning the reluctance of our refractory constituents to bind together is true equally of Belacqua. Their movement is based on a principle of repulsion, their property not to combine but, like heavenly bodies, to scatter and stampede, astral straws on a time-storm, grit in the mistral.[3]

Order in *Pour finir encore et autres foirades*	Headings on English Manuscripts	Dates on English Manuscripts		Published *Fizzles*
"Pour finir encore" (1975)	I	11/73	1	
"Immobile" (1975)	III	12/73	2	
I (= Fizzle 1)	VI	3/75	3	
II (= Fizzle 4)	II	12/73	4	
III (= Fizzle 2)	V	2/74	5	
IV (= Fizzle 6)	IV	Jan. 74–Aug. 74	6	
"Au loin un oiseau" (= 3)	Still	June–July 1972	7	"Still"
"Se voir" (= Fizzle 5)	Pour finir encore	Dec. 1975	8	"For to End" . . .

Fig. 3. Order and dates of translation of "Foirades" as *Fizzles*

By the 1960's, in fictions like *Imagination Dead Imagine*, Beckett's settings increasingly tended to resemble alien planets. In *Fizzles*, Beckett expands his galactic imagery, ventures new stylistic vehicles, and creates a few shining successes like "Still"—even though he himself judges them to be insignificant. Here imitative style displays itself in the pulsating rhythm and pacing of sentences, and in language that collapses upon itself. Each composition is a separate stylistic game, sometimes playing with language like that in *Texts for Nothing* when the linguistic and narrative impasse can be circumvented in no other way. However, Fizzles 1 through 6 (the original "Foirades") do form a progression if they are interpreted as rhetorical responses to the kind of stasis posited in "Still," which is published as Fizzle 7 but had been written before the first fizzle translations. In the six original fizzles the characters shake out their bodies once more and attempt to move in various ways—as Beckett the verbal traveller can never remain quite still. Examining them in their order of English composition illuminates some texts and reveals refracted light between others.

"Still", Fizzle 7, begins with an ironic weather report recalling the initial setting of *From an Abandoned Work*: "Bright at last close of a dark day the sun shines out at last and goes down." This first sentence verbally represents the stillness of the entire text in its stasis caused by verbatim repetition ("at last") and redundancy ("sun shines out" repeats "bright"). Many parts of speech are deleted in these condensed sentences, which are similar to— but not as minimal as—the phrases in *Lessness*. Often articles and the pronoun "I" are omitted, as in "[I] Even get up [in] certain moods and go stand by [the] western window . . ." (p. 47). Usually sitting still, a man follows the sun's semicircular path with his head and eyes, as the word "still" is repeated twenty-four times—the number of hours in a day, of course—reminding us of the sun's cycle. (A similar human sun is depicted in the late playlet *A Piece of Monologue*, where the old protagonist's dwindling life is likened to fading planetary light.) In fact, in Fizzle 7 the character's hand mimics the sun as it "rises" and then "hangs" as if inclined to "sink." Physical movements are described mechanically in "Still" as they are in *How It Is*, and all human positions are rendered angular and precise. Because the protagonist sits in a chair constantly facing south, he must turn his head ninety degrees to see the setting sun in the west. At all times arms are bent at right angles to lie along the armrest; legs are "broken right angles at the knees"; his trunk is straight and therefore at right angles to the thighs. In Beckett's later fictions, the characters, as well as the settings, become artificial constructs, almost machines (and sometimes word machines) as they retreat farther from being human. In "Still" the absence of pronouns, especially the expected "I," means that all the discrete body fragments never sum to a being who is undeniably present,[4] and we are left with merely the illusion of a protagonist.

Just as the sun only appears to revolve around the earth, but in fact is quite still, not everything is what it appears to be in "Still." All is "Quite quiet *apparently*" (my emphasis). The sky appears to grow dark "though of course no such thing just less light"; although the chair appears permanently situated south, it is in fact quite movable. The eyes open and close, but there is "no other movement any kind though of course not still at all." While the character appears static, "close inspection" (a phrase recurring from *The Lost Ones* and *Imagination Dead Imagine*) reveals that he trembles all over and his breast rises and falls with his breathing. Appearances are deceiving in the style of "Still" as well: its language gives the impression of absolute stasis because of numerous present-participle verbs (watching, staring, standing, sinking, fading) and the reiteration of the word "still" (seven sentences begin with some variation of "quite still"). The prose in general is stilled around certain stable repetitions. Also, reiterations of "here" and "same place same position," of "now" and "always," give the illusion of stillness in space and time; and recurrences of the adverbs "normally" and "again" (although they imply some action) also suggest a daily, regular cycle.

Nothing new under the sun, since the prose, as well as the man and the star, travels in a predictable orbit. Cycles and orbits operate within the style itself, where identical phrases reappear for the second and third descriptions of the armchair: always "in small upright wicker chair with armrests." And when the body undergoes its examination, the syntactic form as well as the figure's form stays in place as three consecutive sentences begin similarly: "Legs side by side . . . ," "Trunk likewise . . . ," "Arms likewise . . . ," (p. 48). The narrator himself calls attention to the cyclical quality of his descriptions of the hand with the self-mocking use of "etc." and "ditto": "[hand] hangs there trembling as if half inclined etc."; "thumb on outer edge of right socket index ditto." Aurally too a sameness prevails when vowels are echoed within a phrase, as in "quite still till quite dark," which has cadence as well as assonance.

Yet the language, apparently still, does move somewhat as subtle modulations make the prose tremble. Semantic shifts occur when various denotations and connotations dwell within the repeated words: for example, "still," among its other meanings, can measure degree, as in "less light still" (compare "even less light"). Thus we have difference underneath apparent sameness as the reiterated "still" adapts to its varied linguistic contexts. The title word never stays still, recurring everywhere as a different part of speech: "Here an adverb, here an adjective, here a noun, the word is shifty and unstable: the tenuous morpheme offers us both density and imprecision of meaning."[5] At times the prose oscillates between two possibilities—"such as tree or bush," "if near if far," "starlight or moonlight or both" and "now more now less"—with a kind of binary rhythm (the same binary opposition that linguistic analysis unlocks in *Lessness*); and many sentences begin with a marker of larger possibilities, "Or . . . ." Within other phrases, either oxymoronic or more simply internally inconsistent, the words move and bump against each other semantically: "eyes stare out unseeing," the hands are "clenched lightly" on the armrests, and at the end the man tries "listening to the *sounds* all quite *still*" (my emphasis). Thus the semantics and syntax of the piece are as paradoxical as its content.

However much he is a picture of stasis, the character does turn his head and move his arm. We view a series of snapshots or "stills" which, when flipped through quickly (like sketches for cartoons), magically produce the illusion of movement. That this creature resembles a cartoon robot, with interchangeable parts, is suggested in an almost comic remark on the connections among bodily motions, when the right hand "leaves the armrest taking with it the whole forearm complete with elbow. . . ." Also, the term "deasil" to indicate a right turn adds to the mechanical, scientific atmosphere. We even witness a melodramatic and humorous instant replay of the suspended hand, as if a film is being run backwards: "Here back a little way to that suspense before head to rescue . . ." (p. 50). The final *tableau vivant* is staged in language recalling the conclusion of *Imagination Dead Imagine* ("Leave it so all quite still. . . ."), as both protagonist and reader are at rest, listening for a sound. And the piece closes reverberating with three meanings of its title word: no change over time (the character still sitting), no movement (sitting still), and no sound (stillness).

Many of these stylistic features are explained by a condition of the narrative task at hand: Beckett is attempting to depict very subtle and cyclical movements of a character through slight shifts in prose. "Still" presents a near static world in a near static style: what minimal movement is possible occurs in fragmented phrases and in slow motion, in the illusion of change produced by successive frames, like the juxtaposition of images effecting progression in lyrical poetry—sans logical connectives. Under the burden of transposing the kinetic into the verbal, syntax sometimes breaks down. Particularly in a sentence where the narrator explicitly states the impossibility of his linguistic challenge, the syntax bears the strain: "Quite still then all this time eyes open when discovered then closed then opened and closed again no other movement any kind though of course not still at all when suddenly or so it looks this movement impossible to follow let alone describe" (p. 49). Either absolute stillness is impossible, or it is impossible to capture in language.[6] And of course, this analogy between slight movements in the arm and a minimal expression of them is compounded because the very motions of characters in Beckett's prose become metaphors for his journeys through language. With "Still" the author is giving us a clue about how minutely and carefully the reader has to observe the text in the recent fictions; "close inspection," stylistic analysis, is increasingly essential.

That an extreme image of stasis fascinated Beckett is demonstrated by his repeated returns to it in variations on the same piece, in the unpublished *Sounds* and *Still 3* (what John Pilling terms the "redactions" of "Still"[7]) and in the two-page-long "As the Story Was Told." This recursive little story (1973) places a first-person persona in the same upright chair as the one in "Still" and situates it within the same summer-house appearing in the later fiction *Company* (1980): "At the centre, facing the coloured panes, stood a small upright wicker chair with armrests, as against the summer-house's window-seat. I sat there very straight and still, with my arms along the rests, looking out at the orange light."[8] This "I" in a hut is conflated with a "he," an old dying man being tortured in a tent, who may of course represent the author himself never able to formulate the correct narrative ending: "But finally I asked if I knew . . . what exactly was required of the man, what it was exactly that he would not or could not say. No, was the answer, after some hesitation, no, I did not know what the poor man was required to say, in order to be pardoned. . . ." Beckett too could not yet find silence and was required to go on with fiction.

Fizzle 1 (Foirade I) posits a creature able to move again, and thus Beckett's stories continue the vacillation expressed at the end of *The Unnamable*: "I can't go on" for the fetus in *Lessness*; "I'll go on" for the protagonist of Fizzle 1. Fizzle 1 presents a familiar figure, apparently named Murphy,[9] walking in a bent position like the man in *Enough* through tunnels which are extensions of those in *The Lost Ones*. In the searchers' cylinder, light was literally blinding, but in these tunnels the gloom is too dense to be pierced, so that the protagonist has taken to closing his eyes. At random moments his world may increase grow bright—"the way, the ground, the walls, the vault" (p. 9); the mysterious light source recalls the rotunda in *Imagination Dead Imagine*. Thus the suspicion that Fizzle 1 (not Beckett's most successful fiction) is a fragmented recycling of his earlier works arises in the reader's mind, even without the explicit mention of Murphy. The piece starts with Cartesian man demonstrating to himself that he exists, trusting in the empirical data to be gathered through the sense of touch. Here also is another suffering Christ figure, the artist/martyr, who now has little bloody wounds—reminiscent of the jabs of the can opener in *How It Is*. His pace is so slow that "the little wounds have time to close before being opened again"; in fact, his walk can be frozen in midstride, in a tableau anticipating "Still." Perhaps Beckett as tortured artist needs a respite of healing between each infliction of the pain that writing causes. His alter ego continues a slow and self-conscious journey:

He halts, for the first time since he knows he's under way, one foot before the other, the higher flat, the lower on its toes, and waits for a decision. Then he moves on. . . . he must often, namely at every turn, strike against the walls that hem his path, against the right-hand when he turns left, the left-hand when he turns right, now with his foot, now with the crown of his head. . . . [P. 8]

The motifs of pacing and halting, and of footsteps breaking the silence, prepare the creative ground for the play *Footfalls*, which was to come years later. Moving on, as Beckett moves on artistically, the fizzled pacer "makes his first steps for quite a while before realizing they are merely the last, or latest." Stylistically, the writer imitates his character as he strikes against the walls of language that hem his artistic path, writing in parenthetical qualifications amid many commas, thwarted at every linguistic turn. He proceeds hesitantly through accumulation—phrase by phrase from his initial clauses. Beckett thus provides a metaphor for his own career as a stylist: lately he is narrating by accretion—detail by detail from his earlier fiction.

This new quasi-Murphy lives in the old Beckettian binary world of extremes—of a mind imprisoned in a body, of hills and valleys, of light and darkness, of right and left turns. And Beckett, true to his quest for imitative style, writes of this universe with an ebb and flow of opposites that determines the rhythm of his sentences. The character's hands grope "back and forth" over his body; his feet rub "up and down" his legs. (Beckett substituted "up and down" for "along" in revising from the manuscript to the first typescript, and this and other changes heightened a style of opposites.[10]) Even his clothes, "espousing and resisting the movements of the body, coming unstuck from the damp flesh and sticking to it again," participate in the "x and un-x" structure of the phrases. All this occurs in a silence punctuated with sudden sounds. Indeed, the entire history of the character's life is reconstructed in terms of Giordano Bruno's "maxima and minima" (also used in *Imagination Dead Imagine*),[11] such as "the straightest narrow, the loudest fall, the most lingering collapse . . ." (p. 13). These compressions may represent molecular changes of a dying planet or the fall of a meteor through a galaxy: "The only sounds, apart from those of the body on its way, are of fall, a great drop dropping at last from a great height and bursting, a solid mass that leaves its place and crashes down, lighter particles collapsing slowly" (p. 11). Originally Beckett had "matter" for "particles," both words indicating the context of physics and affirming that for "body" we can read "astronomical body," which returns us to the characterization of Belacqua as a star cluster in "Dream of Fair to Middling Women" quoted at the beginning of this chapter. Yet these scientific events are rendered in poetic language that is almost incantatory, with the cadence and repetition of "a great drop dropping at last from a great height." In *Molloy*, Beckett had also spoken lyrically of a contracting world: "I listen and the voice is of a world collapsing endlessly, a frozen world . . ." (p. 49). In the fictions of the sixties and seventies (especially these starlike Fizzles) he has created those worlds in phrases that themselves linger and then collapse slowly.

Language in general swells and contracts in Fizzle 1 as, in a stylistic expansion of clauses like those in *Texts for Nothing*, Beckett layers on qualifications, digressions, and self-contradictions. Here again a sentence that begins as a descriptive statement ends by erasing itself, tracing the arc of its own indecision. A method of prose analysis invented by Francis Christensen, showing modifiers within hierarchies of subordination, can allow a reader to visualize how Beckett's clauses extend, yet simultaneously demolish, each other.[12] In terms of Christensen's diagramming model—using number 1 for the main clause (the "kernel") and a higher number for each level of modification—a typical long sentence in Fizzle 1 would look like this:

[1] Then for a time his zigzags resume their tenor,
   [2] deflecting him alternately to right and left,
      [3] that is to say bearing him onward in a straight line
         [4] more or less,
         [4] but no longer the same straight line as when he set forth,
            [5] or rather as when he realized he was forth,
               [6] or perhaps after all the same. [P. 10]

No surprise then that the character wonders of his journeys, "Or will they cancel out in the end." The reader wonders whether the fizzles will be deflected and undercut down to nothing. With his many qualifiers and modifiers ("from time to time," "one after another," "each time a little weaker, no, sometimes louder than the time before") the Fizzle 1 narrator contains within himself dialogue echoing the two *Godot* tramps as they imagine aloud and contradict each other to fill the silence. Since the protagonist wears too-short too-tight pants, this recollection of the tramp is not unwarranted.

Despite the purgatorial atmosphere of Fizzle 1 and its mazelike setting, its tone is neither altogether somber nor single-mindedly scientific. The narrator revels in a serpentine syntax recalling that in *The Lost Ones* ("The air is so foul that only he seems fitted to survive it who never breathed the other, the true life-giving, or so long as to amount to never"), and this gives him a stuffy persona, but his garrulousness and sense of humor bring back his charm. Realistically, he takes stock of both body and mind and comically concludes, "No sign of insanity in any case, that is a blessing. Meagre equipment, but well balanced" (p. 10). As in *Texts for Nothing* and *Enough*, plays on words multiply when figurative language is taken literally: ". . . nothing like a ray of light, from time to time, to brighten things up for one." Trying to provide two examples of minima which are "unforgettable, on days of great recall," the first fizzler never finishes: "Or again, second example, no, not a good example" (p. 14). His last sentence ("So with one thing and another little by little his history takes shape . . .") is a summation beginning with "so," like the section endings of *The Lost Ones*, and it implies that his story could go on forever—with "fresh elements and motifs," he says, mocking the traditional novelist's art of orchestrating complex subplots and themes.

Foirade II, Fizzle 4, begins with the defeatist statement "I gave up before birth," and other paradoxes concatenate to the point of absurdity: "it's impossible I should have a voice, impossible I should have thoughts, and I speak and think, I do the impossible, it is not possible otherwise" (p. 31). The type of gallows humor Beckett developed for *Texts for Nothing* continues in this piece (which could easily have been one of the thirteen texts). Using a rhetorical maneuver called *occupatio*, the narrator mentions all the things he will not mention: "that will be the end, I won't go on about worms, about bones and dust, no one cares about them, unless I'm *bored* in his dust, that would surprise me, as *stiff* as I was in his flesh . . ." (p. 32, my emphasis). Along the way, of course, he manages to play on the cliché "bored stiff" and "stiff" meaning corpse. Beckett not only creates puns, but also puns on the very idea of punning (a self-reflexive joke he began as early as *Murphy*). Charles Krance speculates that "the reason for this lies in the etymology of the term: to *pun* is a variant of the verb to *pound*, and its original meaning is that of compacting a substance. By punning on, or comically mistreating, the notion of the pun and by extension, that of the increasing compactness of his own writings," Beckett is opening new time-space "apertures." [13]

Because of the "stiff" pun and other mortal references, death becomes more prominent in Fizzle 4 than in Fizzle 1, as the protagonist returns to a fond wish of *Abandoned Work's* narrator that he could drown. Yet even his death wish is perishing, since now the "he" is driven, compelled by the "I"—as Beckett is urged forward artistically by incessant mental whispers. This hypothesis resonates from the final, *Texts for Nothing*–like litany, a rhythmic passage that can be read as a choral refrain, with the even lines commenting on the odd:

> He'll come to a place and drop,
> why there and not elsewhere,
> drop and sleep,
> badly because of me,
> he'll get up and go on,
> badly because of me,
> he can't stay still any more,
> because of me,
> he can't go on any more,
> because of me . . . [P. 33]

After this the "I" will feed the "he" once more, as an inner voice "feeds" the writer; and Beckett as artist can go on. Many years and several fictions later Beckett's narrator continues to judge that he performs "badly," imagines and writes badly, in *Ill Seen Ill Said*.

Fizzler 1 predicts that "someday he'll see himself," and the prophecy is indirectly fulfilled in Fizzle 2 (Foirade III) when the next character, who usually resists being viewed and had remained secluded for years, decides, "Now I would resume that inspection." Consequently, Fizzler 2 has a friend, named Horn, visit at night and read him notes about his personal history. Since the listener receives his information in the dark, Beckett plays on the meaning and etymology of "elucidation" when he writes, "I thought I had made my last journey, the one I must now try once more to elucidate . . ." (p. 21). "Horn" recalls the horn on the old RCA Victrolas, and because he transmits stored information, the chronicler resembles a human tape recording machine. This third foirade thus becomes a hybrid of *Malone*

Dies and *Krapp's Last Tape* as the hero lies in bed replaying his past. Dramatically, this image eventually materialized on the stage in *Ohio Impromptu* (1981), where a Reader reads to a Listener about a past couple who had read aloud. The premise of *Film* also unfolds here, as the protagonist attempts to hide his face but knows that soon he will allow himself to be seen. Horn *does* let himself be inspected, and his fading face haunts the narrator: "It is in outer space, not to be confused with the other, that such images develop" (p. 21). He argues that closed lids can "banish" such specters; but "as we shall see," puns the narrator, closing one's eyes does not solve the problem, presumably because the mirrors of imagination and memory (inner space) succeed when the physical eyes fail. Thus the narrator perceives the remembered face of Horn more clearly when the real face (in "outer space," a phrase also propelling us far from the confines of our galaxy) merges into shadow. Just as the Unnamable cannot elude his projected characters, and Krapp can never outdistance his past voices, this narrator never escapes the gravitational force of his imagined selves.

For the style of Foirade III (Fizzle 2), Beckett shifts from a distant, third-person history to an immediate first-person memory; from mostly long, meticulous sentences (Fizzle 1) or a lengthy sentence with numerous commas (Fizzle 4) to very short sentences and fragments, with more playful language and less complex syntax. Like Malone, this narrator transforms the commonplace into the alien when he stares at "some such unbroken plane as that which I command from my bed, I mean the ceiling" (p. 21). He occasionally enjoys ludicrously correct, pedantic phrasing: "I thought I had made my last journey . . . the one from which it were better I had never returned" (pp. 21–22). Making a game of speech, the narrator asserts that he had "come to bear everything bar being seen," and highlights a ritualistic, formulaic "five or six" for both the years since the events and the minutes of Horn's visit.

Most important, this narrator is acutely conscious of words that mark chronology, using terms like "now," "then," "before," and "after" so "that we may feel ourselves in time." In fact, though, the concepts of before and after lose meaning because in this recursive world there can be no *last* journey; consequently, he laments near the end of the piece that, "the feeling gains on me that I must undertake another" (p. 22). In revisions to the original manuscript, Beckett added the phrases "again" and "once more" to stress the narrator's recycling behavior.[14] And these infinite cycles, like those in *Endgame* and *How It Is*, are frightening and oddly constraining, for the same reason that the boundless, endless sands of *Lessness* were paralyzing. Man is just a white speck lost in infinite whiteness, a bit of grit in the vast steppe; and a discontinuous fizzle style floats us in an imagined outer space where there are no time coordinates, moving closer to the void.

Foirade IV, Fizzle 6, returns to the quasirealistic world and to the themes of Foirade II, Fizzle 4, as the narrator again desires to end life's journey, to be covered by the "old earth" that has rejected him earlier. Through the metaphor of the beetles called cockchafers—who grow in the earth for three years ("those the moles don't get"), devour foliage for two weeks, and then disappear—the protagonist mourns the brief and meaningless life of man. Accurate about the biological facts on cockchafers (related to the smaller species familiarly called June beetles), Beckett intersperses in Foirade IV many details about their development: that numerous buried grubs are eaten before adulthood, that the adults are attracted to light, and that they eat in the evening and hide during the day. Indeed, Beckett even metamorphoses his human narrator into one of these insects momentarily: "I come home at nightfall, they take to wing, rise from my little oaktree and whirr away, glutted, into the shadows. I reach up, grasp the bough, pull myself up and go in" (p. 43). Even if the narrator does not inhabit the oak tree, identification between him and the beetles arises through a sentence in Italian which is missing in *Fizzles* but occurs in *Foirades* after "shadows": "Tristi fummo ne l'aere dolce" (p. 45). The Italian line was in the same location in the first and second English manuscripts. By the first typescript we get an English translation, "Sad we were in the sweet air,"[15] but its absence in the published version shows Beckett's continuing artistic contraction. The correct Italian sentence, "Tristi fummo/ nell'aer dolce" (*Inferno*, VII, 121–22), is spoken by Dante's bitter sinners who had forfeited earthly happiness; recollections that the dying cockchafers head for the river serve to trigger thoughts of the narrator's earlier loved ones. Like the hero of *How It Is* (who as a Dantesque sinner remembers those "above in the light"), he forms memory-images in the clouds— "see the sky, a long gaze, but no, gasps and spasms, a childhood sea, other skies, another body" (p. 44)—and simultaneously generates aural patterns with echoing /s/ and /g/ sounds and the repeated "other." Despite the serious tone which frames Foirade IV, the narrator does have some fun with language in between: he remembers his past with ". . . happiness too, yes, there was that too, unhappily." Later, echoing the "I" of *Texts for Nothing*, he humorously criticizes his own style: "Ah to love at your last and see them at theirs, the last minute loved ones, and be happy, why ah, uncalled for" (p. 44).

At the close he is standing by a window gazing at the sky, in an attitude similar to the character's position in "Still": "Simply stay still," he tells himself. Concerns about going on with fiction, the "little panic steps" of Fizzles 3 and 4, are eventually quieted, and in Fizzle 5 (Foirade V) instead of jagged phrases separated by commas, we read condensed, sometimes two-word, "sentences"—actually phrases and clauses punctuated solely with periods. In its rhythm of short segments this piece resembles *Ping*, but in its longer sentences, its overall syntax, and its tone it has closer affinities to *The Lost Ones*: "Sum the bright lots. The dark. Outnumbered the former by far" (p. 38). Similarities between the two pieces are so numerous and pronounced that Fizzle 5 (translated from "Se Voir" in 1974) could have been an offshoot of *The Lost Ones* (finished in 1971); in both works the setting consists of three concentric circles with an "arena" in the center. In Fizzle 5 a narrow track separates a central arena from an outer ditch, with a void extending beyond the ditch. This arena holds millions of beings moving and still, who neither see nor touch each other. All along the ditch are millions of small square lots (called "zones" in *Foirades*) and in each lot lies a body diagonal or curled, like the figures in *Imagination*'s dome. The entire arrangement circumscribes a "closed place," parallel to a closed system thermodynamically, which (appropriately, according to the law of entropy) is running down. "In the beginning," says the narrator, echoing Genesis, all the lots were bright, but now most are dark. The dead leaves of the track dry and crumble into dust as they would during a "heat death" of the universe. Perhaps we are metaphorically located on the moon, where the force of gravity is six times less than on earth; analogously, the bodies in the lots "appear six times smaller than life." It is more likely, however, that this piece again pictures inner not outer space. In the tight circumference of a work of fiction, the laws of the arena operate: "There is nothing but what is said. Beyond what is said there is nothing" (p. 37). Thus Beckett represents the three zones of the old Murphy's mind in a new form, and simultaneously depicts the imagination of the artist and of the reader.

So completely is the reader fixed in a creator's mind in the fizzles that each sentence progresses exclusively from the possibilities and necessary consequents generated by its predecessor, in a style of narrative necessity that Beckett would perfect later in *Ill Seen Ill Said*. Thus the fiction consists of step-by-step blueprints for its fabrication, enacting a trend in contemporary literature that Umberto Eco describes in his study, *The Role of the Reader*: "How to produce texts by reading them." [16] Fizzle 5 contains no preconceived arena; rather, each detail of the story is imagined (known), then written, then accepted as given, then elaborated on—to be reconstructed in the reader's mind. "All needed to be known for *say* is known" (my emphasis). This odd usage of "say" transforms it into a noun with the meaning of "the saying of it," "the voicing of it." Later we encounter a piece of causal reasoning still more revealing: "This is known *because* it needs to be said" (p. 37, my emphasis), which implies that if a detail should follow a description then it must be known, created, on the spot. Other streams of artistic logic flow from descriptions in process: "The ditch seems straight. Then reappears a body seen before. A closed curve *therefore*" (p. 38, my emphasis). All these phrases imply an inexorable momentum of the imaginative process. Once a circular ditch is established, other plausible consequences are imagined into being with sentences of synchronous composition: "The track follows the ditch all the way along. [emended to] All the way round. [separate areas are demarcated] It is on a higher level than the arena. [made more precise] A step higher. [Now the imagination starts to envision, to create.] It is made of dead leaves. [Oh no, a natural detail.] A reminder of beldam nature [a mocking narrator]" (p. 38). Beckett teases his faithful readers with this hint that gone is the place of realistic, especially Romantic, fiction; we are now encapsulated in the "closed place" of metafiction.

While time moves too slowly in Foirades I and III, it races in the fifth foirade in the French collection, "Au loin un oiseau" and so do the lives of human beings (Fizzle 3, "Afar a bird" in English). For this last old man, "day dawns, he has only to raise his eyes, open his eyes, he merges in the hedge, afar a bird, a moment past he grasps and is fled . . ." (p. 26). In the original manuscript the final clause in the passage above appeared as "the time he takes to watch and he's gone," [17] where the second "he" ambiguously identifies both man and bird and thus emphasizes the transitory nature of both. Fizzle 3 consists of one long string of phrases separated by commas with no final period; here style imitates content as the words run by in "little panic steps." Like the creature in *How It Is*, fizzler 3 physically and verbally takes ten steps and then stops to breathe. However, instead of crawling, this new traveller walks bowed over a (writing?) stick, recalling earlier Beckett wanderers. Because of these correspondences and Fizzle 3's other images, the split self now suggests father and son, as in *Abandoned Work* (Balfe the roadman makes a reappearance here), or youth and old age, as in *Enough*; but it is more likely that the "I" again represents the mind and "he," the body, as they did in *Texts*. Beckett lends a spatial dimension to the mental voice—"I'll be inside, nothing but a little grit"—and the notion that the "I" dwells inside is repeated five times in three different tenses. The body is born and dies while the mind feeds the head, supplies it with people, places, and phantoms—all that it needs to create. Once more two halves of the composing self are imaginative thought and physical writing, inner voice and outer hand. Finally, he/I parallels author/character ("he seeks a voice for me") and when conjoined forms Beckett's self-conscious narrator.

Like the split selves (inner and outer spaces) of *Texts for Nothing* and *The Unnamable*, the "I" of Fizzle 3-VI lives a now-familiar paradox: he must keep going in order to stop, keep talking in order to be still. Therefore it is natural that this fizzle exploits paradoxical language in the classical form of "I can't go on, I'll go on," as in, "it's impossible I should know, I'll know." Echoing motifs and phrases from the earlier-composed Fizzle 4, including the contradictory "I gave up before birth," Fizzle 3 recapitulates 4 just as some of the texts in *Texts for Nothing* repeat and reply to each other in musical variation. Ironically, the narrator discusses terminal distances and last phantoms even though there is no end to the physical or verbal journeys; typographically there is no final period for his spurt of words. This sixth foirade circles back on itself with the echo, near the conclusion of the piece, of its first phrase "ruinstrewn land," thus forming its own closed system of fiction. The stillness of silence produces one sort of ending, but since *Fizzles* promises no "last journey," and since the still creature is still listening for a sound, the writer must conclude again. In the last piece of the volume, "For to end yet again," the title phrase begins sentences one and three, and introduces the theme of the text, a central concern of Beckett's fiction since *The Unnamable*. In order to stop once more, the writer must, paradoxically, start once more, thus the first sentence of Fizzle 8 ends with "to begin" and its second sentence starts "Long thus to begin." Between these phrases and the phrase "yet another end" in the conclusion, Beckett employs many words indicating finality ("in the end," "its last state," "last ——— of all," "of a last end"), but undercuts this sense of completeness with repeated implications of restarts or continuations ("first change of all," "still," "again"). Each new sentence, each new image moves Beckett closer to, yet farther from, an ending.

For this last piece, an apocalyptic lamentation after six fizzles, the setting slides from the inner space of the skull to the outer space of the universe, all in an underworld that is part mythological and part Christian. Literally, the action consists of two white dwarves carrying monstrous parts of bodies on a litter to their final resting place. Symbolically, this grey world borrows from the *Inferno's* atmosphere of "starless air," of "air forever dark," and describes a Dantesque limbo "of those nor for God nor for his enemies." Since these hollow men are on a litter described as if it were a boat, perhaps the bodies are getting a ride from Charon across the Acheron River. Or maybe it is the River Lethe we are crossing, since the stretcher is "the dung litter of laughable memory." Also, the litter of memory conveyed by dwarves of Habit (their brows show "the bump of habitativity or love of home") enacts the theories on memory that Beckett expressed in *Proust*. Figuratively, Fizzle 8 develops a time-lapse photograph of human life from dust to dust, *Godot's* forceps astride the grave once more. Its creature, less than a human being, again combines both fetus and corpse; echoes of *Lessness*, with its fetal being, resonate throughout: "grey sky," "cloudless," "timeless," "little body," "ruins of the refuge," and "not a breath."[18] He is "expelled" from his shelter in birth like the character in Beckett's early story "The Expelled": "First change of all a fragment comes away from mother ruin and with slow fall scarce stirs the dust" (p. 58). In his last change the expelled one falls but still breathes, and keeps his blue eyes open, recalling the white body in *Ping*. Its final state is a "sepulchral skull" where it dwells unsure whether this is truly the end, or whether there is yet another level of earth and sky through which to descend.

Beckett in 1975 could certainly have been asking the same question of his prose, viewing himself with each last fizzle or fiction as an artistic intelligence that valiantly "makes to glimmer again in lieu of going out." Therefore he places his final persona amidst the dust remaining from the "haughtiest monuments" of his past work, in a story that reads like stage directions for autobiographical drama, a play like *That Time*. Fizzle 8 starts with stage set, props, and lighting instructions: "For to end yet again skull alone in a dark place pent bowed on a board to begin. Long thus to begin till the place fades followed by the board long after" (p. 55). Language that could serve as directions for lighting continues the drama metaphor ("By degrees less dark till final grey or all at once as if switched on") as Beckett recreates his mental theater. The minimal climactic action of this dramatic narrative, a fall of the little body, is depicted with geometric precision so that it can be envisioned and perhaps theatrically reproduced: "Feet centre / body radius / falls unbending as a statue falls / faster and faster / the space of a quadrant" (p. 59, my divisions). This little body, the impotent writer again, reincarnates the creature in *Lessness* who cannot stand or stir and prefigures the man lying flat on his back in *Company*, the next glimmer to appear after *Fizzles*.

The Beckett-like narrator writes not so much for readers of a narrative as for directors or observers of a play or film, so aware is he of what can be perceived and from what (camera?) angle. Throughout Fizzle 8 phrases about vision are insistent: "as far as eye can see," "invisible to any other eye," "seen from above," "[two dwarves] so alike the eye cannot tell them apart," "bird's-eye view," "so soft the eye does not see them go," and "strain as it will the eye achieves no more than two tiny oval blanks." This last clause implies that the two eyes see only themselves. Beckett's obsession with an outsider's eye suggests a watchfulness, a self-consciousness as author; his own blue eyes look beyond the external world to his artistic process and his own product as he writes about writing. Increasingly, both writer and reader must observe with eyes of the imagination, for Fizzle 8 places us in yet another metafictional world devoid of logical reasoning or physical causality: the little body falls as if pushed by a hand, yet there are no other humans present; or as if forced by the wind, yet there is "not a breath."

So we reside in the writer's creative center; and given the language of Fizzle 8, for "skull" one may read "star," as in, "Thus then the skull makes to glimmer again in lieu of going out." This description suggests a nova explosion in which an old star collapses gravitationally and then explodes leaving a small remnant, or fizzle, of itself. Curiously, Beckett described himself as a star, in a complaint about his writing's progress: "If I don't get away by myself now and try to work, I'll explode, or implode." [19] Besides demonstrating that Beckett knew astronomical terms, this statement recalls those he made before *Lessness* about the impotent writer linked to his aborted forms; both character and writer are fetal, unable to stand upright. Implosion offers an exciting metaphor for Beckett's later fictions as well as for the author himself, since imploded stars have a much greater density, analogous to the condensed style of some fizzles (stars). The "first change" of Fizzle 8's "little body," the birth of a star, may result from a large mass of gases condensing, falling in upon the center, imploding. One of the last stellar changes, beginning the end of a star, is the white dwarf stage. An alternating, pulsating rhythm echoing astral movements is present even in the shapes of Beckett's sentences depicting the "carriage immemorial" (the "ageless carriers" in the first typescript,[20] that is, the two white dwarves), since "as one they advance as one retreat hither thither halt move on again." The verbal series here alternates between verbs of motion and those depicting slowing or cessation of motion. Over millions of years, stars diminish in size and intensity to become black holes, almost antistars. White dwarves peopling "For to end yet again" suggest that this fictional world is approaching a void it has yet to reach.[21]

Each of the six fizzles may be seen as responses to the stillness of *Lessness*, as ways of "going on." In reaction to stasis, Fizzle 1 has a protagonist who can and does move, even if his walk is in "zigzags"; and these very zigzags offer an analogy for Beckett's later styles. Just as the traveller in Fizzle 1 alternates right and left turns, Beckett in his later fictions shifts and varies between two extreme styles: long convoluted sentences, and short minimal phrases. "It matters little in any case, so long as he keeps on climbing. . . . so long as he is on the right road" (pp. 10–11). In each of his later fictions, Beckett explores different routes and experiments with various modes in order to keep going artistically. The "I" in the next fizzle (4) mentally moves "step by step" and wonders why the "he" goes "to the left and not elsewither," as one degree of freedom, travel to the right, has vanished. Besides the artist as a quester/walker who must persevere, another notion Beckett returns to is that of the writer as one who hears mental voices and then transcribes them. "Still" ends "listening for a sound," and Foirade II–4 predicts "no one will talk to him, he won't talk to himself." Successful listening, a dramatization of someone prompting the writer, appears in the next fizzle (III–2) as Horn reads his notes to the narrator. Hearing language makes images materialize in the protagonist's mind, and this in turn compels him to overcome his (artistic) stillness: "So I have taken to getting up again and making a few steps in the room" (p. 22). The protagonist in Foirade IV progresses from the "I" in Foirade III who walks a few steps by "holding on to the bars of the bed," to one navigating from window to window "leaning on the furniture." Thus he anticipates the stasis of "Still" ("stand at gaze before the window" and "Standing before a window . . . a long gaze") merged with the halting motion of previous fizzles.

Concluding, the narrator declares of his body that he "wore out the machine" with *too much* movement when younger, "athletics . . . all that jumping and running." This sentence seems incongruous and cryptic until we read it as metanarrative: "My fortieth year had come and gone and I still throwing the javelin." In his fortieth year, in 1946, Beckett was still moving the pen, still active in classical or at least traditional pursuits in fiction analogous to throwing the javelin—writing the three French stories (including "La fin") and the short story "Premier amour" (whose English translation he would not allow to be published until 1972). In other words, Beckett was wearing himself out with composing semirealistic, pretrilogy prose; then he wrote *Molloy* in 1947, when he was forty-one. If Fizzle IV–6 is literary autobiography as well, then "old earth," the realistic world that Beckett has rejected since his forty-first year, now rejects him: "how I gaze on you, and what refusal, you so refused" (p. 43). The "I" perceives the earth "with my other's [the artist's inner] ravening eyes" that can also peer into the window of the soul. Beckett masters fragmented prose for acutely self-conscious narration, and in the process questions the very nature of fictional language.

Fizzle V–5, which begins "Closed place," takes us within the artist's window and frames the self-contained world of contemporary literature. Since one body in the ditch reappears, then we deduce the enclosure is circular, "a closed curve therefore." With its ditch, arena, towers, and tracks, the locale of V resembles the terrain of I–1 containing walls, narrows, and paths at different heights; and of course, both settings represent the coils of the brain, "the great head where he toils" (p. 7). But whereas the activity of walking (albeit fatiguing and difficult) was possible in

Foirade I, in Foirade V the only bodies present are lying still. Perhaps Foirade V impressed Beckett as too closed, dead, static; so for the last foirade he returns to a character moving, to frantic "panic steps," literally and figuratively. Foirade VI–3 combines the settings of I, II, and V in a "ruinstrewn land" of hedges, between road and ditch," and conflates the figures of the other fizzles: Murphy, he/I, and the "trunk horizontal" of "Still." In fact, just as the "I" says "I'll put faces in his head, names, places, churn them all up together" (p. 27), Beckett churns together the creatures, settings, themes, and motifs of Foirades I through V as he merges voices, vision, stasis, and split personas in a medley of short phrases spun off from the earlier pieces:

I see him in my mind, there divining us, hands and head a little heap, hours pass, he is still, he seeks a voice for me, it's impossible I should have a voice and I have none . . . but no more of him, that image, the little heap of hands and head, the trunk horizontal, the jutting elbows, the eyes closed and the face rigid listening. . . . [P. 26]

In the last fizzle, an "I" must provide a "he" with "all it needs to end," anticipating "For to End Yet Again." Its "ruinstrewn land" becomes a "wilderness," the "bones" of Foirades I and VI corrode, and mix with the "dust" of V; even the light of day, which finally overcomes the darkness in "Still," exists only as "remains" in "For to End."

The skull's abiding worry, that he will have to finish yet again, infinitely, is analogous to an ongoing astronomical controversy. One school of thought is that the universe originally exploded in a big bang and will continue to expand until some finite time; the other holds that the universe alternately dilates and contracts in never-ending cycles. Beckett readers have posed a literary question echoing the scientific one: Will his universe be able to expand (or contract) until it reaches an end point? Or has it already been pulsating through numerous cycles? For Beckett, it is not an either/or situation because he returns to his earlier themes and techniques without repeating them formulaically and without exhausting them. He condenses his younger styles without compressing them completely into silence—occasionally pausing, retreating, or veering in a different direction. In the more successful fizzles he continues to explore the inner and outer spaces of man with ever-new forms and styles, never quite collapsing to the black hole stage.

11

Company and *Ill Seen Ill Said*
"Gropings of the Mind"

The next two texts, *Company* (1980) and *Ill Seen Ill Said* (1981), each about sixty pages of very large print, complement each other. Together they eclipse *Fizzles*, as in them Beckett decided to go on with fiction by expanding rather than contracting. Perhaps the previous self-contained worlds seemed too sterile for Beckett, or perhaps personal retrospective stirrings moved the author in his seventies; but for whatever reason, he turned to realistic vignettes within a metafictional frame for *Company*: a man waiting in the dark (the writer) hears voices recalling to him scenes from his childhood. Then, in another shift, after *Company* grew too lyrical, nostalgic, almost sentimental in spots, Beckett apparently felt that he had to bury the ghosts of conventional fiction once again. Thus for *Ill Seen Ill Said* he created, in a new closed system of language, a funereal woman who visits a tombstone and says farewell to the natural world. In the previous fiction, the "I's" and Molloys kept suggesting their maker; and now, as with numbers approaching a mathematical limit, the pronouns come ever closer to meaning Samuel Beckett himself: *Company* presents the writer reflecting on his life,[1] and *Ill Seen Ill Said* reveals the artist reviewing his career. While *Company* is in some passages forthrightly and touchingly autobiographical, *Ill Seen Ill Said* is autobiographical in a metafictional, linguistic sense as its style painfully records the immediate life of the author, the man writing.

In language by turns mathematical, lyrical, and allegorical, Beckett continues to experiment with style, reshaping and further condensing syntax patterns from earlier prose to arrive at spare yet rich sentences that are easier to read than the permuted phrases of the sixties, but no easier to interpret because the imagery becomes increasingly cryptic. More important, in both of these recent texts Beckett innovates brilliantly with narrative technique, creating layers of pronouns in *Company* for recursive speakers and listeners, and inventing strata of observers in *Ill Seen*. The phrase "unformulable gropings of the mind" from *Ill Seen* repeats Beckett's despair over the expressive power of language and his association of artistic and physical journeys: the mind itself gropes through a terrain of fragmented linguistic constructions. Verbal analysis, pushing a reading below or through these recent compressed structures and narrative mazes, allows the reader to perceive Beckett's creative process and his artistic suffering as never before.

Company calls to mind both *Texts for Nothing* and *How It Is*, with several tableaux from childhood and with a succession of voices and scribes (or listeners). Here Beckett metamorphoses images from his past fictions and his past life and affords us a most intimate view of his situation as a writer, his condition as human being, and the human condition itself. As the final word of *Company* proclaims, he, and we, are "Alone"; and yet the memories, fantasies, and stories that Beckett fabricates to soothe his narrator-listener all diminish loneliness. A man lying solitary in the dark ("he") calls up voices, companions, and figments—and addresses himself in the second person—with a style that belies, while it imitates, his real, solitary situation:

The voice comes to him now from one quarter and now from another. Now faint from afar and now a murmur in his ear. In the course of a single sentence it may change place and tone. Thus for example clear from above his upturned face, you first saw the light at Easter and now. Then a murmur in his ear, you are on your back in the dark.[2]

For *Company*, Beckett devises a new narrative technique, a language and structure suited to a being lying motionless and listening for verbal companionship, who is forced to multiply and respond to his own various voices and fragmented selves.

To begin, the narrator posits a given in paragraph 2, a narrative proposal we must accept: "That then is the proposition. To one on his back in the dark a voice tells of a past." This is a hypothetical notion to be "maintained" in the mind like the hierarchical arrangement of *The Lost Ones*. *Company*'s first phrases are also reminiscent of the start of *Imagination Dead Imagine*; but rather than asking the reader to erase his reality and his fancy and then to conjure up something out of nothing, Beckett instructs us in exactly what to envision: "A voice comes to one in the dark. Imagine." This imperative to imagine thrusts two ways—to the reader and to the narrator himself—since the stated "you" in the memory sections is always the listener half of the speaker (plummetting him back to the past), and since the understood "you" of an imperative invokes the reader's participation. We do not enter a fabricated rotunda and view fantastic bodies as in *Imagination*; instead, Beckett calls up realistic and autobiographical memories, and we eavesdrop on these palliatives to loneliness, these minimal additions to company.

As listeners in the dark waiting for *Company's* voice to speak to us, we are, of course, in a position parallel to Beckett's hearer, so that many of his sentences loop back self-referentially and then spin outward toward the reader. The reader too finds a second proposition more plausible after accepting an original hypothesis: "A device perhaps from the incontrovertibility of the one to win credence for the other." In determining his situation and explaining it to himself, the hearer (sometimes called H, or M— like all those Murphy's and Malone's) offers information, yet the subject is mystified by his condition:

In another dark or in the same another devising it all for company. This at first sight seems clear. But as the eye dwells it grows obscure. Indeed the longer the eye dwells the obscurer it grows. Till the eye closes and freed from pore the mind inquires, What does this mean? What finally does this mean that at first sight seemed clear? Till it the mind too closes as it were. [Pp. 22–23]

By asking what the voice means, the hearer expresses our confusion; only with imagination's vision is he able to perceive his true situation. The largest question, for both Hearer and *his* hearer (us), is that of his very existence.

In *Texts for Nothing* the narrator tried to create a self by constructing a character in the present: the "I" had occurred everywhere in the past but must to be "here" and "now" in order to live. By contrast, the *Company* narrator's goal is "To have the hearer have a past and acknowledge it" (p. 34) because only in this way can he attain the first-person pronoun. Regressing linguistically, the narrator in *Company* finds an "I" almost impossible to achieve in any tense: although a "you" exists as listener, it can seldom utter the sentence "Yes I remember." In fact, as Wayne Booth terms it, the arrival of a first-person pronoun "after so many pages of rigorous, even brutal denial" marks the climax of the text.[3] Placement of this initial "I" immediately after the sentence "You were born on an Easter Friday after long labour" suggests that the creature is suddenly and grammatically born out of the long labor of the writing itself, born on a Good

Friday as Beckett alleges that he was. Beckett's creation of "the hearer" and his use of the second and third person instead of the first for most of the text demonstrate how much more critical the problem of identity—and therefore the use of pronouns— has become since *The Unnamable*. (A literalized treatment of the self as divided into "she" and "you" is dramatized in the playlet *Rockaby*, first produced in 1981 and composed at about the same time as *Company*. It depicts a female listener hearing her recorded, internalized, dying voice recounting her life in the third person.) Lately Beckett's protagonists—in both drama and fiction—have become more audience or listener than writer.

The intrusion of memory passages in the second person in *Company* has a seance-like quality; we get the sense that this he/you/I speaks from beyond the grave or that the listener waits for disembodied voices. Another element of this uncanny atmosphere is that the memory vignettes so closely enact scenes from Beckett's biography, for example, his learning to swim and his throwing himself from tree branches when a boy.[4] These seventeen separate and scattered paragraphs about the past (out of the text's fifty-nine paragraphs) float up from the white spaces of the pages: they rise out of the silence to the narrator-listener, then they speak in eerie voices to us as well as to "him" when we share the hearer's recollections, as we subsume the "you" listening in the darkness. And this sense of overhearing provides a heightened version of how literature often speaks to us, drawing us into a dream of words.

Like *How It Is* and *Fizzles*, *Company* blends scientific and quite lyrical prose, formal and informal styles. The two contrasting languages play in counterpoint: "Mind and heart wage a war of words in two competing tempos."[5] Like many of Beckett's later narrators, *Company*'s voice speaks alternately as philosopher, mathematician, and poet. This man lying in the dark, objectively referring to himself as "he," strives for an accuracy he knows is fallible; he early on repeats variations of "So with what reason remains he reasons ill" (p. 12) and later adds the disclaimers "with what judgment remained" and "with what feeling remains." Slowly establishing his present condition and gradually calling up his history, he remains satisfied with his description only temporarily; hence the recurring qualifications "Up to a point," "For the time being," "Within reason," and "for the moment," which often take the form of separate sentences. In Beckett texts of the 1960's and 1970's often a voice describes a setting, but in the 1980's even this staple of fiction is increasingly under-cut; and Beckett incorporates his frustration with descriptive language in the very titles of the next two fictions, *Ill Seen Ill Said* and *Worstward Ho.*

No less an empirical philosopher than other Beckettian nar-rators, *Company's* "he" questions from the beginning whether his physical position can be "verified." He tabulates exhaustively the possibilities of the voice's effect (for example, in paragraph 10) and later admits that there is "logically" no question of the speaker's intended audience being other than himself. Logical reasoning is incongruously applied even to a lover's height in a potential love scene. Beckett readers were not overly surprised when the sadistic and cynical protagonist of *How It Is* performed mental measurements of his victim. But when *Company's* per-sona—who elsewhere wades in nostalgia and sentiment—itemizes his lover's contiguous parts, computes tests, and the-orizes about relative human heights, the effect is laughable. Since their pelvises align, he muses, "Does it follow from this that the loss in height for the body that sits is the same for it that kneels?" (p. 41). These estimates plus meticulous geometrical configurations of the trysting place, a summerhouse, reveal that like the characters in *Enough* who "take flight in arithmetic," this protagonist uses mathematics as an emotional and intellectual escape—in this case, to avoid the fear of his lover's pregnancy. By paragraph 42 he hopelessly concludes that "rare flickers of rea-soning [are] of no avail," but nine paragraphs later, when eval-uating the perceptions of all five senses, he again considers and then rejects some special sixth sense: "Pure reason? Beyond ex-perience" (p. 52). Throughout the narrative, his reasoning bor-rows precision from mathematical language for several pur-poses: to count footsteps as he rambles about the countryside (with or without his father's shade), to calculate the area of the summerhouse floor and then the gazebo's volume, to multiply the heartbeats of a lifespan, to trace the geometry of his crawling postures, and to tabulate seconds on his watch. In all these cal-culations, what he actually seeks, exploiting a deep mathemati-cal pun, is the "constant" of his life. The Beckett voice still ex-pects solace from words, even though he gradually realizes that they cannot bring him certainty. Scientific language does not dispel philosophical doubt,[6] and perhaps this is why the hearer seeks visual images conjured up by words but not circumscribed by them.

We might say that our narrator is cursed with a logical mind that is also fanciful, except that the speaker in the dark is more accurate when he bemoans "A fancy so reason-ridden." As he wonders what may be "reasonably imagined," the stress does not necessarily fall on "reasonably," for it is the imaginative temperament that reigns here, thematically and stylistically. Imagination itself provides continual company—indicated in part by the sheer repetition of the word (thirty-one occurrences). In fact, "imagine" and its variants, surrounded by "devise," "contrive," "visions," "figment," and "fable," form a collocative set of terms saturating the text as the narrator contemplates "Devising figments to temper his nothingness." In addition, Beckett semantically extends the term "imagine," allowing it to take on related meanings; it substitutes for other words, increasing its frequency and importance in the story. We find "imagine" in a colloquial phrase in which one expects to read "thinks": "So he imagines to himself . . ." (p. 33). The creature decides on his favorite position "after due imagination" rather than due reflection, and the imperative to choose for himself, "Quick imagine," translates as "Quick decide." Later "imagination" occurs in a linguistic environment appropriate for "mind" when the narrator tries to "make up his imagination" about whether his alter ego could create while crawling. As the creature, literally and figuratively in the dark, worries about "the place to which imagination perhaps unadvisedly had consigned him," "imagination" comes to mean history, or even fate. The word means "see" and then "describe" in "Imagine closer the place where he lies." Most important, "imagine" becomes synonymous with "create," as it must for the fiction writer: "These are among the matters yet to be imagined." In a self-damning sentence prefacing those to come in *Ill Seen Ill Said*, the narrator regrets that "further imagination shows him to have imagined ill."

Imaginings and memories accompany the lone creature, but most palpably words themselves serve as companions, even the very sounds and structures of words. One criterion for good linguistic "company" is that it be most "diverting" or "least likely to pall"; a more varied voice would be more "companionable." However, repetition as well as variety has its charm; and often a sentence recurs verbatim in the course of a single paragraph, as if the solitary thinker were fondling his phrases. Within the compass of one sentence, words and roots of words echo (as in, for example, "What visions i the shadeless dark of light and shade"), so that both sentences and paragraphs turn back upon themselves. One sentence of resonating words—"Some soft thing softly stirring soon to stir no more" (p. 19)—reminds modern readers of James Joyce's verbal artistry in the last paragraph of *The Dead* with its snow faintly falling and falling faintly. Incongruously, Beckett's prose achieves sonorous qualities similar to Joyce's through short sentences rather than long ones.

In the following passage of *Company*, where "he" relives a peaceful afternoon from childhood, several devices combine to sustain a tranquil atmosphere: parallel structure, an imperative that is more invitation than command, rhythmic sentences (especially a series of three-word prepositional phrases in the second sentence), repetition of words and clauses, and the closural technique of ending the last three sentences identically. (My added dividers and line breaks serve to magnify these poetic effects.)

> You lie in the dark / and are back in that light.
> Straining out / from your nest / in the gorse
> with your eyes / across the water / till they ache.
> You close them while you count a hundred.
> Then open and strain again.
> Again and again.
> Till in the end it is there.
> Palest blue / against the pale sky.
> You lie in the dark / and are back in that light.
> Fall asleep in that sunless cloudless light.
> Sleep till morning light. [P. 25]

Amplifying the repeated "light," Beckett adds alliterative *l*s in "lie" and "light"; echoing *l*s in "till," "fall," "palest"; assonance of strain/again/ end/against; rhyming of sky/lie; and near repetition of asleep/sleep. Also, the first line, reappearing later, is rhythmically cadenced until it scans. One can almost hear the staccato, repetitive chanting of a hypnotist ("You are getting drowsy, very drowsy. Your eyes are getting heavy. Heavier"). Our lonely narrator has sung himself a lullabye just as the incantatory voice coming to the hearer in *Rockaby* rocks her to sleep— or to death.

So pronounced are *Company*'s poetic properties that one of its paragraphs when retyped resembles a short lyric:[7]

> A faint voice at loudest.
> It slowly ebbs till almost out of hearing.

Then slowly back to faint full.
At each slow ebb hope slowly dawns
that it is dying.
He must know it will flow again.
And yet at each slow ebb hope slowly dawns
that it is dying. [P. 17]

The very sounds convey its subject: a diminishing, not yet diminished voice. And the paradoxes, verbal echoes, and other lyrical characteristics of the paragraph recall the hypnotic, incantatory ending of Eliot's "Love Song of J. Alfred Prufrock": alliteration (faint/full, dawn/dying), internal rhyme (slow/know/flow), assonance (slow/hope), and particularly the overwhelming repetition of "slow," occurring twice, and "slowly" four times. To make this word reverberate, Beckett begins the next paragraph with "Slowly." A similar repetitive quality links the final six lines of "Prufrock" (an effect that is produced through the same morpheme recurring in different parts of speech—as in sea/seaward), but Eliot finesses a smoother rhythm because of his langorous three-line sentences, so different in pacing from *Company*'s curt, one-line sentences:

I have seen them riding seaward on the waves
Combing the white hair of the waves blown back
When the wind blows the water white and black.

We have lingered in the chambers of the sea
By sea-girls wreathed in seaweed red and brown
Till human voices wake us, and we drown. [Ll. 126–31]

Whether or not Beckett had Eliot's poem in mind, it is interesting to notice other parallels: both *Company*'s creature and J. Alfred are isolated, self-conscious men who objectify and distance the self by dividing it into a "he" and a "you" or a "you and I," and who use language as a shelter.

Even when *Company*'s voice misses the mark of poetry, it betrays its fondness for language at both the word and phrase levels. Delighting in paradoxical or oxymoronic descriptions, especially about light, the listener calls up Milton's "darkness visible"[8] as he conjoins "shadowy light," "faintly luminous," and "Sunless cloudless brightness." Characterizations of the voice prompt series of parallel structure that loosely scan, as the narrator measures not just words or feet per phrase but also syllables per word, as in "The ideal amplitude for effortless audition." Adapting a humorous pedantic style already perfected in

The Lost Ones, Beckett constructs sentences reflecting the narrator's simultaneous penchants for precision and parallelism, when the voice's "ideal amplitude" is further harmoniously described as "neither offending the ear with loudness nor through converse excess constraining it to strain" (p. 34). Besides lyrical and rhythmically balanced sentences, the creature also relies on contrasting jagged and fragmented sentences to keep himself company. Just as the tramps in *Godot* passed the time with word-game repartee, and the self in *Texts for Nothing* toyed with his various voices, this recluse maintains a playful dialogue with himself.

Beckett also borrows syntax from previous styles to fill in his innovative, layered narrative framework. Like the "I" in *Abandoned Work*, the "he" in *Company* often thinks in short, quick spurts, not bothering to include such minor elements as verbs: "Those [were] its first words. [There was a] Long pause for him to believe his ears . . ." (p. 17); "Other details as need felt" expands to "Other details [can be added?] as [the] need [is?] felt" (p. 57). A related aspect of *Company*'s syntax develops the grammar of afterthought from *Enough*, a natural stylistic feature for a piece self-reflexively termed an "esquisse" (French for a sketch, outline, or rough draft): "Is there anything to add to this esquisse?" (p. 45). In both *Company* and *Enough* the narrator often nostalgically and tentatively evokes visions of the past that gradually take shape in the mind and on the page. Thus short phrases qualifying a description follow the full stop of a period and become (fragmented) sentences of their own, afterthoughts given prominence. This syntax of qualifiers charts the revising pen at work: the voice appeared "At no time from below. So far." Later as "he" remembers his walks through a sheep pasture, he concurrently walks the reader through his reasoning and imagining processes:

The fleeting ground before your feet. From time to time. You do not count your steps any more. For the simple reason they number each day the same. Average day in day out the same. The way being always the same. You keep count of the days and every tenth day multiply. And add. . . . Day after day. The same way. [Pp. 36–37]

Regularity of his ways is echoed with the repetition of "same"; in fact, three consecutive sentences end with this word. Similar short phrase-sentences appear in *The Lost Ones*, although usually as a forethought (since each property of the abode is detailed later) rather than an afterthought, for example, "The light.

Its dimness. Its yellowness" (p. 7). Again, the language in the cylinder's system offers the closest analog for *Company*'s style. Specifically, *Company* shares with *Lost Ones* formal verb phrases ("May not there be another with him . . .") and inverted, convoluted constructions ("In dark and silence to close as if to light the eyes and hear a sound"—p. 19; "Impending for some time the following"—p. 31). Much of this inversion results from passive voice verbs, a natural stylistic choice for a listener anticipating a message: "To its form and dimensions a clue is given by the voice afar" (p. 32). The temporal situation of the listener as dreamer also produces comically severe syntax, as "he" attempts to distinguish his past and present reactions: "What with what feeling remains does he feel about now as compared to then? . . . As well inquire what he felt then about then as compared to before" (p. 22). For the reader these sentences present themselves, *Watt*-like, as riddles to be solved, and recall Joyce's formal, serpentine, and cryptic puzzles and answers in the "Ithaca" chapter of *Ulysses*.

Despite the long, varied stylistic legacy that *Company* bears, one of the most effective features of its syntax belongs to this text alone. It could be called the grammar of regression. Since phrases like "Devised deviser" contain condensed relative clauses (this expands to "deviser who was devised"), many sentences are contracted nestings of embedded clauses echoing patterns of the nursery rhyme "The House That Jack Built." Interestingly, Joyce also uses this recursive pattern, in many variations, throughout *Finnegans Wake*. The structure that Beckett built concerns a being who imagines a voice that creates a being who imagines a voice—or a "devised devisor devising it all for company." (In a contemporaneous playlet, *Ohio Impromptu*, Beckett presents a reader who reads about a reader who reads about a reader who. . . .) Like Chinese boxes or nested Russian dolls, a smaller layer within a larger layer continually unfolds, so that *Company* becomes "The fable of one with you in the dark. The fable of one fabling of one with you in the dark" (p. 63). In the trilogy narrators are transcribers of voices, and so too is the protagonist of *How It Is* with his insistent refrain of "I say it as I hear it." In *Company* the voice might well repeat "I hear it as I say it to myself." Ingeniously, Beckett creates a lone listener who postulates a whole hierarchy of "you"s to populate his world:

Hearing on and off a voice of which uncertain whether addressed to him or to another sharing his situation. There being nothing to show when it describes correctly his situation that the description is not for the benefit of another in the same situation. [P. 44]

Later, as if in linguistic pursuit, the voice closes in on itself, hoping that narrator and listener, "he" and "you," will converge in an "I." Resembling the Unnamable (whose name *Company*'s persona temporarily adopts), this infinitely regressing voice wanders in the interstices of who is addressing—or creating—whom. And like Pim's tormentor in *How It Is*, he asks, "Can the crawling creator crawling in the same create dark as his creature create while crawling?" (p. 52). In asking that question, his playful tone jars with his obvious anxiety over identity (echoing Beckett's personal concern with inner and outer selves).

Ultimately, all these regressions reduce to mere fictions, "figments," when the narrator/listener concedes with his last word that he is "Alone." *Company*'s deviser feels unloved since birth (his parents stooping over the cradle evince "no trace of love," and most images of mother and some of father are negative). Emotionally he recalls Hamm from *Endgame*, but he is a more humble Hamm, content to listen as the verbal photographs surface—though in reality, of course, the narrator himself has created the fiction about listening, as well as each memory. Both heroes measure infinity "grain by grain in the mind," and in both, the craving for company (originating in a sad and silent childhood) motivates the struggle for art. Memory vignettes, plus Beckett's very battle with language in the text, bring *Company* closer to autobiography than this self-protective writer has ever cared to approach.

Verbal striving again assumes the form of a physical journey, a parallel carrying special metaphorical and personal consequences in *Abandoned Work*, *How It Is*, and *Lessness*. Continuing the metaphor of "going on" for motion and fiction, the narrator catalogs what must still be devised and concludes, "But to be going on with let him crawl." A lone creature in the dark, falling, resting, and trying once more to crawl has become one of Beckett's favorite images for the contemporary artist who attempts vainly to express, to grope toward a satisfying language. Patterns of crawling, falling, resting, crawling serve to structure *Company*: each paragraph marks a new departure toward defining either the past or the present, a new quest for some meager comfort in fiction:

Crawls and falls. Lies. Lies in the dark with closed eyes resting from his crawl. Recovering. Physically and from his disappointment at having crawled again in vain. Perhaps saying to himself, Why crawl at all? [P. 54]

Analogously, Beckett has been asking himself for years, particularly since *The Unnamable*, Why write at all? In this same paragraph, at his most sorrowful, as he agonizes over whether he should abandon "bootless crawl and figments comfortless," he/Beckett obliquely compares the artist's suffering to Christ's for at least the second time in the text and the nth time in the canon. The narrator lying "in darkness" remembers that he "first saw the light and cried" on the day "when in darkness Christ at the ninth hour cried and died" (p. 55), and we again recall that Beckett claims to have been born on a Good Friday. Visually, the narrator's posture, with his "crossed feet" and "bowed head," suggests a crucifixion.[9] Our solitary hero grandly suffers "the woes of his kind," and hints at the same writer-martyr equation as in *Ping* and *How It Is*: his pencil is his cross. But Beckett's crucified narrators, dying more slowly than Christ, never reach the peace and finality of death, of silence; and their suffering earns no meaning or redemption.

At the end of *Company*, Beckett bids farewell to his first narrative character, Belacqua from *More Pricks Than Kicks*, as if to the whole body of his early fiction. By the last paragraph of the text the narrator lying in the dark conflates both meanings of the word "lie"—resting and fabling—while he creates wonderful puns about fiction like "From time to time with unexpected grace you lie" and "you resume your fable where the act of lying cut it short." In a crescendo of despair, the narrator repeats the phrases "in vain" and the playfully Shakespearian "labour lost" as he concludes his lament. His next story advertizes creative defeat in its very title: both imagination and composition are vain in *Ill Seen Ill Said*.

Rather than affirming any company or comfort in language, *Ill Seen Ill Said* expresses total frustration with words; unlike the hearer in *Company*, the female protagonist of *Ill Seen* has "no more converse" with herself. One measure of Beckett's increasing disappointment over verbal expression is his subsequent reduction from the complex first-second-third-person layered narrative point of view in *Company*, which is further complicated by a narrator/listener. The simpler narrative voice in *Ill Seen Ill Said* urges himself in the second person "On" to describe a "she" in the third person. Thematically circling around the need to stop writing, *Ill Seen* follows the paths of *Texts for Nothing* and "For to End Yet Again" (Fizzle 8), and in fact, that title phrase reappears here. In its storyline, such as it is, *Ill Seen Ill Said* is a hybrid of *Enough* and "Still" (Fizzle 7): a third-person narrative about an old woman who either wanders about visiting a tomb or sits still peering out her window at the sun, the moon, and Venus. Most closely related in motif to *Imagination Dead Imagine*, *Ill Seen* concerns the disjunction between real and fictional worlds, the writer's powers of perception and creation, and the reader's ability to reconstruct an image.

In style, *Ill Seen* combines characteristics of Beckett's prose of the sixties and seventies: the narrator's self-conscious comments impeding the story, linguistic forays for the precise noun and the correct verb tense, cumulative descriptions, paradoxical language, and in-process creation of minimal character and setting. Of course, because Beckett never employs his stylistic stratagems in quite the same way twice, *Ill Seen* does not simply replay bits of earlier fictions. What is particularly new here is an intensified preoccupation with the process of creation—phrase by phrase—and with the writer's craft, with how exactly to portray these processes stylistically: there is more insistent use of the imperative, more direct evocation of the imagination, and more complex use of visual imagery. Also, another innovative narrative technique (an observing eye interposed between narrator and reader) calls forth new sentence structures and new metaphors. All of this culminates in one of Beckett's more powerful allegories about writing itself.

Ill Seen Ill Said is his most self-conscious fiction so far, every syllable eked out with difficulty. Confronting directly the agonies of composition, *Ill Seen* introduces a perfect metaphor for Beckett's later prose styles: "strangury." A condition of the urinary organs in which urine is emitted painfully and drop by drop serves as an apt image for Beckett's recent languages. After physical objects in the story become "less," the narrator comments, "See now how words too. A few drops mishaphazard. Then strangury."[10] Sentences also become less long, averaging 3.61 words in a paragraph near the end of the text, compared to a slightly longer (but still condensed) 5.63 words per sentence in an early paragraph, and an average of about 11.0 words in *Company*. More than other Beckett fictions, this text is sprinkled with drops of one-word sentences. The narrator in a state of strangury produces a syntax of "less." Although more extended than the fragmented phrases of *How It Is* or *Ping*, the minimal sentences of *Ill Seen* are still far from orthodox in form and sequence. The high proportion of one-word and one-phrase sentences means that two out of three periods could in fact be deleted, or replaced by commas, to result in more conventional English units with standard length and clausal construction. For example, the thirty-five "sentences" of paragraph 26 technically can be reduced to fifteen sentences, if connected with appropriate punctuation and conjunctions. Ellipses condense many of the sentences in the text, rendering them telegrammatic, often omitting both subject and verb: "She [is] as [she was] when [she] fled. Where [she is now is at the same place she was] as when [she] fled. . . . Day no sooner risen [then it is] fallen" (pp. 50–51). The repeated pronoun "she" must often be supplied by the reader, and this extreme contraction suggests that the self, along with "she" (the linguistic marker for the self), is often in danger of vanishing.

Another familiar feature of the language here (as in *Lessness* and *Fizzles*) is a syntax of contrasts, of binary oppositions in words and details. The woman walks either inside or outside the house, and when outside moves to or from a tomb. When not in motion, she is static in her contemplation of Venus, a star that cyclically rises and sets. Her hands "tighten then loosen their clasp. Slow systole diastole. . . . Rhythm of a labouring heart" (pp. 31–32). Later the cabin partition dissolves and reappears, in alternating sentences, and the reasons are both clear and obscure; the narrator self-consciously analyzes his pulsating structure, asking "Analogy of the heart?" (p. 53). Another analogy would be the expansion and collapse of stars that Beckett explored in *Fizzles*. By far the most important dichotomy in *Ill Seen* is between "[t]hings and imaginings," "that old tandem": in the cabin we hear the "imaginary murmur of flakes" of snow and "a real creak." Quite directly, the narrator contrasts the real and the imaginary, "the counter-poison." Natural and fictional worlds, "once so twain," so divisible, are now mingled, and similarly "such the farrago from eye to mind," from observer to writer. No wonder that at the end of the piece Beckett laments the "unspeakable globe."

The old woman sees the sun rise and "rails at the source of all life," and in parallel, Beckett rails at life-like fiction, preferring to fabricate (in paragraph two) an obviously imaginary cabin situ-

ated "at the inexistent centre of a formless place." Beckett's narrator marvels "to think that there is still life in this age." Consequently, he mocks superrealism with his repeated depiction of a
buttonhook as "larger than life," and then burlesques Gothic
settings as he grudgingly adds details to the cabin's description:

South gable no problem. But the other. That door. Careful. Black
too? Black too. And the roof. Slates. More. Small slates black too
brought from a ruined mansion. What tales had they tongues to tell.
[P. 43]

But within the frame of a quasi-Gothic story, the woman is mysteriously drawn to a particular stone: "Rounded rectangular
block three times as high as wide. Four. Her stature now." This
pictures a large tombstone, probably marking the grave of nature
or of conventional fiction. Near the conclusion, Beckett bids
"Farewell to farewell," and thus we learn retrospectively that the
entire text has been a wake for his past narrative art.

To eradicate the real world, *Ill Seen*'s narrator borrows the language of magic, like *Imagination*'s voice with his "vanished" and
his sense of "Presto!" In a universe where things appear and disappear "suddenly," no mundane logic need apply: "She who
looks up no more looks up and sees them. . . . So the unreason-
ing goes" (pp. 23–24). Beckett combines paradox and parallelism to achieve one-sentence tableaux with cinematic and fantastic effects: "She still without stopping. On her way without
starting. Gone without going. Back without returning" (p. 19).
Incorporeal, the woman appears "darkly" and "as though by en-
chantment," seeming to the observer "a mirage" as well as "a figment." Gradually, the reader takes his place in the audience of a
magic show, for "let the eye be distracted," and "suddenly" the
sun is gone: "Pfft occulted. Nothing having stirred." We can remember "pfft" as Pozzo's onomatopoetic signal of night's instant
arrival in his long declamation on time in *Godot*, and "pfft" was
also one of Beckett's early approximations for the word "ping."
"Occulted," an astronomical term meaning "hidden, obscured,
or concealed," recalls the galactic imagery of *Fizzles*. Together,
the words "Pfft occulted" turn Beckett himself into a verbal magician. The narrator says quite explicitly (rather than implicitly
as in the earlier fiction and drama) that we are "[i]n the madhouse
of the skull and nowhere else" (p. 20), yet though located in the
writer's mind once again, we are permitted tokens of the real
world, an old dying woman (a displaced portrayal of Beckett

himself?)[11] in a cabin near a pasture. Thus the natural world metamorphoses into the world of realistic fiction and then into the arena of self-referential narrative. This recent story about writing transmutes autobiographical elements—as *Not I* dramatized images of Beckett as speaker/writer, and *Footfalls* recreated images of Beckett's mother as a pacer in the night[12]—and life becomes art as the character is transfigured into pure "figment."

The Unnamable will go on even though he cannot go on; this latest impossible writing assignment causes *Ill Seen's* narrator to prod himself along with the command "On" three times in the first paragraph, prompting him to complete his exposition. Beckett builds the narrative discontinuously through cumulative detail and added modifiers: "From where she lies she sees Venus rise. On. From where she lies when the skies are clear she sees Venus rise followed by the sun" (paragraph 1). Besides urging himself "On," the narrator also advises himself to be "Quick" (usually to capture the woman in prose before she disappears), to be "Careful," or to proceed "Gently." With these repeated directives, he depicts the setting in a fragmented, revised, yet deliberate way, as had the voice of *The Lost Ones*, but more tentatively at each step: "The cabin. Its situation. Careful. On" (paragraph 2). We overhear the imagination in a hesitant process of creation; as the narrator gives shape to this shapeless, fabricated area, he warily draws two concentric circles for the reader: "The two zones form a roughly circular whole. As though outlined by a *trembling* hand. Diameter. Careful. Say one furlong" (paragraph 3, my emphasis). Especially at the beginning of the fiction, he must return "careful" answers to all questions of narrative possibility, so that he does not admit too much material into the story: "Flowers? Careful. . . . And man? Shut of at last? Alas no" (paragraph 3). Humanity, characters, still intrude into a most distanced metafiction. A man, reminiscent of the master from *Enough*, creeps onto the pages, no matter how much caution the voice exercises; as a potential creature, he occasionally threatens to become an actual character. Not even Beckett, perhaps, can wholly dispel the real world—or can totally exclude himself.

Merely continuing the writing process is uppermost in the narrator's mind: he is content, like the wanderer in *Abandoned Work*, to be simply on his way, not adhering to an orderly sequence in either narration or description. Only after the midpoint of the story does the cabin's interior come into existence, through a now-familiar question-and-answer style, a dialogue between imaginer and writer, and between creator and reviser: "The bed. Careful. A pallet? [a few alternatives evaluated before he concludes] A pallet then flat on the floor" (paragraph 36). It is not until several paragraphs later that the reader receives a full sketch of the setting; Beckett's narrator chides himself almost humorously about this delay, like John Barth's self-conscious narrator in "Lost in the Funhouse" criticizing himself midway for not advancing his plot sooner. By paragraph 41 (of sixty-one) the self-disparaging voice finally envisions the cabin's walls: "White walls. High time. . . . Such the dwelling ill seen ill said. Outwardly. High time." That so much reading time elapses before the narrator arrives at such a basic detail as wall color shows that he operates not on any principle of general to particular, or of physiological, visual process, but as a victim of narrative necessity.

Just as standard syntax rules govern what stylisticians call "linguistic contingency," [13] limiting a writer's succeeding grammatical options in a sentence under construction (based on initial choices), so a novelist's fictional contingency operates in a story; and Beckett self-consciously highlights these constraints. For example, invention of a trapdoor in the cabin necessitates mention of its floor, "For the first time then wooden floor" (paragraph 39); and as the writer is compelled to add appropriate descriptive details, we are granted a glimpse of the artistic process. Employing terms of deductive inevitability like "then" and "therefore," and repeating the word "necessary" and its variants, the narrator composes his story according to what should or must follow from what precedes. Because there are two skylights in the cabin's roof, there can be "No ceiling therefore. Necessarily. Otherwise with the curtains closed she would be in the dark" (paragraph 16). The story's logic and the "careful" building of these details both reflects and enacts the creative process, the tension between free imagination and constrained development. Since there are lambs already present from the beginning, the narrator asserts (three times in paragraph 4) that it would be better to have a moor than a pasture; but alas, he has already created a pasture. Certain elements of the story, then, become axiomatic: "There had to be lambs. Rightly or wrongly." With this sort of language, Beckett mocks the artificiality of sequence and symbolism in fiction; there have to be lambs presumably to represent whiteness, springtime, and innocent martyrdom. In one sense the writer is at the mercy of his thoughts (those voices in the head that Beckett has dramatized so many times), and all details are "Seen *no matter how* and said as seen," (my emphasis) written as imagined. What is the origin of these conceptions, inspirations? The writer appears powerless to predict, to initiate, or to control his early creative impulses.

Conversely, though, other language patterns in *Ill Seen* manifest the supreme power of the author of a supreme fiction—to bring a world into existence on command, with a single phrase. Saying as creating began for Beckett back in *Molloy*, but recently it has become a painfully self-conscious motif and, in fact, a major theme of the fiction itself. In *Company* the phrasing of Genesis ("Let there be light") is invoked for artistic creation: "But there are no flies. Then why not let there be? The temptation is great. Let there be a fly" (p. 28). In *Ill Seen* details of the woman materialize as if by divine intervention: "Let the eye from its vigil be distracted a moment" (p. 19). When *Ill Seen's* woman is still visible in the distance, black against the snow and free of snowflakes, "nothing needed now but for them to start falling again which *therefore* they do" (my italics). Whatever the writer conceives then immediately and magically happens, and a reassuring confidence in this momentum of invention accrues. The fiction writer obviously transcends reality, transforms autobiography, and transgresses time. Of the lone female character we learn "No shock were she already dead. As of course she is. But in the meantime *more convenient not*. Still living *then* she lies hidden" (paragraph 40, my italics). Flaunting authorial control over his character, the narrator makes her appear and vanish successively, killing and resurrecting her with single verbs. When the creator stops imagining, the creature stops in her tracks, turned to stone. An author thus manipulates both action and motivation: "Such helplessness to move she cannot help. Heading on foot for a particular point often she freezes on the way. Unable till long after to move on not knowing whither or for what purpose" (paragraph 1). If author wavers, character wavers: "Have her sit? Lie? Kneel? Go? She too vacillates" (paragraph 45). Regaining control, he stills her as she eats, the bowl midway to her mouth, "Now again in the rigid Memnon pose." Later, she moves slightly, "But before she can proceed she fades and disappears." Erasing her before the next mouthful seems mischievous, yet the writer in turn is being manipulated by the higher power of the imagination. As in Euclidean geometry, where all theories and corollaries follow logically from a few axioms, in fictional space the imagination supplies the givens and then a compelling narrative necessity supercedes.

Gradually, the reader of *Ill Seen* experiences a basic mechanism of fiction: that while an author often motivates and moves the character, he sometimes cannot restrict her, once she is imagined into being, anymore than he can dictate to his creative mind. The woman randomly and autonomously flits in and out of "the madhouse of the skull." She herself is in a symmetrical position vis-à-vis Venus and the constellations ("the twelve"); they "appear and recede" depending on the seasons and the sun, and all she can do is place herself in the right position to observe them. Similarly, the "eye of flesh" and "the other [eye]" (the imagination) watch as character and setting "emerge," an oft-repeated word that implies authorial passivity. *Ill Seen's* narrator, like the listener in *Company*, lies "[i]n wait for her to reappear. In order to resume" (paragraph 11). Her drastic changes, including reincarnations, usually take place at paragraph boundaries, thus freeing the narrator to continue composition—at least for another passage. A list of paragraph openings exposes this design of protagonist reemergence and renewed narration:

She is there. Again. [paragraph 14]
As hope expires of her ever reappearing she reappears. [20]
Seated on the stones she is seen from behind. [26]
Panic past pass on. The hands. Seen from above. [29]
She reemerges on her back. [36]
On resumption the head is covered. [38]
See them [woman and stone] again side by side. [43]
She reappears at evening at her window. [45]
She is vanishing. [46]
The face yet again in the light of the last rays. [47]
Reexamined rid of light the mouth changes. [48]
Back after many winters. . . . She as when fled. [49]
But see she suddenly no longer there. [50]
Alone the face remains. [55]
Full glare now on the face present throughout the recent future. [58]

Since these appearances and visions—of both character and setting—occur "suddenly" (a frequent word in the text), they impart to the reader a sense of entering the writer's imagination, of witnessing fictional apparitions in the brain. The cabin too floats in and out: "Next to emerge from the shadows an inner wall. Only slowly to dissolve in favour of a single space" (paragraph 17). Figments materialize to be ill seen and then ill said by an author who feels only limited control, through a narrator who longs to be finished with all writing, "with not being able," who searches continually for "the wrong word." As early as *How It Is* (1964), Beckett had used the same disillusioned phrases to discuss the difficulty of the artistic enterprise: "my life last state last version ill-said ill-heard ill-recaptured ill-murmured in the mud" (p. 7).

Much earlier (around 1938), Beckett wrote in French an essay on art, whose English title is "The Two Needs." It concerns artistic needs larger than, but related to, the "necessary" local additions of detail that "need" to be said in *Ill Seen Ill Said*. Deirdre Bair's summary of this essay reverberates in our minds because Beckett's original philosophy of art seems to have stretched out over thirty-five years to touch issues and images in *Ping, Fizzles, Company,* and *Ill Seen Ill Said*:

. . ."Les Deux Besoins" continues the development of Beckett's idea that art results from the artist's quest to rid himself of extraneous knowledge in order to refine his perceptions into a clear, distilled vision of the fundamental inner being: art comes from the abandonment of the macrocosm for the pursuit of the microcosm. Man is doomed to failure because he can never commit or abandon himself completely to his inner voice. The eternal struggle to do so—and the artist's constant turning inward—creates conflict, and in turn forces him to create art. This vision of the preordained failure of the artist gives rise in Beckett's noncritical writing to the figure of the quest-hero, doomed to follow the tortuously turning path of his inner self on an endless, timeless plane where there is no real definition, no end and no accomplishment. The goal is always tantalizingly beyond reach. On the one hand, it is a grim, joyless task, this pursuit of art. On the other, it is the true way to find satisfaction—peace lies only in pursuit.[14]

In *Ill Seen*, this self-conscious and doomed quest for appropriate artistic expression is stylistic as well as thematic, and manifests itself semantically and syntactically in structures I have been calling the "grammar of afterthought" and "description by accumulation."

Instead of a sentence embodying a complete thought, an *Ill Seen* "sentence" actually consists of a short phrase amended or

extended by the next phrasal structure: "She is there. Again. . . .
Distracted by the sky. By something in the sky. . . . Without the
curtain's being opened. Suddenly open" (p. 19). This syntax
traces a groping about for the desired modifier, which reflects an
on-going creation (governed by narrative necessity) of further
details or events. *Company's* narrator recognizes a similar composing process and expresses his bridge between imagination
and composition through the same significant word, "need":
"Other details as need felt" (paragraph 55). Though not as pervasive or frantic as the quest for the "right aggregate" and correct verb in *Texts for Nothing,* stylistic searches for the appropriate "wrong" verb tense cause the *Ill Said* narrator to perform
similar immediate revisions: "How come a cabin in such a place?
How came? Careful" (paragraph 2). If correct writing will not
permit an ending, then perhaps bad prose will force the voice to
stop.

Testing verbs and qualifying statements is not enough; the
narrator also must question the origin and plausibility of his setting. However, not even the writer himself can regress too far
back along the road of narrative motivation; certain elements
(the woman and the cabin, for example) are posited at the start
and are thereby fixed, inexplicable, axiomatic. It is curious that at
the beginning of the story the narrator justifies his description of
the woman in the present tense (often the continuous present),
saying, "All this in the present as had she the misfortune to be
still of this world" (paragraph 1). Yet he allows past-tense verbs
to creep into the cabin's depiction: "And none to urge—none to
have urged its demolition" (paragraph 2), perhaps because the
cabin, like *Imagination's* dome, represents the house of fiction. In
many of the seventeen sentences using this synchronous revising construction, a dash explicitly signals the narrator's abrupt
switch to alternative phrasing. In addition to verb tenses, subjects also are revised: "For before they have—before the eye has
time they mist" (paragraph 29). We observe Beckett's narrator not
just composing but also critiquing his prose, at times pleased
with his verbal handiwork as he generates more abstract concepts: "Seeing the black night *or better* blackness pure and simple
that limpid they would shed" (p. 58, my italics). And through
word choices like "limpid," gropings of the mind produce some
fluid literary motion.

Far from being ill said, *Ill Seen's* style gives us a fragile and
complex transcription of the creative mind at work, modulating

roles between imaginer, creator, reader, and editor.[15] Our hesitant composer is prepared to admit when he has chosen too strong a word: "Quick beforehand again two mysteries. Not even. Mild shocks. Not even" (p. 56). In the other direction, he also challenges feeble expressions: "Suddenly the look. Nothing having stirred. Look? Too weak a word. Too wrong. Its absence? No better" (p. 57). That Molloy evinced similar semantic indecision but in much longer sentences, with phrases like these separated by commas rather than by periods, provides one measure of how fragmentary Beckett's syntax has become between the forties and the eighties.

At least once, even the wrong word eludes the ill-said speaker, for "Such now the confusion now between real and—how say its contrary? . . . Such equal liars both. Real and—how ill say its contrary?" (p. 40). Although elsewhere in the text the narrator has at his command the terms "figment" and "imagination," he can now only approximate this crucial contrast metaphorically through the setting's two zones. The zone of pasture (representing nature, the real world) is gradually overtaken by the zone of stones (representing art and artifice). This same metaphor translates to Beckett's own evolving canon: beginning with relatively realistic fictions like *Murphy* (here represented by clover on the cabin and considerable, organic pasture),[16] by the sixties and seventies his structures are hermetically enclosed within the realm of artifice, self-referential fiction (the encroaching, inorganic rock). What matters in the later prose is not the world but the mind creating a world, not substance but the dynamics of its creation: style.

When finally at a loss for wrong words, the narrator settles on the term "less": "With what one word convey its [the chair's] change? Careful. Less. Ah the sweet one word. Less. It is less. The same but less" (paragraph 50). Minimalism has, of course, been Beckett's artistic and stylistic aim since *Texts for Nothing* and his achievement since *Lessness*; with this new text he repeats his wish to create a "void," to reach the silence of "home," the death of words. By the end of the story the narrator wants to delete all "trace" of the woman, to erase all inkling "of what was never"; and in the final paragraph he insists on an ending through three repetitions of "last." In a pseudonarrative with a disjointed or nonexistent plot, a story suffused with the tone of allegory and the structures of poetry, meaning resides in image patterns rather than in sequential events. Two foregrounded motifs, vi-

sual imagery and black/white patterns—especially when analyzed for stylistic cohesion—reaffirm that *Ill Seen*, like other
post-*Unnamable* fictions, is obdurately about writing itself.

Taking his cue from the title, a reader senses the prevalence of
vision throughout *Ill Seen*; indeed, a close examination reveals
that all but a few of its sixty-one paragraphs contain the word
"eye" or some allusion to sight. Watching occurs at three levels:
the woman looking for Venus and other stars, the narrator trying
to envision the woman and her cabin, and the reader (as is common in Beckett's late fiction) asked to recreate character and setting visually. To complicate the picture, Beckett creates a fourth
eye that subsumes those three, an observer entering the story in
paragraph 6 who becomes part protagonist, part self-conscious
narrator, and part reader and visualizer. Although this stealthy
observer acquires the negative associations of a voyeur or peep-
ing Tom, we as readers want him to succeed in his spying because his success offers our only hope for seeing: "To the imaginary stranger the dwelling appears deserted. . . . The eye glued
to one or the other window has nothing but black drapes for its
pains. Motionless against the door he listens long" (paragraph
6). Since our interloper-observer must grasp the character and
pin down her image, at times his language becomes rough and
assaulting: "But quick seize her where she is best to be seized."
That his capturing eye could be lethal is suggested in "close it for
good and all and see her to death" (paragraph 27). The narrator
acknowledges that the woman's face is "defenseless" and asks,
"What is it defends her? Even from her own [eyes]." With her
"lashes jet black" she revives the female image in *Ping*; with her
orbs "washen blue" she portrays Beckett's other author-narrators
or Beckett's inner self. Isolated, the artist suffers from his internal vision, the agony of self-perception.

Both the female character and the narrator-observer perceive
chiefly with the "other" eye of the imagination, the one that requires no light (a qualification repeated three times). Imagination's eye searches inside the narrator's mind—"Far behind the
eye the quest begins"—for a particular phrase as he composes.
Analogously, in a gesture familiar from *The Unnamable* but more
foregrounded here, the character's own eyes turn inward, "dazed
at what seen behind the lids." In fact, occasionally the two views
converge, either through grammatical ambiguity ("the eye" with
no modifier) or because of the passive verb "seen" used with an
object but no subject, no agent: "Where nothing to be seen in

the graying rays but snow." Our attitude toward the eye (usually the observer's) becomes ambivalent as phrases describing it change connotations in various linguistic environments. Besides the neutral phrase "the eye," which is the most frequent depiction, the reader encounters the following images:

> intent gaze
> the eye of flesh
> the eye from its vigil
> the widowed eye
> the relentless eye
> unremittent [eye]
> this filthy eye of flesh
> the staring eye
> the eye exposed to such conditions
> the staring gaze
> the hovering eye
> the eye . . . and its drivelling scribe
> the vile jelly
> still agonizing eye
> the [woman's] eye persistently closed

Without using the word "camera," Beckett implies a camera eye for the observer since it takes a "close-up" of a nail on the wall (until the scene "blurs") and later of a watch dial, and a distant shot of the woman in the snow, appearing as a "stain." A lens captures the chair from "every angle" and shifts focus for the woman's hands "seen from above" and for her face "wooed from below." At times this cinematic optical instrument becomes indifferent or even cruel, causing the grass to shiver under its persistent stare. In this "inspection" mode it resembles the camera-stalker in *Film* and "the eye of prey" in *Imagination*, forcing its victims to shudder. Yet besides producing discomfort, the eye itself—character's *and* observer's—suffers pain, and repeatedly appears tearful or weeping: "Riveted to some detail of the desert the eye fills with tears. Imagination at wit's end spreads its sad wings." Thus the eye represents Beckett the artist compelled to view the world and to transcribe his visions, ill seen, ill written ("the eye . . . and its drivelling scribe"), full of sympathy for the human condition and for the writer's predicament.

Beckett has maintained in his critical statements that only the intangible, the invisible zone of consciousness, is worth writing about. Facing an unruly tangible character, the writer can only close his eyes, do "[n]o more unless to rest. In the outward and so-called visible. That daub. Quick again to the brim the old nausea and shut again" (p. 38). After abandoning the gray zone of being, the author is left with mere realistic fiction—the visible, inferior plaster. The *Ill Seen* woman's imaginary face, caught between fiction and metafiction, contrasts with "true plaster," and her mouth, like the "sewn" body in *Ping*, once gives a "hint of extruding pulp." Through the style of this story we sense an exhausted Beckett who is sick of all fiction, certainly of his earlier prose, "the old nausea"; and food metaphors in this story would suggest that the contemporary writer chokes on his own material. The narrator says of the *Ill Seen* man who enters at the beginning, "Quick enlarge and devour before night falls," and by the end the narrative voice prays for enough time "to devour all. Moment by glutton moment. . . . Not another crumb of carrion left. Lick chops and basta." This gruesome image and harsh tone would strike the reader as an incongruous conclusion unless he recalls a poem Beckett wrote decades earlier, "The Vulture":

> dragging his hunger through the sky
> of my skull shell of sky and earth
>
> stooping to the prone who must
> soon take up their life and walk
>
> mocked by a tissue that may not serve
> till hunger earth and sky be offal

With these lines as one clue to Beckett's aesthetic philosophy, we can decipher many of the image patterns in *Ill Seen*. The suffering artist with a "hovering eye" (the hungry vulture) preys on the carrion of reality, turns dead life into living art within the microcosm of his mind ("skull shell of sky and earth").[17] Transposed further into the motifs of *Ill Said*, the tearful eye stalking a woman who is "already dead" becomes a large bird of prey wanting to devour all sky and earth. Besides the mention of "carrion," another indication of a bird's world is "pip," also used in the last paragraph: "Then in that perfect dark foreknell darling sound pip for end begun." (Curiously, "pip" means, besides to peep or chirp, to break out from the shell—metaphorically here the skull's shell—and also, as a noun, it names a contagious disease of birds characterized by secretion of a thick mucus in the mouth or throat. This condition would hamper the bird-artist too in his song and thus would reduce his communication to "strangury." However, the pip sound is "darling" because it promises the writer he is approaching his end.) The notion that the artist turns life into "offal," kills his subject then resurrects and transfigures it, explains the striking image of the zone of stones overtaking the pasture. There the white stones "bury all," and the small rocks themselves resemble "millions of little sepulchres," indicating merely one way the whiteness of completed metafiction can blank out the real world in *Ill Seen Ill Said*.

Like the set and costumes of Beckett's recent play *Ohio Impromptu*, everything in *Ill Seen* emerges in stark blacks and whites. Stones, the moon, the chalky soil, the lambs all share whiteness; while the night, the woman's shadow, the cabin drapes, and the greatcoats all are funereal. The woman becomes a study in photographic visual contrasts: "the long white hair stares in a fan . . . ancient horror" (like the face in Beckett's autobiographical play *That Time*); her face and hands are "bluish white," giving off a whiff of death, and she is clothed in black. The cabin's white walls set off its black door and slates; and its ebony floor offers monotone background for the pacing figure, "Black on black the brushing skirt" (recalling May in *Footfalls* walking at night). Black dots and darts on a white disc form the watch dial, and in a geologically accurate description of granite (the same rock chosen to mingle light and dark in *Krapp's Last Tape*), Beckett adds that "Black as jade [is] the jasper that flecks its whiteness." Before the middle of the story the narrator dreads both total darkness and total white, revealing a horror of "void" in general. In contradiction, he immediately allows the woman to "vanish" so that there is "Nothing left but black sky. White earth. Or inversely." Next, he erases the natural world, leaving only the colors of words on a page: "No more sky or earth. Finished high and low. Nothing but black and white. Everywhere no matter where. But black. Void" (p. 31). Later he outlines a photographic negative void of absolute whiteness when he has snow bury the woman, her steps, and her cabin. The woman as a black stain on a sheet of white, and the black footprints leaving a "trace" that will be covered by falling or drifted snow replay wording and imagery from *Ping*; and the same interpretation of self-reflexive fiction applies: she and her actions metaphorically diagram "traces blurs signs" that slowly fade to the whiteness of a silent blank (blanc) page. Thus the key to *Ill Seen* is not the actual key in the story but the coffer it opens, more precisely its contents, a yellowing (white) paper which the narrator violently rips into shreds. Then he

stuffs it "Down the plughole. On to the next. White. Quick
blacken." His anger not only betrays frustration with the Sis-
yphean predicament of the modern writer forced to compose
and then recompose, but also implies once again that a void can
be formed either by total whiteness or total blackness, by silence
or by words that obliterate each other, by nothing or texts for
nothing.

Why does the narrator urgently write in order to achieve
blankness? This same paradox has plagued Samuel Beckett and
his readers over the last thirty years: Why does the author go on
with fiction in order to create voids? He too courts yet flees the
silence, and the imperative "on" increasingly carries a heavy personal commitment. When we are inside the recent fictions we
sense ourselves—despite all our aversions to simplistic autobiographical equations—to be inside the author's mind. Beckett's
novels, argues one critic, are "saturated with the feeling of autobiography, a feeling that puzzles the reader because, despite all
the 'I . . . my . . . mine . . . me' discourse, he seems to learn
nothing about the author. The novels seem to hover at the edge
of autobiography, but some evasion, some slipperiness, always
seems to prevent the imminent revelation. . . ."[18] The most important biographical fact about Samuel Beckett is that he is a
writer, and the most secret revelation is how he feels when he
writes, how he imagines, sees, hears, and then transforms images into words; how he perceives inner eyes and inner voices;
how he suspects and perhaps fears an endless succession of creators and scribes within him. It is that knowledge, that limited
yet expansive kind of personal evidence, which the reader
senses in these two recent pieces, especially at the conclusion of
Company:

What visions in the dark of light! Who exclaims thus? Who asks
who exclaims, What visions in the shadeless dark of light and
shade! Yet another still? Devising it all for company. What a further
addition to company that would be! Yet another still devising it for
company. Quick leave him.

With the narrative and stylistic technique of multiple layers of
observers, personas, and pronouns, Samuel Beckett chases not
just the "I" of consciousness in general but the I of his artistic
self.

12

Samuel Beckett's New Worlds

since feeling is first
who pays any attention
to the syntax of things
will never wholly kiss you;
e.e. cummings

Interpretations of Beckett's well-seen, well-said, but difficult-to-understand metafictions that are written in various sorts of quasi-English must begin with analyses of their styles; and perceiving the language as story as well as vehicle becomes crucial for his fiction after *The Unnamable*. Beckett has maintained the technique of imitative style (although some new styles embody their substances more effectively than others in his recent prose) so that the very arrangement of phrases or the absence of verbs speaks one meaning of a text. Since Beckett achieves some measure of imitative style in each fiction, characterizing the language through stylistic analysis must preface or accompany any complete interpretation of the text: the shapes of the sentences diagram the shapes of ideas. With plot, character, and setting all diminished in late Beckett fictions, the only drama remaining is the "drama of the sentence"[1] as the reader experiences suspense not of action but of syntax itself; he wonders not "Will the hero marry or die?" but "Will the narrator ever reach the end of the sentence?" and "What adventures lie between subject and object?"

Tracing the shapes of clauses and phrases provides the only way to decipher such texts as *Ping* and *Lessness*, and experiencing the drama of a sentence results in discoveries about Beckett's innovative narrative techniques that would otherwise escape the reader of works like *Company* and *Ill Seen Ill Said*. In fact, for decoding the more unorthodox styles, which possess what linguists call their own microgrammars, the Beckett reader must gradually recreate the vocabulary and the syntax rules of the text before he can begin to read it as metafiction. Recent Beckett texts demand almost a tactile pulling apart and then a geometric reconstruction: for *Ping*, I actually dismantled the text by writing

244

its constituent two-to-four word phrases on slips of paper and then shuffling them physically as well as mentally. Verbal analysis unlocks many of these self-reflexive stories, yet an unremitting concentration at the word-phrase-sentence level holds its own dangers, so that critical caution and qualification are in order. First, we must not pay so much attention to syntax and word counts that we cease to feel an emotional response—to hear the rhythms intuitively, to register the images visually. Many people have had the experience of hearing Lucky's fast-paced monologue in *Godot* or the streams of anguish from *Not I* in Beckett's theater, and therefore can identify with the narrators of *Texts for Nothing* or *How It Is* as they listen to their inner voices—suspecting that they miss every fifth word. Listening to these fragmented speeches is analogous to reading some of the residual prose, in that we must react through the heart as well as with the head. Beckett's mastery of the language makes us respond even when we cannot understand. What linguistic description can fully capture the mathematical yet lyrical effects of *Company*?

After we intellectually decipher individual phrases, we experience the narrative emotionally in (to borrow Belacqua's words again) the trajectories between phrases; to traverse these trajectories, we must interpret the language of literature, a cultural dialect. Besides treating individual texts stylistically as separate languages or dialects, the reader may identify a broader linguistic framework by viewing literature in general as a language and determining which syntactic analogs apply.[2] As Jonathan Culler explains in *Structuralist Poetics*, just as all competent speakers of English have internalized its grammatical constructions, so competent fiction readers have internalized "a grammar of literature." Beckett's post-trilogy texts flout or test both grammars: his sentences disappoint our expectations about syntax because of their ellipses, convolution, and fragmentation; his stories frustrate preconceptions and paradigms about fiction because of their refusal to begin, to progress, or to end. If overall "[t]o understand the language of a text is to recognize the world to which it refers,"[3] then the reader is as baffled by a short Beckett text as he is by the first few pages of a fantasy novel. In fact, the worlds of *Imagination Dead Imagine* and *The Lost Ones* suggest bizarre amalgams of the fantastic and the familiar, recalling the best science fiction. But even by the last page, and even on a second reading, a recent Beckett story places heavy burdens on our powers of "recuperation" (rescue from the exotic) and "naturalization" (assimilation into our notions of the real world) since everything from phrase to plot is deviant and cannot be "made to seem natural" through the usual frames of discourse.

Authors, especially fantasy writers, purposely "defamiliarize" their environments, write descriptions that make the world strange, that, in Culler's words, go "below the level of functional relevance" (p. 142); Beckett's famous depiction of Watt's walk (which sounds like robotic instructions) would be a classic illustration. In the later fictions Beckett is continually writing below this level of relevance, describing in unnecessary, almost parodic detail, for example, the torture scenes in *How It Is*, the planes and angles in *Fizzles*, and the ladder code of *The Lost Ones*. Furthermore, Beckett defamiliarizes the sentence by pushing modifiers beyond useful relevance (to the verge of incoherence) in long, convoluted clauses, and by abandoning verbs and punctuation (our normal linguistic landmarks) in strings of short phrases. The human mind, though, is flexible enough—or does it inflexibly demand sense?—to "make anything signify" (p. 138). One of Culler's asides, that even a random word sequence can be assimilated by calling it an allegory of chaos, points to *Lessness*. (John Pilling found another way of naturalizing this text—by deliberately reading it as a comfortable, consecutive narrative.)[4] Although Culler may not have had *Lessness* in mind, he does consider Beckett's work generally as he contemplates unusual fictional worlds: "As the example of Beckett shows, we can always make the meaningless meaningful by production of an appropriate context" (p. 138). Of course Beckett's fictions never shun meaning altogether; they merely appear obscure and impenetrable at first encounter. What has not been clear until lately is that for all the post-trilogy narratives, the appropriate context is language processes; a puzzling piece like *Ping* suddenly radiates with meaning when viewed as a synchronous enactment of writing.[5] If Beckett's early work is about art (*Godot* can be read as a play about interpreting, and *Endgame* as a play about composing), then this becomes doubly true for the later fictions: self-reflexive associations hold at the phrase level.

Widening the linguistic net to encompass the language of literature as a whole allows expansion from Beckett's imitative style to a notion of imitative reading: besides style reflecting substance, in the world of late Beckett the reader's activity of groping through the phrases imitates the narrator's or protagonist's behavior. One critic's description of the reading process bears an uncanny resemblance to both an explanation of Beckett's new styles and a blueprint for a residual creature's visual or mechanical movements:

The act of recreation is not a smooth or continuous process, but one which, in its essence, relies on *interruptions* of the flow to render it efficacious. We look forward, we look back, we decide, we change our decisions, we form expectations, we are shocked by their nonfulfillment, we question, we muse, we accept, we reject; this is the dynamic process of recreation.[6]

As we have seen, Beckett's later fictions are so highly unconventional that they call into question the traditional ways of approaching prose. Often requiring that we begin by parsing the language into its minimal units, these texts force us to externalize our usually internal, intuitive paths to meaning. Beckett's first-person narrators and second-person observers force a complicity with self-aware readers, with those not just attuned to the grammar of a story but also newly alert to the many potential grammars of English.

Even though each recent Beckett text comprises its own closed system of language, distinct imagistic terrain, and unique geometrical shape, when viewed together these new worlds make up a recognizable universe, the world of late Beckett. This metafictional world, outside time and space, full of detached observers, self-conscious narrators, and self-reflexive metaphors, is founded on rituals of language and of motion. Habitual movements such as Murphy's rites of arithmetic and Winnie's ceremonies of her toilet are intensified, stylized, and formalized in the rituals of Beckett's later fiction. His recent characters and narrators operate under internally and externally imposed patterns of behavior, and even when these creatures are still, their minds follow certain prescribed tracks. Beckett in turn has placed himself under sometimes arbitrary and sometimes meaningful linguistic rules, and obsessively he traces similar themes with images drawn from a web of compelling patterns.

A near equivalence between language and movement, between the character's physical and verbal journeys, is a constant in Beckett.[7] More precisely, in the later fictions there are numerous specific parallels between a character's nature, position, and motion and the language's construction and syntactical maneuvers. Starting with *Texts for Nothing* and especially in *Lessness*, the Beckett creature is a fetus who cannot "get born" or fashion an identity, and thus cannot finish its own creation. These undeveloped beings find their counterparts in fragments of aborted syntax—the "midget grammar" named by the writer/traveller in *How It Is*—in small, undeveloped phrases, often not fully formed into mature clauses, or else in grotesquely long and tortured constructions. Whether fetal, corpselike, or simply infirm, later Beckett beings are incomplete humans—amorphous, maimed, static—especially in Fizzle 8, where they reduce to "monstrous extremities including skulls stunted legs and trunks monstrous arms stunted faces." Appropriately, they speak, or are spoken about, in incomplete or twisted sentences, in fractured language. With their crawling, some characters recall toddlers (for example, the wormlike bodies in *How It Is*); and at the other end of life's span, many other recent Beckett characters are old men bent over their canes (see *Abandoned Work*, *Enough*, and *Company*), in narratives where walking sticks double as writing sticks.

With their loss of limbs and locomotion, they regress to rudiments of people depicted in rudiments of grammar. Often impotent, sexless, they command only verbless sentences, phrases lacking a center of action. When verbs *are* present, their tense is problematic for Beckett's later characters, who are wandering (if moving at all) in dimensionless suspension. *Company*'s narrator thirty years later echoes the grammatical concerns in *Texts for Nothing*, when Hearer admits, "Say changing now for some time past though no tense in the dark in that dim mind. All at once over and in train and to come" (p. 34). Numerous shifts in tenses, common in later Beckett sentences, produce a halting quality indicative of prose in revision, imitating characters striving toward self-creation. The typical Beckett narrator is what Ann Banfield calls a "timeless subjectivity" who, if he can attain an "I" within a "NOW," creates an utterance that "passes from being a sentence of narration *per se* to being a representation of consciousness."[8] These verbal issues help to explain why the bare and actionless stages of Beckett's later fictions are still compelling: we are intently watching the drama of sentence formation, the difficult progression through uncharted, self-begetting languages.

In the world of later Beckett, measured walking in straight lines is unheard of. Analogously, conventional sentences with linear subject-verb-object alignment are rare. Instead, characters struggle with effort through forbidding landscapes, or run in self-propelled panic until they must stop and pant ("little panic steps" in *Fizzles*). All this crawling and stopping, or moving and falling, is embodied in styles of false starts, of discontinuous phrases, abrupt pauses, verbal about-faces, and long digressions. Sentences run out of energy or lose direction after one phrase—or one modifier, or one preposition. In extended structures there may indeed live a subject (questioned, mocked, cancelled) and perhaps a verb (revised, qualified, contradicted), but these parts of speech are separated by distances so vast that, as the *Texts* narrator puts it, the subject dies before the verb. In the longest sentences, embedded clauses produce parodies of elaborate syntax as characters get entangled in their own physical and verbal patterns. Beckett describes creatures impeded or halting with short jagged and repeated phrases; he depicts wanderers moving in large circles or twisted tunnels with long convoluted sentences. One other common Beckettian travel mode is a zigzag motion, ahead yet deflected at a forty-five degree angle,[9] toward a center then away from it, in an indirect route represented by the paradoxical language of the Unnamable's "I can't go on, I'll go on." Any progress toward stillness implies some sort of hope, and yet the specific configuration of that progress signifies the hopelessness of reaching an end.

Motion is so constricted and circumscribed that for some characters the body cannot go on at all; when the creature as a whole is stalled in space, then the smallest activity of any bodily part becomes momentous. In "Still" (Fizzle 7) the turning of a head or the dropping of a hand assume epic, godlike proportions for an otherwise static figure. *Company*'s listener lying still in the darkness contemplates and magnifies minimal gestures, and this fragmentation occurs stylistically as well as physically in his one-phrase sentences, which permit only slow, disjoint linguistic progression:

Can he move? Does he move? Should he move? What a help that would be. When the voice fails. Some movement however small. Were it but of a hand closing. Or opening if closed to begin. What a help that would be in the dark! To close the eyes and see that hand. . . .
There is of course the eye. Filling the whole field. The hood

slowly down. Or up if down to begin. The globe. All pupil. Staring up. Hooded. Bared. Hooded again. Bared again. [Pp. 20–21]

In *Company*—as well as in *Ping, Imagination Dead Imagine,* and *The Lost Ones*—the flicker of an eyelid shakes the earth. Similarly, small changes in phrasing pulsate the prose and create a quiet humor in the movement of language itself for these later pieces, not as obvious or broad as the comic moments in the trilogy but equally satisfying.

With increasing precision, Beckett writes of a person who is watching relentlessly, trying to catch himself in the act of imagining; and expressing this vigilance becomes one of the many functions of the pervasive eye imagery in his world. Many artists begin by observing the outside world, and some of Beckett's narrators—artists all—assume the objective stance of a camera eye, taking snapshots, capturing their subjects. Yet as early as *Texts for Nothing* (1950) the voice already had begun to say farewell to the realistic "world above." In many of the recent stories the artist must kill his subject, must observe it to death (*Imagination Dead Imagine, Fizzle 8, Ill Seen Ill Said*) in order to recreate it. Besides looking outward, the Beckett narrator looks within, often to establish or reaffirm his own existence or identity. The need to be witnessed (as in *From an Abandoned Work*) makes an observing eye comforting as well as agonizing; and the narrator of *Texts for Nothing* tries to visualize himself into being—to imagine a character's body into which he can infuse himself. When the eyes are destroyed in *The Lost Ones,* the searchers are forced to seek within themselves, thus the artist's self-perception becomes another visual motif in the world of late Beckett, in which the "pale blue" eyes occurring in *Lessness* and suggested elsewhere represent the author's own introspection: "Ruins all silent marble still little body prostrate at attention wash blue [eyes] deep in gaping sockets" (*Fizzle 8*). As the artist searches externally, then internally, and back out onto his own verbal creation, the prose in Beckett's new world reflects this oscillation through repetition; consider the phrase "within without" in *Ping* and the vacillation between "Go in" and "Go back out" in *Imagination Dead Imagine,* whose every structure and detail connotes imaginative vision. Making the imagined tangible is a necessary step of visual reconstruction, as thoughts flow from the mind's eye to the hand (*Enough*) or from the eye of the imagination to the voice of narration (*Ill Seen Ill Said*).

Taking observation one level deeper, Beckett's highly self-conscious narrators perceive themselves as they envision, compose, and revise, especially in *How It Is, Imagination Dead Imagine, Company,* and *Ill Seen Ill Said.* Finally, self-conscious readers—now players in Beckett's new fictional games—also shift focus between an "I" and a "he," the other of the text, as they perceive themselves reading. To analyze a similar recursive sensation, George Poulet uses the image of detached witnessing and the word "prey," which, curiously, recall the language of *Imagination*:

Everything happens . . . as though, from the moment I become a prey to what I read, I to begin to share the use of my consciousness with this being . . . who is the conscious subject ensconced at the heart of the work. . . . A lag takes place, a sort of schizoid distinction between what I feel and what the other feels; a confused awareness of delay, so that the work seems first to think by itself, and then to inform me what it has thought. Thus I often have the impression, while reading, of simply witnessing an action which at the same time concerns and yet does not concern me.[10]

In *Ill Seen* a hierarchy of observers and observed necessitates different sorts of eyes, a visual progression from author to narrator to character to reader. A similar layering is embodied in the shifts of pronouns in *Company* as the reader listens to a creature who listens to himself listening in the dark.

Beckett characters do not merely want to observe themselves or be perceived into being; they strive to perceive being itself and then to create it. In this way, puny and weak as they are, they aspire to divinity: they assume godlike characteristics as creators and as saviors, suffering as they impose the order of art on the confusion of thought, by creating a tiny world syllable by painful syllable. What separates man from machine or animal is not just that he thinks but that he knows that he thinks. Strata of self-awareness in Beckett are expressed in a regression of voices and in the nesting of clauses, both suggesting the uncovering of the "ideal core of the onion," Beckett's metaphor for being in *Proust.* Consequently, the weary voice can never die: there is always another voice waiting to record that death. Beckett is continually writing to infinite regression but never arriving there. Drawing mathematical diagrams, critics agree that his descending linguistic spiral seeks a point (that which has zero dimensions), the infinitely small, but the vanishing point keeps receding—and this reduction and retraction occurs once again in the most recent fiction, called *Worstward Ho*.

Things go from bad to worse in Beckett's fiction, from "ill said" to "missaid" in *Worstward Ho*, as he continues writing but "With worsening words." After the *Ill Seen* narrator begins by inciting himself "On," this little word recurs insistently in its first few paragraphs. In the next piece, *Worstward Ho*, "on" becomes a chant, a compulsion, a dirge—with the same shifting, ambivalent tone as the repeated command for "More" in the concurrent playlet *Rockaby*. The tiny first paragraph contains "on" in each of its six miniscule sentences:

On. Say on. Be said on. Somehow on. Till nohow on. Said nohow on.[11]

This last sentence also ends the entire text. Thus the piece, like *The Unnamable*, concludes with the stoic imperative "on," but undercut by two notions: that instead of going on, the narrator is just saying that he is going on; and that he moves *nohow* on rather than the more positive *anyhow* on (this contradiction, or at least paradox, is echoed in the jarring title "Worstward Ho"). The most recent fictional "going on" proceeds in a manner similar to the drop-by-drop, word-by-word "strangury" in *Ill Seen Ill Said*, through an alternation of "secreting" or "oozing" with stopping: repetitive sentences in short paragraphs and then blanks or white spaces; truncated phrases and then dashes. "Blanks for when words gone. . . . No ooze for when ooze gone" (p. 41), the narrator asserts in a paragraph that paradoxically and humorously repeats "ooze" eight times. To create "Blanks for nohow on," Beckett drops fourteen dashes over his forty large-print pages. With the despairing and oxymoronic phrase "nohow on," the repetition of "on" produces incantatory prose rhythms; and "on" also sets up assonance with the semantically related recurrent words "long" and "gone." As in other late Beckett texts, these effects are more pronounced when short sentences are transcribed as lines of poetry:

Blanks for nohow on.
How long?
Blanks how long till somehow on?
Again somehow on.
All gone when nohow on.
Time gone when nohow on. [P. 32]

Even more so than in *Ill Seen Ill Said*, the language gives the impression that it is running away with itself, that sound is taking supremacy over sense: with alliteration enhancing internal rhyme in "Faintly vainly longing" (p. 37), and with plays on words like "All gnawing to be naught. Never to be naught" and "Vain longing that vain longing go." Like the "I" in *Texts for Nothing*, this narrator becomes preoccupied with a term or a syntactical segment and then must exhaust it before he can advance to another paragraph with either a new fixation (say, the idea of blanks) or else a different narrative element (say, hands or eyes). But these apparent tongue twisters do not exist merely to tease the reader; rather they develop the very themes of the piece, the artist's immediate and frustrating relationship with language. "To last unlessenable least how loath to leasten" (p. 34) is an inflated and comical way of saying that he wants somehow to move on.

Besides "on," the second constant throughout *Worstward Ho* (the very titles reveal despair as Beckett's art regresses from *Ill Seen Ill Said* and *Fizzles*) is the notion of saying. In order to go on artistically, one must say something; and in order to proceed with nothing at hand, one must *say* anything, everything into existence: "No bones but [nevertheless?] say bones" (p. 8). The reader can hear an implied "therefore" in the "but" here, and also between the statements "Say on. Be on" (p. 24). In this next self-consciously creative sequence, an old woman is brought into being gradually and painfully through words, in fact through the mere saying of "the words":

Somehow again on back to the bowed back alone. Nothing to show a woman's and yet a woman's. Oozed from softening soft the word woman's. The words old woman's. The words nothing to show bowed back alone a woman's and yet a woman's. So better worse from now that shade a woman's. An old woman's. [P. 35]

Like the Unnamable, who begins "Where now? Who now?," the narrator worstward bound debates whether to start with the place or the body. He begins to narrate feeling literally sick of his own writing, vomiting up banal words as did the *Ill Seen* voice at the conclusion of that piece. One way to recommence (after he admonishes himself to "Throw up for good") is to will something into being through pronouns, the same linguistic sleight of hand that Beckett developed for *Texts for Nothing*. So by the second page we get "It stands. What? Yes. Say it stands." Repetition of "it stands" allows *it* to acquire substance until the narrator ventures pronouns more personal, then finds them too strong: "No words for him whose words. Him? One. No words for one whose words. One? It" (p. 20). "It" suffices because all that exists is the little body—not even a being, a "one"—the same little body from *Lessness* that could not stand upright. The figure that now is "Somehow standing" (p. 11) is the body of fictional language, the frail creation described in the "midget grammar" of *How It Is*. The narrator speaks of it in some of the most un-English sentences Beckett has produced—like sophisticated baby talk: "Try say. How first it lay. Then somehow knelt. Bit by bit. Then on from there. Bit by bit. Till up at last" (p. 10).

As in *Lessness*, many words are negated in *Worstward Ho* with the suffix "-less": "Thenceless thitherless there" depicts this paradoxical world in which time and space are abolished. Also lessened is sentence structure, until the two-word clause becomes common and the one-word sentence is not infrequent. In the syntactic tradition of *Enough* and *Ill Seen Ill Said*, this text rides on a grammar of accumulation and afterthought—"Other examples if needs must. Of pain. Relief from. Change of"—producing not so much sentences as notes for sentences. Syntax in general is lessened toward the speech of an infantile creature, especially through the deletion of articles and prepositions:

So skull not go. [P. 46]
A time when try see. [P. 11]
How try say? How try fail? No try no fail. [P. 17]

In what fraction remains of plot, character, setting, syntax, and morphology, the motto is "Add? Never. Till if needs must. . . . Others to lessen" (p. 25). Most conspicuously not added in this piece is the pronoun "I," the voice who is doing all the saying and the missaying. Supplying the missing agent and expanding the lessening clauses is demanding for the reader because many possibilities occur to the imagination. Consider the verb "say" (although the very part of speech is questionable) in the following representative passage:

Unchanged? Sudden back unchanged? Yes. Say yes.
Each time unchanged. Somehow unchanged. Till no.
Till say no. [P. 14]

This "say" can mean "[you] say" (an imperative to the narrator himself, as in *Imagination Dead Imagine*) or "[let me] say" or "[I'm going to] assert" or "let us assume" or "the uttering [of it]." Two other problematic words, "for" and "be," produce strained syntax; and sentences bearing these two words plus multiple and consecutive "said"s become almost impossible to decipher:

Said is missaid. Whenever said said said missaid. From now said alone. No more from now now said and now missaid. From now said alone. Said for missaid. For be missaid. [P. 37]

Uncompacting the triple "saids," we might get "Whenever the saying one said something, he missaid something, that is, misspoke himself." In other words, all words are false. And yet only by saying can this impotent narrator create anything; he closes a description of eyes with "Be they so said," a forceful, authoritative imperative reminiscent of "Let there be . . ." from Genesis.

Beyond permitting ambiguous meanings, the narrator also self-consciously questions meaning itself, the connection between word and idea: "Something not wrong with one. Meaning—meaning!—meaning the kneeling one" (p. 20). Here the exclamation implies that we are not at the level of philosophical or semantic interpretation but mere grammatical clarity, the antecedents for the pronoun "one." Elsewhere the narrator settles for the vague language of uncertainty in which antecedents are unknown and unimportant: "Somewhose somewhere somehow enough still" (p. 30). "Somehow" used here later succumbs to "nohow" in greater frequency, culminating—culminating!—in the penultimate paragraph which ends "Nohow less. Nohow worse. Nohow naught. Nohow on."

In *Worstward Ho* the despondent artist watching himself trying to ooze out more words through a narrator, within the soft within the skull ("In that head in that head"—p. 22) requires more eyes than ever before, and more layering of vision, than in the other late fictions. After the body that is posited at the beginning, Beckett introduces "Another. . . . Head sunk on crippled hands," in other words himself, or a close metaphor for himself, an old man suffering from arthritis—especially in his fingers. (The actor Julian Curry tells a moving story about learning from Beckett by mail that Krapp in *Krapp's Last Tape* should on stage embrace his tape recorder with crippled hands, and then when meeting Beckett in person, finding that his fingers outstretched for greeting were curled like a claw.)[12] This author/Another has "Eyes clenched. Seat of all. Germ of all" (p. 10), his vision and imagination again linked. Often in the piece the eyes are depicted as staring, but they also adopt characteristics one normally associates with fists, like hands tightening and clasping: "Clenched staring eyes. Clenched eyes clamped to clenched staring eyes" (p. 23). It is as if the eye itself, the "preying" eye, must reach out and grab the world, or at least the word, some universe waiting to be captured by the artist's conception, "Clenched eyes clamped to all" (p. 23).

Yet as in each of Beckett's new worlds, vision focuses within as well as without; the writer must "see for be seen" in order to observe himself in the act of composing. He is reduced to "Skull and stare alone. Scene and seer of all" (p. 24), that is, seen and see-er of all he creates. The movement in and out intensifies when the narrator conflates the two stares into one eye, "One dim black hole mid-foreskull. Into the hell of all. Out from the hell of all" (p. 44). This idea of a permeable Cyclops membrane is later repeated in language still further compressed and employing again the astronomical phrase "black hole" (for void) appearing in Fizzle 8: "Black hole agape on all. Inletting all. Outletting all" (p. 45). Even at the end, the eye lingers, as does its oscillating motion: "Into [the skull] still the hole. Into what left of soft. From out what little left" (p. 47). Besides witnessing himself, characteristically "in pain" as he writes, the narrator sees three figures, an old man and a child holding hands (shades of *From an Abandoned Work* and *Enough*), and an old woman looking at gravestones with the "names gone and when to when" (the mourner of deceased fiction from *Ill Seen*). This trinity of shadowy characters is represented by the "three pins" in "one pinhole" of the ending, the three most definite objects that the artist's eye perceives, like a primitive camera—two pieces of cardboard, one with a pinpoint hole.

The Unnamable races ahead for several pages and then stops, veers toward a new direction, continues with a different story or train of thought. Beckett's recent narrator plodding worstward reaches such an impasse about every second short paragraph and consequently must begin numerous sentences with "On" or "On back." Beckett goes on by the very saying of exactly why and how he cannot go on, or by the wish to go on "worse"; thus the piece logically ends with "Said nohow on." Reinforcing the recurrence of "on" and "say," and the exploiting of "less" terms, the repetition of carefully chosen words and affixes constructs Beckett's net of linguistic despair. All this calls into question one critic's depiction of Becket's prose starting with *Enough*, and her prediction for the texts after *Company*: "Instead of impasse the pieces project a tranquil diminishing. Instead of falling into exhausted silence, the pieces drift softly to rest."[13] While there is some sardonic humor in *Worstward Ho*, cynicism rather than tranquility prevails. The title word "worse" in many compounds and forms—grammatical or not—both spurs the narrative forward and undermines it, holds it back. "Worse words for worser still" becomes the goal (p. 41). One linguistic method to worsen words is to write them and unwrite them simultaneously with the prefix "un-," which appears pervasively in the text, for example in "unworsenable worst," "uninane," and "unlessenable." Then with two consecutive "un-"s the writer can pretend to make a positive statement [analogously $-(-5)=5$], yet "ununsaid" delivers not the force of "said." The language of paradox, so common in Beckett's later fictional worlds, travels new paths as Beckett moves worstward, especially in the penultimate paragraph of the text, where "No move and [yet] sudden[ly?] all far. . . . At bounds of boundless void." "Void" is the last word in several *Worstward Ho* sentences and the terminus that Beckett narrators both seek and flee. The stylistic features cataloged here combine in a sentence that tries desperately to un-say itself, but which escapes a complete void with the last-minute qualifier/rescuer "almost": "Unmoreable unlessable unworseable evermost almost void" (p. 43).

A writer challenging himself at these profound linguistic levels clearly sets up a series of interpretive hurdles for the reader—one of the features of postmodernist narrative. Since Beckett was a pioneer of postmodernism, one would expect his prose to exhibit in an early stage all the devices now characteristic of contemporary fiction. What is surprising, though, is that Beckett had already introduced these experimental techniques in a developed, mature form by the time of *Texts for Nothing* (1950). In fact, by comparison with the most extreme reaches of recent innovative prose, Beckett's texts have gotten there first and already claimed the stylistic territory. In his earliest fiction, alogic, deletions, repeated patterns, intentional errors, and self-conscious remarks undercut surface realism.[14] Criteria for contemporary fiction, when applied to Beckett's later worlds, can be extended to deeper and deeper fictional strata. Many recent self-conscious fictions have experimented, for example, with shifting narrative levels in order to stress the artificiality of a text. Beckett began

this with the voice in *The Unnamable* asking if he has been created by some Other; by the 1980's in *Company*, as we have seen,
the "narrated object" and the "narrating agent" reverse in mid-
paragraph and mid-sentence. Its series of devised devisors transcends even the narrative complexity of Christine Brooke-Rose's
novel called *Thru* (1975), which describes its own technique in
the sentence, "Whoever you invented invented you too." [15]

While one formulation of the reader's general problem with
contemporary prose is uncertainty that "manifests itself on the
level of narrative rather than style," [16] we have found that sentences in Beckett's new styles display profound indeterminacy at
the level of syntax and semantics. If other contemporary writers
express a global lack of certainty in their shifting character
names and abandonment of the closed ending, Beckett evinces
despair in any security by failing even to begin a story. The Unnamable opens with questions searching for a point of departure
and concludes by spurring himself to "go on"; and the exhausted
voice of *Ill Seen Ill Said*, thirty-two years later, can begin only by
inciting itself "On." Many fictions in between—*Texts for Nothing*,
How It Is, *Enough*, *Company*—commence in the middle of things
or move toward circular conclusions or dead ends, because true
beginnings and endings become philosophically and linguistically impossible. Because residual sentences and phrases self-
cancel, self-destruct, even the smallest units of narrative cannot
begin or terminate.

Other characteristics of postmodernist prose that operate on
plot elements or narrative technique in contemporary American
fiction (which is, in general, more experimental than contemporary British) come into play at the phrase level in Beckett's new
worlds. While Barth, Borges, Doctorow, and other postmodernists practice plot permutation by offering several possible paths
to the conclusion of a narrative, Beckett produces wonderfully
comic effects with permutation of phrases in *Texts* and *Enough*.
Rearrangement of words is *inherently* funny if we accept Henri
Bergson's analysis of the comic as the mechanical superimposed
on the human, and this alone could account for much of the humor of a Beckett prose sequence—particularly when read aloud.
In addition, Beckett's permutations of language [17] have a serious
consequent: they imply the infinite potential of syntax. According to theories of generative grammar, the rules governing conjunction make possible infinitely long sentences by the mere addition of "and" with another phrase; or in Beckett's case, by the

addition of "or." Disjunction, digression, contradiction, authorial intrusion—all of these postmodern devils of discontinuity—are working in his posttrilogy texts; but just as prevalent in the recent pieces is disconnected syntax in fragmented sentences, incomplete clauses, and non-sequitur phrases, that is, discontinuity beneath the plot and paragraph level.

After stretching the sentence in *The Unnamable* as far as Faulkner could, Beckett then contracts it in later texts as much as Vonnegut dares. Few fiction writers—we would have to admit Joyce to this select group too—have played as many variations on the English sentence, or played them as lyrically; Beckett shares the poet's freedom with and delight in grammar. As he is dismissing conventional syntax and punctuation, Beckett is feeding logic to the (Knott household) dogs. When taken to extremes, alogic becomes randomness, and returns us to the chance sequence of *Lessness*, which succeeds as art despite its mechanical ordering because the originally composed sentences are internally well shaped and beautiful: "Little body little block heart beating ash grey only upright." While *Lessness* best captures the Beckett creature in miniature and embodies Beckett's experimentation with language, each later fiction similarly resists reduction to a tale about life and becomes a chronicle about writing itself, in fact, a diagram of the workings of fictional language.

Activity in the real world becomes increasingly constrained for Beckett characters after Murphy, and since 1960 one of the few permitted movements has been to look inward to the self. The only way for Beckett to write is to secrete or "ooze" words drop by drop—"strangury"; the only prose to write is self-conscious, self-referential fictions. How tiresome to keep reading about the impossibility of writing, interjects Robert Scholes, who obviously prefers fabulators to metafictionists.[18] Displaying the same short-temperedness as some reviewers of *Company* (return, circular Reader, to the first page of Chapter 1), Scholes complains that recent self-reflexive narratives often lack either of his criteria for fiction: sublimation (escape) and feedback (new vision). This critique continues in a chapter he entitles "Imagination Dead Imagine," an allusion to Beckett not pursued and not altogether complimentary. Surely some readers choose not to "go on" with Beckett after *The Unnamable*, but those who do will discover the aesthetic enjoyments one always anticipates in a great stylist fabricating new styles, and the intellectual joys of altered perspectives on language, on reading—and perhaps even our world and how to interpret it. New visions, then, about both prose and perception itself.

Jonathan Culler makes even larger claims for experimental fiction, that it helps us interpret not just the outside world but also ourselves:

the most challenging and innovatory texts . . . are precisely those that are difficult to process according to received modes of understanding. An awareness of the assumptions on which one proceeds, an ability to make explicit what one is trying to do, makes it easier to see where and how the text resists one's attempts to make sense of it and how, by its refusal to comply with one's expectations, it leads to that questioning of the self and of ordinary social modes of understanding which has always been the result of the greatest literature. [P. 129]

Passive reading of the later fictions is out of the question. As Ruby Cohn says about *Imagination*, "Beckett defies the reader *not* to pick up a pencil," and about *Ping*, "Beckett compels the reader to become a fellow-writer." [19] Whether one is an active reader or a hyperactive stylistician rearranging permuted phrases, the reader feels as if she is de-composing the prose. Actually she performs a grammatical version of Barthes' thematic and imagistic dissection in *S/Z*: "It is that kind of reading, disrespectful because it cuts up the text, and fascinated, loving (éprise) because it returns to it and feeds on it, that I have tried to write." [20] Beckett's repetitive languages, for instance, provide static backgrounds against which new phrases, divergent memory passages, and swerves in style—as in the autobiographical images of *How It Is* and *Company*—are foregrounded; and the reader must locate, cluster, and interpret these highlighted elements with a sensitivity to each word. After abandoning our lists and recombining the fragments, we learn to kiss a text as well as to pay attention to the syntax of things.

Every time a writer sits down at his desk he in a sense reinvents the language, and Beckett accomplishes this in multiple dimensions by creating new dialects of English, and by writing *about* language, fiction, and his own career through highly self-conscious narrators. If we can define a language simply as a set of words with syntax rules for linking those words correctly, then for many later pieces, Beckett has devised a new grammar— different minimal constituent units (either words or phrases) and self-imposed regulations for their arrangement. Another property of a language, freedom within constraint, permits an end-less generation of grammatical constructions. Words move in regulated structures, behaving like the Lost Ones climbing on their ordinance-governed ladders. *Ping* originated as lists of phrasal elements and rules for their pairing and sequencing; *Lessness* demonstrates, almost parades, both facets of language—finite rules and infinite combinations—producing a text about grammar, about the possibilities of prose. Exploiting a circum-scribed phrasal vocabulary, Beckett generates ten sentences de-riving from an image, for each of six images. With these sixty sentences of a finite variety (the same constituent phrases per-muted in different ways) the author then lets loose chaos to-wards artistic order; he rolls linguistic dice to determine haphaz-ard sequencing of sentences and random lengths of paragraphs.

Beckett literally makes a game of chance and skill out of lan-guage, surpassing all the games and systems used simply as motifs in his earlier fictions: astrology, arithmetic, chess, and ge-ometry. In the later prose he plays end games of grammar, and toys with geometries of narration. Paradoxically, this view of the writer as the inventor of a matrix for each text both endows him with control and strips him of power. Godlike, Beckett creates a new system, but because his linguistic network is based on such a circumscribed, self-limiting diction and grammar, his degrees of linguistic freedom are constrained. Then, with an added layer of irony, this supposedly impotent artist demonstrates his crea-tive powers in a virtuoso performance, like a poet intentionally choosing the villanelle form with which to challenge and display his verbal expertise.

Each Beckett fiction defines its own world, its own closed sys-tem of language (most obviously in *The Lost Ones*), creating a structure—cylinder, oblong, dome—in which the artist or the reader is enclosed. But these stark, confining worlds are de-picted with such scientific precision and such poetic lyricism, and the linguistic limitations are overcome so deftly, that the stark fictional constructs possess what mathematicians term ele-gance. Beckett is a verbal Houdini who, manacled at ankles and wrists, locks himself in a trunk submerged in water—and then brilliantly escapes. Of course, a performer does not earn endur-ing fame and respect by repeating the same feats, but by invent-ing fresh routines to perform, each one more daring than the last. Although Beckett has occasionally retreated to earlier, safer styles, with most of the later pieces he perseveres onward to some new challenge, as he did when he exploited the second person pronoun with layers of consciousness in *Company*. However, these later pieces are not just dazzling linguistic performances for their own sake, but are vehicles for exploring being, language, and imagination. Another self-reflexive author, Raymond Federman, has said that for his own work and in the fiction he reads and admires (including, of course, Beckett's), "to write a novel is not only to tell a story, it is a process of interrogation about the creative process."[21] And herein lies our continuing fascination with Beckett's fiction even when it appears exasperatingly unreadable: we sense that he is allowing us to experience literature at its genesis, to glimpse, to discover, in his creation and our recreation of a text, the very workings of the human brain, profound complexity in simple words.

In attempting to overcome his artistic impasse after *The Unnamable*, Beckett has created a temporary impasse for the reader. As he goes on with fiction, he calls for a new type of reader who will go on with a more intense kind of reading—one who is able to approach prose as if it were poetry and, simultaneously, as if it were a sample text of a foreign language. When analyzing the style of recent fictions, each babel of silence and words, we appreciate Beckett's solutions to linguistic problems as we recreate those stratagems. Instead of simply experiencing a fictional universe, we must first reconstruct it, must fabricate a something out of very little—unreal settings, vanishing characters, and nonsentences. In our difficult verbal journey we form an artistic partnership with narrator/protagonists or narrator/observers and with the author himself, as we share their struggles with issues as large as narrative technique and as small as the choice of a word. Thus in wrenching story and grammar beyond their normal limits, Samuel Beckett extends us beyond our original limitations and expands our abilities as readers, out past the figments of dawn and dusk.

Notes

Chapter 1. Beckett's New Styles

1. Samuel Beckett quoted by Harold Hobson, "Samuel Beckett: Dramatist of the Year," *International Theatre Annual I* (1956), p. 153.

2. See Hannah Copeland, *Art and the Artist in the Works of Samuel Beckett.* 3. Richard A. Lanham, *Analyzing Prose* (New York: Charles Scribner's Sons, 1983).

4. David Lodge, *The Language of Fiction: Essays in Criticism and Verbal Analysis of the English Novel* (New York: Columbia Press, 1966).

5. Majorie Perloff, "Between Verse and Poetry: Beckett and the New Poetry." See also Chap. 6 in Perloff's *The Poetics of Indeterminacy: Rimbaud to Cage* (Princeton, N.J.: Princeton University Press, 1981).

6. Samuel Beckett in Israel Shenker, "Moody Man of Letters," *New York Times*, May 6, 1957, sec. 2, p. 1.

7. Beckett, *Proust*, p. 67.

8. Beckett, "Dante . . . Bruno . Vico . . Joyce," in *Our Exagmination Round His Factification for Incamination of Work in Progress* (1929; New York: New Directions, 1972), p. 14.

9. Fish, "What is Stylistics and Why are They Saying Such Terrible Things About It?" in Seymour Chatman, ed., *Approaches to Poetics*, p. 150n.

10. Fish, "Literature in the Reader: Affective Stylistics," in Jane P. Tompkins, ed., *Reader-Response Criticism: From Formalism to Post-Structuralism*, p. 74; reprinted from *New Literary History* 2, no. 1 (Autumn 1970): 123–62.

11. Lawrence E. Harvey, *Samuel Beckett: Poet and Critic*, p. 168.

12. H. Porter Abbott, *The Fiction of Samuel Beckett: Form and Effect.*

13. Especially good is Ludovic Janvier, "Style in the Trilogy," in J. D. O'Hara, ed., *Twentieth Century Interpretations of "Molloy," "Malone Dies," and "The Unnamable"*, pp. 82–90. This piece first appeared as part of Janvier's book *Pour Samuel Beckett* (Paris: Editions de Minuit, 1966); translated here by O'Hara.

14. Hugh Kenner, "Shades of Syntax," in Ruby Cohn, ed., *Samuel Beckett: A Collection of Criticism*, pp. 21–31.

15. Curtis W. Hayes, "A Study in Prose Styles: Edward Gibbon and Ernest Hemingway," in Donald C. Freeman, ed., *Linguistics and Literary Style*, pp. 279–96. Hereafter this book will be cited as *LALS*. Hayes's article is reprinted from *Texas Studies in Literature and Language* 7 (1964): 371–86.

16. Richard Ohmann, "Generative Grammars and the Concept of Literary Style," in Freeman, ed., *LALS*, pp. 258–76, rpr. from *Word* 20 (1964): 424–39.

17. Also see Enoch Brater, "Dada, Surrealism, and the Genesis of *Not I*," *Modern Drama* 18 (1975): 49–59.

18. Susan Brienza and Enoch Brater, "Chance and Choice in Beckett's *Lessness*," *ELH* 43 (1976): 244–58.

19. Maurice Nadeau, *The History of Surrealism*, trans. from the French by Richard Howard, p. 49.

20. Jolas, *transition* 3 (June 1929): 179. Quoted in Barbara Reich Gluck, *Beckett and Joyce: Friendship and Fiction*, p. 22.

21. Quoted in Sighle Kennedy, *Murphy's Bed* (Lewisburg, Pa.: Bucknell University Press, 1971), p. 274.

22. "'Syntax Upended in Opposite Corners': Alterations in Beckett's Linguistic Theories," in Morris Beja et al., eds., *Samuel Beckett: Humanistic Perspectives*, p. 125.

23. James Peter Thorne, "Stylistics and Generative Grammar," in Freeman, ed., *LALS*, pp. 182–96, rpr. from *Journal of Linguistics* 1 (1965): 49–59.

24. Richard M. Ohmann, "Prolegomena to the Analysis of Prose Style," in Harold C. Martin, ed., *Style in Prose Fiction*, English Institute Essays (New York, 1959), p. 9.

25. Tzvetan Todorov, "The Place of Style in the Structure of the Text," in Seymour Chatman, ed., *Literary Style: A Symposium*, pp. 30–31.

26. Jan Mukarovsky, "Standard Language and Poetic Language" in *LALS*, pp. 40–56, rpr. from *A Prague School Reader on Esthetics, Literary Structure, and Style*, selected and translated by Paul L. Garvin (Washington, D.C.: Georgetown University Press, 1964), pp. 17–30.

27. M. A. K. Halliday, "Descriptive Linguistics in Literary Study," in Freeman, ed., *LALS*, pp. 57–72, rpr. from G. I. Duthie, ed., *English Studies Today* (Edinburgh University Press, 1964), and Geoffrey Leech, "This Bread I Break—Language and Interpretation," in Freeman, ed., *LALS*, pp. 119–28, rpr. from *A Review of English Literature* 6 (1965): 66–75.

28. Bruce F. Kawin, *Telling It Again and Again: Repetition in Literature and Film*, p. 155.

29. Brian Finney, "*Assumption* to *Lessness*: Beckett's Shorter Fiction," p. 76; in Katherine Worth, ed. *Beckett the Shape Changer*, pp. 61–84.

30. *Ulysses* (1922; New York: Random House, 1961), p. 704.

31. DavidRead, "Artistic Theory in the Work of Samuel Beckett," *Journal of Beckett Studies*, no. 8 (Autumn 1982): 18.

32. See Harvey, *Samuel Beckett*, p. 441 and p. 249. Quoted in Read, p. 20.

33. Samuel Beckett to John Fletcher, quoted in Finney, "*Assumption* to *Lessness*," p. 75.

34. Brian Finney, *Since "How It Is"*: *A Study of Samuel Beckett's Later Fiction*. Also see note 30.

35. See J. E. Dearlove, *Accommodating the Chaos: Samuel Beckett's Nonrelational Art*.

36. See Ruby Cohn, *Back to Beckett*.

37. Beckett letter of June 21, 1956, quoted in Samuel Beckett, *Disjecta: Miscellaneous Writings and a Dramatic Fragment*, ed. Ruby Cohn (New York: Grove Press, 1984), p. 107.

38. Beckett letter of October 15, 1956, quoted in *Disjecta*, p. 107.

39. Samuel Beckett, *Stories and Texts for Nothing*, p. 82.

40. See Ben-Zvi's now-classic article, "Samuel Beckett, Fritz Mauthner, and the Limits of Language," *PMLA* 95 (March 1980): 183–200.

Chapter 2. *Texts for Nothing*

1. Samuel Beckett, *Stories and Texts for Nothing*, p. 125. All citations refer to this edition.

2. Ruby Cohn, *Samuel Beckett*: *The Comic Gamut*, p. 169.

3. John Fletcher, *The Novels of Samuel Beckett*, p. 196; and Eugene Webb, *Samuel Beckett: A Study of His Novels*, p. 154.

4. Cohn, *The Comic Gamut*, p. 154.

5. From a corrected and revised typescript of *Texts for Nothing* at Washington University, St. Louis.

6. Seen to imply "the meaning that there is no meaning" in Hannelore Fahrenbach and John Fletcher, "The 'Voice of Silence': Reason, Imagination and Creative Sterility in 'Texts for Nothing.'" *Journal of Beckett Studies*, no. 1 (Winter 1976): 30–31.

7. Brian Finney, "*Assumption* to *Lessness*: Beckett's Shorter Fiction," in Katherine Worth, ed., *Beckett the Shape Changer*, p. 73.

8. Samuel Beckett, *Nouvelles et textes pour rien* (Paris: Éditions de Minuit, 1958), p. 139.

9. *Textes pour rien*, pp. 156–57.

10. *Textes*, p. 179.

11. *Textes*, p. 201.

12. J. E. Dearlove, *Accommodating the Chaos: Samuel Beckett's Nonrelational Art*, pp. 80–83.

13. H. Porter Abbott, *The Fiction of Samuel Beckett: Form and Effect*, p. 131.

14. Abbott, *Fiction of Samuel Beckett*, p. 133.

15. Cohn, *The Comic Gamut*, pp. 174–75.

16. Bruce F. Kawin, *Telling it Again and Again: Repetition in Literature and Film*, p. 133.

17. Richard Coe, "God and Samuel Beckett" in J. D. O'Hara, ed.,

Twentieth Century Interpretations of "Molloy," "Malone Dies," "The Unnamable", p. 112.

18. Francis Michael Doherty, *Samuel Beckett*, p. 139.

19. Mary Ann Caws, "A Rereading of the Traces," *L'Esprit Créateur* 11, no. 3 (Fall 1971): 15.

20. Marilyn Gaddis Rose, "The Lyrical Structure of Beckett's *Texts for Nothing*," *Novel* 4, no. 3 (Spring 1971): 224.

21. From materials at Washington University, St. Louis.

22. John Pilling has perceived some of these correspondences and reaches a similar conclusion on the importance of *Texts for Nothing* for Beckett's later development. See James Knowlson and John Pilling, *Frescoes of the Skull: The Later Prose and Drama of Samuel Beckett*, pp. 41–61.

Chapter 3. *From an Abandoned Work*

1. In Samuel Beckett, *First Love and Other Shorts*, pp. 39–49. All subsequent citations for this story refer to this edition.

2. J. E. Dearlove, *Accommodating the Chaos: Samuel Beckett's Nonrelational Art*, pp. 129, 132.

3. See Richard N. Coe, *Samuel Beckett* (New York: Grove Press, 1966), p. 79.

4. H. Porter Abbott, *The Fiction of Samuel Beckett: Form and Effect*, p. 138.

5. John M. Coetzee, "The English Fiction of Samuel Beckett: An Essay in Stylistic Analysis," (dissertation, University of Texas at Austin, 1969), pp. 125–32.

6. Coetzee, "The English Fiction," p. 148.

7. Ruby Cohn, *Samuel Beckett: The Comic Gamut*, p. 108.

8. Michael Robinson, *The Long Sonata of the Dead: A Study of Samuel Beckett*, p. 212.

9. Quoted in Lawrence Harvey, *Samuel Beckett: Poet and Critic*, p. 155.

10. *Poems in English* (New York: Grove Press, 1961), p. 36.

11. Harvey, *Samuel Beckett: Poet and Critic*, pp. 86–87.

12. Martin Esslin, "Samuel Beckett's Poems," in John Calder, ed., *Beckett at Sixty: A Festschrift*, pp. 58–59.

13. Samuel Beckett, trans. in collaboration with Ludovic and Agnes Janvier, *D'un ouvrage abandonné* in *Têtes-mortes* (Paris: Éditions de Minuit, 1967), p. 29. Other French quotations refer to this edition.

14. Ruby Cohn, *Back to Beckett*, p. 243.

15. Oddly, Dearlove sees no "crossing out lines or deleting passages" in *Abandoned Work*. See *Accommodating the Chaos*, p. 132.

16. James Knowlson, *Light and Darkness in the Theatre of Samuel Beckett*, p. 34.

17. See the typescripts, with corrections in Beckett's hand, in the Beckett collection at Washington University, St. Louis.

18. Stephen Ullmann, *Language and Style*, p. 90.

19. See Deirdre Bair, *Samuel Beckett: A Biography*.

20. Samuel Beckett, *Proust* (1931; New York: Grove Press, 1957), p. 23.

21. Edith Kern, *Existential Thought and Fictional Technique: Kierkegaard, Sartre, and Beckett*, p. 226.

22. Cohn, *Back to Beckett*, p. 241.

23. Peter Murphy notes that "Balfe" is an anagram of "fable" (in a paper on *Abandoned Work* presented at Columbus, Ohio, Beckett Symposium, May 1981), which tends to support my reading of the narrator as artist.

24. *Proust*, p. 2.

25. Cohn, *Back to Beckett*, p. 243.

26. Vivian Mercier, "Beckett's Ango-Irish Stage Dialects," *James Joyce Quarterly* 8 (1971): 314–15.

27. E. M. Scarry, "Six Ways to Kill a Blackbird or Any Other Intentional Object: Samuel Beckett's Method of Meaning," *James Joyce Quarterly* 8 (1971): 282.

28. Cohn, *Comic Gamut*, p. 103.

29. *Proust*, pp. 66–67.

Chapter 4. *Enough*

1. Ludovic Janvier, "Place of Narration/Narration of Place" (trans. by Ruby Cohn), in Ruby Cohn, ed., *Samuel Beckett*, p. 107.

2. At the Mark Taper Forum in Los Angeles, March 15–18, 1984.

3. E. M. Scarry, "Six Ways to Kill a Blackbird or Any Other Intentional Object: Samuel Beckett's Method of Meaning," *James Joyce Quarterly* 8 (1971): 285–89.

4. Samuel Beckett, *Enough*, in *First Love and Other Shorts* (New York: Grove Press, 1974), p. 53. All other references to this story are to this edition.

5. Brian Finney, *Since "How It Is": A Study of Samuel Beckett's Later Fiction*, p. 33.

6. In a letter from John Fletcher to E. M. Scarry, in Scarry, p. 289.

7. Scarry, "Six Ways to Kill a Blackbird."

8. Brian Finney, *Since "How It Is,"* p. 28.

9. This is Edith Kern quoting Gessner in "Beckett's Knight of Infinite Resignation," *Yale French Studies* 29 (1962): 54. Kern's translation is from Gessner's *Die Unzulanglichkeit der Sprache*.

10. Peter Murphy, "The Nature and Art of Love in *Enough*," *Journal of Beckett Studies*, no. 4 (Spring 1979): 33.

11. Ruby Cohn, *Back to Beckett*, pp. 245–46.

12. Cohn, p. 246.

13. Peter Murphy, p. 33.

14. From *Têtes-mortes* (Paris: Éditions de Minuit, 1967), p. 43.

15. Ruby Cohn, *Samuel Beckett: The Comic Gamut*, p. 96.

16. J. E. Dearlove, *Accommodating the Chaos: Samuel Beckett's Nonrelational Art*, p. 146.

17. Kristin Morrison, *Canters and Chronicles: The Use of Narrative in the Plays of Samuel Beckett and Harold Pinter*, pp. 52–81.

18. Giacomo Leopardi, *Poems and Prose*, trans. by Edwin Morgan (Bloomington, Ind.: Indiana University Press, 1966), pp. 66–69.

19. Francis Doherty, *Samuel Beckett*, p. 146.

20. Stephen's association between intense fear of death and his desire for immortality through literature is discussed in an unpublished manuscript on *Ulysses* by Professor Margaret McBride, University of Texas at San Antonio. The parallel to *Enough's* narrator is my extension.

Chapter 5. *How It Is*

1. *The New Yorker*, 40 (Dec. 19, 1964): 166.

2. Samuel Beckett, *How It Is* (New York: Grove Press, 1964), p. 7. All other page references for *How It Is* refer to this edition.

3. Ruby Cohn, *Back to Beckett*, p. 233.

4. David Lodge, "Some *Ping* Understood," *Encounter* 30 (1968): 85–89.

5. Suggested by John Pilling in personal communication.

6. Ruby Cohn, *Back to Beckett*, p. 239.

7. Dougald McMillan, "Samuel Beckett and the Visual Arts: The Embarrassment of Allegory," in Ruby Cohn, ed., *Samuel Beckett*, p. 127.

8. Hugh Kenner, *A Reader's Guide to Samuel Beckett*, p. 138.

9. P. N. Furbank, "Beckett's Purgatory," *Encounter* 22 (1964): 72.

10. These parallels are analyzed in an unpublished paper by Ms. Suzy Holstein.

11. *The Divine Comedy*, trans. by Thomas G. Bergin (New York: Grossman Publishers, 1969).

12. See the excellent article by Frederik N. Smith, "Fiction as Composing Process: *How It Is*," p. 108, in *Samuel Beckett: Humanistic Perspectives*, ed. by Morris Beja, S. E. Gontaraki, and Pierre Astier, pp. 107–121.

13. In composition notebooks labeled "PIM" in the Humanities Research Center at the University of Texas, Austin.

14. In the *Comment c'est* notebook, Humanities Research Center, University of Texas at Austin.

15. This analogy is also used in Eric P. Levy, *Beckett and the Voice of Species: A Study of the Prose Fiction*, pp. 87–88.

16. In the notebook marked "PIM IV," p. 14, Humanities Reaserch Center, Austin.

17. Marjorie Perloff, *The Poetics of Indeterminacy: Rimbaud to Cage*, pp. 229–47.

18. J. E. Dearlove, *Accommodating the Chaos: Samuel Beckett's Nonrelational Art*, p. 97.

19. Francis Doherty, *Samuel Beckett*, p. 129.

20. Hugh Kenner, *Samuel Beckett: A Critical Study*, p. 189.

21. Michael Robinson, *The Long Sonata of the Dead: A Study of Samuel Beckett*, p. 213.

22. For example, it is Dearlove's hypothesis that *How It Is* is a flashback told from the perspective of part 3. See *Accommodating the Chaos*, p. 94.

23. Again in the "PIM IV" notebook at Austin.

24. John Pilling also discusses the narrator's groping about for the correct verb tense in his *Samuel Beckett*, p. 51.

25. Hannah Copeland, *Art and the Artist in the Works of Samuel Beckett*, p. 102.

26. James Knowlson and John Pilling, *Frescoes of the Skull: The Later Prose and Drama of Samuel Beckett*, p. 68.

27. John Pilling finds this true for much of Beckett's fiction, and he discusses its philosophical significance in *Samuel Beckett*, p. 31.

28. H. Porter Abbott, *The Fiction of Samuel Beckett: Form and Effect*, p. 139.

29. Hugh Kenner, "Shades of Syntax," in Ruby Cohn, ed. *Samuel Beckett: A Collection of Critical Essays*, p. 29.

30. Kenner, "Shades of Syntax," p. 30.

31. See the picture of this in Deirdre Bair, *Samuel Beckett: A Biography*, opposite p. 114.

32. Lawrence Harvey, *Samuel Beckett: Poet and Critic*, p. 373.

Chapter 6. *Imagination Dead Imagine*

1. Hugh Kenner, *A Reader's Guide to Samuel Beckett*, p. 178.

2. Samuel Beckett, *Imagination Dead Imagination*, in *First Love and Other Shorts* (New York: Grove Press, 1974), p. 63. All later references to this piece will be to this edition.

3. Samuel Beckett, "Dante . . . Bruno . Vico . . Joyce," in *Our Exagmination Round His Factification for Incamination of Work in Progress*, 2d ed. (1929; New York: New Directions, 1962), p. 6.

4. Lawrence E. Harvey, *Samuel Beckett: Poet and Critic*, p. 32.

5. The manuscripts and typescripts containing these revisions are in the manuscript collection of Washington University at St. Louis.

6. Professor Rubin Rabinovitz (in private communication) notes that this is one tenet of Gestalt psychology, a field both Murphy and Neary are concerned with. And of course, this school of psychology centers on problems of perception.

7. Raymond Federman, "Samuel Beckett's Film on the Agony of Perceivedness," *James Joyce Quarterly* 8 (Summer 1971): 369.

8. John E. Grant, "Imagination Dead?," *James Joyce Quarterly* 8 (Summer 1971): 340.

9. Samuel Beckett, *Cascando and Other Short Dramatic Pieces* (New York: Grove Press, 1968), p. 75.

10. Grant, "Imagination Dead?" pp. 340–41. Grant's italics.

11. Beckett's words quoted in James Knowlson's "Editorial," *Journal of Beckett Studies*, no. 3 (Summer 1978).

12. *All Strange Away*, p. 7. *All Strange Away* was printed in *Journal of Beckett Studies*, no. 3 (Summer 1978), pp. 1–9, and republished in Samuel Beckett, *Rockaby and Other Short Pieces* (New York: Grove Press, 1981), pp. 37–66.

13. Brian Finney, "A Reading of Samuel Beckett's *Imagination Dead Imagine*," *Twentieth Century Literature* 17 (April 1971): 70.

14. James Knowlson, *Light and Darkness in the Theatre of Samuel Beckett*, p. 18.

15. Knowlson, p. 26.

16. George Berkeley, *Three Dialogues Between Hylas and Philonous* (1713; New York: Bobbs-Merril, 1954).

17. Lawrence Harvey, "A Poet's Initiation," pp. 171–84 in Melvin Friedman, ed., *Samuel Beckett Now*, p. 184.

18. Harvey, p. 183.

19. John Mood, " 'Silence Within': A Study of the *Residua* of Samuel Beckett," *Studies in Short Fiction* 7 (1969): 390.

20. Ruby Cohn, *Back to Beckett*, p. 247. Cohn also notes the precision, "like a physics text," undercut by approximation (p. 248).

21. David Hesla, *The Shape of Chaos: An Interpretation of the Art of Samuel Beckett*, pp. 57–58.

22. This notebook, dated Michaelmas 1931, is available on microfilm in the manuscript collection of Trinity College, Dublin.

23. Henri Bergson, *Creative Evolution* (1911; New York: Modern Library, 1944), p. 303. Other Bergson quotations are from this edition.

24. Evidence that Beckett was interested in and influenced by Henri Bergson can be found in the many Bergsonian concepts of time, intellect, and artistic vision woven into his lectures on the French novel found in the Beckett Manuscript Collection at Trinity College, Dublin. In addition, Professor Rubin Rabinovitz in personal communication mentions that one of Beckett's teachers at Trinity, A. A. Luce, who introduced Beckett to Berkeley's work, was a Bergson scholar.

25. Samuel Beckett, *Imagination morte imaginez*, in *Têtes-mortes* (Paris: Les Éditions de Minuit, 1967), p. 51. Other references to the French original are to this edition.

26. G. C. Bernard, *Samuel Beckett: A New Approach* (New York: Dodd, Mead & Co., 1970), p. 80.

27. James Hansford, "'Imagination Dead Imagine': The Imagination and Its Context," *Journal of Beckett Studies*, no. 7 (Spring 1982): 59.

28. Ludovic Janvier, "Lieu du retrait de la blancheur de l'écho," *Critique* 23 (February 1967): 224.

29. Finney, "A Reading of . . . *Imagine*," p. 66.

30. See, for example, John Pilling, *Samuel Beckett*, p. 57. Conversely, Ruby Cohn notes "the resonant series of 'or' possibilities" and the fact that the series ends with "what they are doing"—and only living creatures can *do* anything (*Back to Beckett*, p. 250).

31. Finney, "A Reading of . . . *Imagine*," p. 67.

32. Hansford, "'Imagination Dead Imagine,'" p. 66.

33. Kenner, *A Reader's Guide*, p. 178.

34. Harvey, *Poet and Critic*, p. 315.

35. Pp. 9–10. A photocopy of this unpublished novel is in the Beckett Archives at the University of Reading Library, England.

36. Daniel Albright, *Representation and the Imagination: Beckett, Kafka, Nabokov, and Schoenberg*, p. 166.

Chapter 7. *The Lost Ones*

1. Christopher Ricks, "Beckett First and Last," *New York Review of Books*, Dec. 14, 1972, p. 42.

2. Raymond Federman, "Samuel Beckett: The Liar's Paradox," in Edouard Morot-Sir et al., eds., *Samuel Beckett: The Art of Rhetoric*, p. 138.

3. Samuel Beckett, *Waiting for Godot* (New York: Grove Press, 1954), p. 29.

4. Samuel Beckett, *The Lost Ones* (New York: Grove Press, 1972), pp. 15–16. Other page citations for this piece refer to this edition.

5. Colin Duckworth, "The Making of Godot," in Ruby Cohn, ed., *Casebook on "Waiting for Godot"* (New York: Grove Press, 1967), p. 95.

6. Richard L. Admussen, "A New Dimension in Beckett Studies: The Manuscripts," in Walter C. Kraft, ed., *Proceedings: Pacific Northwest Conference on Foreign Languages* (Twenty-fourth Annual Meeting, May 4–5, 1973, Western Washington State College), vol. 24 (Corvallis: Oregon State University, 1973), p. 180.

7. Ruby Cohn, *Back to Beckett*, pp. 259–60.

8. Samuel Beckett, *Le Dépeupleur* (Paris: Les Éditions de Minuit, 1970).

9. A. Alvarez, *Samuel Beckett*, p. 125.

10. Ludovic Janvier, *Pour Samuel Beckett* (Paris: Union Générale D'Éditions, 1973), p. 371.

11. Lawrence E. Harvey, *Samuel Beckett: Poet and Critic*, p. 388.

12. "The Impossibility of Saying the Same Old Thing the Same Old Way—Samuel Beckett's Fiction Since *Comment c'est*," *L'Esprit créateur* 11 (Fall 1971): 21.

13. Donald Davie, "Kinds of Comedy," *Spectrum* 2 (Winter 1958): 24.

14. Brian Finney, *Since "How It Is": A Study of Samuel Beckett's Later Fiction*, pp. 12–16.

15. Finney, p. 32.

16. This parallel with Kafka's world was suggested to me by Professor Jeffrey Rubin-Dorsky in conversation.

17. For example, Alvarez, *Samuel Beckett*, p. 127.

18. David Hesla, *The Shape of Chaos: An Interpretation of the Art of Samuel Beckett*, p. 52.

19. Quoted by David Hesla, p. 52.

20. Bell Gale Chevigny, ed., "Introduction," *Twentieth Century Interpretations of "Endgame,"* p. 4.

21. Samuel Beckett, "Kottabista," *Hermathena*, 115 (1973): 19.

22. Cohn, *Back to Beckett*, p. 260.

23. Fritz Mauthner, quoted in Linda Ben-Zvi, "Samuel Beckett, Fritz Mauthner, and the Limits of Language," *PMLA* 95 (March 1980), 187.

Chapter 8. *Ping*

1. On a small note card inserted with the typescripts in the Samuel Beckett Collection, Washington University, St. Louis.

2. Ruby Cohn, *Back to Beckett*, pp. 254–55. See the entire section on *Ping*, pp. 250–56, for an excellent close reading.

3. Samuel Beckett, *Ping*, in *First Love and Other Shorts* (New York: Grove Press, 1974), pp. 69–72. All references will be to this edition.

4. Edith Kern, *Existential Thought and Fictional Technique: Kierkegaard, Sartre, Beckett*, pp. 238–39.

5. John Pilling discusses *Ping* as a reaction against *The Lost Ones* and a reduction of other works, and proposes that the black eye staring at the protagonist is "destroying the solitude he has been intent on perfecting," thus suggesting *Murphy*. James Knowlson and John Pilling, *Frescoes of the Skull: The Later Prose and Drama of Samuel Beckett*, p. 171; see pp. 168–71.

6. David I. Grossvogel, *Four Playwrights and a Postscript: Brecht, Ionesco, Beckett, Genet* (Ithaca, N.Y.: Cornell University Press, 1962), p. 105.

7. Rosette Lamont, "Beckett's Metaphysics of Choiceless Awareness," in Melvin J. Friedman, ed., *Samuel Beckett Now*, p. 209.

8. Cohn, *Back to Beckett*, p. 194.

9. Hans-Joachim Schulz, *This Hell of Stories: A Hegelian Approach to the Novels of Samuel Beckett*, p. 111.

10. G. C. Barnard, *Samuel Beckett, A New Approach: A Study of the Novels and Plays* (New York: Dodd, Mead & Co., 1970), p. 84.

11. Hugh Kenner, *A Reader's Guide to Samuel Beckett*, p. 179.

12. Notes taken by Rachel Burrows née Dobbin on Beckett's lectures

on the novel, dated Michaelmas, 1931. On microfilm at Trinity College, Dublin.

13. Henri Bergson, *Creative Evolution*, p. 332.

14. "Beckett's Recent *Residua*," *Southern Review* 5 (1969): 1050.

15. See Knowlson, *Light and Darkness in the Theatre of Samuel Beckett*, pp. 34–41.

16. William H. Gass, *Fiction and the Figures of Life* (New York: Alfred A. Knopf, 1970), pp. 12–13.

17. Gass, p. 13.

18. In the manuscript collection at Washington University, St. Louis.

19. David Lodge, "Some *Ping* Understood," *Encounter* 30 (1968): 85.

20. Lodge, p. 88.

21. Lodge, p. 86. But to interpret the *life* of the white body as being "over" may be invalid; the summoned vision of an Other could just as well be over at the end.

22. John J. Mood, "Silence Within': A Study of the *Residua* of Samuel Beckett," *Studies in Short Fiction* 7 (1969): 398–99.

23. Elisabeth Bergman Segrè, "Style and Structure in Beckett's 'Ping': *That Something Itself*," *Journal of Modern Literature* 6 (Winter 1977): 127–47.

24. In *Têtes-mortes* (Paris: Éditions de Minuit, 1967), pp. 61–66.

25. A copy of the typescript is at the University of Reading Library.

26. Ludovic Janvier, "Le Lieu du rétrait de la blancheur de l'écho," *Critique* 237 (Feb., 1967): 233.

27. Lawrence E. Harvey, *Samuel Beckett: Poet and Critic*, p. 342.

28. Quoted in Harvey, *Samuel Beckett*.

Chapter 9. *Lessness*

1. Samuel Beckett, *Lessness* (London: Calder & Boyars, 1970). Originally published in French as *Sans* (Paris: Éditions de Minuit, 1969). Manuscripts from the Beinecke Rare Books and Manuscript Library, Yale University. I am quoting with Mr. Beckett's permission.

2. A. J. Leventhal, "Samuel Beckett: About Him and About," *Hermathena* 114 (1972): 16.

3. Edith Fournier, "'Sans': Cantate et Fugue pour un Réfuge," *Les Lettres Nouvelles* (March–Oct., 1970), p. 151.

4. J. M. Coetzee, "Samuel Beckett's *Lessness*: An Exercise in Decomposition," *Computers and the Humanities* 7 (1967): 197.

5. John J. Mood, "Samuel Beckett's Impasse-Lessness," *Ball State University Forum* 14 (Autumn 1973): 78.

6. J. E. Dearlove, *Accommodating the Chaos: Samuel Beckett's Nonrelational Art*, p. 118. Also see pp. 119–27.

7. John Fletcher, *The Novels of Samuel Beckett*, 2d ed., p. 235.

8. This approach derives from the method of James Peter Thorne,

"Stylistics and Generative Grammars," in Donald C. Freeman, ed., *Linguistics and Literary Style*, p. 189. Hereafter referred to as *LALS*.

9. Rulon Wells, "Nominal and Verbal Style," in Freeman, ed., *LALS*, p. 304.

10. Approach adapted from Geoffrey Leech, " 'This Bread I Break'—Language and Interpretation," in Freeman, ed., *LALS*, pp. 119-28. See Chapter 5.

11. See Susan Brienza and Enoch Brater, "Chance and Choice in Beckett's *Lessness*," *ELH, A Journal of English Literary History* 43 (Summer 1976): 244-58.

12. Brian Finney, "*Assumption* to *Lessness*: Beckett's Shorter Fiction," in Katherine Worth, ed., *Beckett the Shape Changer*, p. 79.

13. Enoch Brater, "*Noah, Not I*, and Beckett's 'Incomprehensibly Sublime,' *Comparative Drama* 8 (Fall 1974): 254-63.

14. Lawrence E. Harvey, *Samuel Beckett*: *Poet and Critic*, p. 358.

15. John Fletcher, "Beckett as Poet," in Ruby Cohn, ed., *Samuel Beckett: A Collection of Criticism*, p. 48.

16. Ross Chambers, "Beckett's Brinkmanship" in Martin Esslin, ed., *Samuel Beckett: A Collection of Critical Essays*, p. 154. Reprinted from *Journal of the Australian Language and Literature Association*, no. 19 (May 1963).

17. *The Village Voice*, Feb. 5, 1958, p. 7. Quoted in Bell Gale Chevigny, ed., *Twentieth Century Interpretations of "Endgame"*, p. 3.

18. Leventhal, "Samuel Beckett," p. 17.

19. Colin Duckworth, *Angels of Darkness*: *Dramatic Effect in Samuel Beckett* (London: George Allen & Unwin, Ltd., 1972), p. 62.

20. Finney, in Worth, *Beckett the Shape Changer*, p. 80.

21. Lawrence Harvey, *Samuel Beckett*, p. 196. This is Harvey's paraphrase.

22. Quoted by Harvey, p. 247.

23. Quoted by Harvey, p. 249.

24. Quoted by Harvey, p. 249.

25. Samuel Beckett, quoted in Israel Shenker, "Moody Man of Letters," *New York Times*, 6 May 1956, sec. 2, p. 3.

26. Harvey, *Samuel Beckett*, pp. 419-20.

Chapter 10. *Fizzles*

1. Samuel Beckett, *Fizzles* (New York: Grove Press, 1976); *Pour finir encore et autres foirades* (Paris: Éditions de Minuit, 1976).

2. Sighle Kennedy, *Murphy's Bed* (Lewisburg, Pa.: Bucknell University Press, 1971).

3. Quoted in Samuel Beckett, *Disjecta*: *Miscellaneous Writings and a Dramatic Fragment*, ed. Ruby Cohn (New York: Grove Press, 1984), p. 46.

4. Enoch Brater, "Still/Beckett: the Essential and the Incidental," *Journal of Beckett Studies*, no. 6 (Feb. 1977): 10.

5. Brater, p. 8.

6. Brater, p. 9.

7. Pilling, "Review Article: 'Fizzles,'" *Journal of Beckett Studies*, no. 2 (Summer 1977): 98.

8. At Reading University Library, manuscript 1396/4/14.

9. What kind of reincarnation of Murphy this character might be remains unclear because of the ambiguous sentence in which "Murphy" appears: "The legs notably seem in good shape, that is a blessing, Murphy had first-rate legs" (p. 9). I will call him "Murphy" on occasion so as to increase the ambiguity.

10. See items 1550/1 and 1550/2 in the Beckett collection at Reading University.

11. See Chapter Six.

12. Francis Christensen, "A Generative Rhetoric of the Sentence," in his *Notes Toward A New Rhetoric*, 2d. ed. (1967; Harper & Row, 1978), pp. 23–44.

13. Charles Krance, "Odd Fizzles: Beckett and the Heavenly Sciences," in *Science and Literature*, ed. Harry R. Garvin (Lewisburg: Bucknell Univiersity Press, 1983), pp. 102–103.

14. See the Reading University manuscript 1550/10.

15. See items 1550/15 and 1550/16 in the Reading University Beckett collection.

16. Quoted in Shlomith Rimmon-Kenan, *Narrative Fiction: Contemporary Poetics*, p. 117. Also see the entire chapter entitled "The text and its reading," pp. 117–29.

17. Item 1550/23, Reading University.

18. For a detailed comparison between *Lessness* and *Fizzle 8* and a study of the motifs linking all of *Fizzles*, see Rubin Rabinovitz, "*Fizzles* and Samuel Beckett's Earlier Fiction," *Contemporary Literature* 24 (Fall 1983): 306–321. Also good on resonances among the fizzles, and echoes from other Beckett works, is James Knowlson and John Pilling, *Frescoes of the Skull: The Later Prose and Drama of Samuel Beckett*, pp. 132–35.

19. Samuel Beckett to Alan Schneider, quoted in Deirdre Bair, *Samuel Beckett: A Biography*, p. 458. Also quoted in Charles Krance, "Odd Fizzles: Beckett and the Heavenly Sciences," p. 96.

20. See item 1551/3 in the Reading University Beckett collection.

21. Astronomers use the proportion of white dwarves to measure the age of a system: "That white dwarfs, of immense density, are a final stage in stellar evolution has been supported by direct observations. The older stellar clusters, for example Hyades and Praesepe, contain many white dwarfs, while the younger clusters, for example the Pleiades, contain few." I. S. Shklovskii and Carl Sagan, *Intelligent Life in the Universe* (New York: Dell Publishing Co., 1966), p. 84.

Chapter 11. *Company* and *Ill Seen Ill Said*

1. John Pilling speculates that Beckett, after the Bair biography, wanted to "establish the proper conjunctions and disjunctions" between his life and his art. "Review Article: 'Company' by Samuel Beckett," *Journal of Beckett Studies*, no. 7 (Spring 1982): 127.

2. Samuel Beckett, *Company* (New York: Grove Press, 1980), paragraph 11. All references are to this edition.

3. Wayne C. Booth, *The Rhetoric of Fiction*, 2d. ed., p. 451.

4. See Deirdre Bair, *Samuel Beckett: A Biography*, pp. 15–17.

5. Enoch Brater, "The *Company* Beckett Keeps: The Shape of Memory and One Fablist's Decay of Lying," in Morris Beja, et al., eds., *Samuel Beckett: Humanistic Perspectives*, p. 168.

6. Linda Ben-Zvi describes this condition of uncertainty as "the Mauthner equation": "what cannot be formed in words, cannot be known." See "Fritz Mauthner for Company," *Journal of Beckett Studies*, no. 9 (1984): 75.

7. Marjorie Perloff's analysis of *Ill Seen Ill Said* as poetry influenced these thoughts. See "Between Verse and Prose: Beckett and the New Poetry," *Critical Inquiry* 9 (Dec. 1982): 415–33.

8. Pilling notes that this line from Milton is "purloined (not for the first time)," in his "Review Article," p. 129.

9. Eric Levy sees in the allusion to "Black basalt" (in conjunction with Good Friday) an intimation of a sepulchre and argues that "the experience of the pure reflection [the mirror structure and imagery that Levy finds in the text] is parallel with the experience in the tomb." See Eric Levy, "'Company': The Mirror of Beckettian Mimesis," *Journal of Beckett Studies*, no. 8 (Autumn 1982): 103.

10. Samuel Beckett, *Ill Seen Ill Said* (New York: Grove Press, 1981), paragraph 50, p. 52. All references are to this edition.

11. See H. Porter Abbott, "A Poetics of Radical Displacement: Samuel Beckett Coming up to 70," *Texas Studies in Literature and Language* (Spring 1975): 219–38.

12. See Deirdre Bair, *Samuel Beckett: A Biography*, pp. 10–11.

13. Victor Erlich, "Roman Jakobson: Grammar of Poetry and Poetry of Grammar," in Seymour Chatman, ed., *Approaches to Poetics*, p. 26.

14. Bair, *Samuel Beckett*, pp. 294–95. The French original, "Les Deux Besoins," is reprinted in Samuel Beckett, *Disjecta: Miscellaneous Writings and a Dramatic Fragment*, ed. Ruby Cohn (New York: Grove Press, 1984), pp. 55–58.

15. Frederik Smith has noticed a similar in-process writing style in *How It Is*. See his excellent article, "Fiction as Composing Process: *How It Is*," in Morris Beja, et al., eds, *Samuel Beckett: Humanistic Perspectives*, pp. 107–121.

16. Rubin Rabinovitz shows that in a complex network of Beckettian

metaphors, ruins of the structures from earlier fictions appear in the later stories. See "Samuel Beckett's Figurative Language," *Contemporary Literature* 26 (Fall 1985): 317–30, especially p. 322.

17. See Lawrence Harvey's interpretation of "The Vulture" in *Samuel Beckett: Poet and Critic*, pp. 112–16.

18. Daniel Albright, *Representation and the Imagination: Beckett, Kafka, Nabokov, and Schoenberg*, p. 171.

Chapter 12. Beckett's New Worlds

1. Jonathan Culler also uses this phrase, but with a different meaning. See his *Structuralist Poetics*, p. 263.

2. Culler's *Structuralist Poetics*, pp. 113–30.

3. *Structuralist Poetics*, p. 135.

4. James Knowlson and John Pilling, *Frescoes of the Skull: The Later Prose and Drama of Samuel Beckett*, pp. 172–76.

5. Culler suggests, without discussing *Ping*, that this vantage point of writing as metaphor can naturalize some works.

6. Wolfgang Iser, "The Reading Process: a Phenomenological Approach," in Jane P. Tompkins, ed., *Reader-Response Criticism: From Formalism to Post-Structuralism*, p. 62.

7. Ruby Cohn has argued repeatedly for this.

8. Banfield, *Unspeakable Sentences: Narration and Representation in the Language of Fiction*, pp. 164–65.

9. Rubin Rabinovitz, "*Fizzles* and Samuel Beckett's Earlier Fiction," *Contemporary Literature* 24 (Fall 1983): 308–309.

10. George Poulet, "Criticism and the Experience of Interiority," in Tompkins, ed., *Reader-Response Criticism*, pp. 47–48.

11. Samuel Beckett, *Worstward Ho* (New York: Grove Press, 1983), p. 7. All other page references are to this edition.

12. Recounted at the Beckett conference in Austin, Texas, March 1984.

13. Judith Dearlove, "'Syntax Upended in Opposite Corners': Alterations in Beckett's Linguistic Theories," in Morris Beja et al., eds., *Samuel Beckett: Humanistic Perspectives*, p. 127. While "Still" may possess "a sense of sufficiency," a new serenity and lack of urgency certainly is not evident in *Company*.

14. See Rubin Rabinovitz, *The Development of Samuel Beckett's Fiction*.

15. Quoted in Schlomith Rimmon-Kenan, *Narrative Fiction: Contemporary Poetics*, p. 94. See the entire chapter entitled "Narration: levels and voices," pp. 86–101.

16. David Lodge, *The Modes of Modern Writing: Metaphor, Metonymy, and the Typology of Modern Literature*, p. 226. Also see pp. 224–25.

17. Patricia Waugh finds permutation inherent in metafiction. See *Metafiction: The Theory and Practice of Self-conscious Fiction*, pp. 43–46.

18. Robert Scholes, *Fabulation and Metafiction*, pp. 210–18.

19. Ruby Cohn, *Back to Beckett*, p. 251.

20. Roland Barthes in *Figaro littéraire*, March 9–15, 1970. Quoted in Hugh M. Davidson, "Sign, Sense, and Roland Barthes" in Seymour Chatman, ed., *Approaches to Poetics*, p. 38.

21. Interview with Federman, *Contemporary Literature* 24 (Fall 1983): 303.

Bibliography

BECKETT TEXTS USED

Cascando and Other Short Dramatic Pieces. New York: Grove Press, 1968.
Company. New York: Grove Press, 1980.
Disjecta: Miscellaneous Writings and a Dramatic Fragment, ed. Ruby Cohn.
  New York: Grove Press, 1984.
Endgame. New York: Grove Press, 1958.
Ends and Odds. New York: Grove Press, 1976.
First Love and Other Shorts. New York: Grove Press, 1974. Contains *From
  an Abandoned Work, Enough, Imagination Dead Imagine*, and *Ping*.
Fizzles. New York: Grove Press, 1976.
Happy Days. New York: Grove Press, 1961.
How It Is. New York: Grove Press, 1964.
Ill Seen Ill Said. New York: Grove Press, 1981.
Krapp's Last Tape and Other Dramatic Pieces. New York: Grove Press, 1960.
Lessness. London: Calder & Boyars, 1970.
The Lost Ones. New York: Grove Press, 1972.
Malone Dies. New York: Grove Press, 1956.
Mercier and Camier. New York: Grove Press, 1974.
Molloy. New York: Grove Press, 1955.
More Pricks Than Kicks. 1934; New York: Grove Press, 1972.
Murphy. 1938; New York: Grove Press, 1957.
Not I. London: Faber and Faber, 1973.
Poems in English. New York: Grove Press, 1961.
Proust. 1931; New York: Grove Press, 1957.
Rockaby and Other Short Pieces. New York: Grove Press, 1981. Contains
  the story "All Strange Away."
Stories and Texts for Nothing. New York: Grove Press, 1967.
The Unnamable. New York: Grove Press, 1958.
Waiting for Godot. New York: Grove Press, 1954.
Watt. 1953; New York: Grove Press, 1983.
Worstward Ho. New York: Grove Press, 1983.

SELECTED WORKS ON BECKETT

Abbott, H. Porter. "Farewell to Incompetence: Beckett's *How It Is* and
  Imagination Dead Imagine. Contemporary Literature 11 (1970): 36–47.
———. *The Fiction of Samuel Beckett: Form and Effect*. Berkeley: University
  of California Press, 1973.

————. "A Poetics of Radical Displacement: Samuel Beckett Coming Up to Seventy." *Texas Studies in Literature and Language* 17 (Spring 1975): 219–38.

Admussen, Richard L. *The Samuel Beckett Manuscripts: A Study*. Boston: G. K. Hall & Company, 1978.

Albright, Daniel. *Representation and the Imagination: Beckett, Kafka, Nabokov, and Schoenberg*. University of Chicago Press, 1981.

Alvarez, A. *Samuel Beckett*. New York: Viking Press, 1973.

Atkins, Anselm. "Lucky's Speech in Beckett's *Waiting for Godot*: A Punctuated Sense-Line Arrangement." *Educational Theatre Journal* 19 (1967): 426–32.

Bair, Deirdre. *Samuel Beckett: A Biography*. New York: Harcourt, Brace, Jovanovich, 1978.

Barge, Laura. "'Coloured Images' in the 'Black Dark': Samuel Beckett's Later Fiction." *PMLA* 92 (1977): 273–84.

Beja, Morris, et al., eds. *Samuel Beckett: Humanistic Perspectives*. Columbus: Ohio State University Press, 1983.

Ben-Zvi, Linda. "Samuel Beckett, Fritz Mauthner, and the Limits of Language." *PMLA* 95 (March 1980): 183–200.

Booth, Wayne C. "Beckett's *Company* as Example." In Wayne C. Booth, *The Rhetoric of Fiction*, 2d ed., pp. 441–57. University of Chicago Press, 1982.

Bruns, Gerald L. "Samuel Beckett's *How It Is*." *James Joyce Quarterly* 8 (1971): 318–31.

————. "The Storyteller and the Problem of Language in Samuel Beckett's Fiction." *Modern Language Quarterly* 30 (1969): 265–81.

Calder, John. "Beckett—Man and Artist." *Adam—International Review* 35 (1970): 70–71.

————, ed. *Beckett At Sixty: A Festschrift*. London: Calder and Boyars, 1967.

Caws, Mary Ann. "A Rereading of the Traces." *L'Esprit Créateur* 11 (Fall 1971): 14–20.

Chevigny, Bell Gale, ed. *Twentieth Century Interpretations of "Endgame."* Englewood Cliffs, N.J.: Prentice Hall, 1969.

Chicago Review 33 (1982), no. 2. Special issue on innovative fiction and Beckett.

Coetzee, John M. "The English Fiction of Samuel Beckett: An Essay in Stylistic Analysis." Ph.D. diss., University of Texas at Austin, Texas, 1969.

————. "Samuel Beckett's *Lessness*: An Exercise in Decomposition." *Computers and the Humanities* 7 (1973): 195–98.

Cohn, Ruby. *Back to Beckett*. Princeton, N.J.: Princeton University Press, 1973.

————. "Beckett's Recent *Residua*." *Southern Review* 5 (1969): 1045–54.

————. "*Comment c'est*: de quoi rire." *French Review* 35 (May 1962): 563–69.

————, ed. *Samuel Beckett: A Collection of Criticism*. New York: McGraw-Hill, 1975.

————. *Samuel Beckett: The Comic Gamut*. New Brunswick, N.J.: Rutgers University Press, 1962.

————. "Samuel Beckett Self-Translator." *PMLA* 65 (1961): 613–21. *College Literature* 8 (Fall, 1981). Special Beckett issue.

Copeland, Hannah C. *Art and the Artist in the Works of Samuel Beckett*. The Hague: Mouton, 1975.

Davie, Donald. "Kinds of Comedy." *Spectrum* (Santa Barbara City College) 2 (Winter 1958): 25–31.

Dearlove, J. E. *Accommodating the Chaos: Samuel Beckett's Nonrelational Art*. Durham, N.C.: Duke University Press, 1982.

Dobrez, Livio. "Samuel Beckett's Irreducible." *Southern Review* 6 (1973): 205–221.

Doherty, Francis Michael. *Samuel Beckett*. London: Hutchinson University Library, 1971.

Driver, Tom F. "Beckett by the Madeleine." *Columbia University Forum* 4 (Summer 1961): 21–25.

Eliopulos, James. *Samuel Beckett's Dramatic Language*. The Hague: Mouton, 1975.

Erickson, John D., ed. *L'Esprit Créateur* 11 (Fall 1971). Special issue on Samuel Beckett.

————. "Objects and Systems in the Novels of Samuel Beckett." *L'Esprit Créateur* 7 (Summer 1967): 113–22.

Esslin, Martin, ed. *Samuel Beckett: A Collection of Critical Essays*. Englewood Cliffs, N.J.: Prentice Hall, 1965.

Fahrenbach, Hannelore, and John Fletcher. "The 'Voice of Silence': Reason, Imagination and Creative Sterility in 'Texts for Nothing,'" *Journal of Beckett Studies*, no. 1 (Winter 1976): 30–36.

Federman, Raymond. "'How It Is' With Beckett's Fiction." *French Review* 38 (Winter 1965): 459–68.

————. "The Impossibility of Saying the Same Old Thing the Same Old Way: Samuel Beckett's Fiction Since *Comment c'est*." *L'Esprit Créateur* 11 (1970): 21–43.

————. "Samuel Beckett's Film on the Agony of Perceivedness." *James Joyce Quarterly* 8 (Summer 1971): 363–70.

———— and John Fletcher. *Samuel Beckett: His Works and His Critics: An Essay in Bibliography*. Berkeley: University of California Press, 1974.

Finney, Brian. "A Reading of Beckett's *Imagination Dead Imagine*." *Twentieth Century Literature* 17 (1971): 65–72.

————. *Since "How It Is": A Study of Samuel Beckett's Later Fiction*. London: Covent Garden Press, 1972.

Fletcher, John. *The Novels of Samuel Beckett*, 2d ed. New York: Barnes & Noble, 1970.

————. *Samuel Beckett's Art*. London: Chatto & Windus, 1967.

Fournier, Edith. "Pour que la boue me soit contée . . ." (rev. of *Comment c'est*). *Critique* 17 (May 1961): 412–18.

———. " 'Sans': Cantate et fugue pour un refuge." *Les Lettres Nouvelles* (1970), 149–60.

Friedman, Melvin J. "Review-Essay: Samuel Beckett and His Critics Enter the 1970's." *Studies in the Novel* (North Texas State University) 5 (1973): 383–99.

———, ed. *Samuel Beckett Now*. University of Chicago Press, 1970.

Gluck, Barbara Reich. *Beckett and Joyce: Friendship and Fiction*. Lewisburg, Pa.: Bucknell University Press, 1979.

Gontarski, S. E. *Beckett's "Happy Days": A Manuscript Study*. Columbus: Ohio State University Libraries, 1977.

Grant, John E. "Imagination Dead?" *James Joyce Quarterly* 8 (1970): 336–62.

Harvey, Lawrence E. "Samuel Beckett on Life, Art and Criticism." *Modern Language Notes* 80 (1965): 545–62.

———. *Samuel Beckett: Poet and Critic*. Princeton, N.J.: Princeton University Press, 1970.

Hassan, Ihab. *The Literature of Silence: Henry Miller and Samuel Beckett*. New York: Alfred A. Knopf, 1967.

———. *Paracriticisms: Seven Speculations of the Times*. Urbana: University of Illinois Press, 1975.

Hayman, Ronald. *Samuel Beckett*. New York: Frederick Ungar Publishing Company, 1973.

Hesla, David. *The Shape of Chaos: An Interpretation of the Art of Samuel Beckett*. Minneapolis: University of Minnesota Press, 1971.

Hoffman, Frederick J. *Samuel Beckett: The Language of Self*. Carbondale: Southern Illinois University Press, 1962.

Iser, Wolfgang. *The Implied Reader: Patterns of Communication in Prose Fiction from Bunyan to Beckett*. Baltimore, Md.: Johns Hopkins University Press, 1973.

Janvier, Ludovic. "Le Lieu du rétrait de la blancheur de l'écho." *Critique* 23 (Feb. 1967): 215–38.

Johnson, Raymond. "Waiting for Beckett." *Adam—International Review* 35 (1970): 74–75.

Journal of Beckett Studies, nos. 1–9.

Journal of Modern Literature 6 (Feb. 1977). Special Beckett issue.

Kawin, Bruce F. *Telling It Again and Again: Repetition in Literature and Film*. Ithaca, N.Y.: Cornell University Press, 1972.

Kellman, Steven. "Beckett's Fatal Duel." *Romance Notes* 16 (Winter 1975): 268–73.

Kenner, Hugh. "Art in a Closed Field." *Virginia Quartely Review* 38 (Summer 1962): 597–613.

———. "Beckett Translating Beckett: *Comment c'est*." *Delos* 5 (1970): 194–211.

————. *A Reader's Guide to Samuel Beckett*. New York: Farrar, Straus & Giroux, 1973.

————. *Samuel Beckett: A Critical Study*. Reprint, Berkeley: University of California Press, 1968.

Kern, Edith. *Existential Thought and Fictional Technique: Kierkegaard, Sartre, and Beckett*. New Haven: Yale University Press, 1970.

Knowlson, James. *Light and Darkness in the Theatre of Samuel Beckett*. Text of a public lecture delivered at Trinity College, Dublin, on February 7, 1972. London: Turret Books, 1972.

———— and John Pilling. *Frescoes of the Skull: The Later Prose and Drama of Samuel Beckett*. New York: Grove Press, 1980.

Krance, Charles. "Odd Fizzles: Beckett and the Heavenly Sciences." In *Science and Literature*, ed., Harry R. Garvin, pp. 96–107. Lewisburg, Pa.: Bucknell University Press, 1983.

Krieger, Elliot. "Samuel Beckett's *Texts for Nothing*: Explication and Exposition." *Modern Language Notes* 92 (1977): 987-1000.

Leventhal, A. J. "The Beckett Hero." *Critique: Studies in Modern Fiction* 7 (1965): 18–35.

————. "Samuel Beckett: About Him and About." *Hermathena* 114 (1972): 5–22.

Levy, Eric P. "The Metaphor of Ignorance: Time and Personal Identity in *How It Is*." *Renascence* 28 (Winter 1975): 27–37.

————. *Beckett and the Voice of Species: A Study of the Prose Fiction*. Totowa, N.J.: Barnes & Noble, 1980.

Lodge, David. *The Novelist at the Crossroads, and Other Essays on Fiction and Criticism*. Ithaca, N.Y.: Cornell University Press, 1971. Contains "Some *Ping* Understood," originally pub. *Encounter* 30 (1968): 85–89.

Mercier, Vivian. Beckett/*Beckett*. New York: Oxford University Press, 1977.

Mood, John J. "Samuel Beckett's Impasse-Lessness." *Ball State University Forum* 14 (1973): 74–80.

————. "'Silence Within': A Study of the *Residua* of Samuel Beckett." *Studies in Short Fiction* 7 (1969): 385–401.

Moorjani, Angela B. "Narrative Game Strategies in Beckett's *Watt*." *L'Esprit Créateur* 17 (Fall 1977): 235–44.

Morot-Sir, Edouard, Howard Harper, and Dougald McMillan. *Samuel Beckett: The Art of Rhetoric*. Chapel Hill: University of North Carolina, Department of Romance Languages, 1976.

Morrison, Kristin. *Canters and Chronicles: Narration in the Plays of Samuel Beckett and Harold Pinter*. Chicago: University of Chicago Press, 1983.

Murch, Anne C. "Encore un pas." *Critique* (Paris) 27 (1971): 45–47. A review article on *Lessness* and *Têtes-Mortes*.

————. "Tirer l'échelle? *Le Dépeupleur* de Samuel Beckett." *French Studies* 27 (Oct. 1973): 429–39.

O'Hara, J. D., ed. *Twentieth Century Interpretations of "Molloy," "Malone*

Dies," "The Unnamable": A Collection of Critical Essays. Englewood Cliffs, N.J.: Prentice-Hall, 1970.

Perloff, Marjorie. "Between Verse and Prose: Beckett and the New Poetry." *Critical Inquiry* 9 (Dec. 1982): 415–33.

Pilling, John. "Beckett After *Still*." *Romance Notes* 18 (Autumn 1977): 280–87.

———. *Samuel Beckett*. London: Routledge & Kegan Paul, 1976.

———. "The Significance of Beckett's *Still*." *Essays in Criticism* 28 (April 1978): 143–57.

Rabinovitz, Rubin. *The Development of Samuel Beckett's Fiction*. Urbana: University of Illinois Press, 1984.

———. "*Fizzles* and Samuel Beckett's Earlier Fiction." *Contemporary Literature* 24 (Fall 1983): 307–322.

———. "Samuel Beckett's Figurative Language." *Contemporary Literature* 26 (Fall 1985): 317–30.

Ricks, Christopher. "Beckett First and Last." *The New York Review of Books*, 14 Dec. 1972, pp. 42–44.

Robinson, C. J. B. "A Way with Words: Paradox, Silence, and Samuel Beckett." *Cambridge Quarterly* 5 (1971): 249–64.

Robinson, Michael. "Beckett: At Another Impasse." *Journal of European Studies* 1 (1971): 353–61.

———. *The Long Sonata of the Dead: A Study of Samuel Beckett*. New York: Grove Press, 1969.

Rose, Marilyn Gaddis. "The Lyrical Structure of Beckett's *Texts for Nothing*." *Novel* 4 (Spring 1971): 223–30.

Scarry, E. M. "Six Ways to Kill a Blackbird or Any Other Intentional Object: Samuel Beckett's Method of Meaning." *James Joyce Quarterly* 8 (1971): 278–89.

Schulz, Hans-Joachim. *This Hell of Stories: A Hegelian Approach to the Novels of Samuel Beckett*. The Hague: Mouton, 1973.

Shadoian, Jack. "The Achievement of *Comment c'est*." *Critique* 12 (1970): 5–18.

Shenker, Israel. "Moody Man of Letters." *New York Times*, 6 May 1956, sec. 2, pp. x, 1, 3.

Starnes, Patrick. "Samuel Beckett: An Interview." *Antigonish Review*, no. 10 (Summer 1972): 49–53.

Szanto, George H. *Narrative Consciousness: Structure and Perception in the Fiction of Kafka, Beckett, and Robbe-Grillet*. Austin: University of Texas Press, 1972.

Webb, Eugene. *Samuel Beckett: A Study of His Novels*. Seattle: University of Washington Press, 1973.

Worth, Katharine, ed. *Beckett the Shape Changer*. London: Routledge & Kegan Paul, 1975.

OTHER REFERENCES

Banfield, Ann. *Unspeakable Sentences: Narration and Representation in the Language of Fiction*. London: Routledge & Kegan Paul, 1982.

Beckett, Samuel. "Dennis Devlin." *transition* 27 (1938): 289–94.

———. La Peinture des van Velde." *Cahiers d'art* 20–21 (1945): 349–54.

Bergson, Henri. *Creative Evolution*. 1911; New York: Modern Library, 1944.

Berkeley, George. *Three Dialogues Between Hylas and Philonous*. 1713; New York: Bobbs-Merrill, 1954.

Breton, André. "Surrealism Yesterday, Today and Tomorrow." Trans. by Edward W. Titus. *This Quarter* 5 (Sept. 1932): 7–44.

Chatman, Seymour, ed. *Approaches to Poetics*. New York: Columbia University Press, 1973.

———, ed. *Literary Style: A Symposium*. New York: Oxford University Press, 1973.

———. *Story and Discourse: Narrative Structure in Fiction and Film*. 1978; Ithaca, N.Y.: Cornell University Press, 1980.

Chatman, Seymour, and Samuel R. Levin, eds. *Essays on the Language of Literature*. Boston: Houghton Mifflin Co., 1967.

Culler, Jonathan. *Structuralist Poetics: Structuralism, Linguistics, and the Study of Literature*. Ithaca, N.Y.: Cornell University Press, 1975.

Eco, Umberto. *The Role of the Reader: Explorations of the Semiotics of Texts*. Bloomington and London: Indiana University Press, 1978.

Enkvist, Nils Erik. *Linguistic Stylistics*. The Hague: Mouton, 1973.

Fowler, Roger, ed. *Essays on Style and Language: Linguistic and Critical Approaches to Literary Style*. London: Routledge & Kegan Paul, 1966.

———. *Style and Structure in Literature: Essays in the New Stylistics*. Ithaca, N.Y.: Cornell University Press, 1975.

Freeman, Donald C., ed. *Linguistics and Literary Style*. New York: Holt, Rinehart and Winston, 1970.

Grossman, Manuel L. *Dada: Paradox, Mystification, and Ambiguity in European Literature*. New York: Pegasus, 1971.

Jacobs, Roderick, and Peter Rosenbaum . *Transformations, Style, and Meaning*. Lexington, Mass.: Xerox College Publishing, 1971.

Jolas, Eugene. "Literature and the New Man." *transition*, June 1930.

———. "Paramyths." *transition*, July 1935, p. 7.

Korg, Jacob. *Language in Modern Literature: Innovation and Experiment*. New York: Barnes Noble, 1979.

Lee, Vernon. *The Handling of Words, and Other Studies in Literary Psychology*. Lincoln: University of Nebraska Press, 1968.

Leed, Jacob. *The Computer and Literary Style*. Kent, Ohio: Kent State University Press, 1966.

Lodge, David. *Language of Fiction: Essays in Criticism and Verbal Analysis of the English Novel*. New York: Columbia University Press, 1966.

————. *The Modes of Modern Writing: Metaphor, Metonymy, and the Typology of Modern Literature*. Ithaca, N.Y.: Cornell University Press, 1977.

Nadeau, Maurice. *The History of Surrealism*. Translated by Richard Howard. New York: Macmillan, 1965.

Nowottny, Winifred. *The Language Poets Use*. London: Athlone Press, 1962.

Perloff, Marjorie. *The Poetics of Indeterminacy: Rimbaud to Cage*. Princeton, N.J.: Princton University Press, 1981.

Rimmon-Kenan, Shlomith. *Narrative Fiction: Contemporary Poetics*. New Accents Series. London and New York: Methuen, 1983.

Sebeok, Thomas A., ed. *Style in Language*. Cambridge: Massachusetts Institute of Technology Press, 1960.

Tompkins, Jane P., ed. *Reader-Response Criticism: From Formalism to Post-Structuralism*. Baltimore, Md.: Johns Hopkins University Press, 1980.

Tufte, Virginia. *Grammar as Style*. New York: Holt, Rinehart & Winston, 1971.

Ullmann, Stephen. *Language and Style*. Oxford: Basil Blackwell, 1964.

————. *Meaning and Style, Collected Papers*. Oxford: Basil Blackwell, 1973.

Waugh, Patricia. *Metafiction: The Theory and Practise of Self-Conscious Fiction*. London: Methuen, 1984.

Index

287